Beth Junor was born in 1958 in Lanark. She visited Yellow Gate Greenham Common Women's Peace Camp from 1983 while organising in the peace movement in Scotland, before living and working full-time at the camp from August 1986 – February 1990. She produced the camp's Newsletters during this period, as well as a Handbook on non-violence, *Resist the Military*. She is a published poet; her play *Hunger* was read on Radio Pirate Woman, Galway, before receiving a second professional production in the 1993 Edinburgh Festival Fringe. Beth was educated at St Andrews University and at Yellow Gate Greenham Common Women's Peace Camp. She continues to support the work of the camp and now also does full-time paid work in the Scottish health service. She has served 7 prison terms for her non-violent actions against the military.

Katrina Howse was born in England in 1958. After graduating from Sheffield University, she worked as a community mural artist while organising in the women's and peace movements, helping to set up Waddington Women's Peace Camp in resistance to the Falklands War. Katrina began living and working full-time at the Women's Peace Camp on Greenham Common in August 1982 and has lived and worked full-time at Yellow Gate since. She is a professional mural artist who exhibits and sells her work nationally and internationally. She has served 19 prison terms for her non-violent actions against the military, including one 6-month sentence.

GW00391704

"Punishment Cell" 1982 Katrina Hawse

# GREENHAM COMMON
## WOMEN'S PEACE CAMP:
## A HISTORY OF NON-VIOLENT RESISTANCE
## 1984 – 1995

**Written and Edited by Beth Junor**

**Illustrations by Katrina Howse**

**WORKING PRESS**

Published in 1995 by
Working Press
54 Sharsted Street
LONDON SE17 3TN

British Library Cataloguing in Publication Data.
A catalogue record for this book  is available from the British Library.

ISBN 1 870736 93 1

Typeset by The Caseroom, Peebles EH45 8AT, Scotland

Printed and bound by
Antony Rowe Ltd., Chippenham SN14 6QA, England

# Contents

## DEDICATION

*This book is dedicated*
*to the memory of*
*Helen Thomas, Hiro Sumpter, Teresa Smith, Irene Mkwayi*

and

*to all women who struggle daily*
*against poverty, injustice, cancer*
*and other consequences*
*of the military-industrial complex.*

# ACKNOWLEDGEMENTS

I wish to thank *Mairi McPhail & Rory Bagnall*, for taking me into their home when I had to cease living at the camp, and for helping me to find the shelter which made this project thinkable. My gratitude also to *Sue Frazer* for all her support.

Thanks also go to *Henny Smoes, Isla Williams, Michael & Aileen Brownlie, Christa Knellwolf, Alison Jackson, Margaretta D'Arcy, Erica Wilson, Judith Walker, David Partridge, Ethel Carlsson and Janet Tavner* for generous support.

Thank you to *Rosy Bremer, Louise Blakley, Siân Evans, Frances Vigay, Sarah Hipperson, Mary Millington and Abigail Adams* for help in the final stages.

Thank you to *Stefan Szczelkun* of Working Press for care taken and generous sharing of knowledge & skills.

Thank you to all contributors, with especial appreciation to the women who devoted time and care to recording their work while also taking on the work of the camp: *Katrina Howse, Sarah Hipperson, Aniko Jones, Rosy Bremer, Jean Hutchinson and Peggy Walford.*

*Katrina Howse* has provided constant help, support and inspiration throughout the project – thank you for everything.

# PHOTOGRAPHERS

Cover photography by Colin Cavers

1. King's Cross Women's Centre
2. King's Cross Women's Centre
3. King's Cross Women's Centre
4. Camp photo
5. King's Cross Women's Centre
6. King's Cross Women's Centre
7. King's Cross Women's Centre
8. King's Cross Women's Centre
9. Bee Ring
10. King's Cross Women's Centre
11. David Hoffman
12. Eva Lie
13. King's Cross Women's Centre
14. King's Cross Women's Centre
15. Camp photo
16. Camp photo
17. Camp photo
18. Camp photo
19. Ian Longthorne
20. Frances Vigay
21. Frances Vigay
22. Frances Vigay
23. Camp photo
24. Nigel Goldsmith
25. Camp photo
26. Nigel Goldsmith
27. Frances Vigay
28. Frances Vigay
29. Frances Vigay
30. Camp photo
31. Frances Vigay

All illustrations are by Katrina Howse.

# INTRODUCTION

If you travel south-west of London onto the Newbury to Basingstoke (A339) road, you will soon begin to see signs for New Greenham Park (new road signs, which as recently as six months ago read Greenham Common*). If you look closely through the embankment of trees on the left-hand side of this road, you may catch glimpses of perimeter fencing. This fence encloses over 1,000 acres of Common land, which from 1941 until October 1992 had been occupied by the military. It is now a temporary community recreational and small-business park – still Common land, still under the control of the Ministry of Defence.

When you reach the slip-road leading from the A339 to the entrance gates to the Common, underneath the poplars you will see two small caravans. If you stop to visit and walk across the slip-road, you will see it is still marked with paint and pitted with the fires which were part of the resistance to cruise missile convoy exercises. In the area of the encampment you'll find a herb garden underneath the forsythia bush and across from this, a circular flower garden around a young fir tree marked by a small sign, 'Helen's Garden'. Up the path towards the fence is a lavender patch, and in late summer at least, beans climbing up their bamboo frames, some tomato plants, marrows and a compost heap. Beyond Helen's Garden to the east is a clearing in the gorse, where two more small caravans are parked. This is Greenham Common Women's Peace Camp. Since September 5th 1981, for every minute of every day, there have been women on this land and should you arrive today there will still be women there to welcome you.

Greenham Common became a major base for the United States Air Force (USAF) during the Second World War, when local people believed they were temporarily sacrificing Greenham Common for the war effort. They called the Common 'the lung of Newbury.' Once in place, however, the military never returned the open Common land to the people. Greenham Common became a major base for the United States Air Force during WW11. Following a brief respite after the War, the USAF returned in 1951 to build the longest military runway in Europe to accommodate their heavy bombers. In 1961, 77 acres were bought by the Ministry of Defence. By the mid-1960's access to large parts of the Common was only possible through gaps in the perimeter

*The road signs were altered when the Ministry of Defence stepped up their plans to sell their part of the Common to the highest bidder. The name change also reflects a desire on the MoD's part to separate the new business developments from the history of the Women's Peace Camp.

fencing. In 1978, strong local protests prevented the stationing of huge KC-135 tanker planes at the air base. On the 12th of December the following year, NATO decided that 96 USAF ground-launched cruise missiles would be stationed at the base. Underground silos would be constructed for this purpose, and the entire base upgraded to accommodate the personnel needed to operate the missile system. The majority of local people were relieved that this system would not create the amount of noise and disruption to their lives as had been threatened by the KC-135's. Exercises would not create the overhead noise of heavy aircraft, but would take place on the roads, quietly, in the dead of night. The NATO decision held the promise of wealth for the Newbury community. Each nuclear warhead would have the killing capacity of 16 Hiroshima bombs.

The 1979 NATO decision to site nuclear cruise missiles at Greenham Common and elsewhere in Europe was seen as a dangerous escalation in the arms race, particularly since the characteristics of cruise missiles suggested they were first strike nuclear weapons. On September 5th 1981 a group of women, together with some children and men, reached the destination of their walk for peace which had begun ten days earlier in Cardiff, Wales: the Royal Air Force/United States Air Force base at Greenham Common. The march itself was a leaf from the book of successful non-violent actions for peace and justice, and was to become part of an international history of resistance which includes Gandhi's marches with Indian miners in South Africa and against the British salt monopoly in India, as well as the US civil rights marches. The marchers' intention was to hand in a letter to the Commander of the base, which expressed their fears for the future. Four women chained themselves to the fence adjacent to the base's Main Gate. Later there was a request for dialogue – a public debate with the Secretary of State for Defence, Francis Pym. This was refused.

From the initial chaining action the idea of maintaining a more permanent presence on the land outside the air base evolved. Someone put up a sign which read, 'Women's Peace Camp,' and the movement which was to catch the imagination of people world-wide had begun. The camp outside the Main Gate grew in numbers. In February 1982, by majority decision, the camp became women-only in preparation for a major eviction, and has remained a women-only camp since. Throughout 1983 other women's peace camps were being set up around the nine-mile perimeter fence. The camps were named after the colours of the rainbow: Red, Orange, Yellow, Green, Blue, Indigo, Violet. The original camp outside the Main Gate was Yellow Gate. Later still, more camps sprung up for periods, then faded – Woad, Emerald and Jade.

Over the years, all of the camps have faded and disappeared, some returning for periods, with the exception of Yellow Gate. 14 years later, Yellow Gate remains in unbroken resistance. It is now the foundation from which actions are taken against this country's Trident nuclear weapons programme.

An incalculable number of women, many hundreds of thousands, have passed through the women's peace camp at Greenham Common since September 5th 1981. Thousands of women have visited or lived on the Common outside the perimeter fence for periods lasting from an overnight stay to (in fewer numbers) permanent residence of months and years. Many more thousands of women, some children and some men have supported the camp.

September 5th 1995 marks 14 years of non-stop non-violent resistance to the military from Yellow Gate, Greenham Common Women's Peace Camp. It would be misleading, and a great denial of the hard work of a few individual women, to give the impression that it has been the chance occurrence of a continuous, ever-changing rota of women which has kept Yellow Gate going non-stop for these 14 years. The reality is that it is the continuity of a few women, holding onto that small piece of ground whether as a camp of three or four or as part of a camp of twenty, thirty or fifty, that has been essential to the continuous survival of this camp.

There is a period in every resistance movement which catches the world's attention – 30,000 women joining hands around the perimeter at Greenham Common, the encampment in Tiananmen Square, mass demonstrations in Wenceslas Square, the gathering at the Berlin Wall and its dismantling by the people; behind each of these historical landmarks is a smaller group of determined dissidents, who had worked for years previously and who – survival permitting – would work for years afterwards in pursuit of justice, peace and democracy, long after the cameras have gone elsewhere.

Katrina Howse, for example, first came to live at Yellow Gate in August 1982. She made Yellow Gate her only home, and has remained working and living here permanently since: 9 of these 13 years in a tent. Her longest absence from the camp was for a period of four months in 1985, when she was serving a six month custodial prison sentence. It is this kind of commitment which has established the continuity of the camp outside the Main Gate.

To say this, that Yellow Gate could not have maintained its non-stop resistance for 14 years without great commitment from a few women is in no way to dismiss, or even detract in the slightest from the value of the contributions of others, although articulating this commitment is often misinterpreted as such. These two aspects of the peace camp, the women who have been committed to living permanently over a period of years, and all of those who have passed through the camp or have lent support, are inseparable, like the two sides of a leaf: the side exposed to the wind, rain and snow is inseparable from the nourishing network of veins running underneath. Not even thousands of women passing through the camp over the years would have ensured such continuous resistance as has been maintained at Yellow Gate, as is evidenced by the demise of the other camps. However, if the state believed that the camp was wholly reliant upon three or four individuals, they would have succeeded in their aim of closing down the camp long ago. The state knows that the camp is being watched and supported by many others, both nationally and internationally. All of those who support the peace camp and continue to believe in its value are dependent upon the long-term investment which a few are willing to make.

This continuity of a small group of women at Yellow Gate is one of the camp's greatest strengths in its struggle against the military. The continuity of experience is often the only thing which prevents further abuses of power by the military, police, bailiffs, press and the surrounding hostile community. A wealth of knowledge and experience is kept alive in the camp and is one of its greatest protections against the many forms of violence which the women continually face.

The history of the first years of the peace camp, from 1981-84, has been recorded in several publications. The last book to be published which gave voice to the women living at the camp ends its chronology of events with 9th March 1984, as the first, partial, cruise missile convoy exercises begin to leave the base. A major eviction, called 'The Final Solution' by the authorities, took place less than a month later, on April 4th 1984. Film of the eviction was broadcast in Australia, Canada, the US and throughout Europe. Then there was silence. No news of events at the peace camp could get much further than the local weekly paper. The British media became suddenly and unanimously uninterested. Women from the camp phoning the Press Association had the phone put down on them. Internationally, the impression had been created that the major eviction had ended the protest.

The history of resistance to each cruise missile convoy exercise to leave the base after March 9th 1984 remains untold. So too does the history of non-violent resistance to the British Army, of the resistance in courts and inside prisons, of the killing of Helen Thomas and her mother's struggle to get to the truth about Helen's death. These are some of the things we would like to record and discuss in this book. These are things you will not have read about in the papers, seen on television or heard on the radio. Or perhaps you will have heard rumours, or heard the reports of others on some of these things and now say, 'So that's what really happened.'

We are against censorship in all its forms, and therefore celebrate the publication of this book as a victory for freedom of expression. All of the voices are those of women who live or have lived at Yellow Gate or of those who support the camp. Many accounts were tape-recorded, transcribed verbatim, then edited for inclusion in this history. Some accounts are taken from the camp's Newsletters, which have been in the public domain since 1986 – articles harassed out of women who were already overworked with the daily physical, mental and emotional work of the camp. Other accounts have been sent to me throughout the book's compilation, as memories resurfaced. The chronology of camp events has been gleaned from Yellow Gate's daily diaries and from volumes of court papers and correspondence. Fact appears as fact and opinion is clearly delineated as opinion. All facts, as well as events referred to in the personal accounts, are verifiable by reference to several sources.

This book has not attempted to record any of the history of the other camps around the perimeter, but has confined itself to what we know best, our own experiences of work and life at Yellow Gate. When reference is made to one of the other peace camps, this is clearly stated.

We often say that the truest history of the Women's Peace Camp's work is to be found in the Criminal Records Office. Here we are able to tell the story behind each conviction and prison sentence. We hope this record of our resistance will inspire others to act, and give affirmation to all who struggle daily against injustice.

*A luta continua!*

Beth Junor
September 5th, 1995

# 1984
# THE FINAL SOLUTION?

Newbury District Council's so-called landscaping scheme of 1982 had enhanced the slip-road to the Main Gate of the air base by dropping tons of Somerset soil, rocks and boulders haphazardly over the area of the women's peace camp. This new moon-scape remained until the spring of 1984, when it then had to be removed for a road-widening scheme. This road-widening work would leave the A339 road narrower in places; it was yet another elaborate and expensive eviction plan, but the authorities had named this version 'The Final Solution'. Women at Yellow Gate began the year still living in simple constructions on top of the Somerset hillocks, constantly anxious about the impending eviction, having seen the document with its title copied from the Nazis.

**JANUARY 1st, 1984:** *Sarah Hipperson* – I was determined to start the year of 1984 on Greenham Common.

I had been in London, recovering from a water only fast in Holloway Women's Prison which had lasted from November 1st until December 1st, 1983. The fast was never intended to be a 'Hunger Strike' – it was an offering, as so many offerings were made by other women to bring about a change of heart and mind. On the 14th of November I had listened on my radio to the first of the consignment of 96 ground launched cruise missiles arriving by plane over the heads of the women waiting to blockade the roads. By choosing to bring them in this way there was an acknowledgement that the women were serious about their determination to resist the cruise missiles. As I listened to the voices of women I knew, committing themselves to the struggle, I felt strong and empowered to continue the fast. I remember thinking, 'Now the real work starts – we will have the missiles removed; it will take ten years, but it will be done.' The quality of commitment was there and women were prepared to live in an entirely different way from their previous experiences. It was exhilarating to come to the realisation that this disparate group of women could come together for the purpose of taking on the greatest military power in the world, with the strongest belief that they had the right to do so, and set about doing so with absolute determination.

Once out, I was desperate to get back to the camp, but I knew living on the Common needed more strength than I had at the time. I'd lost 2 1/2 stone of body weight.

During the December weekend demonstration, women pulled down the base's perimeter fence by hand. The uprights had been loosened with winches, ordered by Jane Dennett. I wasn't able to take part in the action because of my health, but I witnessed it. As women set about taking down the fence, I stood by a tree watching with amazement the concentration and utter determination on women's faces as the fence came tumbling down. It was so symbolic of what I knew would be the eventual outcome of this confrontation between the military and the women. We would make it impossible for them to carry out their work behind the security of the fence.

Extra police were drafted into the area but they couldn't stop the fence coming down. The Paratroop Regiment, 'resting' from 'duties' in Northern Ireland, were billetted inside the base and were only too willing to do their bit. I was horrified to see the US airmen handing out sticks to the Paras. They beat women on their fingers to loosen their hands from the fence. A number of women received injuries. Jean Freer and another woman managed to break through the ranks of the military and were held, charged with Criminal Damage and later went to court.

Then I was sent back to Holloway for a week over the Christmas period by Bow Street Magistrates Court (London), for marking the Ministry of Defence building with members of Catholic Peace Action, a Christian group of which I am a founder member. The group is based on resistance to the nuclear deterrence defence policy through faith and acts of civil disobedience.

I arrived back on the Common on New Year's Eve to fulfill my commitment to start 1984 on Greenham Common.

**JANUARY 2nd, 1984:** challenge to newspaper announcement that women from the peace camp would no longer be served at Little Chef restaurants.

*Sarah Hipperson* – Since I hadn't been able to take part in the December action, I thought I could take part in this one. Four of us caught an early bus from the camp and arrived in Newbury at the Little Chef at 8.30 am. Already there were a number of customers enjoying breakfast.

As I walked in, I heard the manageress and one of the waitresses draw in their breaths, almost simultaneously. I headed for a table as far into the restaurant as I could go. Liz Beech was to follow after a short interval, then Barbara Gordon, then Maria Lundstrom.

The manageress approached and asked in hushed tones, so as not to disturb her customers, 'Can I ask where you have come from this morning?'

Addressing all the diners, I asked, 'Have you all been asked where you've come from this morning?'

The other women started to come in. Panic was written all over the faces of the staff, and the customers tried to pretend that nothing unusual was happening. A freelance reporter who happened to be there offered to buy me a cup of coffee. This seemed to be the last straw for the manageress and she called the police.

An Inspector and four police constables duly arrived. We were asked to leave but we insisted we had the right to be served, we hadn't done anything wrong.

In Newbury at that time, living at the women's peace camp was enough reason to be banned from any community services or activities. In keeping with this attitude we were carried out of the place and dumped in the nearest puddle.

A police guard was mounted at the entrance of the Little Chef for days. Sarah Green and her six-month-old child Jay were held in the police cells in Newbury for a number of hours for daring to refuse the banning order which was enforced by Thames Valley Police.

It was no secret that Rocco Forte, owner of Trust House Forte's Little Chef restaurants was an admirer of Mrs Thatcher, who had threatened to 'eradicate' us.

A nationwide boycott of The Little Chef by the peace movement accompanied with stickers everywhere saying 'Little Chef-NO THANKS' ensued, and was effective in helping to stop the ban. Mr Forte recanted, discovering as so many bigots before him have, that when the cost of exercising prejudice means a loss of profit, then it is time to stop the exercise.

Late in January, while I was still recovering from the fast, I undertook an action with four other women. (The others were not from the peace camp.) The action took place at the Soviet Embassy in London and was in support of Olga Medvecova, who was going on trial in Moscow for a dissenting act against the Soviet state. It was said she was expecting to be sent to a prison camp in Siberia.

Our action was to gain admission to the Embassy and to hand in a letter requesting visas to attend Olga's trial.

We were well received and offered coffee which we duly accepted while the First Secretary, Uri Mazure, read our letter. When he finished reading he was polite but told us our request could not be complied with.

We then said we would remain in the Embassy until he understood our position. We talked for nearly an hour but he kept repeating that it was not possible to grant visas to us.

I said we would have a silent vigil for an hour to give him more time to think. We all sat very peacefully for an hour.

An official (possibly a KGB agent) was called and sounded angry as he spoke in Russian to Mr Mazure. He seemed to be telling him to get rid of us. In reply Mr Mazure indicated with a lift of his shoulders and his upturned hands that he had already tried that and it hadn't worked.

After a stand-off lasting 7 hours we were carried out of the Embassy and roughly handled by the special police who deal with diplomatic incidents. Uri Mazure seemed uncomfortable with the way we were removed. I think if he had been free to do so he would have granted our request.

I like to think that our action had an influence on the Soviet authorities in dropping the charges and setting Olga free. Meeting Olga in Moscow five months later seemed like a miracle.

**FEBRUARY 14th 1984**, House of Commons: during a series of questions about MPs visits to the base at Greenham Common, Mr Boyes, MP asks whether the Minister of State for the Armed Forces, John Stanley, was aware that the barbed wire inside the base is "equivalent to four-inch knives, and that if anyone goes near it he [sic] could have his fingers chopped off?" Amid interruptions, the Minister of State replies, "I am sure that it was an instructive question, but I am afraid that I did not hear it." The House went on to other business.[1]

**MARCH 9th 1984**: first cruise missile convoy exercise. 100 Police with dogs surround women at Blue Gate to prevent them alerting other camps that three convoy vehicles have left the base. An hour later, however, women manage to follow the convoy's route.

**MARCH 13th 1984**, House of Commons: an MP asks the Secretary of State for Defence if he will take the opportunity to "congratulate all the British and American personnel who took part in last Friday's exercise involving cruise missile launchers, the success of which was satisfying to a great many patriotic people" in the country. John Stanley welcomed the suggestion, and added, "I should also like to thank the Thames Valley police."[2]

**MARCH 22nd 1984**, Reading Crown Court: Department of Transport granted a possession order on land at the Main Gate. The hearing was in chambers, with no public or press access.

**MARCH 23rd 1984**: Sarah Tisdall, a junior MoD employee, sentenced to six months imprisonment for passing documents to the Guardian newspaper which showed how the government planned to handle the public relations aspects of the arrival of cruise missiles at Greenham Common. Gerald Kaufman MP described the sentence as a warning of the Government's determination to diminish freedom of expression and suppress dissent. Sarah Tisdall herself said in a television interview that she felt it immoral for the Secretary of State to evade parliamentary criticism of the arrival of cruise missiles at Greenham

Common. On April 9th, Sarah Tisdall was refused leave to Appeal her sentence.

**MARCH 29th 1984**: cruise missile convoy leaves Greenham Common in the early hours, escorted by hundreds of Police, for RAF Lyneham, near Chippenham. Evictions at the camps in the afternoon; women converge on the busy Main Gate, blocking it for about three hours.

**APRIL 1st 1984**, Reading Crown Court: fifteen women due to appear, for beginning of trial of Criminal Damage charges of July 8th, 1983. Trial expected to last at least two weeks.

NOT TO BE PUBLISHED BEFORE 0300 HOURS THURSDAY 15 MARCH 1984
THE PRESS COUNCIL
*PRESS RELEASE NO. U10427/1646 – Page 3*

The Press Council's adjudication was: The DAILY EXPRESS chose not to produce evidence to defend its front page lead story about the Greenham Common Peace Women but to say that the editor is satisfied of its accuracy. In the light of evidence from the complainants and information from the Secretary of State for Defence, the Chief Constable of Thames Valley, and Newbury District Council, the Press Council is satisfied that the story was untrue. It was published with extraordinary prominence and should have been very carefully researched, checked and cross-checked. The Press Council concludes that this was not done. The Council is satisfied that the particular top secret delivery of missile casings described in the story did not take place and the resistance to the delivery, which was also described in the story, did not take place. No evidence has been put before the Council that areas around the Women's Peace Camp are totally polluted as the story alleged. Although according to the Director of Environment Services for Newbury arrangements for sanitation and food hygiene are rather primitive he has said he does not consider that a public health nuisance is being created. The complaint that the DAILY EXPRESS account was inaccurate and prejudicial is upheld and the newspaper censured. To the extent that it relied upon that account for its facts, the newspaper's editorial was unjustified. It was also abusive. While the newspaper was entitled to make such an attack in a leading article it should have given those it attacked an opportunity to reply. The complaints about the DAILY EXPRESS editorial article is, therefore, also upheld.

**END APRIL 1994**, Ragusa, near Comiso, Sicily:

*Mary Millington* – Twelve women, including Bee, Skeeter and myself from Yellow Gate, had been imprisoned following an international women's blockade of the Comiso cruise missile base in Sicily in March 1983. Following our expulsion from Italy, we petitioned the Italian consulate in London for either an apology for our unlawful imprisonment or a fair and public trial.

We were granted the trial in Ragusa in April the following year.

Ten of us stood trial, our countries of origin being Italy, Ireland, the Netherlands, Germany, Britain and Denmark. Italian peace women had raised money for us to have excellent lawyers, and we found the charge against us, 'blocco stradale', had been changed in order to avoid having to give us a long prison sentence. We were sentenced to a conditional suspended fine, but three of us decided to challenge the decision since the new charge, 'violenza privata', sounded like an insult to our non-violence. We lost at the court of appeal in Catania the following year, but we had gained a great deal from our experience of international women's solidarity.

**APRIL 2nd 1984**: eviction of camp outside the Main Gate due to take place today, but post-poned, due to numbers of women present (approximately 200).

**APRIL 3rd 1984**, House of Commons: in response to a Written Question, the Secretary of State for the Home Department, Leon Brittan, reveals Thames Valley Police estimated the cost of policing Greenham Common in 1983-84 to be £2.8 million; central Government "contributed about £2.1 million through the special payment of £1.5 million and Police grant of £0.65 million."[3]

**APRIL 4th 1984**, 0600 hrs: 400 Police surround benders at the Main Gate. Women are awoken with threats of rape and of being "gassed like animals" in their shelters.[4] were gone, there was just a strip of land in between the base and what we called the 'mini-base', the new construction site for the 'road-widening'. You couldn't stop on the road near where the camp had been, they had earth-movers on there. They had caravans and a private security firm, and they had picket fencing all the way round. It was really, really painful to see. There were women over the main road, around belongings. I remember Myra Hughes and Peggy Walford were there, and a group of women. They'd returned from having been forced to walk down the road. One woman described it, 'We were told to pick up our belongings, and walk into Hampshire.'

Some women tried to stay on the land, and were dragged off. They were still wandering over the original site. The stand-pipes for getting our water had been taken. There were a lot of shocked women. The camp was still there. Some of us weren't happy about all of us staying over the road. We had to be on the land where all that emotional energy had gone in. We felt that that was our land, not in a possessive sense but in a spiritual sense and in terms of the resistance. We felt that our struggle was there, and that if they took that away from us they took our struggle. We returned to the original site.

*Sarah Hipperson* – The BBC sent a car to the camp in the afternoon to take Liz Beech and I to their studios to give a response to the eviction. We arrived there clutching our belongings, looking like refugees. We were so dishevelled after the ordeal of the eviction that we asked for and were allowed to have showers, before appearing on the Newsnight programme. The interview was conducted by John Tusa. The unruly, 'yob'-like behaviour of the police during the eviction was defended by Ivan Lawrence, QC, MP. He more or less dismissed our complaints as coming from 'hysterical women'. I was able to challenge his prejudiced assumptions on the factual basis that I had personally woken up to the sound of heavy footsteps aggressively stamping around my bender, male voices demanding that I come out, with the chilling threat of rape and that we should be 'gassed like trapped animals' in our benders. Revealing this truth on national television was an effective answer to the parliamentarian who failed to carry out his duty to determine the facts before condemning the victims.

The coverage by the media brought forth very good support from the mining community, who were making the connection between our experiences, especially with the 24-hour policing we were being subjected to.

Lord Longford arrived the day after the eviction. He had been sent down to 'do a piece' on us by some publisher. He couldn't understand that a non-hierarchical group could carry on the protest, and without office facilities. He seemed stunned when we told him that we were now forced to live without any shelter. It was very cold, and he was obviously feeling it. He was without a top coat (he told us he had lost it), so I wrapped a blanket around him and pinned it at the neck. Later he wanted to go up to the base. We walked up with him and I introduced him, still wrapped in the blanket, to the policeman at the Gate, saying, 'This is Lord Longford.' The policeman raised his eyebrows in disbelief and replied, 'Really.' He took some convincing.

Tony Benn also made the journey to give his support by making a statement at the Gate. He has always been willing to give us help when we ask. Other Labour MPs came to the camp at that time – that was when the heart of the Labour movement was unilateralist. Now it isn't fashionable.

APRIL 5th 1984: Galaxy aircraft delivers more cruise missiles and launcher vehicles to Greenham Common – the first Galaxy to land since the first missiles were delivered in November 1983. Women at other camps around the perimeter evicted again, just before the arrival of the Galaxy.

**APRIL 5th 1984**, House of Commons: MP Mr Bob Clay describes visit to Greenham Common yesterday, with MP Mr Tony Benn:

On arriving at the Greenham Common air base on Wednesday, we discovered the conspiracy hatched up by the Ministry of Defence, the Ministry of Transport, Berkshire County Council and the Police last year. I presume that all hon. Members have read the minute about which one of my hon. Friends spoke earlier in the week. The documents state, "What shall we do about these peace protesters? We shall devise a road widening scheme." It is an ingenious use of public money for a monetarist Government to devise a road-widening scheme specifically for the purpose of clearing away peace protesters. It was not reported in the media, but that road-widening scheme will go on for a long time, because there is a great deal of common land around the base and the women will camp on that common land.

Fencing around the area which goes on and on is preventing access by our citizens to common land. I wonder whether that is legal. It reminds me of the history of earlier troubles and developments in society. It is ironic that it is not the first time that people have moved in and started fencing off common land without so much as a "by your leave". That is now going on around Greenham Common to prevent peaceful protesters from getting anywhere near the base.

. . . It has nothing to do with security, official secrets or anything else; it is just that the Government are no longer prepared to tolerate what is symbolic of the most peaceful protest that has been carried out consistently in this country for years.

Gentle, pacifist women who have offered no violence throughout their protest outside the base are cleared away because they are an embarrassment to the Government, and for another reason – while they are there, they see things. They see, as one of my hon. Friends and I did three weeks ago, an enormous United States air force transport vehicle come out of the base and smash straight into two private cars. If the women had not been there they would not have seen that. When similar vehicles come out with cruise missiles, if the drivers are as competent as those two Americans, the women would not be able to say, "God help us when they come out with the cruise missiles."

. . . What else have the Police done to try to clear away the women? They had a policy of trying to put as many of those women in gaol as possible under any pretext. A woman who has been arrested for obstruction, for example, can go to No.1 court at Newbury magistrates' court and ask for bail or time to pay a fine. When asked for her address she can say, "Greenham Common Women's Peace Camp." The magistrate will refuse to accept that address and send her to prison for 14 or 28 days. In court No.2 next door, a woman can appear on an identical charge and give Greenham Common Women's Peace Camp as the address and have it accepted.

Every 14 days, Mrs Jane Dennett receives her war widow's pension from the Ministry of Defence addressed to Mrs Jane Dennett at Greenham Common Women's Peace Camp, but when she went to Newbury magistrates' court and gave that address, the magistrates sent her to Holloway for 28 days because she refused to give any other address.

Another lady who appeared before the court was told that Greenham Common Women's Peace Camp was not an acceptable address, so she said, "But I live there." The magistrate said that she must provide other addresses, so she gave him three others. Then the magistrate said, "But you have already told me that you live at Greenham Common peace camp. I cannot accept these other addresses because I know that you will not be there if we require to re-arrest you," so he sent her to gaol as well. [Interruption] Let us have it on the record that Conservative Members are saying, "Quite right; let us have more of it."

All that is being done to try to disguise from the public what is going on inside an American base over which the British have no control. The women see the yellow, green and black alerts when American officers who live in the surrounding villages come screaming into the base at 5 am. All the Americans on the base go down the bunkers, and the game continues until eventually we have either won the war, or we are all dead, or both. Then the black flag goes up . . . The Government want to get rid of the women so that they cannot see those games.

I began by referring to the miners' dispute, and I said that I observed in Nottinghamshire the same sort of road blocks as I observed being organised by the Police in Berkshire this week. It disturbs me that, wherever we turn these days, we see the elimination of protest, attacks on protesters and intolerance towards dissent. Conservative members are cheering it on. It frightens me more than anything that I have seen in my my limited life has frightened me- [HON. MEMBERS: "Good."] Conservative Members say, "Good." It will be good for them, will it not, when Members of Parliament who disagree with them are frightened as well? That is what we are moving towards, and the sooner that the mass of working people and peaceful protesters recognise it, the sooner we shall save ourselves from the authoritarian state towards which they are taking us.[5]

*Sarah Hipperson* – For a period of time there were early morning exercises carried out by the USAF to establish a code of behaviour in the event of a nuclear attack. The siren would sound about four a.m., calling the families who lived outside in the surrounding area to come to the base, to enter the nuclear bunker. As soon as we heard the eerie sound of the sirens we would pull on our clothes and emerge from our tents to sit on the approach road to the base, blocking their cars from entering the base. The children would be sitting in the cars next to their mothers, all still in their nightwear, and visibly frightened. They never knew whether it was an exercise or the real thing. Because it was meant to simulate the real circumstances that would occur in the event of a nuclear attack no one was informed that it was an exercise.

The police would arrive after our blockade was established, the cars with the families in them would be stopped, and they would then start dragging us away. They were very brutal. I remember one elderly woman who had come to do a night watch being dragged by the arms so badly that she had to go to hospital in an ambulance with a dislocated shoulder. Eventually these exercises were abandoned because we made them unworkable.

**APRIL 8th 1984**: 28 women arrested outside the base after trying to re-occupy land from which they had been evicted.

**APRIL 9th 1984**: 19 further arrests.

**APRIL 9th 1984**: DAILY EXPRESS, despite recent admonishment from the Press Council, publishes a series of articles about the camp featuring an 'under-cover' reporter, 'Sarah Bond'. Trial of 15 women an Reading Crown Court disrupted by publication of these articles; the case was adjourned, and the women on trial were subjected to the bail condition that they sign on at Newbury Police Station every day.

*Sarah Hipperson* – The placing of Sarah Bond as a 'spy' within the camp was not coincidental to the planned eviction. In fact, I believe she was essential to the grand plan. Her role was to discredit certain women, at the very time that 15 women were going on trial in Reading Crown Court.

The 1984 eviction was a combined effort by Berkshire County Council, Newbury District Council, Ministry of Defence, USAF, Thames Valley Police, and previously discredited members of the press. There were less obvious participants in the plan – the Courts, and the local vigilante group RAGE (Ratepayers Against Greenham Encampments, who had publicans and shopkeepers amongst their members). That is why they believed they had 'The Final Solution' to the Greenham 'problem'.

***Katrina Howse*** - As soon as the first week of that abortive case was over, we really concentrated on holding the camp. It wasn't right, all of us being over the road. We felt a huge sense of loss. A group of seven or eight of us, after all this confusion and upheaval, just walked round the back of the common, up to the fence, and set up camp at one of the old locations we'd had before, where women had been wandering since the eviction. It was painful. When we got there, I just burst into tears – it felt as though that land had been occupied, and we'd just won it back, by simply taking action, even through all that feeling of powerlessness. We'd acted through that feeling of powerlessness and it was very energising. As soon as we got there we all felt instantly better. We lit the camp fire and one woman hung up cut-out silver shapes over the fire and in the trees – stars, and little animals. We were physically separated from the other women, who were over the main road. Some women from over the road started calling themselves 'Downstairs' and us 'Upstairs'. Upstairs there was Jane Dennett, Sarah Hipperson, Hazel Rennie, Mary Hedger, Liz Beech, Setareh Campbell and myself. Naomi Griffiths was there, too, and slept in her car. The rest of us were on the Common.

The next ten weeks were an intensive phase of fighting to hold that peace camp, in between the base fence and the construction fence. Meanwhile all the 'road-widening' work was going on. We couldn't put tents up. As soon as we put tents up they were pulled down by the police or we were told by the police to take them down. We had a constant guard of a full van of police, parked up by the Main Gate. They were Thames Valley Police in this van, but they were given help by the Ministry of Defence (MoD) Police, who were normally on guard at the Gate. Every time we lit a fire they would come and put it out. So we'd light a fire again, they'd put it out again. There was a series of silver fire extinguishers, lined up outside the Gate to one side.

***Sarah Hipperson*** - The fire extinguishers were clearly the property of the USAF – proof of their involvement in the grand plan.

***Katrina*** - Yes. These would be filled by the MoD Police and handed out to the Thames Valley Police. Those became such an enemy to us, those silver fire extinguishers, because every time we lit a fire they would pick up the fire extinguisher, and put the fire out. Then we'd light the fire again, and they'd come over again. We'd light it fifty times in ten minutes, sometimes, and sometimes we'd just leave it out, wait 'til they were in the van or maybe having a break, then light it and try and cook something.

There were times when it used to be a real battle to try and keep that fire. We'd blockade around the fire, hold up plastic and try and deflect their jet of water. Many times we got soaking wet. They would just fire it over us or between us. They'd always manage to put the fire out.

For several weeks we were trying to cook with a kind of burner; basically it was just a metal container like a drum, that you could pick up with a handle, with a grill at the front. We would build a fire in there and put a pot over that. The Police would come over, then someone would have to run off with a saucepan with the mushrooms, someone would run off with the tomatoes, someone would run off with the frying pan. We'd run down the path by the fence, or to the Downstairs camp. The Police would follow, with the fire extinguisher. As long as you had a fire, you could go a mile and a half and they'd still be following you, two Police with a fire extinguisher.

One time we had the portable fire at night. The Police came up to the camp and we ran off with the can with the fire in it. They followed us, then we thought they'd lost us. Suddenly, they dived out of the bushes with the fire extinguisher and this jet of water came at the fire. They had been hiding in the bushes. Such disgraceful, such cruel behaviour went on for ten weeks.

We slept in survival bags, or Gore-Texes, as we couldn't have any shelter up. We had no privacy. Sometimes the Police would walk over and look at women sleeping in their Gore-Texes – just look at them. They hoped that we'd get so fed up that we'd just leave, that this kind of mental and physical torture would just drive us away.

We were also being evicted by Newbury District Council bailiffs. After they'd evicted Blue Gate they came 'round to us. Even though we didn't have tents up, we had to move everything.

**APRIL 29th 1984**, Florennes, Belgium: 15,000 anti-nuclear campaigners join hands around the perimeter of the local USAF base in protest at the scheduled installation of 48 cruise missiles.

*Sarah Hipperson* – The projected installation of cruise missiles in Florennes was also a factor in the eviction – the Prime Minister Wielfried Martens and members of his government pointed to Greenham as a situation they had no wish to see repeated in Belgium. The eviction was to prove that they had finished off the protest at Greenham. The mounds of earth piled up in front of the peace camp on the reclaimed land outside the main gate were placed there to further make the point to the world that women were no longer on Greenham Common. The police presence at this time on Greenham Common was also an exercise to test the working together of personnel from different

Police Authorities. This was a political decision in preparation for the intense policing of the miners when picketing at their workplaces.

**MAY 7th 1994:** *Sarah Hipperson* ⁻ There was a gathering of women and children at the camp, which was still under seige by the police. Suddenly there was a huge explosion in the gorse on the other side of the road and smoke rose high in the sky, well above the poplar trees. A woman who was visiting her daughter – a young woman who had just come to live at the camp after seeing the eviction on the television – collapsed with shock. She thought her daughter was in that area, as she had been earlier, but fortunately she had left just before the explosion, and was safe. The explosion was caused by a petrol bomb attack. The gorse was tinder dry at the time – there hadn't been rain for weeks. There was a great danger to the whole Common. The fire was put out by USAF firefighters. The police never found the attacker, yet weeks later, summoned two women to court for lighting a camp fire on the 7th of May. In court the inconsistency of the evidence offered was pointed out to the Magistrates. The policeman who was giving the evidence had been on duty at the time of the petrol bomb attack but could not remember it. Yet he could remember all the details about a small fire being started to make a cup of tea. The case was dismissed.

**MAY 13th 1984:** 'Visibility Action': approximately 30 women take non-violent direct action to make their struggle visible again, after media silence following the big eviction.

*Katrina Howse* ⁻ After we were evicted, there was nothing about us in the press, absolutely nothing. We really felt there was a D-Notice [government directive to the media, listing subjects not to be covered 'in the interests of national security'] on the camp. We knew that pictures of the eviction had gone round the world. They had been seen in Australia, Canada, America, Europe. Then there was nothing about us.

I remember feeling such frustration one morning, after the construction fence had gone, reading in the Guardian that the women's peace camp was back. We never went away! According to the state line, we hadn't been there for ten weeks, we'd just moved back. The newspapers covered up all that struggle and state torture of us, saying "they've gone back". That was such an insult, after ten weeks of such intense struggle.

The regular evictions by Newbury District Council continued.

The silos fence was cut; all the women were arrested, held in Newbury Police Station, then released without charge. Women returned to the silos fence and cut it again. Some were charged on two counts of Criminal Damage, others returned to cut the fence for a third time.

Those charged were held in custody to appear in Court the following day, when the MoD successfully applied for bail conditions prohibiting women from going within five miles of the base. Women living at the camp could not agree to this bail condition and approximately 20 women were remanded in Holloway for 8 days. After 8 days the bail condition was altered to prohibit the women from going within five metres of the perimeter fence; those on remand agreed and were released from custody.

This series of events was not covered in any media, nor was much of what follows.

**MAY 16th 1984**, House of Commons Defence Committee: The Physical Security of Military Installations in the United Kingdom: Mr A Ward warns the Committee – '. . . The process of consulting about bylaws runs the risk of spreading the knowledge about their existence. This is a fact that has to be taken into account sometimes.'

This extract is later presented by Jean Hutchinson of Yellow Gate to the House of Lords, in D.P.P. v Hutchinson 1990, Z Ac 783, where five Law Lords allow Jean and Georgina Smith's appeal in their challenge to the validity of the Greenham Common Byelaws (1985) and hold that the law-maker had exceeded his powers in framing the Byelaws so as to prevent access to Common land.

**MAY 20th 1984**: 1,000 women pensioners hold vigil for peace at Greenham Common.

**MAY 30th 1984**: National Union of Miners delegation visits peace camp (coalminers strike had begun on 10th March 1984). This visit was one of many made by striking miners to the peace camp.

**JUNE 12th 1984**: six women from Greenham Common are examined for radioactive contamination following non-violent direct action at the nearby Aldermaston Atomic Weapons plant.

**JUNE 26th 1984**: Cruise missile convoy exercise. 15 women break into the base, 8 arrested. The exercise took place at a wood called Blackball Firs, on Salisbury Plain.

**JUNE 28th 1984**: Cruise missile launchers return to base with help of massive Police presence.

**JUNE 25th – JULY 22nd 1984**, Sweden: summer peace camp in Stockholm.

**JULY 8th 1984**: more than 500 coaches, cars and vans bring women to Greenham Common to celebrate "Common Women's Day". Two women reveal they had been camping inside the base for a week.

**JULY 1984**, Reading Crown Court: trial of 15 women at Reading Crown Court, which had been disrupted by DAILY EXPRESS articles, resumes.

*Mary Millington* – A large number of women had taken part in the early morning fence-cutting action on the North side of Greenham, but only a chosen minority of us were arrested and charged.

The Metropolitan Police, who had been drafted in to practice techniques they would use on miners pickets, were using horrendously violent crowd control tactics, isolating individuals and then attacking them in groups of 6. Sarah Green, holding a two-week-old baby Jay, and deliberately keeping well away from the fence, was one of those attacked in this way.

There were 14 women in court, including 3 of us who had 'confessed' after failing to be arrested, but there were 18 pairs of bolt-cutters exhibited by the prosecution. Had some of us been using 2 pairs at once?! The fact was that the police had learned by now that the prisons could not cope with a lot of us at once, but they had not yet learned to keep the damage calculation down to below the Crown Court level.

We caused chaos in Reading Crown Court. At first they searched us every morning on our arrival, in spite of the fact that we were all on bail. Some women insisted on stripping to avoid being touched by the prison officers, which caused such embarrassment to the court that the searches were discontinued. The prosecution's video showed Katrina calling, 'Hecate!' inside the base, and women sitting at the fence triumphantly singing, 'Building bridges between our divisions...'

Sarah Hipperson, who had come to support, challenged the collusion of the judge with the prosecution and got carried out of the court.

Katrina discredited a lying police witness in cross-examination.

One of our barristers, Dora, spoke out against the way a copy of 'The Greenham Factor,' which had been accepted as evidence, had been wrapped up so that the jury could not read the text.

All this wore them down.

It would have worn them down more if we had all followed through, done the prison and continued taking action. As it was, only a minority of us were driven off to prison at the end of the case.

4 months suspended sentences handed down to Katrina Howse, Mary Millington, Arlene Trudell, Ann Francis, Jane Dennett.

**JULY 24th 1984**, House of Commons: in response to a written question from Newbury MP Michael McNair Wilson, the Minister of State for the Armed Forces states that investigations have already been carried out into the presence for six days of two women protestors inside the perimeter fence of RAF Greenham Common.[6]

**SUMMER 1984**, Denmark: women's peace camp planned for the

Ravnstrup NATO command centre in Jylland.

**JULY 24th 1984:** cruise missile convoy leaves base for Tidworth Army camp, Salisbury Plain. Non-violently resisted at Yellow Gate.

**JULY 31st 1984:** more arrests after women break into base.

**AUGUST 8th 1984:** US soldiers remove women from the Main Gate area as they blockade the return of US trucks on military manoevre.

**SEPTEMBER 12th 1984:** a High Court judge excludes a 20-foot strip of land from an eviction order granted to the Ministry of Transport against women at Greenham Common.

**SEPTEMBER 20th – 30th 1984:** 'Ten Million Women for Ten Days': this demonstration was inspired by the belief that at least 10 million women all over the world were with the women at Greenham Common in Spirit against the base. An estimated 50,000 women camped and passed through the peace camps over the ten days, many taking non-violent direct action inside the base.

**OCTOBER 15th 1984:** President Ceausescu of Romania welcomed by the government on three-day official visit to UK.

**OCTOBER 30th 1984,** 1100 am: 26-vehicle, full cruise missile convoy leaves base. 15 women lay in the road, and are held back by two dozen Police. One woman has her leg run into by a Police motorcyclist, her leg is sprained. Convoy is followed to Bulford Camp on Salisbury Plain.

Yellow Gate is evicted.Evening: convoy at Beach's Barn, Salisbury Plain. 14 women walk onto the Plain and are met by a line of soldiers and Police 1/4 mile from the convoy. The women sit down and sing, for hours.

**OCTOBER 31st 1984, HALLOWE'EN:** 30 women go into base, one group converges on the air traffic control tower, demanding that resources be spent on food for Ethiopia, not on war exercises. Two women get int a Police car, but unknown to them the US soldiers' guns were inside – one US soldier smashed the windscreen with his rifle butt. Two women taken to hospital with superficial cuts. Another group were surrounded by five US soldiers with guns, one of whom shouts "Stop!" and clicks back his automatic rifle to prime it. Doesn't aim it, though; the women walk calmly on. Women stand in a circle and sing.

Later: two women go into base on their own.Exercises go on all day – yellow flag, red, then black. The sirens go off at black, US soldiers put gas masks on. Five minutes after they let the last woman out of the base, sirens start for black alert.

These exercises go on for days.

**NOVEMBER 1st 1984:** the convoy is tracked to a wood called

Ablington Furze on Salisbury Plain. The previous night, a woman's van drives along Salisbury Plain and becomes the 23rd vehicle of the convoy. The MoD blockade the van and let the tyres down.Ten women go into the base and get onto the side runway in daytime.Early evening: three women go in and cut the inner silo fence. They are surrounded by soldiers and charged with Criminal Damage.

NOVEMBER 1st 1984: three RAF aircraft fly to Ethiopia carrying food, technical equipment and medical supplies. The decision to use military aircraft to get food to the starving quickly was taken by the Government amidst a row over Government aid policy. On October 23rd BBC television had shown film of the terrible scenes of starvation and death at the Korem refugee camp; aid charities were deluged with donations from the public of all ages and classes, and there was a demand for the use of military aircraft to carry food to the area. The Foreign Secretary told the Commons that the Government was adding £5 million to its previous aid programme for Ethiopia, plus 6,000 tonnes of food. The row erupted when the Minister for Overseas Development, Timothy Raison, revealed that the £5 million was not an addition to Britain's provision for help to the Third World but would come from the existing aid budget.[7]

NOVEMBER 2nd 1984: the convoy seems to disappear from the Plain, the exercise appears over. The women wait.

NOVEMBER 3rd 1984: women overhear that the convoy will be back in an hour – 0215 am. Three women go into the base and reach the inner silo fence. Convoy sighted leaving Salisbury Plain, comes back in to the base at 0630 am.

NOVEMBER 4th 1984: 21 women take a USAF bus in the base and drive to the inner silo fence, start to cut it. 18 charged with taking the bus, 3 charged with Criminal Damage. A further 10 women walk to the silos.

NOVEMBER 5th 1984: National CND chairwoman, Joan Ruddock, in Beijing, China.

NOVEMBER 15th 1984: full cruise missile convoy leaves the Main Gate at 0100 am. Women encircled by Police. Convoy tracked to Longmoor Ranges, Hampshire.Six women go into base and get close to silos fence. When the women were released one woman had her head banged hard by two soldiers, against the vehicle door frame.Several other women enter the base, several women arrested on Longmoor Ranges.

NOVEMBER 16th 1984: two women go to Longmoor Ranges and are arrested by soldiers and held in a barbed wire compound. One soldier armed with machine gun. Later released from Aldershot Police station without charge. Three local women and one young woman were held in an open air pit for 11/2 hours. Many years later, compensation is paid to these women.

NOVEMBER 17th 1984: Women go on to the Ranges and are ordered off.

NOVEMBER 18th 1984: 5 women go onto the Ranges. Many women involved in vigils outside Longmoor.

NOVEMBER 19th 1984: four women go to prison, having received 7 and 14 days sentences.

NOVEMBER 20th 1984, 0230 am: two women in the base. 0300 am: convoy comes in at Blue Gate. The women track it to a hangar near Yellow Gate and get to the runway, in front of four launchers going back to the silos. Police presence at Yellow Gate was a decoy. One hour later a 15 vehicle convoy without launchers comes in at Yellow Gate.

NOVEMBER 21st 1984: a missile launcher cab in garage compound is occupied by 8 women for 15 minutes. Women get through two sets of fence, barbed wire and razor wire. One woman gets into the cab with the driver and stands next to the steering wheel. Inside the cab are the controls – the button the military intend to press to kill millions. Other women on top of cab.More rolls of barbed wire and razor wire going up throughout base.

NOVEMBER 22nd 1984: Sarah Hipperson sentenced to 28 days imprisonment, plus 14 days for Criminal Damage. Georgina Smith sentenced to 7 days.At night, two women get into vehicle compound and paint 30 USAF vehicles with messages and symbols. Both charged.

EVICTIONS EVERY DAY – NO WOMAN IS EVER EVICTED, ONLY HER BELONGINGS.

[Information about actions taken between October 30th – November 2nd, and between November 15th – November 22nd 1984 is taken from two handwritten sheets of paper, produced by camp women at the time. The events recorded on these papers give some indication of the level of resistance – unfortunately many hundreds of similar actions go unrecorded.]

NOVEMBER 23rd – 25th 1984: National CND conference at Sheffield. National CND membership now stands at 110,000. Members of the 1,500 local groups bring the total number of paid-up supporters to around 400,000. Hundreds continue to join every week. Despite this, National CND support for Greenham Common Women's Peace Camp remains negligible.

A resolution at the conference calls for CND to "campaign vigorously" against Soviet weapons and policies, and criticises the scarcity of CND material aimed at the Soviet bloc. The resolution, put forward by the CND group from Canterbury, Kent, was not voted on, after delegates approved a constitutional ploy to avoid taking a vote on the resolution. The "no-vote" ploy was put forward by Communist Party (CP) member Ian Davison. Jon Bloomfield, also of the CP, said that the "political thrust" of the resolution was wrong. Mary Brennan of the CP suggested the way forward was to have more contact with the Kremlin-sponsored official Peace Committees.

**NOVEMBER 24th 1984:** Tory MP for Huntingdon, and future Prime Minister, John Major, assures the villagers of Molesworth,Cambridgeshire (near the second proposed site for cruise missiles in Britain) that the Government plans to prevent "another Greenham" at the base gates.

**DECEMBER 11th 1984:** tenth cruise missile convoy exercise begins. Non-violently resisted.

**DECEMBER 13th 1984:** Anthony Meyer, of RAGE (Ratepayers Against Greenham Encampment) lodges objection with the Electoral Resistration Officer for Newbury to the presence of names of several women living at the peace camp on the Electoral Register.

**DECEMBER 1984:** Several thousand women commemorate the Anniversary of the decision of 1979 to site cruise missiles in Britain, by coming to Greenham Common.

**DECEMBER 15th 1984:** Mikhail Gorbachev in London for official visit.

**DECEMBER 16th 1984:** Mrs Thatcher says in BBC interview, "I like Mr Gorbachev – we can do business together."

**DECEMBER 22nd 1984:** Blue Gate, Greenham Common woman Deirdre Sainsbury murdered. A 37-year-old sales representative who had given her a lift in his car was gaoled for life the following year.

PEACE CAMP

PROTEST GREENHAM COMMON ♀

Six ♀ Years

PRISON

K. Hearn 87'

# 1985
# VOTES FOR WOMEN!

*arah Hipperson* ‒ It became obvious that The Final Solution had failed in clearing women from the Common. They had succeeded in reducing the numbers of women, but what they never managed to do was demoralize the core of women who refused to give up the struggle to have cruise missiles removed from Greenham Common. It was this factor that they finally came to recognise – that a core of women would remain until the military and their weapons had gone.

In 1985 they still held on to a slim belief that they could effect a show of state power that would bring them the result of proving that these women were marginalised 'weirdo's' no one would want to support; a well tested political ploy designed to encompass the population into their scheme.

The press stood by and let them get on with it. When you phoned to tell them a cruise convoy was leaving Greenham there was little or no response; as women were evicted in the coldest weather, there were few who showed any interest.

Newbury, with the exception of a few honourable and brave women, had long set its face firmly against the women from the peace camp and slammed their doors singly and collectively closed. The Empire Bakery and Restaurant was an exception in this hostile environment and continues to make us welcome.

It was in this atmosphere in 1985 that the state set about trying to dislodge the group of women that previous treatment had failed to shift. ‒

Early in 1985 the local RAGE (Ratepayers Against Greenham Encampment) group began to display a broadening of tactics, the vigilante attacks of previous years having been unsuccessful by themselves. When Anthony Meyer of RAGE successfully argued in an Electoral Court that the women at the peace camp had no right to vote since the encampment should not legally qualify as a place of residence, many women living outside the Main Gate were disenfranchised.

A group of seven of the disenfranchised women argued against the Electoral Court's ruling. Sarah Hipperson, Rebecca Johnson, Caroline Rebecca Wynn Griffiths, Naomi Griffiths, Sarah Green, Muriel Jane Dennett and Katrina Howse won their Appeal on March 13th 1985. The Newbury County Court judge ordered that the seven women be reinstated on the Register of Electors.[1]

'It wasn't just that they didn't want us to vote, they wanted to brand us as illegal, an illegal encampment where the women had no rights, then the state could do exactly what it liked to us,' says Katrina.

The RAGE advertisement which had appeared in the local press in 1984 now resurfaced as evidence submitted to the Court of Appeal by the Solicitors for Anthony Meyer, along with copies of numerous injunctions served upon the women, demanding that they appear in Court to hear Applications from Newbury District Council that they leave the land at Greenham Common – both, presumably, illustrations that 'they had been warned'.[2]

By March, however, the women had learned more about the political forces behind Anthony Meyer, in particular, that RAGE had connected up with the far-right Coalition for Peace through Security, which had received aid from a right-wing US pressure group, the Committee for the Survival of a Free Congress (CSFC). The CSFC had also given aid to the far-right ARENA party in El Salvador, closely linked with El Salvador's death squads.

JANUARY 7th 1985, Council Offices, Market Street, Newbury: hearing before Electoral Registration Officer, Mr W J Turner, in which women living at the peace camp are disenfranchised. One of the witnesses who gave evidence against the women was Mr Loveday, a researcher working on this occasion for the Coalition for Peace through Security. Later in the year the GUARDIAN reported Mr Loveday as working for the Freedom Association, in the same capacity, in connection with the UDM, the newly formed miners union set up in opposition to the National Union of Mineworkers.

Extract from the proceedings:

Witness for the Applicants cross-examined by SARAH HIPPERSON:

Q. You did not say what your interest was in this; you gave a London address?

A. Yes. I am self-employed as a researcher. One of the groups that I do some work for is a group called Coalition for Peace through Security, of which I am regional organiser; and I make no secret about it; it is on our headed notepaper.

A Speaker: Yet his barrister started off saying that the issue of cruise missiles was not the concern of this Court; the barrister who called him said that. I think that is dishonesty of the grossest kind. We at least admit that what is going on here is political.

Mr. Mitchell [barrister]: Sir, I feel it is encumbent upon me to deal with that point. The witness is a witness of fact, a witness of the observations which he himself made together with another person, of what he saw and of the photographs which he took . . . That is all that this witness is testifying to. His political beliefs, whatever they are, are totally and utterly irrelevant. The Court can only go on the basis of his testimony; and the applicants can only challenge that testimony by seeking to undermine what has been said by witnesses or by this witness if they feel that this witness has not given an accurate account of life at the camp. That is the issue.

*Sarah Hipperson:* It is not quite the issue. Can I just say to speed this up, I think that what he has just said he could have said in two or three words. I hope that we are not going to have the whole of our day used up by him parading his law skills here. Because it is a human rights issue here that is at stake. As far as he is concerned, he brought a political witness on to this or into this hearing. We have not got before us Anthony Meyer or Miss J Bowes; we have not got them. So if they had been here, it would have been more understandable, since they are residents presumably of this area. But this gentleman comes from London. He is not, by examining these pictures, a professional photographer. He is in this situation by dint of his political stance; and he has come from London; and he has come particularly belonging to a political group which is anti-peace activists; and we here are working for peace. So the whole idea somehow that the issues at stake in that area should not be discussed I think must be discredited right now.

. . . *Sarah Hipperson:* Were you in the aircraft [from which the witness made observations of the peace camp] around the beginning of April?

A. I cannot exactly remember the time that I was in the aircraft; but I believe it was on the earlier occasion.

A. Can I ask you if at that time the plane was carrying a banner?

A. Yes.

Q. 'Go Home Girls'?

A. It may well have been that banner. As you are probably aware, the Coalition has been involved in a number of banners over Greenham from time to time.

*Cross-examined by MISS GREEN*

Q. Do you have the vote?

A. Yes.

Q. Do you believe in a democracy that everyone should have a vote?

*Mr Mitchell:* I object to that question.

*Mr Turner:* I do not really think this is material.

*Miss Green:* I thought we were talking about voting.

*Mr Mitchell:* The witness's beliefs about voting are totally irrelevant. He can only testify to what he has seen or heard with his own eyes or ears.

*Miss Green:* I will ask him something else. Have you ever heard of Emily Davison?

A. That is certainly a question of fact. I do not believe I have heard of Emily Davison.

*Miss Green:* She was the Suffragette who died to get women the vote. I would just like everyone to remember that today. That is all.[3]

**JANUARY 16th 1985**: cruise missile convoy leaves base – despite icy road conditions, in which the vehicles have poor handling ability. Women enter the base and occupy a transporter cab.

**FEBRUARY 1985**: the first play to be written about the women at the peace camp on Greenham Common, 'The Fence', premieres this month at the Alexandra Theatre, Bognor Regis, Sussex.

**FEBRUARY 3rd 1985**: 50 women arrested after getting into the base and lighting bonfires on the runway, to celebrate Candlemas (Imbolg) – the start of Spring.

**FEBRUARY 5th 1985**: an operation begins to fence off the second UK cruise missile base at Molesworth – a disused airfield in Cambridgeshire, where a peace camp of women and men had established itself. Shortly before midnight, Ministry of Defence Police arrived to evict the protestors. 1500 Royal Engineers began to fence off the site – the Minister of Defence, Michael Heseltine, was present, wearing an army flak-jacket.

**FEBRUARY 6th 1985**, House of Commons: Heseltine makes statement about the previous night's exercise. MPs suggested that the exercise was more consistent with a Police state than with a democracy, that it was an eastern-European type operation, and that because of the tremendous resistance of the women at Greenham, Heseltine was now using the iron fist at Molesworth. It was revealed that the exercise had taken three months' planning.[4]

**FEBRUARY 12th 1985**, House of Commons: Defence Committee discusses a 'full security option' at Greenham Common. Land swap is proposed; the committee looks forward to the introduction of byelaws at Greenham Common:

228. With respect to security generally at places like Greenham (I am not knocking Greenham – anywhere where you have nuclear weapons, and you have more sensitive areas and less sensitive areas), you seem to take the view that it does not matter all that much if people break through the outer peritmeter as long as they do not get through the second perimeter and penetrate the crucial sensitive area at the centre. Am I maligning you or do you regard incursions of the outer fence as sensitive? Where do you draw the line? Are you going to suggest, because someone has gone through an armoured fence a couple

of miles away, it does not matter much as long as they are just strolling along a couple of miles from the really sensitive area? At what point do you start to get seriously alarmed? Is it only when they actually try to climb up the final fence of the GAMA [the silos area] ?

(*Mr Gooderham.*) That is a very difficult question to answer, because ideally we do not want them in any of the defences at all. I think one does tend to breathe a sigh of relief if they only manage to get through the outer fence and certainly do not get through the inner fence, but it is all a matter of relativity. How often does this occur? Is it a passing phase?

(*Mr Ward.*) The only site with regular incursions in a very sensitive site is Greenham Common where it would take up a disproportionate expenditure of manpower and money to keep them out of the entire 800 acres, which does not mean you throw away 750 acres and concentrate exclusively on the GAMA, but the GAMA has to be where you put the weight of available resources.

229. Why do you need 800 acres?

(*Mr Ward.*) It is an airfield.

230. How much of it do you actually need for an operational airfield?

(*Mr Ward.*) As an airfield I am assured by American colleagues it is not all that big. Although in these times it sees only delivery flights by single transport aircraft, as a wartime standby base it has a very good runway, some say the best runway in the United Kingdom. Associated with that are the two parallel taxi-ways and a number of hard standings. The acreage is determined by the length of the main runway.

231. Indeed. There are parts of the perimeter where the terrain favours an intruder: rather than trying to keep the intruder out have you looked at the possibility of retrenching any of the perimeter to make life easier?

(*Mr Ward.*) There are parts of the perimeter where observation is so difficult as to be in some conditions almost impossible, as you rightly say. We considered giving up territory to a fence line more easily observable and, in fact, are in the process of confidential discussions with the district and county councils with a view to swapping some land with each other, if I may so put it. What we are talking of swapping is all common land, as you realise, and we are not allowed to increase our net holding in common land. This will have certain aims such as improving security possibly at the main gate and the quality of other areas of the perimeter notably in the immediate vicinity of GAMA where we would like to see the outer fence a little further away from the GAMA itself. This is in hand. We hope that we will achieve some results fairly soon. But you appreciate it is quite an involved process.

233. That is very helpful. I do not have any further questions.

(*Mr Ward.*) Just for the record, it might be relevant to know it has been decided to introduce byelaws under the Defence (Lands) Act in respect of Greenham Common and Molesworth, which, if all goes well, could be in force by Easter. [5]

**FEBRUARY 16th 1985:** Katrina Howse and Sarah Hipperson wrongly arrested for Criminal Damage to the perimeter fence, during a black alert exercise in the base.

*Katrina Howse* – The weeks the cruise missile convoys weren't out, the base was getting so active – they were going on special nuclear alerts, from yellow alert to red alert to black alert. It was a terrific strain on the camp, because we knew we had to resist it in some way. They were direct nuclear war exercises. We used to deliberately time it to go in on black alert.

I used to go in a lot with different groupings of women, from Yellow Gate, mainly. I had a four months suspended sentence for Criminal Damage, and it was a difficult time for me because more and more, I was being followed around the fence.

I was followed by a PC Potts – I think he was specially assigned to me in some way – who was hoping to catch me cutting holes in the fence. I remember him hiding behind a rock and me just being able to see his hat, above the rock. On another occasion, we'd just cut a hole during the day and then suddenly PC Potts was shouting at me, from the other side of the fence, 'There's a hole, look, you've done this hole!' and I was saying, 'Now, then, you must give the whole truth, and nothing but the truth!' They didn't get me, at that time.

I knew I had very little leeway, but at the same time, there were very few women around who were really taking on these nuclear alerts. So what happened was, the fateful day of February 16th, I went off when they started another nuclear alert, going from yellow to red to black. I went round between Yellow Gate and Orange Gate with a group of about five or six women. It was a part of the fence that had already been cut; there were clips holding it together. Some of the women started on it first, because everyone was aware I was in this position.

One woman was proceeding to undo the clips with a tool – it wasn't bolt-cutters. She'd done quite a few, then I unwound three strands and we went in. It was during the day, and we hadn't got very far when a Security Police patrol with two USAF men inside got out and apprehended us. Then PC Potts came round and arrested us.

We got to the Processing Centre and suddenly it became apparent that everyone was going to be released except me. I was going to be charged with Criminal Damage. I knew they couldn't have had the proper evidence, because they were going on about seeing me with bolt-cutters, and everything.

While I was being held, Sarah Hipperson was saying to the Police at the Gate, 'Release Katrina Howse, or we'll do a mass raid.' There was a hole in the fence, she went through it, and then they got her, as well! They arrested her for Criminal Damage.

I was taken down to Newbury Police Station and I said to the custody Sargeant there, Cox, 'Look, this is a fixed-up charge and you can't go ahead with it.' He just went ahead with it. The MoD CID [Criminal Investigation Department] Sargeant, Williams, was really pleased with himself.

As soon as I got that charge, I just knew I was looking at four months in prison, at least, and that they'd got me on what they wanted.

*Sarah Hipperson* – I was taken to Newbury Police Station with two other women by Sgt. Williams. Sargeant Cox refused to accept the charge – Sgt. Williams was told he hadn't produced any evidence of Criminal Damage. Six weeks later, a summons was issued against me, but not against the other two women. It was becoming obvious to me that there was something sinister going on; Katrina's situation was very serious because of the earlier outstanding suspended sentence.

When my case finally came to Newbury Magistrates Court early in November, I thought I wouldn't have any real difficulty having the case dismissed.

I called the two women who had previously been arrested with me on the 16th of February. They gave evidence that supported my contention that I hadn't been anywhere near the fence when they were arrested for the offence of Criminal Damage.

I called Custody Sgt. Cox, who had refused to charge me on the 16th of February, and I called Sgt. Williams to give evidence that Sgt. Cox had refused to accept his charge against me on that day.

On demand from Sgt. Williams, I had to pay him £40.00 cash to get him to be a witness.

I was shocked when, after a full day in court, I was found Guilty. I was convicted on trumped up evidence concocted between the MoD Police and two USAF servicemen.

I took the case to appeal and it was thrown out after the prosecution witnesses failed to support the charge of Criminal Damage with evidence.

After Judge Murchie announced that there was no case to answer, I asked – through my barrister – for Costs. The Judge made the following statement: 'I will not give her one penny piece. If ever a woman brought a prosecution on herself, it is Sarah Hipperson.' I was astonished at his attitude, especially as I hadn't spoken a word in Court, and he had dismissed the prosecution's case.

**FEBRUARY 17th 1985**, Washington, US: Appeal Court rejects the case of 'Greenham Women Against Cruise'.

*Katrina Howse* – This was a network of women not from the camp, and not accountable to the women who were at the camp. The case concentrated on legally challenging the US military only, whereas the camp was against all military states.

**MARCH 1985**: notice in CND's monthly magazine 'SANITY' announces closure of the peace camp's Caledonian Road London office, and advises all mail be sent directly to the peace camp. For years afterwards, however, groups and individuals world-wide continue to claim to represent or maintain offices for the peace camp, with little or no accountability to the women living at the camp. The plea to send all mail directly to the camp still stands. Our postal address is: *Yellow Gate, Greenham Common Women's Peace Camp, nr. NEWBURY, Berkshire, England RG19 6HN.*

**MARCH 11th 1985**: death of Soviet Union President Chernenko announced. Succeeded as general secretary of the Soviet Union Communist Party by Mikhail Gorbachev.

**MARCH 15th 1985**: Belgian Prime Minister announces that deployment of 16 of the 48 cruise missiles to be stationed in Belgium is to go ahead immediately.[6]

**MARCH 18th 1985**: cruise missile convoy leaves base at 0300 hrs for Salisbury Plain. Non-violent protests at Yellow Gate.

MARCH 20th 1985, US: President Reagan's request for $1,500 million funding for a further 21 MX intercontinental ballistic missiles approved by the Senate, then by the House of Representatives on March 26th and 28th.[7]

**MARCH 27th 1985**: NATO nuclear planning group endorses for the US the 'star wars' strategic defence initiative.[8]

**APRIL 1st 1985**: Greenham Common Byelaws come into force, creating the new offence of Criminal Trespass for entering the base.

*Katrina Howse* – I think it was so many women going into the base so many times that led them to bring in the Greenham Common Byelaws. There were a lot of British Army around the silos, but not many around the rest of the perimeter fence. We'd cut holes in the fence with bolt-cutters and go in. We mostly went in at night but we would also go in during the day, if there was a nuclear alert on. It was this going in over and over again that meant, from the state's point of view, the Greenham Common Byelaws had to be drawn up. They were brought into force on

April Fool's Day 1985 and were immediately broken, exactly at midnight.

**APRIL 11th 1985**: Ann Francis, from Abergavenny, Wales, sentenced to twelve months imprisonment at Aylesbury Crown Court for Criminal Damage to the perimeter fence at Greenham Common.

**NIGHT OF APRIL 11th 1985**: Hazel Rennie and Jane Powell severely beaten at their recently established camp opposite the convoy vehicle compound (Jade Camp). Before the attack, nearby lights in the base were turned off; the two men attacking remained completely silent throughout the attack. The women suffered broken ribs and internal injuries. Both returned to the Common, once recovered.

**APRIL 24th 1985**: cruise missile convoy leaves base for exercises on Salisbury Plain. Non-violently resisted at Yellow Gate.

**APRIL 30th 1985**: cruise missile convoy returns to base in early hours, from Salisbury Plain. Stopped by women at Yellow Gate, one of whom climbed onto a launcher and was driven into the base unseen by the Police.

**APRIL – MAY 1st 1985**, London, Court of Appeal: Hipperson and Others v Electoral Registration Officer for the District of Newbury and Another.

Before Sir John Donaldson, Master of the Rolls, Lord Justice Stephen Brown and Mr Justice Glidewell.

(Judgement delivered May 1st)

'The Greenham Common women who had lived on an encampment outside the airfield in an area which spanned both Department of Transport and common land were resident there for the purposes of the Representation of the People Act 1983 and their voting qualification was not destroyed by reason of illegality or unlawfulness of residence.

The Court of Appeal ... dismissed an appeal by Mr George Anthony Meyer from Judge Peck at Newbury County Court on March 13, 1984, who ordered that the names of Sarah Hipperson, Rebecca Johnson, Caroline Rebecca Wynn Griffiths, Naomi Griffiths, Sarah Charmain Green, Muriel Jane Dennett and Katrina Howse be reinstated on the Register of Electors for the Constituency of Newbury for 1985.

The MASTER OF THE ROLLS, giving the judgment of the court, said that voting rights lay at the root of parliamentary democracy.

The seven ladies had all made a point of telling the court that each was committed to the anti-nuclear cause and Katrina Howse made it very clear that she held strong views about the position of men in society. Those facts were recorded because the ladies would wish them to be recorded, but the court disregarded them for all purposes.

Mr Meyer's objection related solely to rsidence. He contended that their residence lacked the necessary factual attributes for electoral purposes and that it had a criminal or quasi-criminal character which prevented their being treated or accepted as resident for electoral purposes.

. . . all the Greenham ladies had been living on the encampment for a substantial period and it was nothing to the point that, in theory, they might have been required to leave shortly thereafter.

. . . It was quite clear that if criminality was relevant, it could only be in relation to the criminality of residing at the qualifying address, as contrasted with the activities carried on at or from that address. Were it otherwise, burglars and brothel keepers would be disenfranchised . . .

. . .The Court rejected the submission that the franchise was affected by the fact that the qualifying residence was illegal or unlawful . . .'

**Katrina Howse** – It has to be remembered, while all this was going on, we were suffering harsh weather conditions from January right through to Spring, with very few women; also we were trying to track the cruise missile convoy and find out which woods it went to on Salisbury Plain. We not only had to keep the camp going, we also had to go out and try and track the convoy. At that stage it was difficult to find out where it was. We were doing a lot of ground work, sometimes with not much success – we weren't familiar with Salisbury Plain.

The High Court was quite nerve-wracking, because each one of us knew we were required to say something about why we shouldn't have the right to vote taken away from us, from Greenham Common.

Also we had to challenge the structure of the Court. The set-up of the Court was oppressive – we were speaking in front of High Court judges, and the Master of the Rolls, at that. It was a very formal atmosphere and you had to crane your neck up to even see the judges, because they were on one of those very old, high Victorian benches, very high up above you. The atmosphere was very alienating, but we all spoke out – we were nervous, but we knew we just had to give it all we'd got.I think we said what we had to say, and in the end, legally, they couldn't justify taking the vote away from us again – even in Thatcher's Britain.

Naomi Griffiths was represented, but the rest of us represented ourselves. I felt that, if they did take the right to vote away, at least I would've argued it myself, rather than have left it to barristers. It was too important, and it wasn't just dry legal arguments, the reason we were there was also important politically.

**APRIL 30th – MAY 5th 1985:** Reclaim Salisbury Plain Women's Walk.

This walk, organised mainly by Mary Millington, took approximately 150 women and some children over Salisbury Plain, from Avebury to Redhorn Hill at the top of the Larkhill Artillery Ranges, through the Artillery Ranges, past one of the cruise missile convoy sites called Blackball Firs and on to Stonehenge.

The vast lands of Salisbury Plain have contained military training areas for centuries, but earlier still, the land was of immense spiritual significance to the communities settled upon it. Today, the Salisbury Plain military training area covers 93,000 acres (and they are asking for more), within which there are 1,700 ancient monuments, in addition to the well-known monuments of Avebury and Stonehenge. Some areas are open to the public when firing is not taking place. Firing is signalled by red warning flags and red lights on the perimeter of the training areas.

*Mary Millington* – After it became clear that 'melting into the countryside' (which was what the military said cruise missiles would do!) actually meant having war-game exercises on Salisbury Plain, an idea began to grow in some of our minds: Salisbury Plain should be reclaimed by non-violent women.

Women from outside the camp took on the publicity. So many of us gathered at Silbury Hill on May Eve that there were very few women left at Greenham; credit should go to Sarah Hipperson and others for keeping up the 24-hour presence until we returned.

The following day we mustered at Redhorn Hill, on the northern boundary of the Larkhill Ranges. After a long meeting, it was the strong wills of Katrina, Sarah Green and Missy which got us all over a barbed wire fence and on to military land. Only a handful of arrests were made. The MoD police were quite inadequate in numbers to prevent our passage, and firing on the ranges had to be stopped as we tramped through on our Reclaiming path down the Centre Range Road.

*Katrina* – We were facing certainly over fifty MoD Police who were determined we weren't going to go on. What we did was, instead of going through them we went around them: over a barbed wire fence, around them, onto the Range and then straight down the road. They went berserk. They were running around shouting at us, 'Don't you know there's live firing!' although it was a clear road and we had some distance to go before we would get to the point where they were shelling.

The police were trying to stop women and they didn't succeed. We were spiralling around holding hands. I had a heavy rucksack on and at one time I was knocked onto my back. I couldn't get back up again with this rucksack. I was half propped up against the bank, desperately holding women's hands on either side and women were spiralling round and round, with this MoD man trying to pin me to the ground.

It was so confused, they just couldn't hold this kind of spiral walk, they couldn't stop it because we'd just spiral around them. They really tried to use violence, to push women down, hold women down, and it just didn't work in the end.

Then they started running towards us saying, 'OK, OK, just slow down, we'll get them to stop the firing.' And sure enough, a couple of minutes later, as we walked slowly on, we saw the shelling stopped and we saw the British Army retreating. Huge waves of dust were thrown up into the air from tanks that had fired shells. They were going, the British Army was retreating and it felt amazing, like this must be the first time the British Army had been defeated by non-violent women.

We continued – we could not walk off that road running down Larkhill Artillery Range because on either side there are unexploded bombs. As we stopped for lunch, who should come down the road, in what I thought looked like a tea-van, but was actually some kind of Property Services Agency vehicle, but "Stitcher" Williams, Sargeant Williams who had stitched me up on that Criminal Damage charge (he was calling himself "Stitcher Williams" by this stage). I think he was sent down to identify which camp women were on the walk. As he came past I shouted at him, 'Three black teas and no sugar!'

After lunch we carried on down that road. It was a very joyful thing.

*Mary Millington* – We set up camp beside the Bustard pub, and were awoken next morning to an angry tirade of shelling, tanks and helicopters: the military were very strongly resentful of our success in stopping them the day before!

We insisted on walking through Larkhill army camp, Missy shouting, 'Stop playing wars!' at the top of her voice.

Then Stonehenge came into view, already fenced 'round in preparation for the war against the Solstice festival (about to become legal if it should be held for a 12th year). They gave us the overflow car-park as a camp-site, then the eclipse of the moon was celebrated with dancing, chanting and drumming among the stones.

The next day some of us took off for Beach's Barn, a site on Bulford Ranges which had been used for cruise missile exercises. As we reclaimed this copse, we were arrested and charged.

From this until mid-1990, Yellow Gate women were

repeatedly arrested while interrupting cruise missile exercises on Salisbury Plain.

MAY 25th 1985: 'No Name Action': between three and four hundred women Trespassed in the base and approximately forty refused to give names. 'No Name' women were taken to Newbury Police cells to appear in Court immediately. Those whom the Police were unable to identify were sentenced to seven days imprisonment and sent to Holloway identified by numbers. These women were then dispersed to various women's prisons.

JUNE 3rd 1985: Katrina Howse found Guilty of stitched up Criminal Damage charge in Newbury Magistrates Court. Katrina refused to accept bail conditions and did 19 days on remand in Holloway. She was committed to Reading Crown Court for sentencing, and appealed her conviction to Reading Crown Court.

JUNE 3rd 1985: 'Katrina Tank Action': new British Army artillery tank stopped and occupied on A34 by women returning to the camp after having attended Katrina's trial in Newbury Magistrates Court. All women arrested give their name as 'Katrina', in solidarity with Katrina Howse.

JUNE 1985: riots in Holloway Women's Prison. Male officers drafted in.

JUNE 14th 1985: Ann Francis's twelve months sentence reduced on Appeal to six months plus six months suspended.

JUNE 14th, 1995: 41 women travel by bus to the Soviet Union. *Sarah Hipperson* - The trip was originally intended to be a trip by Greenham women. However, the cost was too expensive for many camp women so the trip was shared with women who had no connection with the camp – therefore we were not able to make contacts with regard to Soviet nuclear policy.

We did make a connection with Olga Medvecova, a Soviet dissident woman. In light of the situation she had been in five months previously, meeting Olga in Moscow seemed like a miracle but in reality was due to the work of Jane Dennett, who on other occasions had bravely spoken out and made contact with other dissidents. I learned from Jane also to speak out in these situations.

Olga was under house arrest but in true Greenham fashion Barbara Gordon and I did a 'sit in' outside her apartment, eventually wearing down the KGB agents so that we were able to have tea with her and accompany her, her husband and baby to their local police station to ask for the release of a young dissident man who had been arrested for trying to make contact with the Medvecovas.

This young man was released 15 minutes after we returned to

their flat, and we had the chance to meet him.

Some years later when the Medvecovas were allowed to leave the Soviet Union, Olga came to visit the camp, but I didn't have the opportunity to talk with her.

Two entries in my diary of that trip remind me that my mind was not far from Greenham: 16th June – a visit to the Berlin Wall – on it I wrote the message, 'Free Ann Francis and Katrina Howse'. 25th June – from Kiev I made a phone call to my friend Aileen Brownlie in Wanstead. She had agreed to take messages from the camp for me. The good news was that Katrina was out of prison, having been granted bail on the 21st June. The camp was strong. I sent my love to them and went off to share the good news with the other camp women on the trip.

JULY 1985: British Nuclear Fuels Ltd. (BNFL) convicted on three charges of mismanagement and negligence as a result of a serious leakage in November 1983 from their nuclear reprocessing plant at Windscale, Cumbria (later renamed Sellafield).

JULY 10th 1985, New Zealand: Greenpeace ship 'Rainbow Warrior' is sunk in New Zealand harbour and crew member Fernando Pereiro is killed. Consensus in French media is that the DGSE, French Secret Service, are responsible.

JULY 26th, 1985: Sarah Hipperson sent to Holloway for 7 days, for Trespass of 1st April 1985.

*Sarah* ⁻ This was not my first prison sentence, but one I wish to record principally because I believe I was sent down as a result of a corrupt, politically motivated government decision to remove me and other women from Greenham Common, to stop our protest against the preparations for nuclear war being carried on there minute by minute, hour by hour, daily. I'd been convicted of Trespass, under a law brought into being to give a legal gloss to this abuse of power by the Secretary of State for Defence, Michael Heseltine.

This was one more bankrupt scheme amongst so many others. I kept wondering how people in these positions of power fail to reach any understanding about our commitment, when every day it was demonstrated to them by our resistance to all their plans.

On the 1st of April when Michael Heseltine instituted the Greenham Common Byelaws, a huge number of women entered the base one minute into that day, to demonstrate to him that his threat would not work. After hours of arresting and charging women, the MoD police may have realised that the date on each charge sheet would read 1st April, and wondered whether this was an April Fool's joke.

I remember going off to prison on the 26th July thinking the Byelaws charges are going to keep them all busy – the police, the courts and the prisons. Serves them right.

**JULY 10TH – 27th 1985**, Nairobi, Kenya: conference to mark end of the United Nations Decade for Women.

**JULY – AUGUST 1985**: many Greenham Common Byelaws offences tried in Newbury Magistrates Court. For non-payment of fines imposed, women are sentenced from one day in Police cells to seven days in Holloway, to three months imprisonment to Katrina Howse for refusing to be bound over to 'keep the peace' (released after four days).

**AUGUST 11th 1985**: women lodge an official complaint after personal belongings destroyed in the course of an eviction.

**AUGUST 20th 1985**: cars smashed and turned over at Green Gate at around midnight.

**AUGUST 27th 1985**: woman hit by USAF cruise missile convoy support vehicle, while demonstrating against cruise deployment. Taken to hospital with a crushed leg.

This incident was later listed in a USAF year-end list of achievements, a document leaked to the peace camp.

**SEPTEMBER 8th – 9th 1985**: fourth birthday celebrations for the peace camp. Thousands of women, including Jacoba Seman and Maria Pangelinan from Saipan in the Pacific come to Greenham Common.

Large numbers of arrests for Trespass.

One woman strip-searched at Newbury Police Station in presence of two male Police officers.

**SEPTEMBER 17th – 18th 1985**: Katrina Howse sentenced to six months imprisonment at Reading Crown Court for Criminal Damage to perimeter fence, i.e. stitched up charge of February 16th.

*Katrina* – In June in Newbury Magistrates Court, the two USAF men had obviously been tutored in their Prosecution statements. Just one difference in wording had been inserted between them, obviously just a slight change from an original format they'd been given. I couldn't get through it, at Newbury Magistrates Court.

That summer was taken up battling to get Witness Summonses out. The particular one I wanted to be witness summonsed was Sgt Williams,'Stitcher' Williams.

That first day at Reading Crown Court was a shambles for the Prosecution, an absolute shambles. I tried to pull out the way in which the two USAF statements showed an orchestrated similarity. In the course of the trial, the typewritten version of these two men's statements against me were produced, and then the written versions, in their handwriting. The written version of each one was quite substantially different from the typewritten version – whole phrases were different.

I couldn't believe it, because I'd only seen the typed version – and neither could the Prosecution barrister. The Judge saw it. The Prosecution barrister was saying, 'Bloody hell, bloody hell! What's all this about?' – swearing away. The Judge just said to the Prosecution, 'How can you explain this?' and the Prosecution were saying, 'Um, could we have an adjournment?'

The Judge was angry it had been exposed in Court in that way. After that was exposed, he had to do the work of holding the case together. The Prosecution case had fallen to bits. The Judge was angry not at the potential false evidence, he was angry because he had to hold it together for them, because the two main Prosecution witnesses had been exposed.

I got to question Sgt Williams, which was good. But when I came to my defence case, I had to say I had unwound three strands of fence. I also said that, as a child, over the Cuban missile crisis my Mum had tucked us into bed and thought, well there may not be a world tomorrow, but I'm going to make sure they're as comfortable as possible. My father had died in the November, and I felt his presence quite strongly in the court.

I went down to the cells, came back again and the Judge said, 'Guilty'. When he pronounced sentence on me, he turned his head away and said something like, 'Clearly in breach of suspended sentence; four months, plus two months for the commission of this offence – six months in all.'

I said, 'Look me in the eye, look me in the eye when you sentence me.' He wouldn't, he just looked down.

I went down, and I just couldn't believe it. It took me two weeks to begin to find my feet. The first week was just a nightmare. Compared with what most women are doing in there, six months isn't a lot, but when it happens to you, six months is a long time.

I couldn't stand to be in Holloway any more, to be surrounded by the concrete of it. I knew I'd be better once I got moved to the country. There was a shipment out to Bullwood Hall, and I was on it.

Once I got to Bullwood Hall, I started coping. I had a friend in Bullwood Hall, a Ghanaian woman I'd met the August before. She'd been in for about 30 months, and at the end of September, shortly after I got to Bullwood Hall, she was released. That was really good, to see her go out.

Although psychologically Bullwood Hall was better for me than Holloway, it also is a huge dump of a place. You have to 'slop out' – there aren't toilets in the cells. You're locked in some nights, if you don't get association, from five o'clock until eight o'clock the next morning, and they won't unlock the doors unless women are really, really ill.

I was on a vegan diet [containing no animal products whatsoever], which consisted a lot of the time of frozen vegetables and salads, with huge chunks of raw onion in them. It was deficient in everything: fat, protein, carbohydrates, vitamins and minerals. Nearly every day, I would make a Governor's App. [an application to complain to the prison's governor or assistant governor]. I would tell them what I'd had to eat that day, say if there had been an improvement on the previous day or if the diet had worsened. Improvements were generally short-lived. I had to complain all the time, because the budget for each prisoner just wasn't enough and that's all they'd say to me. But I still complained, almost daily, right to the end of my sentence.

At the start, they really seemed to have no idea about what a vegan could eat. They even thought I could digest half a raw onion, whole. By the end, the diet had improved.

Over the years, the vegan diet in prisons seems to have further improved, through the constant complaints of vegans in prison. –

Katrina's trial in Reading Crown Court and sentence were not reported in any media.

**SEPTEMBER 18th 1985**, Brixton, South London: Police shoot Mrs Cherry Groce.

Home Secretary, Hurd, approves use by Police of tear gas and plastic bullets to respond to unrest in inner cities. Promises new Public Order Bill at Tory Party Conference in October.

**NOVEMBER 19th -20th 1985**, Geneva: President Reagan and Gorbachev meet, the first such summit meeting for over six years.

**DECEMBER 5th 1985**: Year End Report, Headquarters 501st Security Police Group, USAF, which was subsequently leaked to the peace camp:

To: All Personnel

1. The 501st Security Police Group has had another outstanding year. As the year draws to a close we find ourselves reviewing and preparing documents that recount the many accomplishments of the unit. It could not have happened without your support and dedication.

- You were selected Best SP[Security Police] Group in 3AF, USAFE and USAF for 1984.

- You are a member of the largest GLCM[Ground Launched Cruise Missile] SP Group with the largest SP fleet in USAFE . . .

- . . . We've had crime prevention displays for National Police Week and Crime Prevention Month. Four hundred arrests of peace women were made . . .

- The Greenham bylaws went into effect, the superfence was

constructed and we hit one peacewoman with a vehicle.

– We had four wing quarterly award winners . . .

2. It's been a busy year. It's been a productive year. You should be proud of your accomplishments. Let's make 1986 an even better one than 1985. As we enter the holiday season we and our wives wish you a very Merry Christmas and a prosperous New Year.

[signed]DAVID P. MILLS, Lt Col, USAF Commander
and WAYNE H. COX, CMSgt, USAF Chief Enlisted Manager"

**DECEMBER 14th -15th 1985:** an estimated 12,000 women attend Widening the Web demonstration at Greenham Common.

*Sarah Hipperson* – At this gathering, the Wages for Housework Campaign, who are based at the King's Cross Women's Centre in London, acknowledged our work and made a vital political connection with the camp. They worked with us to create themes for the workshops held at 7 of the Gates.

The overall theme, 'PAY WOMEN NOT THE MILITARY' made a clear statement on which we could recognise each other's work. The Wages for Housework 1985 leaflet said, 'GREENHAM HAS HELPED TO MAKE VISIBLE WHERE THE WEALTH OUR WORK CREATES IS BEING SPENT. WHILE WOMEN DO TWO-THIRDS OF THE WORLD'S WORK FOR 5% OF THE INCOME AND 1% OF THE ASSETS, THE U.S. ALONE SPENDS $28 MILLION EVERY HOUR ON THE MILITARY.'

**DECEMBER 27th 1985:** Katrina Howse released from Bullwood Hall women's prison.

**On non-violence:**
'Vigorous resistance to violence
without perpetuating abuse.'
- *Katrina Howse*

# 1986
# THIS SACRED LAND WE WALK UPON

The first day of the New Year had, since the dawn occupation of the missile silos construction site on the first of January 1983, become a day for affirming and renewing the camp's commitment to active non-violent resistance to the military.

On New Year's day in 1986, President Reagan and General Secretary Gorbachev also promised to work for peace, in simultaneous television addresses to each other's countries. As the two leaders of the most powerful military states in the world attempted to warm up super-power relations, inside Greenham Common air base some twelve women sat shivering in their cells in a prison bus. The United Nations' International Year of Peace had begun.

**JANUARY 1st 1986:** *Aniko Jones* was visiting Green Gate at this time − I'd arrived at Green Gate a few days after Christmas. We'd decided one of the best ways to celebrate the New Year was to go into the base, and start the New Year resisting. So we went in − about twelve women, at half-past eleven the night before, so that we'd be in the base at midnight. We walked along the runway. The stars were shining, it was cold and frosty, but it was so clear, and there was a lot of energy. At midnight we all sat down in the middle of the runway, where there's a grass area, and looked up at the stars.

We continued walking along the base and eventually we were arrested, put in a van and taken to the Processing Centre, which I think was near Orange Gate then. There were two empty Portakabins, but instead of being placed into the empty Portakabins we were put into what's called a prison bus. That was one of the very old prison buses, and the cells were even smaller than the ones they have now. A prison bus is about the size of a large horse-box and it's got sixteen cells in it, eight cells on either side. Each cell is just like a metal box; they're so small that you can just about stand up in them and there's no room to put your legs, you can't even cross your legs in it. There's just one straight wall in front of you.

I remember 1985 was one of the coldest years we've had on record, and this bus had no heating. When we were put in, we were told we were only going to be in there for a few minutes, then we were going to go to the Portakabins − they were just waiting for them to warm up or something. But after an hour we were still all there, and had not been processed. I was one of the last to be processed, so I'd been in about an hour and a half.

One woman had been arrested for cutting the fence, but she said she hadn't done it. There were no witnesses, so they had to drop the charge on her. A Ministry of Defence Policeman then said it wasn't her, it was me. I was taken out of the prison bus. They said, 'Is it possible that you cut the fence?' This was the first time I'd come up against a situation like that and I was silent, I didn't know what to do. I was put back in the prison bus.

There was a metal bar in the cell, so I started bashing at the grate. I made a hole in the grate – which I was pleased about, because I was so angry about being put in that place. I didn't feel it was right for us to be put in there, and hopefully it would prevent them from using that bus for a while afterwards. I was taken out and arrested for Criminal Damage to the door of the prison bus cell, then I was put back in and four and three-quarter hours later I was taken out of the prison bus and transported in one of the American Police cars to Newbury Police station.

I was absolutely freezing. When I look back and remember that night, I can clearly recall being able to look down on myself. I could see my body sitting in that metal box as if my real self was not in the cell, but above it. I watched myself being taken from one place to another. Nothing seemed real; I think I went into that mental state as a form of protection against the treatment we'd received and the complete feeling of powerlessness. If I withdrew as much as I could from the situation, then the less they could affect me.

JANUARY 9th 1986: Secretary of State for Defence, Michael Heseltine, resigns during 'the Westland affair' and is replaced by George Younger.

JANUARY 25th 1985: military periodical JANE'S DEFENCE WEEKLY publishes cover story 'Soviet Spetsnaz at Greenham', claiming Soviet women agents called Spetsnaz had infiltrated the peace camps at Greenham Common. The ultimate purpose of the Spetsnaz agents was to 'attack the missile sites under war or surprise conditions in a pre-emptive strike', but 'the initial purpose is to incite protesters to mount protests and demonstrations to test the defending forces' reaction times and to monitor security arrangements and timings of cruise missile convoys leaving Greenham.' Women are trained in camps in 'wild and isolated' areas of the Soviet Union, where 'Western nuclear-capable weapons systems are simulated by life-size inflatable dummy models'. An artist's impression of a Spetsnaz training camp illustrates the mock-up systems – complete with inflatable ground-launched cruise missile launchers.

This article was given wide coverage in the British media. Newspaper, radio and television reports meant that the phrases 'trained

Soviet Spetsnaz spies' and 'Greenham women' had been linked, however confusedly, in the public mind.

*Katrina Howse* — There always had been slurs about us working for 'Kremlin gold'. At Yellow Gate we were clear about our non-aligned position, being against all the military super-power states. Nothing ever came into the Press in a big way now but state propaganda about us. The state had decided to hit out at us again, but behind this was an awareness of our strength and an inability to deal with it.

I knew they were talking about the dedicated actions we had planned and carried out but they couldn't believe that non-aligned women would be able to do this unaided by the 'enemy' super-power state. Actions were always generated by the peace camp, and the strength to carry out these actions could only come from a genuine independence from military states. We also determinedly held on to the autonomy of the peace camp at Yellow Gate, against any outside network of women trying to speak for us, whether to International gatherings or to the Press. The state had branded us the 'enemy' once again, but the truth was we were the enemy of all militarists, everywhere.

**FEBRUARY 1986**, US: President Reagan calling for a further 40% increase in US defence spending over the next five years, but his Administration's request for a $320,000 million budget for 1987 was slightly cut by Congress to $295,000 million in August. Despite this cut, 1986 saw weapons systems which had been the focus of political controversy for a decade or more at last appearing in active service. B-1 bombers became operational in October, and by the end of the year there were ten MX missiles deployed in fixed silos in Wyoming.

In Britain this month there was a further (see July 1985, above) series of major leaks from Sellafield (formerly Windscale), Cumbria, including the release of a 'plutonium nitrate mist'. Construction workers at the site stage protest strikes.

**MARCH 1986**: US naval forces at the Gulf of Sirte. Naval aircraft flew south on March 23rd, and on March 24th three ships sailed south into the area of the Gulf which Libya claimed as territorial waters. Libya fired at the aircraft, none of which were hit. The US attacked, both on the 24th and on the following day. US officials said the attacks on the 25th were in response to further Libyan missile attacks, but later acknowledged that none had taken place. US spokesmen said 'at least two' Libyan ships had been sunk. This caused the loss of between 56 and 97 Libyan lives.[1]

**APRIL 2nd 1986**: bomb explodes on a US TWA plane, killing four passengers.

APRIL 5th 1986: bomb explodes in West Berlin discotheque frequented by US servicemen, killing a Turkish woman and a US soldier and injuring about 200 others.

US officials said there was 'strong circumstantial evidence' of Libyan involvement, and during the next days US officials repeatedly accused Libya of responsibility for terrorist attacks. There was speculation that an attack on Libya was imminent.

APRIL 15th 1986: at 0200 local time, US aircraft bombed Tripoli and Benghazi in Libya. The aircraft used were F111's based at air bases in Oxfordshire (Upper Heyford) and Suffolk (Lakenheath), England.

GUARDIAN newspaper carries the headline 'Situation normal at USAF English bases'. David Fairhall reports red alert standby merely refers to a practice exercise: 'A USAF spokesman said that the intense activity was part of a four-day exercise for which plans were made last August.'

AFTERNOON OF APRIL 15th 1986: eight women from Greenham Common enter Upper Heyford air base.

*Sarah Hipperson* – I recall waking up to the news on my radio that the American military had bombed Libya and that the planes had left from Upper Heyford. I had never been there before but I knew that before the day was over I would visit there.

I was due in court to act as a McKenzie friend (legal supporter and adviser) to a young woman who had just served 3 months within a short time of living at the camp and was expecting to go to prison again. She was appealing for a suspended sentence on this occasion. This was granted and I was then free.

Katrina Howse was waiting for me to finish in court and after a very short conversation we decided to take action at Upper Heyford. We found 6 other women and set off in Missy's green van, with red paint and a pair of bolt cutters.

When we arrived near the base we had to run over a deeply ploughed field to get to the fence. As we ran I could hear this farmer shouting at the top of his voice, 'This is private land!' I half expected to hear him shoot his gun over our heads, but nothing could stop us.

We cut the fence and entered the base, to the astonishment of the airmen sitting at their machine guns, pointed at us. Before they had time to react we were pouring the red paint on the approach road, where the F111's were. We wrote 'MURDERERS' on everything around, before we were arrested.

As we were driven through the base to the holding cells we hung our arms, dripping with red paint, limply out of the windows; with our keening voices we created a frightening spectacle to the many bystanders.

While we were being held I developed a suspicion there was going to be a cover-up of our effective action, so I decided to make a statement which could not be ignored.

I stood trial months later in Banbury Magistrates Court in front of a very nervous bench. The Chairwoman had all the women from the camp dragged from the court and locked out of the proceedings.

Time had passed since the bombing of Libya. There had been much hollow justification from the apologists for the US attack, but decent thinking people would not accept Reagan's assertion that he had 'direct, precise irrefutable evidence' of Libyan involvement in the Berlin disco bombing, and that this gave him the right to undertake the attack under Article 51 of the UN Charter.

I was found Guilty of Criminal Damage and sentenced to a month in prison after claiming that the US bombing of Libya was in violation of UN Charter Article 2 (4) which states 'all members shall refrain in their international relations in the threat or use of force against the territorial integrity or political independence of any state or in any manner inconsistent with the purposes of the UN.'

**NIGHT OF APRIL 15th 1986:** cruise missile convoy returns to Greenham Common. Blockades at Main Gate.

*Sarah Hipperson* − After we were released from Upper Heyford we returned to a very sombre camp. The ground launched cruise missile convoy was expected back from Salisbury Plain. Myra Hughes came over to Katrina and I saying how glad she was to see us back at the camp. There were a good number of women, all standing silently on the pavement of the slip road. Some of these were Cruisewatch women. On this occasion they had made a decision to observe radio silence and not to take action against the convoy, or do anything that might make the convoy 'vulnerable to terrorists'. Myra didn't agree with this and neither did Katrina or I.

Katrina, Myra, Joan and I dragged the fire onto the approach road and took on the incoming convoy as we always did − this was our work.

As far as we were concerned, the terrorists were already with the convoy and would not receive any protection or cooperation from us. Cruisewatch's muddled thinking would again appear in 1987 when a similar scenario would present itself, the US in dispute with Iran and the nuclear convoy being taken to Salisbury Plain. All those who threaten nuclear war are terrorists. I have no sense of wanting to protect 'our' nuclear terrorists in preference to 'foreign' terrorists.

**APRIL 17th, 1986:** the trespass which was to lay the foundation for the legal challenge to the Greenham Common Byelaws (1985) takes place.

For years previously, women had been continually entering the base to disrupt exercises and challenge the presence of the USAF. As a result, Byelaws were introduced which would criminalise women for doing so. Despite this, women saw no reason to desist from this work and continued to disrupt the military's activities inside the base, with the aim of making the Byelaws unworkable through sheer volume of cases brought to court.

*Jean Hutchinson* – Georgina Smith and I were monitoring vehicles in the base – we heard the vehicles starting up and decided to go in because we believed the convoy could be about to come out. We saw a cruise missile launcher and ran, shouting, 'Stop!' We were arrested and charged under the Military Lands Act (1892) Byelaws for Greenham Common.

Little did we know then, that the case started by this action would run for over 4 years.

The Byelaws, which came into operation on the 1st of April 1985, made good April fools of the MoD, especially Michael Heseltine. Many times at Yellow Gate we speculated about the ways in which they might be illegal because we felt by instinct that they were wrong. Sarah Green had an idea that they were a duplication of other laws. I said they seemed rather American because I had been charged in 1983 for conspiring to trespass at Williams International in Michigan – the factory which made 75% of cruise engines.

We knew England did not have trespass laws, where damage had not been done. These thoughts and others were expressed in our court cases in Newbury Magistrates Court *ad infinitum*.

We were bailed until 23rd July, and we knew from the moment we went into Newbury Magistrates Court that we would appeal to the Crown Court.

APRIL 21st 1986: second bombing of Libya feared, under guise of large F111 exercise. Five women enter Upper Heyford base, occupy hangar housing two F111 planes. Three wrote on planes, two occupied an F111. All charged with Criminal Damage and immediately remanded in custody. The planes were grounded for extensive checks.

*Katrina Howse* – We were in Court for something and a woman came in as we were spectating and said, 'I've heard on the radio that there's going to be an exercise at Upper Heyford and Lakenheath, and the BBC are saying, don't worry, it's not going to be another bombing.'

We thought, 'Well, we have to act again.' So we came back to the camp that evening, a group formed, and we went off to Upper Heyford.

We were driven at night by a woman who was visiting.

We cut the fence and walked in. We decided we were going to walk very, very slowly. Hand in hand, we walked right up onto the runway, to a hangar where they were working on two F111's. We got into the hangar and then three of the women started writing on both the F111 planes. There were two USAF men working on the planes. One got really aggressive, and started threatening women with a spanner. He was saying, 'Get away from my plane!' Carol, Juley and Gaelle wrote messages condemning the bombing of Libya, with black felt marker pens.

Lorna and I decided we weren't going to do any Criminal Damage, myself because of the six month sentence I'd done. So, we got up onto the F111, and we sat in the cockpit. Then I thought, oh no, this machine is so dangerous, and I got out and we sat on a wing. Then the USAF set the alarm off and all these men trooped in, with machine guns. We were singing, 'We are gentle, angry women,' a song by Holly Near, very softly and very calmly.

We were all rounded up and put in Police Sherpa vans. We were taken out onto the middle of the runway and searched. It was pitch black, we couldn't see, and we were searched by a USAF woman in the middle of the runway. I think I knew then that we'd done a very successful non-violent direct action because they were so angry. And we actually still thought that the planes were going to go off, to bomb Libya at that time, so we were shouting and calling out.

We were taken to a bunker-like building and processed. When we were in the Processing Centre I just thought, oh, thank goodness we've done something. And it was such a good action.

Then of course the CID [Criminal Investigation Department] came through and took statements.

**Record of Interview:**

Q. Did you cause any damage to any aircraft or property here at Upper Heyford earlier today?

A. I non-violently occupied an F111 plane nuclear bomber that had been used to kill hundreds of people one week ago. I sat in it and on it as the best non violent means I have of protesting that murder and the potential murder of all the bombs that were stacked next to it.

Q. Did you sit in the cockpit of the aircraft?

A. I did to non violently make my presence felt. To do no damage physically but to stop it in the only way I can through to power of my spirit.

Q. Did you cause any damage to the aircraft by writing any slogans on the aircraft or any property in the hangar?

*A.* My intention was not to do that and I did not do it.

*Q.* Did you touch any equipment in the cockpit at all?

*A.* The F111's are machines of mass murder. I took special care to touch nothing.

*Q.* I am terminating this interview.

Interviewees signature: Katrina Howse

Interview commenced: 04.12 am. Concluded: 04.25 am.

It seemed like ages we were waiting. Then we found out we were going to Court the next day. We were going to be held over. We were all charged with Criminal Damage. I just knew then that we'd gone too far, as far as they were concerned, and they weren't going to set us free.

We spent the night in Banbury Police Station. We appeared before the Magistrates Court that morning, and were all remanded. They said they wanted to check over how much damage had been done, before we got bail. We all got sent down to Holloway for the next 8 days.

Apparently those two planes didn't take off that night, because they had to check all the computer equipment. That's something that came out in the Court case. Although I'd said at the time that I didn't touch anything in the cockpit, and I certainly wouldn't have messed with anything there, they had to check it all.

We were in Holloway for 8 days on remand, and during that time, one of the prison warders came up to me and said, there had been a bad radiation leak, from the Soviet Union. She got me a copy of the paper that normally circulates round the wing. That's when I first heard that there'd been a serious nuclear accident at Chernobyl and that radiation had been released. So that felt like a double blow, in a way – being in prison when Chernobyl happened. It underscores your vulnerability – you can't get out and run.

We went back to Court on Beltane, April 30th, and came out to learn about the effects of Chernobyl.

**APRIL 26th 1986**, Ukraine, Soviet Union: explosions at Chernobyl nuclear power station. the world's worst nuclear power accident.

**MAY 2nd ONWARDS 1986**: radioactive cloud from Chernobyl passes over Britain.

*Beth Junor* – I was visiting the camp at the time. It was such wet weather – it seemed to be raining all the time. Everything was soaked, and everyone was soaked. It was that kind of incessant rain, in which you just can't keep dry at the camp. We all knew the rain had the fall-out from Chernobyl in it, but the constant evictions meant there was no 'indoors' for us to go to.

There was a lot of scepticism about the information being given out in Britain at the time. It was just generally assumed that the information in the media, descriptions of effects and so on were all underestimates.

When I got back to Aberdeen, I heard on the radio that there was a lab at the University where you could take things to get them monitored for radioactivity, so I kept the gore-tex [sleeping bag cover] I'd borrowed, and the waterproof coat I'd been wearing at the camp rolled up in a bag. One day after work I cycled down to this lab. That was about a week after I'd returned. A man went over these things with a device which made a ticking noise, which he said was 'just background radiation'. Then he ran it over the gore-tex and the coat and the machine's ticking increased in frequency, especially round the seams, which were still damp. I saw the needle on the machine going up and up. He said there were above-normal readings of certain types of radioactivity, but that it was 'nothing to worry about'. I remembered the figures and wrote them in a letter to the camp at the time. And, he'd said, if I'd had the reading done a week before, it would've been that much again, because the half-life of one type of radioactive material is about a week.

I've since read that amongst the many tonnes of radioactive materials that were sent up into the atmosphere by Chernobyl, was iodine-131, which has a half-life of eight days, and which is easily absorbed by living tissue. Another type easily absorbed was caesium, which has a half-life of thirty years! We don't know yet how much damage was suffered by the plants, animals and people living in the vast fall-out areas, nor by the women living at the camp that May, nor by homeless people, who were of necessity outdoors all the time. But there was nothing they could have done to protect themselves – being evicted all the time means you can't build any proper shelter for yourself. There was no place they could hide, from a disaster like that.

MID-MAY 1986: danger of a meltdown of the Chernobyl reactor's radioactive core apparently averted, but many rescue workers suffered sever radioactive contamination. Official figures said 299 were hospitalised and that there were 24 deaths by June 5th – in addition to the 2 killed in initial explosions. On August 6th, PRAVDA criticized supply and discipline problems in the clean-up operation; later in August, the Estonian-language daily newspaper of the Komsomol (Young Communists) in Estonia reported that military conscripts involved in the operation had protested over being required to spend long periods in the contaminated areas.

MAY 10th 1986: letter from Yellow Gate women to members of the International Year of Peace Council, London:

As women committed to working for peace and to living at Greenham Common, we oppose the inclusion of Coalition for Peace through Security, and Women and Families for Defence on the IYPC. From our personal experience over a long time, we have seen both these organisations try to discredit what we see as sincere efforts for peace. While we are open to working with people who have different views, we cannot work with two organizations who are openly oppressive: sexist, homophobic, racist and classist. CPS and WFFD should not be able to gain credibility by sitting on the Council with others they have worked against in the past. The logical extension of allowing Coalition for Peace through Security and Women and Families for Defence to sit on the Peace Council is inviting the British Movement and the RAF to work alongside other peace groups.

If CPS and WFFD are allowed to remain on the IYPC, we will publicly withdraw our support from this farce and ask every other group to do the same.

Signed by 17 women.

*Sarah Hipperson* – Back in early March, Siân Evans from the Wages for Housework Campaign, who I'd known since 1983 when she lived at Orange Gate, was on a visit to Yellow Gate. She wanted to know if the camp had been informed of the meetings going on in London with regard to the International Year of Peace (IYP). I said I hadn't heard anything, and other women said the same. We hadn't been invited to take part in the Council of the IYP. We were shocked, then, to find out that the Coalition for Peace through Security (CPS), Women and Families for Defence (WFFD) and Peace Through NATO (PTN) were acceptable to the IYP Council and active on committees and in working groups.

The proclamation of the IYP stated 'the promotion of international peace and security requires continuing and positive action by states and peoples aimed at the prevention of war, the removal of various threats to peace – including the nuclear threat' and also listed the 'elimination of racial discrimination and apartheid', among other aspirations.

All three of these right-wing groups failed in the first instance. They supported the Conservative government's defence policy based on a willingness to use nuclear weapons. Mrs Thatcher had given that assurance to the supporters of this policy by stating at a press conference (1/6/83, reported in the GUARDIAN), saying she would be prepared to fire the weapons – referring to nuclear weapons.

At Greenham we had first hand experience of the work of the CPS when they attempted to disenfranchise us and have our residence on Greenham Common undermined. Also, Olga Maitland of WFFD came to the USAF base to offer her organisation's support to the men who carried out the monthly preparations for mass murder when operating the cruise missile convoys.

**MAY 12th, 1986**, London, International Year of Peace Council meeting: the Wages for Housework Campaign represented by Wilmette Brown and Greenham Common Women's Peace Camp represented by Sarah Hipperson, and supported by 50 letters representing groups and individuals, ask for the expulsion of the CPS, WFFD and PTN from the IYP Council. The Council fails to expel these three extreme right-wing, pro-war organisations.

Wilmette Brown said, 'It is not possible for this Council to stand for peace and war at the same time, for NATO and for the Peace Movement, for organisations acceptable to the National Front and for Black people's interests, for the bomb and against it, for increasing and for decreasing military expenditure. We do not accept the Orwellian notion that war is peace.' Wilmette made it clear that, despite a Council vote for confidentiality, she was responsible to and would be reporting back to the widest possible public.

Responding to the many delegates, including the British Council of Churches and 2 Quaker organisations who said the pro-war members were necessary for peaceful dialogue and debate, Sarah Hipperson said, 'When I venture away from Greenham, I find people more interested in the club and the rules than whether we'll survive in this world . . ..Every time I'm evicted five times a day in the pouring rain, every time people are dying in Africa, I know why – it's because the Peace Movement is debating how to get along together.'

The National CND Executive representative, though mandated to support Wages for Housework and Greenham's call for the expulsion of CPS and WFFD (but not PTN), and to withdraw CND from the Council if this did not take place, in the end came out against voting on the issue.[2]

The Wages for Housework Campaign and the women's peace camp were equally visible and vocal in this challenge, yet, at every level, during the meeting and in public letters to PEACE NEWS, Greenham's work in exposing this outrage was studiously ignored by Sheila Oakes and other members of the Council.

This experience certainly alerted me to a greater understanding of how colonialism works – as long as we remained on the Common, did not give voice to opinions going deeper than platitudes, and were happy to see the peace movement as a 'club' we belonged to, we would be tolerated and given financial support. Some of us just would not put up with this treatment.

National CND was eventually persuaded to leave the IYP Council through the work of some Greenham women, in particular Sarah Hipperson, together with the Wages for Housework Campaign and many CND local groups and other grassroots peace and anti-racist activists.

JUNE 1986: reprieve at Yellow Gate from monthly convoy deployment exercises over the Summer Solstice month, due to insufficient numbers of Police available to Police both the cruise missile deployment and the Stonehenge site.

Evictions of the camp continue at rate of five or six per week.

JULY 1986: Women's camp at Green Gate folds.[3]

JULY 23rd, 1986, Newbury Magistrates Court: Jean Hutchinson and Georgina Smith tried for Trespass.

*Jean Hutchinson* – On the morning of the Magistrates Court trial, both Georgina and myself read of some Mildenhall magistrates finding a man named John Bugg Not Guilty of a charge under the Military Lands Act (1892) Byelaws.

Although claim to invalidity of the Byelaws was made before the Magistrates we were found Guilty – we thought, because we didn't have sufficient legal points, but it turned out we didn't have the *one* essential point, the *proviso* (see below).

Technically, the Byelaws had been written in such a way as to allow no defence and even if we had known of the proviso at that point, the Magistrates would have run scared. The question was, would prison follow as usual for unpaid fines?

Now began a process of discovery – examining the Military Lands Act (MLAct) itself we came across the proviso, under Part II of the Act. We could not think as lawyers, we only had our Greenham instincts.

The material written by me is never written in a purely legal way, but more importantly, from a Greenham woman's view of the missiles *and* the Common. Section 14 of the MLAct reads, 'the Secretary of State for Defence is enabled to exercise his powers in the making of byelaws,' but the power is limited by the proviso which states that 'no byelaws promulgated under this section shall authorise the Secretary of State to take away or prejudicially affect any right of common.' Like a miracle, the Byelaws were wrong because Greenham Common was (and is) a registered Common under the Commons Registration Act 1965 (with individual Commoners needing to re-register their rights by 1973). The registration was described as *final*. We began to learn the legal phrases, 'the Byelaws are *ultra vires* the Military Lands Act' – that means they are outside, extra to what was possible, and therefore invalid.

Now we sought legal advice. We wanted a Barrister for one of us and the other one to represent herself. The advice, when it came in a meeting in London, was stunning: 'There is no legal merit in the case.' We were dumbfounded. I remember walking up Kingsway, where we stopped in our track and said, 'Damn it, we'll do it anyway!' The Greenham spirit rises even in dumbfounded women.

In our preparation for Reading Crown Court we threw in everything but the kitchen sink. It seemed incredible that the one legal point of the proviso would be sufficient, so we went on gilding the lily! Some of the points were gut reactions, some were good solid legal points too numerous to mention here including the Byelaws as duplication of the Official Secrets Act, also a brief mention of the Mildenhall case which was quite different from ours because no Common was involved. We planned to keep our best points to the end, i.e. the ones relating to the Common, the Commoners and the MLAct proviso.

AUGUST 4th, 1986: *Peggy Walford:* - On Friday 4th August, a group of British and American peace activists flew from Heathrow Airport on a BA bargain trip costing I think £283.00. The American group had flown into London from Brooklyn, New York, the previous day. Two of them, Ann-Maria Hendrikson and Bob McGlyn were very positive peace activists in the USA.

2½ hours later we touched down in Moscow's airport. We were loaded onto a coach and after a half-hour's run we arrived at the Cosmos Hotel. Around six of us were together on the 25th floor. Later on, we all came together in the hotel's restaurant, where we had a nice meal together.

We left the hotel and went to the nearest Metro station. Half a dozen of us went to visit Yuri and Olga Medvedev. Both are oceanographers. At their flat we met other dissidents, Nina Kowelenko and her daughter Knisia, who were involved with the Helsinki Accord. Nina Kowelenko was born in Siberia and later came to live in the Ukraine. She never saw her parents again. Nina was a devout Roman Catholic, as was her daughter. Yuri and Olga were Jewish people and were most friendly with Andrei Zakarov and his wife Helena Bonar who were banished to closed towns.

On Saturday night we went to visit Irena Badenova and met her young son Misha. She told us her mother Ina Badenova had been expelled in June. We stayed the night making plans for the following day, when we were all to meet at Gorky Park.

On the Sunday we left Irena's flat and made our way on the Metro to Gorky Park. Ann-Maria, Bob and I produced leaflets which we

67

had brought from London. On the front page 'No More Chernobyls, No More Hiroshimas' was written in English and on the back page the same words were in Russian. We had handed them out en route in the Metro and in the queue to the Park we handed out the whole lot we'd brought. Ann-Maria had boards over her shoulders with the same messages in English and Russian. As we advanced towards Gorky Park to buy our tickets two men who looked like soldiers came over to Ann-Maria and asked her to take off the boards. They took them from her and escorted her into their office nearby. Bob McGlyn was told to go there as well. Yuri and Olga were by this time nearly at the Gate and ready to buy all our tickets. Olga asked if I would go and find out what was happening to Ann-Maria and Bob. I agreed to go and asked David Bransfield, a student of Russian from Warwick University, to come with me.

I did go into the office or Police station and asked for an interpreter to be called so all could understand what was taking place. I was told to shut up and sit down, which I did! We were told we would be released and sent out of the country the next day, which we were. We were told we would be watched. When we came out the front door a good sized crowd who had received our leaflets cheered us and said we were very brave people.

During the afternoon we went with Yuri to a synagogue. Although not allowed in, we talked to a crowd of men and women outside.

Back to Olga's flat until nearly 2 in the morning, when we took taxis back to the Cosmos and were promptly told we had to be out of the hotel by 12 o'clock.

At 2 o'clock that afternoon we boarded our flight. The stewardesses brought us the Observer and other Sunday papers stating we had been arrested and why.

I returned to Greenham the following week.

I later met Ina Badenova in London. She had to make her way from Italy to London where families in the Jewish community looked after her. I visited her there and stayed from time to time. Ina was a gifted translator and interpreter, a Professor in modern languages. When she lived in London she went to work for the BBC. When Gorbachev came to power she would have been allowed to go back to the Soviet Union. Her daughter Irena had had a daughter, Sophia. Ina was deliriously happy about going back, and seeing her new granddaughter. However, sadly it was too late for Ina. She died of cancer in the throat.

I lost contact with Irena after that. I have phoned and written many times. Irena spoke excellent English but now anyone who answers that phone seems confused and Irena never comes to the phone. I think they must have lost that flat.

During 1937 I had joined the Young Communist League in Brechin, Scotland, my home town. The Spanish Civil War was on, and we Young Communist Leaguers were committed to supporting Basque refugees who were brought over at that time for their safety's sake. In 1938 I joined the Communist Party of Great Britain and remained a Party card carrier until around 1990-'91, when the Party folded and later became known as the Democratic Left. However, some of us stayed, regrouped, and are now the Communist Party of Britain. Although a CP card carrier, I was also very much aware of the Soviet people's lack of human rights and total lack of democracy. I was aware of many wrongs going on in the Soviet Union.

AUGUST 6th – 9th 1986: anniversaries of the bombings of Hiroshima and Nagasaki commemorated by a series of occupations, blockades and protests at a number of military installations.

The camp called women to come to Greenham Common to take action at Greenham Common, at Welford [USAF bomb store], Aldermaston [Atomic Weapons Establishment 8 miles from Greenham Common], Burghfield [Royal Ordnance Factory where Polaris nuclear warheads were reconditioned for the Polaris submarines] and at Upper Heyford again. Different groups of women protested at different sites in an intense three day period. Over 50 women revisited Upper Heyford, and did a circle-blockade on the main road which runs through the base.

AUGUST 1986: Yellow Gate women support women raped at the Molesworth mixed peace camp in Cambridgeshire.

*Katrina Howse* – About July of 1986 we found out that first one woman, then another, and then another woman living at Molesworth peace camp had been raped by men living at the peace camp. One woman had been raped twice. Three women and four rapes – we were horrified.

One of the women visited us and we had a meeting. Listening to the pain and anger, I knew we had to support these women as musch as we could. The women had already taken down a wooden Peace Camp sign, and for this they were being condemned by sections of the peace movement as being violent.

A group of women from Greenham went to support the three women. When we got to Molesworth, I felt the horror again. The three rapists had gone but the atmosphere was still awful. Men and women still at the peace camp were denying the atrocity, excuses were being made, anything was being said but facing up to what had happened.

We went again, to support whatever the three women felt they had to do. People who opposed us plus others circulated untrue reports that we had trashed the peace camp. We were called violent, we were called rapists! At first I could hardly believe how sections of the mixed peace movement were behaving.

There was a meeting in London at a pacifist centre to talk about the rapes. By this time the three women wanted Molesworth peace camp to close down or become women-only. There was an opposition to this; every time we said it at Molesworth or elsewhere there was opposition. Large sections of the peace movement just wanted it covered up, talk but no action, talk but no justice and change.

Eventually, a few articles were published in peace periodicals talking about the rapes. Too few words, too late. At the National CND Conference that autumn, a supportive woman took the platform and started speaking about the rapes – she wasn't listened to, the Conference wanted to get on with 'the real business' of talking about nuclear weapons systems.

All three women were very courageous and got rebuff after rebuff from the National CND politicians. They just wanted to cover it up and keep their safe careers. Yet, despite them, the women did expose the rapes and confront the rapists. Clarity was finally achieved on this due to the three women's courage. The disgrace was that the rapes had happened, and at a so-called peace camp.

This wasn't the end of our clashes with the mean minded bureaucrats of National CND, as 1987 was to show.

**SEPTEMBER 2nd 1986:** trial of the five women charged with Criminal Damage to two F111's begins in Banbury Magistrates Court. Stipendiary [legally qualified and experienced, paid] magistrate brought in to hear the case, the same one who in August 1985 had sentenced one of the defendants, Katrina Howse, to three months imprisonment for refusing to be bound over to keep the peace. The Court ruled that another Defendant, Gaelle Rous, whose first language is French, must use an interpreter appointed by the Court, not the interpreter she had invited herself. Gaelle argued against this, and was ordered to the cells; three of the remaining Defendants followed in support. Katrina Howse began cross-examination of Prosecution witnesses on her own.

**SEPTEMBER 4th 1986,** Banbury Magistrates' Court: stipendiary magistrate finds the three women who had written on the planes Guilty of Criminal Damage, and the two who had occupied the planes Not Guilty of Criminal Damage.

**SEPTEMBER 5th 1986:** camp's fifth birthday. Many women visit Yellow Gate.

**SEPTEMBER 1986:** US and Soviet Union talking about weapons controls – talks on chemical weapons in Berne, talks on nuclear testing in Geneva, talks on strategic and intermediate-range nuclear weapons.

At Yellow Gate women's peace camp, talks about how to get to Salisbury Plain to disrupt the regular cruise missile convoy exercises.

*Sarah Hipperson* writes about non-violence – Each of recognises the anger and helplessness that rises in us when confronted with denial of rights, oppression, loss of liberty. The horrendous occurrences of the concentration camps, the dropping of nuclear bombs on Hiroshima and Nagasaki, the inhuman apartheid laws of South Africa, the segregation of Black people in the US, the Vietnam War, the present day war in Northern Ireland (the list is endless) – fill us with a sense of urgency, a need to find some power, to counteract the evil that lies at the very root of the thinking which makes these crimes against humanity possible.

As we reach for some effective way to channel our abhorrence and anger, in an attempt to stop these happening, we often just thrash around in self destructive behaviour, and become powerless in the face of the 'steam road roller' of the state. Feeling helpless and disillusioned, we end up apathetic and indifferent to suffering. In this condition we easily become encompassed in the corruption of the state.

Some believe the solution can be found in political theories and practice – but on their own, without a conversion to non-violence and justice, these end up creating the same injustices and crimes against humanity that they genuinely set out to correct. Unless there is true respect for humanity and the life force, all the energy put into overcoming evil will be squandered. We will fail in our defence of those who are immediately in the path of the particular evil we hope to overcome.

The women who live at Yellow Gate choose the power of non-violence to counteract the power of evil, generated from inside the base by genocidal nuclear weapons. There are 101 cruise missiles – each with the explosive power of 16 Hiroshima bombs – held in six silos on Greenham Common in Berkshire in the lush green countryside of rural England. The base can best be described as a nuclear concentration camp, where preparations for mass murder are carried out daily. This is accepted as normal behaviour by most people in Britain, but not by the small group of women who protest vociferously all attempts to normalise, and make acceptable, this nuclear concentration camp. Each month when the cruise missile convoy leaves the base to go to Salisbury Plain we resist strongly but non-violently this practise for mass murder – the consequence of taking this action is that we will serve prison sentences.

Non-violence is neither an easy nor a soft option, it is a clearly chosen path of confrontation with the state and the military. It is not a posture to be struck in an attempt to avoid human responsibilities or the risk of losing privileges. Not taking stands in order to appear non-judgemental is not non-violent, it is a clear dereliction of responsibility, as is rhetoric without practical commitment. Direct action becomes non-violent with the acceptance of the full consequences – the willingness to choose to go to prison even when given the corrupting choice to pay fines by the court. The non-violent action remains non-violent only by the refusal to make deals, financial or otherwise (e.g. the promise of 'good' behaviour).

We work non-violently in faith because we know it works. We believe it is realistic and practicable, also, its results are measurable.

Non-violence is an energy that gives you the power to overcome powerlessness. Whatever the occurrence, you know that there is some action you can take to interrupt, disrupt, or stop deliberately, so that the 'occurrence' does not work as it was intended to do. Evil depends on being thorough and efficient; non-violent direct action makes it unworkable at the time. It also gives a chance to change the thinking behind the ideas that promote these crimes against humanity.

The women's peace camp on Greenham Common provides the perfect place for women to develop non-violent skills, as a living experience, 24 hours a day. Learning to dwell on the land amidst Nature, your senses become heightened. You become like a receiver, ready to pick up signals in the constantly changing daily patterns, and ready to take non-violent direct action when it is called for.

I believe that non-violence is a spiritual energy – a primitive response of resistance to events and circumstances that we find intolerable. It is a precious resource and has an infinite life, if treated with respect.

SEPTEMBER 26th 1986: British Nuclear Fuels Ltd. (BNFL) publishes annual report which confirms publicly for the first time that it was involved in the UK nuclear weapons programme.

SEPTEMBER 28th 1986: at Labour Party conference, leader Neil Kinnock says a Labour government would scrap nuclear weapons in Britain, close American nuclear bases and reject the American nuclear shield.

OCTOBER, 1986: The Greenham-Zimbabwe Exchange:

*Mary Millington* –    A Quaker from Oxford who had been working for Oxfam in Zimbabwe mentioned in ministry a woman he had met there, Sithembiso Nyoni, who told him she thought Greenham was the most exciting thing happening in Britain. He gave me her address and I wrote. Her response was to invite Greenham women to

Zimbabwe. Shirley of Blue Gate and Suzanne of Yellow Gate agreed to go, and money was raised for them to stay there for a month in October 1986.

They were hosted by the YWCA and ORAP (a rural development organisation), and the high point of their time there was a 4 day conference, 'Women, Peace and Development,' in a rural area near Bulawayo.

Two years later, Busi Ncube of ORAP and Edna Mhlanga of the YWCA made the return visit.

**OCTOBER 18th – 19th 1986**, London: the Wages for Housework Campaign hold a peace camp at Argyle Square, King's Cross, to make Greenham's work more visible in London. The theme is 'Welfare not Warfare'.

**OCTOBER 25th, 1986**: Green Gate is opened for the weekend by the Wages for Housework Campaign, who spend their 'Time Off for Women' days on Greenham Common, to 'share the work of 24-hour-a-day resistance to nuclear madness, and to count this work, together with women's work for peace within our communities and around the world.'

*Sarah Hipperson* – During the weekend the camp was self-sufficient, working as an entity, and developed good workshops followed by discussion. I gave a history of Greenham and escorted the Campaign women, and introduced them, to women at all the other Gates. Siân Evans and Kay Chapman (both previously from Orange Gate, now with the Wages for Housework Campaign) encouraged visiting women to join the rota they organised on behalf of Yellow Gate. Every two weeks the rota women from the King's Cross Women's Centre in London held the camp, to allow women time to go into Newbury to sign on, shop, do our laundry, and so on. This was a great help to camp women.

**OCTOBER 30th 1986**: Norman Tebbitt, Conservative Party Chairman, upbraids the BBC for alleged bias, innuendo and imbalance in its reporting of the US bombing of Libya. Party members are asked to send in examples of broadcasters' bias for Conservative Central Office to compile a dossier.

**OCTOBER 30th 1986**: cruise missile convoy leaves base for exercises on Salisbury Plain.

Article by Katrina Howse in 1986 camp newsletter:

The convoy came out on October 30th at 01:30 am. Three of us were in the base for it lining up, and were only caught at 0100 am because American soldiers literally bumped into us where we were hiding outside a parked vehicle. We were charged with breach of

Byelaws, but one of us was held till the next afternoon and then stood trial, because the MoD Police wouldn't accept that she lived at Greenham. That's one of the bad consequences for women who live at the camp because women don't turn up for their Court cases. Women at the camp have no option, we have to turn up for our Court cases as we are going to continue in this struggle.

The three of us, Beth, Janet and myself wanted to be on Salisbury Plain the whole time the convoy was on the Plain, on the basis that it needs women's power facing it the whole time it's out, as well as when it comes out and goes back in. Many women go up, take action by getting to the wood where the convoy is, and come back to Greenham. We wanted to take this a step further, as long as the convoy's out we're out!

There is so little transport at camp, at the moment we use buses, but in the middle of winter when it's really cold we could do with a back up vehicle. As it was we managed without a car, and it can be done, and it feels very adventurous going out with a pack of essentials, plus a large plastic sheet and rope to string between two trees for a shelter. (Water can be picked up along the way in garages, cafes and pubs.) There are buses to Amesbury from Andover; and from Amesbury there are few buses to Tilshead, which is the village closest to West Down Camp. The convoy was on West Down in East Down Plantation, a walk of about two miles from Tilshead. Tilshead is nine miles from Amesbury, and there are no buses after about 5 pm. We finally got to Tilshead late on Hallowe'en, and set up camp on White Barrow, an ancient burial mound about 11/2 miles outside Tilshead. All the land around here belongs to the MoD, but they've got to see you to stop you! We'd walked from Amesbury, about 8 miles, but we still decided to go on after the convoy. There seemed to be a lot of MoD around, so we went on a circular route onto West Down where we saw lots of torches in plantations. They'd upped the security since the last convoy, and had more MoD out, but we just went around them, and got up to East Down Plantation by dawn. The wire was up, the convoy was silent, and the British soldiers were outside the barbed wire around the wood. We sang and chanted and shouted "Blood on your hands!". The soldiers called the MoD and we were arrested and taken to the Processing Centre at West Down Camp. We were charged with breach of the Larkhill and West Down Byelaws, given a Court date in Devizes and let out at Tilshead.

The next night, Saturday, 15 women from Greenham got up to the wire. Sunday night we went on again, we'd been turfed off White Barrow by MoD Police in the morning. They were very anxious that we accept a lift back to Greenham, we declined. They warned us that all the land belonged to the MoD, we told them we'd walk on the road. They don't own the roads. We went into Tilshead and were tailed by MoD for the next two hours. Whatever happened we were a threat whether seen and followed, or not seen, and however much followed we could always lose them at night. They don't want us up on the Plain when the convoy's out, they want us all back at Greenham (when we are at Greenham they quickly want us anywhere else).

*Janet Tavner* – One thing I remember about this is that I had severe blisters, because I'd just walked nine miles! But on the other hand, I remember walking up this hill towards the convoy, and thinking, well where else should I be, if the convoy's out on the Plain. I just felt, this is the only place I want to be.

My first encounter with the convoy was at Greenham, when it was travelling on the road – I was absolutely terrified. I still felt very good about taking action, but I was really shocked by it, physically shocked. On the Plain it felt better, in a way, because you're moving round on a great piece of land, walking on it, and you can really work with the land – you're hiding in the grass, and walking up in the dark, and it feels more that the convoy is an intruder, than you are, when you're walking on the Plain.

The security was enormous – there were Police everywhere, and you just felt, if you could get up to that convoy, you could get through anywhere. It's like crossing some sort of, not minefield, but land mined with human beings – there were Police and soldiers everywhere, searching with lights. You felt that the only thing you had was your gut instinct, about what was right and what was wrong. That's the way you had to walk on.

There were flares being sent up every now and again, to try and spot us in the darkness, and there were trip-wires set up around the wood that would set off flares as soon as anyone touched those wires. There were Police drafted in from all over the South of England.

**NOVEMBER 17th 1986:** cruise missile convoy leaves base again for exercises on Salisbury Plain, only two weeks after return of previous convoy.

*Beth Junor* – extract from Notebook written at the time:

The convoy left the base again late on Monday night, November 17th – while the moon was still full. A lot of women snaked through the woods to meet it on the road when it left the gate – the Police were confused by us but finally put a lot of Police at the bottom of the woods to stop us from getting onto the road.

Then, six women went out onto the Plain: Dina and Janice from Orange Gate, and Sarah, Janet, Katrina and I from Yellow Gate. We walked straight towards the convoy and saw it lined up in the wooods called Little Folly. The USAF were scuttling round their vehicles – which had been helpfully illuminated by flares put out by the soldiers guarding the wire. It was the first time I'd actually seen the convoy on the Plain – before, it had always been hidden, in the middle of the woods. We sang 'I am a witness to your war crimes, and I will remember your face' loudly, also 'women are watching you.' We made our presence very much felt. The the MoD came and, as always, they asked what we were doing there. We were arrested, and four of us were charged, two of us Warned Off.

We met Alison in her van in Tilshead, and she dropped Katrina, Janet and I off in Amesbury, to begin our second stay on the Plain. Dina and Janice seemed pleased about our action and went back to the camp with Sarah.

The three of us headed straight for the only cafe in Amesbury, the Friar Tuck. On previous visits we'd always appreciated some beans on toast and a hot drink here. As we approached this morning, all three of us were very aware that we were becoming known in this small town, women with rucksacks on ur backs, heavy walking boots and outdoor clothing; it was well past the tourist season. And sure enough, when I walked into the cafe, the man behind the counter asked, 'Are you from Greenham Common?'

'Yes, we are,' I answered, but with the vision of beans on toast and hot coffee rapidly fading in my mind's eye.

'Well,' he says, 'we're not going to serve you.'

Just as simple as that. I asked him for a reason, and after a long pause he made up a lie so I just walked out, and told the others. Katrina opened the door again to add, 'We would sue you, if we had money!' Amesbury appears to be following the same path as Newbury.

So, we got out of Amesbury pretty quick, and set up camp. That night we walked up to a military post called the Bustard Vedette, to meet another woman, and although we missed the connection, it was a good action for us to make ourselves visible.

We went back onto the Plain again on Wednesday night/Thursday morning, to Little Folly. The convoy had stopped operating as it was about 0430 am, so Katrina shouted, 'WAKEY, WAKEY!!', before we sang and called out. Again the MoD Police arrived and asked us what we were doing there. The three of us were charged once again. We were warned not to communicate with each other by shouting across the processing centre, or we would be taken out and dropped in Tilshead separately. Anyway, we were dropped in Tishead all together, and had an early morning walk to Shrewton, the next village, about four miles away, where we caught a bus back to a spot near our hidden camping place. The bus happened to drive past the Bustard Vedette, so we shouted at the MoD, 'We'll be back!'

We'd been seen by the Army and MoD walking along the Tilshead to Shrewton road, and now the Army and MoD saw us walking along the road to Stonehenge! Their radioed messages must've been very confusing.

We had to return to Greenham that Thursday, as we were all becoming flat broke, what with all the bus fares and food requirements. When one of us is skint, one of the others always seems to have enough for our fares home, though.

On Saturday we enjoyed the luxury of a lift to the Plain, from Jenny. The convoy had been on the land for five full days now. Even early on Sunday morning, we could hear shelling on the Artillery Range a few miles from our camping spot. Their preparations for killing are incessant.

We returned to the Danger Area on Sunday night – there were increased numbers of MoD Police, and at one point we lay down for about three-quarters of an hour, while they practically tripped over us in their searches for us! We left that spot and were picked up as we were watching the ocnvoy for possible signs of it leaving the Plain.

They must've decided by this point they'd had enough of us, as we were refused bail, and taken to Devizes Police cells for the night, to appear in Court in the morning.

**NOVEMBER 24th 1986:** Devizes Magistrates Court: counsel for the Ministry of Defence make an Application for bail conditions to be imposed on Katrina Howse, Janet Tavner and Beth Junor, failure to comply resulting in the three being remanded in custody.

Katrina Howse argues, successfully, that it is illegal to impose bail conditions/remand in custody for a non-imprisonable offence, such as breach of Salisbury Plain byelaws. The three women are released.

**NOVEMBER 1986:** Sir Robert Armstrong, coordinator of the two secret services (MI5, and MI6 which the Cabinet Secretary didn't admit existed) travels to Australia to persuade a Court in Sydney to prevent publication of Peter Wright's, a pensioner of MI5, book 'Spycatcher'.

**NOVEMBER 1986:** Public Order Act comes into force. The Act is widely seen as a move to widen and strengthen Police powers, while interfering with rights of protest.

In a debate on the Bill in the House of Commons on 13th January 1986, the Government justified Clause 5, which made 'disorderly conduct' or behaviour 'likely to cause alarm, harassment or distress' a new offence by saying that this Clause is aimed at protecting those who are most vulnerable in the community – 'particularly the elderly and people from ethnic minorities'. An opposition MP pointed out that the Government had not taken the opportunity to make racial harassment a specific criminal offence.[4]

In practice, one of the implementations of this Clause has been against Yellow Gate women shouting in protest at the cruise missile convoy on exercise, in a rural area away from domestic housing, when Police officers claimed they had been distressed and alarmed by such protests. The Act has never been used against vigilantes attacking the peace camp.

The MP for Meirionnydd Nant Conwy, D E Thomas, stated in the House on 13th January 1986, 'This is not a public order Bill; it is about extending the control of the state over public disorder. Much of that disorder is created either directly or indirectly by the activities of the state.'[5]

**DECEMBER 13th – 14th 1986:** Reclaim Our Lives demonstration at Greenham Common. Hundreds of women Trespass inside the base, and are charged under the Greenham Common byelaws.

**DECEMBER 19th 1986:**
*Beth Junor* – extract from Notebook:
Today was the first day of real coldness at the camp. The bracken has turned brown and dry, the gorse is drying and losing its brilliant greenness. This morning there was a sheet of ice on the fly-sheet plastic covering my tent, and all evening we've huddled by the fire, burning our shins while our backs froze in the wind. –

The task of surviving another winter begins. Evictions continue, at a rate of 5 – 6 per week.

*Beth* – When I first began living at the camp, every eviction induced a state of panic. The first woman to see the trucks and police escort arriving would shout out a warning, then there was a great commotion as we tried to save the living utensils at the front of the camp: the water containers were always carried off first, then the pots and pans and the prams of food, and we would try to save as much wood as possible. The bailiffs would try to grab whatever they could. They always put the fire out.

They would often come at first light in the morning, having started at the crack of dawn on the north side, which gave us just enough time for a woman at Yellow Gate to have the fire lit and the kettle on for the first cups of tea of the day. Often the first thing you would hear in the mornings in summer was, 'Move your tents off the Common,' and men's feet tramping around the clearing. Or they would come just as the sun was going down (they could only evict during daylight hours) or at any time in between. Sometimes they would come several times in one day. We tried to discern a pattern, but there was none. It was impossible to predict.

I had to learn to organise my tent so that I could be evicted on waking in the morning. I kept my radio, a book and a plastic bag by the side of my sleeping bag so I could keep the radio and the book dry during evictions. Your clothes had to be ready so you could dress very quickly. Your bedding had to be rolled up in one go, and carried to Gladys, the transit van, which would be driven off as soon as the last bedding roll had been thrown in. Different Quaker groups had donated tents called Getaways, which could be dismantled in a minute and carried to the van under your other arm. All the time the bailiffs were pacing, looking for something they could grab. I had to learn to suppress the panic, to do the evictions while appearing to be calm and unperturbed. Humour helped and occasionally we would joke with each other while doing the eviction, but all the while you would be screaming with rage inside.

Later I heard about South African women in the townships who would bury their belongings in sand to prevent them from being taken during evictions. Women in Northern Ireland would have their homes continually raided by the British Army. Evictions are extremely violent events, and all who have had to survive them on such scales are practising great non-violence on a daily basis.

Sometimes when visitors witnessed an eviction they would say, 'It's a bit of a farce, isn't it? You're back again already,' and we would always reply that although it is pointless on their part, it is no farce. It's impossible to imagine what we could have built up if we hadn't been continually evicted.

# 1987
## GROWTH, STRUGGLE, SURVIVAL

1987 marked a turning point in the peace camp's history. In June, the Conservative Party in Britain won a third successive general election victory, with 42 per cent of the vote in a turnout of around 75.4 per cent. All of British politics was being drawn further to the right: the Labour Party leadership implemented purges of the Left within the Party, and activists of every Left-ish persuasion in mainstream politics were marginalised and ostracised. Only the so-called radicals of the Right were safe, and were becoming more confident. The Police, implementing the increasingly oppressive legislation of the Thatcher government, also grew in confidence. This shift to the right and the ostracisation of all left-wing radicals would also manifest itself within grassroots movements in 1987.

At the same time, politicians were beginning to echo, in faint terms, the calls for disarmament which had come so loudly from the grassroots in the early 1980's. In order for these echoes to be heard, it was necessary to silence the troublesome source from which the calls had originated. The media increasingly focused on the politicians' negotiations to eliminate less than four per cent of their total nuclear armoury – the very weapons which had been the focus of the non-violent protests at Greenham Common and subsequently around the world: intermediate range nuclear forces, that is, cruise missiles and SS-20's. The media acquiesced in the consistent censorship of the originating voices of dissent, and now visited the peace camp only to ask when we would be leaving.

As a result of the combination of these factors, there was a general attributing of the weapons reductions moves not to the grassroots – above all, not to ordinary women – but to the magnanimity of two of the world's most powerful men: Gorbachev and Reagan.

This state erasure of the work of the grassroots movements was further aided in 1987 by some elements within the peace and women's movements. At the centre of events which led to a witch-hunt of Yellow Gate women and other grassroots campaigners (in particular from the King's Cross Women's Centre in London, but also including some independent individuals) who were stubbornly refusing to 'join the party' in praise of Gorby, as he affectionately came to be known, was a conference in Moscow of the World Congress of Women, entitled 'Towards the Year 2,000 – Without Nuclear Weapons! For Peace, Equality, Development.' The determination of the women from the peace camp attending the conference to speak out against Soviet nuclear power, Soviet nuclear weapons and Soviet prisons, together with our condemnation of a racist incident at a Greenham workshop at the conference, incurred the wrath of the pro-Soviet networks within the British peace and women's movements.

On our return from Moscow, a network called Greenham Women Everywhere lined up against the women living on the common at Yellow Gate peace camp, and the witch-hunt began. A smear campaign was launched by the pro-Soviet network in the very papers which had consistently censored and attacked the work of the women's peace camp in previous years, thus sowing the seeds of doubt, suspicion and rumour upon which a witch-hunt thrives.

The women at Yellow Gate continued non-violently resisting the military, while fending off not only the attacks of the state but now the added attacks of those within the movement who were livid at the realisation that they could no longer credibly use the peace camp for their own political ends.

By the end of the year, as the INF Treaty was being signed, Yellow Gate was emerging from the year's struggles with clearly articulated principles: non-violence, non-alignment, anti-racism and autonomy as women. Although as a result we were no longer receiving the support of the networks which had formed during the peace camp's earlier years, we were also publicly independent from their pro-Soviet politics and had begun to build a solid basis of support with like-minded women all over the country, and internationally.

**JANUARY 1st 1987**: women enter the base and paint the hangars which hold the cruise missile convoy support vehicles with slogans such as 'Give up war work.'

Large sections of fence are taken down.

**JANUARY 1987**: three further radioactive leaks from Sellafield, resulting in the closing down of reprocessing activities in the first half of February.

**LAST WEEK IN JANUARY 1987**: small groups of women cut the perimeter fence every night.

Evictions are continuing at a rate of five – six per week. Many non-violent actions are taken within the base, and on Salisbury Plain.

**FEBRUARY 1987**: SOCIAL TRENDS (No. 17, HMSO, Feb. '87) reports that the gap between rich and poor in Britain is continuing to widen.

**FEBRUARY 3rd – 26th 1987**, US: nuclear weapons tests are conducted on February 3rd and 11th. The Soviet Union ended its 18-month moratorium and carried out a nuclear weapons test on February 26th.

**FEBRUARY 18th 1987**: Yoko Ono spends her 54th birthday at Greenham Common, and faces the return of cruise missile convoy support vehicles together with the women from the peace camp.

*Sarah Hipperson* – Yoko Ono, returning from Moscow where Mikhail Gorbachev had hosted a gathering for the 'famous and beautiful' to explain his ambition for a world free of nuclear weapons, was making a stop-over in London.

Through an intermediary she made contact with Wilmette Brown of the King's Cross Women's Centre, and let it be known that she wished to spend time on Greenham Common on her 54th birthday.

I called for her at the Dorchester Hotel in London where she and some friends were staying, and we travelled to Greenham in style in a chauffeur driven limousine to Yellow Gate. She was inundated by photographers and reporters but made it clear that she was interested in the work going on in the camp and witnessed at first hand the non-violent resistance of convoy support vehicles returning to the base from Salisbury Plain. I escorted her around the base where she stopped at each camp and spent time with the women.

As we journeyed back to London she commented mostly about the cold and uncomfortable conditions that women were living under.

She made a financial contribution to the camp, which later enabled us to purchase the land known as the Sanctuary. This is a third of an acre of land surrounded by Common on three sides and the perimeter fence of the base on the fourth, from which the bailiffs cannot evict women nor our possessions. The buying of this land created a tension between some women living on Greenham Common about the politics of land ownership – aired at a minuted meeting held at Yellow Gate in 1986. This resulted in a complete absence of interest in the land until the women of Yellow Gate placed two tipis on the land in January 1988.

Yellow Gate women, who had hosted the meeting in 1986 when this land was up for sale, provided the vision and direction needed, being clear that the land should be purchased with the proviso that it should be for the use of women who keep the camps open and functioning as places of resistance to the cruise missile programme. It was also agreed at the meeting that the land should provide a place for rest and re-creation for these same women who had no other secure place to carry on their creative work and not be vulnerable to the eviction destructiveness of Newbury District Council.

Women who wanted to write or weave or paint as in the case of Katrina Howse, an artist who had lived on the Common since August 1982, keeping her craft/art alive under the most hazardous conditions, could now look forward to painting without the daily threat of her work being destroyed by the bailiffs acting for Newbury District Council.

MARCH 13th – 16th 1987, Sydney, Australia: a Court refuses to grant the UK government an injunction preventing publication of a book of memoirs by Peter Wright, former MI5 agent, 'Spycatcher'. UK Attorney General announces on March 16th that the UK government would appeal the ruling.

MARCH 1987: the Government's Central Office of Information produces a 30-minute film, 'Keeping the Peace,' at a cost of £180,000, for use in schools and colleges.

MARCH 28th 1987: UK Prime Minister Margaret Thatcher on official visit to the Soviet Union, March 28th – April 2nd.

*Sarah Hipperson* – On hearing of Margaret Thatcher's visit to the man she had said she could 'do business with,' I joined a group of women protesting outside the Foreign Office in London on the 27th March. The police arrived and arrested three of us for wearing placards in the vicinity of Parliament while it was in session. Kay Chapman and Siân Evans of the King's Cross Women's Centre and myself were held in Cannon Row Police Station cells for a few hours until the demonstration was over, then released without charge – a way of stopping us from protesting, without having to be accountable at law for having done so.

APRIL 2nd and 3rd, 1987, Reading Crown Court: appeal of Georgina Smith and Jean Hutchinson of conviction under the Greenham Common Byelaws.

*Jean Hutchinson* – We went into the Crown Court armed with all the material from our legal researches, including a fierce argument about why we should be heard, but Judge Lait seemed eager to hear what we had to say. Here was a judge who was ready to listen – I don't believe we'd met one before, with the exception of the Master of the Rolls, Lord Donaldson.

We took a day and a half to go through everything, including Georgina's amusing description of the 60 or 70 Commoners rights, which includes grazing rights for this list of animals (I include the lot for full impact): 17 goats, 12 horses, 6 sheep, 47 cattle, 6 cows, 4 pigs, 2 ducks, 2 geese, 16 ponies, donkeys unspecified number.

Judge Lait wanted to know if the cruise missiles could really be held up because of 20 pigs on the runway. We said, 'Oh no, don't worry, there are only 4 pigs allowed.' The ridiculous nature of the situation was well illustrated and was to be continued later.

Maybe our most risky submission, or so we thought at the time, was that the Byelaws were a duplication of existing law which covers the place anyway, namely the Official Secrets Act. Georgina even provided a sketch of the base, indicating where we were arrested (sketches are forbidden under the Official Secrets Act). Was there some MoD or legal megalomaniac working in Whitehall who would like to make a name for him/herself by changing our charges? Under the Official Secrets Act, Greenham Common is a Prohibited Place (with the Byelaws it is a Protected Place). Any of the thousands of women convicted under the Byelaws could have been charged with breaking the Official Secrets Act. But no, we were and are safe from this because there is a big snag for the MoD in that each arrest under the Official Secrets Act needs to be reported to the Attorney General, which would have been a huge upheaval they did not have the stomach for. Thousands of women being reported to the Attorney General would have caused embarrassment even for a government which does not seem to know the meaning of the word shame.

The Greenham Common Byelaws were clearly designed to convict and criminalise women quickly, automatically and without fuss.

When it was time for a reply by Mr Dalgleish, the MoD lawyer, he only had replies to the Mildenhall case. The rest of our submissions about the proviso and the Commoners were a dreadful shock to him and he begged for 2 months' adjournment to prepare his reply. I took a teacher's delight in pointing out he'd not done his homework! He was given time via an adjournment. The case continued on the 17th of June.

**APRIL 13th – 15th 1987**, Moscow: US Secretary of State George Schultz visits Moscow for talks with Mikhail Gorbachev and delivers invitation to Gorbachev from President Reagan for a summit meeting later in the year.

*Sarah Hipperson* – We had heard at the camp about a proposed conference for women which was to take place in Moscow in June. I had heard that this conference was the next step in the plan being implemented by Gorbachev in his determination to relieve his country of the onerous defence budget created by the nuclear arms race. The conference was to be part of his campaign to introduce Glasnost (openness) and Perestroika (reconstruction) to the people of the USSR.

On the 28th April, letters were sent from the camp to Elsie Watson, Secretary of the National Assembly of Women, who had charge of allocating the places for the conference. We wondered why this conference with the profound sounding title, 'Towards the Year 2,000 – Without Nuclear Weapons' hadn't thought of inviting the very women whose lives and work it was to prevent a nuclear attack being launched against the Soviet Union.

Elsie Watson promised to come to the camp but never did; our only response to our efforts came after a phone call to her. After a phone call to the Soviet Embassy and a conversation with Yuri Mazur, we discovered there had been 50 places allocated to the contingent from the UK. He also promised that if we could get places, we could have our visas within a few days. Phone calls were also made to the GDR to a Ms Kubesch of the Women's International Democratic Federation.

The block to us going to Moscow was clearly put up by the pro-Soviet UK organisers of the British contingent who held all the power of deciding who would attend.

The camp appealed by letter to Raisa Gorbachev. This brought forth four airline tickets on the 11th June. In the meantime, as a result of the pressure applied at many levels, Elsie Watson eventually found two places for 'Greenham'. Newbury resident Lynette Edwell and Annie Ingold of Cruisewatch, who visited Orange Gate, indicated they wanted to go, so it was decided to let them have these two places. The camp managed to make a substantial financial contribution to their air fares. I also discovered some time after our return that there had been a collection amongst the MORNING STAR staff towards their fares.

Sometime while we were having all this difficulty four women from Camden made a visit to the camp and stopped by Yellow Gate, asking for an update on what was happening at the camp and inside the base. During the conversation it was revealed that their group had been allocated *four* places for the Moscow conference. I still remember the outrage I felt when I heard this – a support group, operating from the comfort of their homes in London were deemed to be worthy of greater representation than those working against nuclear weapons than the women who were living in hazardous conditions outside a nuclear base.

This situation, following on from the treatment afforded us by the IYP Council, was yet another step in my understanding of the manipulation that was going on within the 'peace movement'. We were regarded within the hierarchy of the 'peace movement' as tokens to be cashed in when needed, but more symbolic than real. I recall saying to the Camden women, Rose Walters, Janet Richardson, Gilly Little and Anne Driver, that they should not represent the camp when camp women were not being invited. I thought they agreed to keep their representation within the parameters of a Greenham support group, but as events in Moscow were to reveal, they didn't.

MAY 6th 1987: another cruise missile convoy due to leave the base. Five women enter the base on the night of May 6th and throw approximately 40 bags of paint over a missile launch control vehicle, then drop a potato down the exhaust pipe. The potato-stricken vehicle broke down as it reached the first roundabout on the A339 road to Salisbury Plain.

**MAY 6th 1987:** Prime Minister Thatcher rejects demands for an independent inquiry into allegations that the security service had in the mid-1970's sought to destabilise the then Labour government.

**JUNE 7th 1987:** Greenham Common Liaison Committee: the Wing Commander of the base states, referring to the peace camp, 'numbers remained low at about 20 but incidents remained frequent; on the legal problems from the conflict between commoners rights and the Military Lands Act, research continued on this complex problem.'

**JUNE 11th 1987:** general election in Britain. Conseratives won 375 seats, Labour 229 seats, the Alliance 22 seats – the third election victory for the Conservatives.

The left of the Labour Party would undergo more purges. A pamphlet published towards the end of July, 'Labour's Next Moves Forward,' bluntly put the case for appealing to the 'home-owning, credit-card-carrying majority.'

**JUNE 17th – 18th 1987**, Reading Crown Court: challenge to the legality of the Greenham Common Byelaws (1985) continues. The judge concedes that the case brought by Georgina Smith and Jean Hutchinson is of substance and *bona fide*, but adjourns it for Judicial Review at the High Court, declining to make a ruling himself.

*Jean Hutchinson* – Our case continued, this time with Barrister Beverley Lang acting as my McKenzie Friend!

The same legal points were put again, with the use of slightly more legal language. The four of us (including solicitor Barbara Cohen) worked hard and successfully to get it right, and by now we knew we had it right, including our attempt to witness summons Michael Heseltine.

It seemed to us, when Dalgleish came to reply, he only had foolishly ineffective replies. However, he had some success with one of them, namely that challenges to Byelaws should not be heard by lower courts (i.e. Magistrates and Crown courts). His second point went totally wrong – it was that the rights of Commoners are not prejudiced, they can exercise them!

We were able to deal with this on the spot by talking about the actual rights again – rights of grazing 20 horses, 12 goats, 2 geese, etc. etc., all through the barbed wire! Dear, oh dear! The judge said, 'This is not common sense.' At this point I came in with what Commoners are allowed to take away, gravel, etc. Under the Official Secrets Act, taking anything from the base would be a felony. I asked the Prosecution if they were really inviting Commoners to become felons overnight.

I think it is clear why they needed the time wasted by the jurisdiction point. Time to get Heseltine and all of them off this awful hook.

It could be said Dalgleish's only success was to work with the lawyer sent by Heseltine to excuse him from coming and confirm his unaccountability.

Judge Lait said he wanted to rule and that we had a case which was 'of substance and bona fide'. But, he grasped at the Crown Prosecution Service point about striking down byelaws in lower courts and became nervous (there is an ancient right to have byelaws struck down in lower courts). If the byelaws are made by the Secretary of State for Defence, it seems it's a bit of a nightmare for a Crown Court judge. Judge Lait sent the case for Judicial Review on this jurisdiction point.

I knew we'd won our main point, but I got angry. I made a plea for all the women coming before the Magistrates Court in Byelaws cases. Judge Lait made a statement not legally binding on the Magistrates Court, but helpful to use as advice to women.

JUNE 18th 1987: in response to the outcome of the above hearing, eleven women cut sixteen sections of perimeter fence near a public road in daylight hours. Police appear to have had prior knowledge of the plans for this action, as several van-loads of Police were spotted in a lane in the nearby village of Thatcham by Kay Chapman from the King's Cross Women's Centre as she returned to London from a day at the camp. Kay turned back to warn the women at Yellow Gate and the site of the action was altered at the last minute.

All women who cut the fence are arrested and charged with Criminal Damage, with the exception of Lynette Edwell, a Newbury resident associated with the peace camp and with the Cruisewatch organisation (generously financially supported by CND, a group of women and men who track the movements of the cruise missile convoy on exercise).

JUNE 23rd – 27th 1987, Moscow: World Congress of Women conference, 'Towards the Year 2,000 – Without Nuclear Weapons! For Peace, Equality, Development!'

Despite difficulties which the camp women experienced obtaining tickets from the National Assembly of Women in Britain, four women from the camp were able to attend on behalf of the peace camp as a result of the last-minute plea to Raisa Gorbachev: Indra Morris, Sarah Hipperson, Katrina Howse and Beth Junor.

In addition to the four women from the peace camp attending were four women from the London group, Camden Greenham Women: Rose Walters, Janet Richardson, Gilly Little and Anne Driver. Lynette Edwell and Annie Ingold were also in attendance.

Wilmette Brown of Black Women for Wages for Housework and Selma James, founder of the Wages for Housework campaign, were attending the conference representing the International Wages for Housework Campaign. King's Cross Women's Centre, where the Wages for Housework campaign is based, had a long-standing history of involvement with Greenham Common Women's Peace Camp.

JUNE 25th 1987, Greenham workshop at the Moscow conference:

All of the above women attend this workshop. Sarah begins the Workshop by outlining the history of the camp, and then tries to draw all of the camp women as well as women who support the camp into the discussion. Lynette, Annie, Rose and Katrina speak. When Wilmette, the first Black woman to speak, begins, all of the Camden women leave the Workshop. Wilmette is subsequently racially attacked in the Workshop by Lynette Edwell, who had remained. A Native North American woman speaks about the racism she, too, has faced in the peace movement in the US.

Subsequent efforts to meet with Lynette Edwell, Annie and the four Camden Greenham Women during the conference fail. Significantly, the four camp women are told that we would be unable to return to Britain at the same time as the rest of the British delegation; Lynette and Annie, together with the Camden Greenham Women therefore arrive back in Britain a few days before the camp women. The camp women return to the Common to find that the camps around the perimeter (apart from Yellow Gate) and their supporters have banded together in defence of Lynette Edwell and the Camden Greenham Women, with whom they share the same social circle. When Yellow Gate women visit the other camps on our return, to deliver a gift from Moscow to each, women there seem mistrustful of us. We are still angry about the behaviour of the Camden Greenham Women and the racist attack, but there seems little interest in what happened in the Workshop and no questions are asked about the conference, in general.

The almost sacrosanct feminist principle of supporting a woman who says she has been wronged was exploited to full capacity by the Greenham Women Everywhere network, as this alignment was to call itself; in this instance, however, the principle was manipulated so as to apply to only one side in the dispute, in defence of Lynette Edwell. The entire pro-Soviet network of which she was a part refused to listen to what Black women had to say about the racist incident in Moscow, and to Yellow Gate women about the importance of non-alignment. The opportunity to openly attack Yellow Gate women – who had always been a thorn in the sides of the other Gates – was, it seemed, too good to miss.

It was a hard lesson to learn, that truth is not only the first casualty of war, but it can also be the first casualty in disputes in the peace movement. The advantage for the military state of lies in both instances is clear.

In the political climate in Britain at this time, in which 'Left-wing infiltration of the Labour Party' was a newspaper headline intended to shock, it was far easier for many in the peace movement to go along with the majority than to defend principles to which an already marginalised minority seem to stubbornly adhere.

JUNE 29th 1987, Moscow: text of message left for the American Peace March, due to arrive in Moscow a few days after the departure of the camp women:

Salyut Hotel, 29 June '87

Moscow

Greenham women came to Moscow to take part in the World Congress of Women – Towards the Year 2,000 Without Nuclear Weapons! For Peace, Equality, Development!

We spoke out against the Soviet state and its weapons with the same commitment and conviction that we speak out against the British and American states and their weapons.

All states have a vested interest in the arms race.

We also spoke out against the entrepreneurs of peace – those making a career off our struggle for peace.

As women who go to prison as a consequence of our work, we spoke out for women in prison in the Soviet Union.

We also spoke out against nuclear power.

We are sorry we are unable to meet the Peace March. We had to return to Britain to continue our work against the cruise convoy which is expected out tonight, the 29th June. We'll be back on the Common when the convoy comes out. We will be taking action on behalf of Soviet women and have had our slogans translated into Russian.

JULY 8th 1987: cruise missile convoy containing seven launcher vehicles (each with the capacity to fire four cruise missiles) leaves the base for exercises on Salisbury Plain. Non-violently resisted at Yellow Gate.

JULY 10th 1987: women from Yellow Gate trespass on Salisbury Plain, disrupt convoy exercises.

JULY 11th 1987: women who have been doing the night shift on Salisbury Plain return to Yellow Gate at 0600. Eviction at 0800.

JULY 14th 1987: the MORNING STAR, Communist Party daily paper, publishes account of the Moscow conference entitled 'Greenham goes to Moscow', in which it is stated: 'The majority of peace women who attended the recent World Congress of Women in Moscow have returned home with positive impressions of the Soviet Union . . . they found . . . a total commitment to peace and disarmament...' Complaint lodged with the Press Council by Beth Junor, on behalf of Yellow Gate women.

JULY 15th 1987: cruise missile convoy returns to the base. Three women protesting down the A339 road are arrested on suspicion of Criminal Damage, severely beaten and handcuffed. One woman is knocked unconscious by the Police. All are taken to Newbury Police Station, searched, interviewed, held for four hours, then all released without charge.

JULY 15th 1987: vigils against Police violence outside Reading Police Station and outside Newbury Police station.

Message hand-delivered after vigil outside Reading Police Station reads:

Thames Valley Police – Reading:

Last night you handcuffed then beat non-violent women; one was beaten into unconsciousness, so that the USAF cruise missile convoy could return to Greenham Common.

Shame on you!

Shame on PC2262!

Shame on PC1761!

Shame on WPC478!

We will condemn you publicly, until your violence stops!

Signed,

Beth Junor, Janet Tavner, Miriam Moss, Dina Gilholy, Katrina Howse, Jean Hutchinson.

JULY 22nd, 23rd, 24th 1987, Royal Courts of Justice, London: Judicial Review in the High Court decides Judge Lait (Reading Crown Court, Greenham Common Byelaws Challenge) can rule and an Order of Mandamus of 31st July orders him to do so.

The Director of Public Prosecutions seeks a hearing of appeal in the House of Lords. This necessitates another delay, this time of 7 months.

JULY 23rd 1987, Newbury Magistrates Court: pleas entered to Criminal Damage charges arising out of fence cutting of June 18th. Sally from Orange Gate witholds evidence for the defendants' case (photographs she had taken of the action).

JULY 26th 1987: statement issued 30th July:

On Sunday, July 26th, a second meeting took place at Greenham Common Women's Peace Camp, to acknowledge that a racist incident where six women: 4 from Camden, 2 from Cruisewatch, walked out when Wilmette Brown, a Black woman, was speaking. A more blatant racist attack followed, all in the Greenham workshop in Moscow, by a Cruisewatch woman. Once again, by refusing to acknowledge the racist attack in Moscow, racist attitudes were much in evidence at Greenham. Racist behaviour was even more blatant than before, in the way that some women tried to prevent Wilmette Brown from speaking. Similarly, the only other Black woman at the meeting was heckled, sneered, jeered, laughed at, and attempts to undermine her confidence were made. In the words of Wilmette, 'a lynch-mob' had formed, and was allowed to continue because other women would not stop them.

We, the undersigned, who have experienced the growing spread of racism in Greenham, will not keep quiet about this racism at Greenham, for the sake of protection a white women's peace camp. Greenham is for all women. We disassociate ourselves from the women who made up, and who protected the lynch-mob.

[Signed] Beth Junor, Margaretta D'Arcy, Miriam Moss, Katrina Howse, Janet Tavner, Sarah Hipperson.

Yellow Gate, Greenham Common Women's Peace Camp.

JULY 28th 1987: peace camp raided by Ministry of Defence Police detectives, under the authority given by the 1984 Police and Criminal Evidence Act, prior to exit of cruise missile convoy later the same night. Press release issued at the time:

On the evening of July 28th, MoD Police conducted a 2-hour raid of Yellow Gate, at Greenham Common Women's Peace Camp, before the cruise missile convoy left the base on exercise. Ostensibly looking for a plan of ROF Burghfield, they went away with women's personal notebooks and diaries, boltcutters, paint, photocopies of old and widely circulated military documents, and some Bicarbonate of Soda.

Every woman's personal belongings were scrutinised, and women were photographed. When women asked for receipts of their property, they were told they would not be given because they refused to sign. Margaretta D'Arcy said this was not true, she wanted to sign as her notebook was valuable to her. A detective, Mr Bull, replied, 'It's up to me to say whether you want to sign or not, and I say you've refused to sign. Documents can disappear, and so can photographs.'

Yellow Gate women later built a huge fire on the road leading to the base, to disrupt the cruise convoy exercise. They placed traffic cones and a road sign in front of the fire to warn motorists. Despite this, one American motorist drove over the cones, and then attempted to run down a woman trying to warn him, by swerving onto the grass verge where she had run for protection.

A group of 30 women went down the A339 (convoy route), as a

statement against previous Police violence towards small groups of women.

Margaretta D'Arcy was injured by PC4781 while stopping convoy support vehicles from leaving the base.

AUGUST 1st, 1987: convoy exercising on Salisbury Plain. Seven women walk past sleeping British soldiers into the wood named Little Folly.

AUGUST 4th, 1987: cruise missile convoy returns to base. Three women mark the vehicles with paint. Many actions are taken at Yellow Gate to stop support vehicles, including a fantastic circus, featuring – the rope trick (convoy is stopped with rope held across the road), the blue gloop trick (convoy mysteriously marked with secret recipe mixture), and other amazing acts and words which cause much confusion amongst Police and military.

AUGUST 4th, 1987: picket of the MORNING STAR newspaper, who had refused Sarah Hipperson right of reply to their article 'Greenham goes to Moscow'. Statement released at the time:

On Tuesday 4 August, about twenty women – women living full time at Greenham, and supporters – picketed the MORNING STAR offices in protest against misrepresentation and censorship of Greenham women in that newspaper's coverage of a recent international women's peace conference in Moscow.

After sending a letter appealing to Raisa Gorbachev, women who live at Greenham Common received four free air tickets and invitations to attend the World Congress of Women – Towards 2000 Without Nuclear Weapons! For Peace, Equality, Development, held in Moscow 23 – 27 June 1987.

The tickets arrived just before the deadline for the Congress. The obstruction came from the National Assembly of women, who are mostly Communist Party members, and who were trying to marginalise and minimise our contribution to this Congress.

On arrival in Moscow, in the midst of so many delegates washing the feet of the Soviet state with tears of gratitude, Greenham women Katrina Howse, Beth Junor and Sarah Hipperson spoke out against Soviet nuclear weapons, Soviet nuclear power, and for women in prison in the Soviet Union. We also spoke out against those who would make careers from our struggle – those who would applaud Greenham as long as they don't take our autonomous, independent and non-aligned stand outside Greenham.

During a Greenham workshop in Moscow a racist attack took place, where four Camden Greenham women and two Cruisewatch women walked out on Wilmette Brown of Black Women for Wages for

Housework and the King's Cross Women's Centre Peace Collective, as she was speaking. She is the author of *Black Women and the Peace Movement* – and an elected member of CND National Council. The walkout created an international incident.

The MORNING STAR, by reporting the happenings of Moscow in a trivial way, sought to suppress two important issues. One was women from Greenham speaking clearly about our non-aligned, autonomous and independent position on nuclear weapons. The second was this racist incident.

On Tuesday 4 August, Greenham women who live at the camp and who had been refused space to reply to this article in the MORNING STAR, took direct action together with supporters, and picketed the newspaper with these demands:

1. An apology from the MORNING STAR to the women of Greenham Common Women's Peace Camp.

2. That the MORNING STAR print Sarah Hipperson's protest letter in full.

3. That when the Press Council has responded to Beth Junor's letter protesting about the article, the MORNING STAR should print the full exchange of letters between Ms Junor, the Press Council and the MORNING STAR, whatever the outcome.

As a result, the MORNING STAR called the Police, and we were subjected to barely contained violent behaviour from some of the male staff. Following our request to meet the editor, which did not receive a positive response, we non-violently blockaded the main entrance of the building. At 4.30 pm, nearly four hours after the picket began, Sarah Hipperson and Wilmette Brown, nominated by the picket, were finally invited in to see Mary Rosser, the Chief Executive who had called the Police earlier, and George Wake, the General Manager of the building. This invitation was brought to the women blockading by the Police, who the MORNING STAR relied on as go-betweens. The editor had refused to meet with us.

Mary Rosser was very reluctant to hear any criticism of the journalist Janey Hulme who had written the article, or of the editor. After she heard the details of the misrepresentation and censorship, Mary Rosser said she would make full enquiries and get back to Sarah Hipperson.

Sarah said that the MORNING STAR had greatly damaged the non-aligned position on which all Greenham's work has been based for nearly six years. Sarah asked Mary Rosser why it had taken so long to meet us – nearly four hours. Despite her reassurances that the MORNING STAR fully supported the Greenham women, it was evident that their tactic was to wait us out and break our demands. This showed that only lip service is given to Greenham's work.

It was only by using the same non-violent direct action we use on the Common that we were allowed a meeting – which, however, was unsatisfactory. When Newbury District Council wants us off the land, when the US Air Force and the Ministry of Defence want to bring out the cruise convoy, they call the Police to remove the women.

It is ironic that the MORNING STAR, which claims to have supported us since Greenham began, resorted to the same methods, also calling the Police.

AUGUST 6th, 1987: 42nd anniversary of the atomic bombing of Hiroshima is commemorated at Yellow Gate.

AUGUST 9th, 1987: 42nd anniversary of the bombing of Nagasaki.

AUGUST 13th, 1987: unscheduled cruise missile convoy leaves the base in the early hours, amidst growing tension in the Gulf region. Because of this international tension, Cruisewatch maintains radio silence. Radio contact between Cruisewatch and Yellow Gate had previously warned women at the peace camp of the impending arrival of the Police, the approach of returning convoy vehicles, etc.

Eight women arrested and charged with Criminal Damage for painting the hangars, a Police van, an RAF jeep and the processing Portakabins. Detained overnight in Newbury Police cells. In Court the following day, the Prosecution applies for seven days remand in custody for all of the women. Application challenged, and refused. (An account of the trial of this action is given in the following chapter.)

AUGUST 15th-16th, 1987: eight women Trespass on Salisbury Plain, in an attempt to find exact location of the convoy. The convoy is on the Imber Ranges – this is the first attempt to find the convoy here, and the group were to walk for six hours over the Plain at night in an attempt to find it (a gruelling experience, now affectionately referred to as The Long March). The women remain undetected and no arrests are made. The knowledge they bring back with them to the camp, however, enables three women to reach the convoy at Imber on the night of 18th August and stop the convoy working.

AUGUST 18th, 1987, Devizes Magistrates Court: stipendiary magistrate refuses to accept the peace camp as an address, and asks for another – since the women were unable to give another address, the three were immediately sent to prison for a week. It was submitted to the Court that the Master of the Rolls, Lord Donaldson, had ruled in the High Court that the peace camp is a recognised address, but this submission was dismissed. The women served their sentence in

Pucklechurch Remand Centre, near Bristol.

**AUGUST 19th, 1987:** cruise missile convoy support vehicles return to base. No information given to Yellow Gate women by Cruisewatch, another manifestation of the growing witch-hunt against Yellow Gate women by the mainstream British peace movement.

Massacre in the nearby town of Hungerford, where a man dressed in military fatigues kills 14 people before killing himself. Two others died later. This was Britain's worst-ever mass-shooting incident. One of the two who died later was Ian Playle, Clerk to the Justices in Newbury Magistrates Court. Mr Playle, like Jessica Hill, was one of the Clerks who would curb the excesses of the prosecution, and was respected by the women at Yellow Gate for his consistent fairness. Mr Playle also refused an invitation from the USAF for an all expenses paid trip to the US (see OCTOBER 6th 1987). Colleague Jessica Hill later wrote in an affidavit prepared at the request of Yellow Gate women, '. . . both he and I acknowledged that the idea of accepting such an invitation was totally out of the question as we were Public Servants and therefore should not accept such gifts. Furthermore, as Clerks in Court dealing with prosecutions arising from incidents at RAF Greenham Common, it would be improper to accept such an invitation as it could seriously jeopardise the appearance of impartiality which is essential for all people involved in the administration of justice. Ian Playle then wrote refusing the invitation.' Mr Playle died on 21st August 1987.

**AUGUST 23rd, 1987:** at Cruisewatch meeting in Newbury, several members express opinion that Yellow Gate women should not receive messages via the Cruisewatch CB radio system.

**SEPTEMBER 3rd, 1987:** responsibility for producing the camp's Newsletter, which is accepted by the Gates in turn, falls on Yellow Gate this month; other Gates hold a meeting to withdraw funds for printing costs (the Newsletter contains first-hand accounts of the Moscow conference, and articulates Yellow Gate's stands on anti-racism and non-alignment).

Cruise missile convoy leaves base at midnight. Non-violently resisted at Yellow Gate.The few women from other Gates who had previously taken an interest in the convoy did not attend for the exiting of this convoy, nor for subsequent convoys.

**SEPTEMBER 5th, 1987:** storms the previous night had soaked everything; eviction at 0800, in the rain.

Sixth birthday of the camp outside the Main Gate. Many women gather at Yellow Gate to celebrate.

**SEPTEMBER 21st, 1987:** no women at Orange Gate, the Gate which had been instrumental in spreading smears about Yellow Gate following the Moscow conference. Women who had previously not been involved in the day to day work of the Gate came in from London and other cities to spread misinformation and whip up antagonism towards the women at Yellow Gate. For example, Fiona Shand, who became a regular visitor to Orange Gate over this period, published an article attacking Yellow Gate and the King's Cross women in the periodical MARXISM TODAY.

*Beth Junor* − One of the most disturbing and frustrating things about the attacks on us was the fact that these women had more resources than us yet came down to the Common in their flash cars from their secure homes to attack women who were living in tents and being evicted every day.

We were being exhausted by our living conditions, by the almost daily harassments either in person by visiting women or in the press, by continually fighting the convoys and by having to deal with the Police and military violence. We were pushed to our very limits, and we knew this network was banding together to divert us from our primary purpose for being at the peace camp − which was to resist militarism through non-violent direct action. The women in Greenham Women Everywhere were driving down to the camp from the comfort of their indoor shelter, having locked their doors behind them and with no fear of an eviction while they were gone. Not only were they witholding their resources from us (for example, photographs for our defence in Court, or transport to Salisbury Plain, which we desperately needed a car for) but they were actively attacking us. We were not equal adversaries. We were at the end of our tethers and they would come and wind us up and provoke us until we lost our tempers and told them to go away and leave us alone. Then they would triumph in our anger, go away satisfied that all the vile rumours they'd heard about us were true, have a rest in their homes, then write their articles or return refreshed for another attack.

They would accuse us of being violent because of our anger, and they believed that they themselves were being non-violent. Although none of them actually hit us (on occasion they came near it, but they were careful not to actually carry out the threat), their behaviour was a clever violence against us because of the inequalities between us, and because they were widening the inequalities between us. State violence is like that too − it doesn't always entail a direct physical hit, but can consist of deprivation of resources or of silencing people's voices, or of a continuous harassment on a rota basis. Non-violence does not always mean being soft-spoken − if you believe in it, you've got to defend it, without insulting another personally. It was never a personal thing between us and these women who harassed us, what we objected to was the way in which they were undermining our principles of non-alignment, non-violence, anti-racism and autonomy as women – everything that we'd worked so hard to establish at the peace camp.

In the end, they took away nearly all the resources we'd had. We were left with nothing but our principles. At this time, the King's Cross women were the only outside group who shared their resources with us, never hesitating to give us lifts to Salisbury Plain so that we could stop the convoy working, for example.

If there's one thing I learned from all this nightmare of harassment,it is that if anyone with less resources than yourself, or anyone whose life is harder than your own, tries to tell you about their life, then the least you can do is listen. That's the least you can do. It is a moral imperative. Then you must help to redress any injustice. The worst thing you can do is use the benefit of your resources to attack those who have less than yourself.

**SEPTEMBER 26th, 1987:** READING WEEKEND POST publishes front-page article alleging a 'Black Mafia' invasion of the women's peace camp at Yellow Gate, quoting local resident Lynette Edwell. This was one of the first in a long series of articles smearing Yellow Gate women and the King's Cross Women's Centre, Wilmette Brown of Black Women for Wages for Housework in particular.

**SEPTEMBER 29th, 1987:** it is announced in the Communist Party's daily paper, the MORNING STAR, that the women of Blue, Woad and Orange Gates have disassociated themselves from Yellow Gate.

*Sarah Hipperson* – In 1987, our principles of non-violence, non-alignment, anti-racism and autonomy as women were not as yet publicly defined. We believed these principles were understood by the 'peace movement', particularly on Greenham Common. This belief was severely tested by the events of 1987. The test revealed how shaky the foundations of this self-defined movement were.

Recording the disassociation of the other camps around the perimeter from Yellow Gate, I wrote, 'The women who remain at Yellow Gate fully accept this separation – we do not look on it as a disagreement, a rift that can be healed, but as a positive separation.'

The need to defend our principles was greater than the need to hold Greenham Common Women's Peace Camp within the feminist/peace movement network. We could not let this network, as powerful as it is, take risks with our non-aligned and anti-racist position. Our credibility and protection were built upon our stand against the nuclear weapons of both the Eastern and Western blocs, protection which has enabled us to remain on Greenham Common to this very day.

The lack of political progress in the feminist/peace movement networks has meant that its numbers have dwindled; they have become little more than one large encounter group, dependent upon 'networking', 'contacts' and collating information for tracts and periodicals, etc. This can create the illusion that what is being done will bring about change – it won't.

The genocidal policy inherent within HM Government's defence policy requires more than this as a response. Any woman who is serious about getting rid of nuclear weapons to create a more just society and can live without networks and the power politics of the 'alternative system' can have a very good productive life at the Women's Peace Camp on Greenham Common.

**OCTOBER 1st, 1987:** Yellow Gate women inform Newbury Quaker Meeting, by letter, that they no longer wish to use the facilities provided for all peace camp women at their Meeting House. The letter details harassment of Yellow Gate women at the Meeting House by Lynette Edwell, an attender at the Quaker Meeting, and by the gutter press as a result of the activities of those who also use the facilities of the Meeting House. No reply received to date.

**OCTOBER 2nd, 1987:** two women from the recently established Woad Gate arrive at Yellow Gate to inform us that from this date our post would be delivered to Woad Gate, on the north side of the base. This was the result of a delegation of women from the other Gates meeting with the Newbury postmaster, which included a woman claiming (falsely) to be from Yellow Gate. The delegation had informed the postmaster that a meeting on the Common between all of the camps had decided that all post should be delivered to Woad Gate.

Thus the postal delivery to the peace camp was disrupted for the first time. Yellow Gate women were subsequently told by the Post Office that this request had raised the issue of the delivery of post to the peace camp in general, within the Post Office. The Postmaster advised that if a secure post-box was set up at the camp outside the Main Gate, postal deliveries would continue to named women there – general camp post would all go the the North side.

A post-box was constructed, inspected by the postmaster and passed as secure; bailiffs arrived the following morning at approximately 0700 and attempted to remove the post-box.

Sarah Hipperson in particular campaigned over the following months for the postal delivery to continue to the original and only permanent camp outside the perimeter of the air base. Postal delivery to Yellow Gate was maintained.

The camp at Woad Gate later folded.

OCTOBER 6th, 1987: Newbury ADVERTISER prints a small article revealing that four 'distinguished citizens' of Newbury have been invited by the USAF to join an all-expenses paid trip to the USA, which would include a tour of the White House and lunch at the Pentagon.

The local worthies include the Chief Crown Prosecutor at Newbury Magistrates Court (where the vast majority of trials of peace camp women take place), two executives of Newbury District Council (the public body responsible for the regular evictions of the peace camps outside the perimeter of the base) and president of Newbury's Chamber of Commerce. This information was repeated in the GUARDIAN's Diary column two days later.

OCTOBER 5th, 6th and 7th, 1987, Newbury Magistrates Court: trial for Criminal Damage to the perimeter fence on June 18th 1987. Two of the original group of eleven women did not attend for trial. All nine women tried are found Guilty. Sarah Hipperson of Yellow Gate is sentenced to three months imprisonment. Georgina Smith of Yellow Gate is sentenced to two months imprisonment. Jean Hutchinson, Maryan Spring, Janet Tavner, Merle Gower and Beth Junor all of Yellow Gate are released on surety until October 30th, pending Social Enquiry reports, before sentencing. Emily Post and Ely Smyly of Blue Gate are described by the stipendiary magistrate as 'ladies of clean character' and given Conditional Discharges.

On October 30th, Jean Hutchinson is sentenced to two months imprisonment, Beth Junor to one month in prison. Maryan, Merle and Janet are sentenced to one month in prison suspended for two years. We later learned that the Home Office investigations of Janet Tavner began at this time.

Sarah, Georgina and Jean appealed against their convictions and sentences. Sarah and Georgina were released from Holloway on stiff bail conditions pending their Appeal. Both were banned from visiting or living on Greenham Common. These Appeals did not commence in Reading Crown Court until 1991. Beth was taken to Holloway and later transferred to Bullwood Hall.

OCTOBER 6th, 1987: (above trial in progress): cruise missile support vehicles leave the base during the day. Non-violently resisted at Yellow Gate.

At night, a group of women from other Gates around the perimeter converge on Yellow Gate and attempt to take our van, Gladys, containing all of our belongings. They leave before the main cruise missile convoy vehicles leave the Main Gate.

Cruise missile convoy out at midnight – non-violently resisted at Yellow Gate.

Another lie brought to the Common from London at this time was that Janet Tavner and Beth Junor of Yellow Gate, as well as some women from the King's Cross Women's Centre in London, were members of the CIA. It was said that the journalist Duncan Campbell had proof of this on computer files. We asked to see this proof, but none was produced. This lie was yet another contribution to the witch-hunt, and it did help to whip up the fear and hatred against us.

*Beth* – A woman from the north side came round to observe Janet and I. She leaned against one of the poplar trees and watched our every move, but she quickly got bored watching us tend the fire and collect water. I resolved to mention at intervals I had to make a phone call to America. We had to laugh about it – again, humour was one of our mechanisms for dealing with an attack.

We have no doubt that state agents were involved in the split between the Gates, and we are as certain as we can be who they were.

OCTOBER 13th, 1987: cruise missile convoy returns in early hours. Support vehicles follow, the next day. Both non-violently resisted at Yellow Gate.

OCTOBER 15th-16th, 1987: south-east of England struck by the worst storm for nearly 300 years. In the following week, torrential rain fell in several parts of the country, particularly in Wales and the Home Counties.

OCTOBER 25th, 1987: a brightly decorated anti-cruise convoy travels to Yellow Gate from the King's Cross Women's Centre in London to celebrate Time Off for Women day. A wonderful morale-boost!

NOVEMBER 4th, 1987: *Sarah Hipperson*, letter to Lord Hailsham, the Lord Chancellor:

Sir,

On the 5th November 1987 I will be appearing in the Magistrates Court, Newbury, Berkshire to answer charges brought by the Crown Prosecution Service on behalf of the Ministry of Defence.

I am enclosing a photocopy of an article that appeared in the Diary column of the Guardian newspaper on the 8th October 1987, the day after I had been sentenced to three months imprisonment by stipendiary magistrate Mr Volcker.

This article calls into question the integrity and suitability of John Wilcox, Chief Crown Prosecutor in the Newbury Magistrates Court. Integrity and suitability necessary for me to feel confident that the cases brought against me are free of prejudice, corrupt and unethical influences. And, that the democratic right to protest is not hindered by the proffering and/or acceptance of gratuities by a representative of a foreign power, namely the United States. Especially when this foreign power's presence and purpose lies at the heart of this protest. Women living at the peace camp are called to court in Newbury, to answer charges arising out of our non-violent direct action resistance to both the presence and purpose of the USAF at Greenham Common RAF base. Ground launched cruise missile convoys regularly leave Yellow/Main Gate, to practice and perfect first strike nuclear attacks against the Soviet people. We regard it as our duty and responsibility to raise awareness of, and to draw attention to, this illegality that breaks at least the following negotiated and signed laws: *The Hague Convention* (war must be confined to military engagements and targets only) – 1899, 1907; *The Genocide Convention* (the prohibition against the wanton killing of civilians) – 1948 and ratified by Act of Parliament 1969; and the laws that govern Common land.

On the 13th October I was granted leave to appeal the judgement by Mr Volcker. I was granted bail on £1,000.00 surety and banned indefinitely from visiting or living on Greenham Common.

(signed Sarah Hipperson)

NOVEMBER 5th, 1987: Sarah challenges the right of the court to hear her case when the Crown Prosecutor's impartiality had been compromised by his acceptance of a gift from the USAF.

We learn from Jessica Hill, a Clerk in Newbury Magistrates Court, that the court had also been invited. She tells us they treated the invitation with the contempt it deserved, realising it would compromise the court officials professionally. Jessica Hill, respected by us as a fair Clerk, left her work in Newbury Magistrates Court soon afterwards, and wrote us an Affidavit for our future legal challenge of this corruption.

NOVEMBER 11th, 1987, Reading Crown Court: Sarah Hipperson applies for changes to her banning conditions, to allow her to return to the Common. Judge Murchie interrupts Sarah's application with, 'You use the court to make political statements,' and 'You always plead Not Guilty to get maximum publicity.' Sarah had never given evidence before this judge.

The application is refused and Sarah is threatened with contempt of court. Sarah then had to wait another month before obtaining a hearing in the Court of Appeal.

NOVEMBER 13th, 1987: Beth is released from Bullwood Hall women's prison and is met by Katrina Howse and Sarah Hipperson; the three resolve to bring the matter of the corrupt acceptance of gifts from the USAF by public officials to justice through the courts, Beth having studied the Prevention of Corruption Acts while inside. The women have a meal together in London, then Beth and Katrina return to the camp. Sarah must remain in London, under her banning order.

Cruise missile convoy leaves base for Salibury Plain at 0200 am. At 0400, two women chain the Main Gate of the base closed. One woman's fingers are smashed by the MoD Police, resulting in a fracture to one finger and tearing of most of the tendons of the hand.

A US serviceman at the Gate holding a mug of coffee declares, 'My coffee's gone cold,' and throws coffee through the Gate, over one of the women.

MoD Police take no action on these assaults.

Jean Hutchinson is arrested and charged under the Public Order Act, for allegedly using 'words or behaviour which is threatening, abusive or insulting or [using] disorderly behaviour within the hearing or sight of a person who is likely to be caused alarm or distress thereby.' *Jean* − The words I used are words I would not normally use, but at the time two officers were twisting my arms behind my back and dragging me about 75 yards at the same time. I expected that at least one arm would be broken. Compared to the alarm and distress they were causing me my words were as nothing. [The Magistrates in Newbury court agreed with Jean and she was found Not Guilty at her trial − see next chapter.]

NOVEMBER 19th, 1987: cruise missile convoy returns to base. Two women arrested on the A339 road, taken to Newbury Police station, held for two hours then released without charge.

NOVEMBER 20th, 21st and 22nd 1987, Hackney, London: CND'S annual conference.

It is revealed that the Cruisewatch organisation received a grant from the Campaign for Nuclear Disarmament of £10,000 (the women's peace camp received no financial support from National CND).

The conference buildings displayed grafitti against the King's Cross Women's Centre. During the conference the front door of the King's Cross Women's Centre in London was covered in abusive grafitti. Consistent attempts were made to prevent Wilmette Brown from speaking to the conference.

Sarah Hipperson and Wilmette Brown stood for election to the National Council − both were, not surprisingly, defeated: the November issue of National CND's magazine, SANITY, had contained a smear article on Wilmette Brown by Communist Party spokeswoman Bea Campbell. The article had been commissioned by Meg Beresford. This was an unprecedented public denouncement of candidates standing for election to the Council.

NOVEMBER 30th, 1987: cruise missile convoy support vehicles out in morning − non-violently resisted at Yellow Gate. Main convoy vehicles leave the Main Gate at 0100 the following morning, followed by more support vehicles – all non-violently resisted.

DECEMBER 3rd, 1987: four women from Yellow Gate Trespass on Salisbury Plain and find convoy in a wood named Little Folly.

DECEMBER 5th, 1987: Yellow Gate women attend 'Working Together to End Strip Searching' conference at Lambeth Town Hall in London. Paintings depicting scenes from life at the women's peace camp at Greenham Common hang on the walls of the conference room, despite the fact the chairwoman of the conference, Linda Bellos, had co-authored a pamphlet attacking the work of the peace camp ('Breaching the Peace', 1983). The campaign against strip searching subsequently highlighted the case of one woman strip-searched in the processing centre at Greenham Common. In fact hundreds of women were strip-searched within the base; in the early stages of this policy women were less aware of their rights in custody and complaints were therefore unrecorded.

DECEMBER 7th, 1987: 'Here to Stay, Here to Verify' banner hung at Yellow Gate, marking our determination to continue our work of 24-hour-a-day resistance against militarism beyond the INF agreement between the United States and the Soviet Union. The slogan is written in both English and Russian to reaffirm our non-aligned stand.

DECEMBER 8th, 1987: INF Treaty signed. Reagan and Gorbachev thereby resolve to eliminate land-based intermediate-range nuclear weapons on both sides. INF missiles – cruise and pershing missiles, SS20's and their successors – represented less than four per cent of the total nuclear armoury. A formidable stockpile of sea-launched and air-launched missiles already occupied the gap between battlefield and intercontinental weapons.

DECEMBER 9th, 1987, Court of Appeal, London: banning order on Sarah Hipperson is dropped, on application in person by Sarah. Several bail conditions are imposed in their place: Sarah was not to enter the base, not to commit Criminal Damage, not to obstruct any vehicles entering or leaving Greenham Comon, and not to incite others to do any of these, in order to be allowed to return to the Common. Sarah stated she only agreed to the conditions imposed because the INF Treaty had been signed the previous day.

DECEMBER 12th and 13th 1987: Take Action on Racism – annual December demonstration on Greenham Common marked, as always, by workshops and non-violent direct action.

DECEMBER 14th, 1987: after Defence Ministers of France and the UK meet, it is reported considerable progress has been made towards collaboration in developing a new nuclear-armed air-launched cruise missile, with a range of up to 300 miles, for deployment by the air forces of each country by the end of the century.

1. The aftermath of an eviction. As always, women remain on the land. Early 1986. Katrina Howse far right.

*2. Hiroshima Day 1986. Horses refuse to trample women blockading the slip-road from the A339 to the Main Gate of teh air base …*

3. . . . . the police have to do their own dirty work.

4. *Stopping cruise missiles convoy support vehicles.*
*January 1987.*

5. Wilmette Brown speaking at a workshop at Green Gate. "Time off for Women" day, October 1986

6. Yoko Ono (left) celebrates her 54th birthday on Greenham Common and faces return of cruise missile convoy support vehicles. February 18th 1987. Sarah Hipperson on right.

*7. Cruise missile convoy support vehicles leaving the Main Gate.*
*12th February 1987.*

*8. Resisting the deployment of cruise missiles (main convoy of launcher and control vehicles):*
*chain between lamp-posts and preparing to burn the household furniture.*
*Early 1987.*

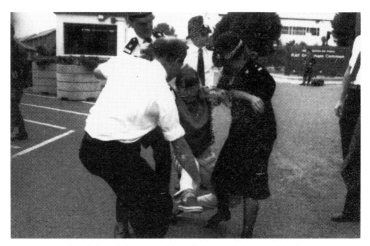

*9. Beth Junor being removed from the base, resisting non-violently.*
*4th August 1988.*

*10. Aniko Jones captures cruise missile convoy support vehicle.*
*1987*

11. *Sarah Hipperson arrested in Whitehall, for demonstrating while Parliament is sitting, on eve of Thatcher's departure for visit with Gorbachev.*
*27th March 1987.*

*12. Janet Tavner (left) Margaretta D'Arcy at Yellow Gate.
October 1987.*

*13. Yellow Gate,
December 1987.*

*14. Katrina Howse (centre) and Wilmette Brown (right) at end of workshop, December gathering 1987.*

*15. Busi Ncube (left) sharing rural survival skills. October 1988.*

16. St Giles Church occupation on 45th anniversary of forced eviction of Imber Villagers. 17th December 1988.
Top row, left to right: Katrina Howse, Abigail Adams, Catherine Wenden, Aniko Jones, Allison Lovell, Sarah Hipperson.
Kneeling: Beth Junor (left) and Janet Tavner.

*17. Banner by Abigail Adams.*

*18. Evictions continue on a regular basis.*
*1989.*

# 1988
## RECLAIM SALISBURY PLAIN

In 1988, the INF treaty between the two military superpowers was ratified. Promises of a more enlightened, peaceful era were still being generated by the media, but the experience of the women living outside the Main Gate of the air base at Greenham Common was very different. Contrary to a public statement by the government, cruise missile convoys continued to leave the base for regular exercises on Salisbury Plain. While the public were being lulled into a false sense of security by continued press coverage of the INF treaty, the base at Greenham Common maintained its capability to use nuclear cruise missles, and in fact continued to actively prepare and practise for their use.

Each of the superpowers continued to suppress protest in their own country, while relations between the US and Soviet Union strengthened to the extent that in 1988 they began observing nuclear tests together. The military personnel in the base who had been saying for years that they had to be there 'in case the Russians take over Britain,' now saw coach-loads of Soviet military personnel being driven with their hosts, under heavy British security, to a local pub for a friendly pint. With no significant reductions in military budgets, and no halt to weapons modernisation programmes, the question arose, who were their new enemies going to be?

At Yellow Gate, women told anyone who would listen, 'the INF treaty is a con'. But the rings of censorship around the camp were ever-tightening, and in 1988 drew close enough to involve the mainstream British peace movement and parts of the feminist movement, thus leaving women more vulnerable to police violence. The Yellow Gate camp became increasingly isolated, by obstinately refusing to join in on the Gorby-mania. Women from the other camps around the perimeter stopped gathering at the Main Gate to oppose the cruise missile convoy exercises together with Yellow Gate women, and their supporting networks followed suit. Many Yellow Gate women were assaulted by Ministry of Defence Police and by civilian police guarding the cruise missile convoy. Some were knocked unconscious.

There were at least 129 arrests of Yellow Gate women during the year. In 21 instances, no charges were laid and in four instances, charges were subsequently dropped. All other arrests resulted in charges being made, which meant an endless succession of court cases and prison sentences throughout the year.

Regular evictions of the peace camp by Newbury District Council continued. There were 87 recorded evictions, in all weathers, in

1988. The evictions were most frequent during January and November, and eased off slightly during warmer, drier weather. On average, there was never a period of more than four days without an eviction. The violence of this frequency of evictions lies largely in the fact that a tent, easily movable, is the most shelter one is allowed. It is not difficult to imagine the consquences for physical health this entails, in Britain's damp climate – in general, chronic low level symptoms and fatigue (rather than the more dramatic seasonal fluctuations in health experienced by those who live indoors). The only medical practice in Newbury which would allow women from the peace camp on its premises still refused to register us; in consequence, no medical records are kept.

In addition to the non-violent direct action against the convoys and the extra work created by the Police, military and Newbury District Council violence, there were several legal challenges in 1988.

The challenge in the courts to Greenham Common Byelaws (1985) continued, and the Crown Court declared the Byelaws invalid.

The Ministry of Defence's occupation of Greeenham Common was also challenged, and an order for the removal of the fences, gates, buildings and works on Greenham Common was lodged in the County Court on March 1st.

The Ministry of Defence instituted proceedings to extinguish Commoners' Rights on Greenham Common, to pave the way for revised legislation which would give the MoD Police renewed powers to arrest and charge women entering the base. Yellow Gate women challenged the Secretary of State for Defence on the legality of this procedure.

Challenges to the military's manipulation of Salisbury Plain byelaws continued, at Crown Court level. Unable to obtain a hearing for our arguments here, we resolved to take two sets of Salisbury Plain byelaws to Judicial Review the following year.

The land was held for another year, and in turn the land replenished and nurtured the women who fought by all non-violent means to drive the military off the Common.

JANUARY 2nd,1988: deterioration of the National Health Service continues. Leading article in the British Medical Journal states the NHS is moving towards 'terminal decline'.

JANUARY 14th,1988: first cruise missile convoy since the signing of the INF Treaty leaves the base for exercises at the deserted village of Imber, on Salisbury Plain. Both the convoy support vehicles during the day and the main convoy vehicles leaving the main gate at midnight are non-violently resisted by Yellow Gate women. Several arrests.

JANUARY 17th, 1988, Imber Village: four women reach the

convoy deployment site through thick fog and are arrested and charged with Trespass contrary to the Imber Ranges Byelaws.

JANUARY 19th, 1988, House of Commons: demonstration outside by seven Yellow Gate women, who pin banners to their clothes to inform the public that the cruise missile convoy is out on exercise. (It is an offence to demonstrate in the vicinity of the House while parliament is sitting – but what if there is a message on one's clothing?) Police have to give up trying to take the banners off the women, who walk up and down the pavement while Parliament is sitting. They confront Margaret Thatcher as she is driven into the House in a limousine.

JANUARY 21st, 1988: cruise missile convoy returns to the base in the early hours.

*Janet Tavner* – For the convoy's return, Katrina, Beth and I dressed up as Police constables (!) and with a torch, the appropriate body language and right arm signals, stopped the third cruise missile launcher erecter vehicle, and the whole convoy behind it.

During the confusing minutes when the Police sergeants tried to find out why 'their constables' had interrupted the convoy, three more women came out from the woods (Allison, Lucy and Aniko) and four women climbed onto a launcher. Aniko and I remained on top of the launcher for ten to fifteen minutes, and the convoy remained at a halt.

Two of us were arrested, but not charged.

Meanwhile at the Main Gate, the military who had gathered to cheer the convoy in, as well as the 'sight-seers' or groups of families in civilian clothes inside the base who similarly gather to cheer the return of the convoy, were also being demoralised – Bee, Jean and Joan were burning American, British and Soviet flags.

JANUARY 25th, 1988: the government announces it is not going to prosecute officers of the Royal Ulster Constabulary who had previously been acquitted following incidents in late 1982 which had given rise to allegations of a 'shoot-to-kill' policy.

JANUARY 28th, 1988, Court of Appeal, London: appeal by six Irishmen known as the Birmingham Six, wrongly convicted for bomb attacks on two Birmingham pubs in 1974, is rejected. This and the announcement of January 25th cause deterioration in British-Irish government relations.

JANUARY 28th, 1988, Camden Council Meeting, London: 100% cut in the grant to King's Cross Women's Centre is approved, as a result of the press smear campaign against the Centre. The Review Panel admitted their decision was on purely political grounds which neither they nor the Council officers would or could specify.

The only 'evidence' the Review Panel offered to justify cutting three women's jobs was a series of articles attacking Wilmette Brown, the Centre's Black joint co-ordinator, for challenging racism in the peace movement.[1]

**FEBURARY 2nd, 1988**, Candlemas: very bad weather at the camp with hailstones, snow blizzards and lashing rain.

**FEBRUARY 3rd, 1988**, House of Lords: Greenham Common Byelaws challenge continues. At today's oral hearing the Director of Public Prosecutions is refused leave to appeal to the House of Lords.

*Jean Hutchinson* – The extreme brevity of this hearing showed up this time wasting and frivolous application by the MoD. The Clerk of the Court in Newbury had informed us that all Greenham Common Byelaws cases are adjourned *sine die* (without day – indefinitely). No wonder there was a trip to the House of Lords, the MoD had been desperately clutching at straws to save their byelaws, their base and their cruise missiles.

We were to appear in Reading Crown Court again on the 25th of February.

**FEBRUARY 8th, 1988:** UK Home Secretary announces setting up of an independent inquiry into the presence of Nazi war criminals in the UK.

**FEBURARY 9th,1988:** due to high winds, all non-essential military and civilian personnel in the base are relieved from duty. This announcement over the load speaker system was followed a few minutes later with the afterthought, 'all personnel must ensure that ALL doors and windows are secured and fastened, before leaving.' As they are aware, it is not only the wind that will open unlocked doors . . .

**FEBRUARY 11th, 1988:** cruise missile support vehicles begin leaving the base at 8.00 am; main convoy leaves the Main Gate at midnight. As a result of the effective non-violent action taken on the A339 on the 21st January, for the first time in the convoy's history there are no Police down this road.

As is usual after the convoy deployment, there is a morning eviction of the camp the following day.

**FEBRUARY 17th, 1988:** cruise missile support vehicles return to the base during the afternoon. Non-violently resisted – one woman chains herself to the front of one of the vehicles, slowing its progress towards the Main Gate to a slow walking pace.

**FEBRUARY 18th, 1988:** cruise missile launcher and control vehicles return to base in the early hours.

*Janet Tavner* – For its return to Greenham Common Airbase, Katrina, Beth, Jean and I broke into the base to meet and stop the convoy. We were discovered and arrested before the convoy returned, but while being held in custody inside the base we overheard a message on a Policeman's radio, saying that the convoy would be parked outside Hangar 303 (inside the base) for an hour.

As if following an instinct, after being released we ran to reach Hangar 303 on the other side of the base. A second time, we broke into the base and made our way towards the convoy vehicles.

The launcher erecter vehicles, which carry the missiles, and the control vehicles carrying the complex computer equipment necessary for launching the missiles, were all being washed outside the hangar building. We quietly walked up to the side of the control vehicle, and climbed on it. No-one took any notice until one woman stood up in her full height on top of the big vehicle.

Ministry of Defence Police arrived and arrested us, but before that, there was a sparkling confrontation between angry women and convoy men.[2]

**FEBRUARY 25th, 1988**, Reading Crown Court: Greenham Common Byelaws challenge continues. Judge Lait rules that the Byelaws are *ultra vires* the Military Lands Act (1892) and that therefore, the Secretary of State (Michael Heseltine) had exceeded his powers.

*Jean Hutchinson* ~ We had proved that the Byelaws written at the instigation of Heseltine were invalid. The re-registering of Greenham and Crookham Commons on a register completed as recently as 1973 began to look like a miracle.

The actual judgement reads, 'In our judgement, byelaw 2(b) takes away the rights of Common (certainly so long as the Byelaws are in force) and prejudicially affects such rights.'

We were also vindicated in the witness summons we had served on Heseltine who was now severely brought to book, legally and politically, because the judgement goes on, 'In our judgement the Secretary of State exceeded the power given to him and byelaw 2(b) is ultra vires and invalid.' We knew this – and we counted him culpable.

As a spin off from 2(b) being illegal 2 (a),(c),(d),(g),(j) and (l) were also *ultra vires* (this would later be taken up by the High Court under the legal concept of 'severability'). In plain terms at least two things are being said: 1) the law will not allow what was done to the Common land by means of the Byelaws and 2) the Secretary of State for Defence did not follow the law. It seemed to us that the government was a regime which was blatantly lawless.

The last sentence of the Crown Court judgement read beautifully, and applied to hundreds of women in thousands of cases: 'Accordingly we quash the convictions of these two Appellants.'

Part of our Press Release read, 'We are outraged that the government has exploited its position of power and has used bad law to criminalise us.' The criminalisation of thousands of women we regard as a crime by the government; with each conviction a woman had been denied her liberty if she chose not to pay the fine, as many of us did.

Now began a desperate legal and political struggle by the MoD to save their Byelaws. On the 12th of May, the Crown Prosecution Service lodged an appeal in the High Court and the hearing took place over 5 days in July.

In the meantime, women entering the base at Greenham Common would be escorted off the base without being charged with Trespass.

**FEBRUARY 25th,1988:** Soviet Union publicises the first withdrawals of Soviet intermediate-range nuclear missiles from East Germany and Czechoslovakia, to be destroyed under the terms of the INF treaty.

**MARCH 1st, 1988:** an order for the removal of the illegal works and fences on Greenham Common is lodged at the County Court of Berkshire by Sarah Hipperson, Katrina Howse, Jean Hutchinson and Elizabeth Junor, on behalf of all Yellow Gate women.

**MARCH 2nd-3rd 1988,** NATO meeting, Brussels: final declaration of the meeting states, about the controversial issue of modernisation of US nuclear weapons, that these weapons 'would continue to be kept up to date where necessary'.

**MARCH 3rd, 1988:** four women leave Yellow Gate for a visit to Northern Ireland, to join the International Women's Day picket outside Maghaberry Prison.

**MARCH 6th, 1988:** Mairead Farrell, Daniel McCann and Sean Savage, all unarmed, are summarily executed on a street in Gibraltar, by members of the British security forces.

*Sarah Hipperson* – We went to Northern Ireland as a result of a lot of work that Margaretta D'Arcy has put into Greenham Common. Through knowing her we became aware of the war going on in Northern Ireland. Through understanding her natural anger about it, we decided to go there. Margaretta arranged for us to stay with a wonderful family in West Belfast: Eileen Loughlin's. We met her daughter Ann Marie, and they gave us a lot of information about the Troubles, and about the pain that was particular to their family. Ann Marie at 15 was hit by a plastic bullet and Eileen, her mother, spent years worrying and caring for her. She was in an intensive care unit, and it was a matter of whether she would live or die. She'd been hit in the head and had a loss of speech, and there were gaps in her life that had been blotted out. At 23, she has epilepsy. It happened eight years ago and no compensation has come to the family. We were met with great hospitality by them, and given the freedom to come and go. It was a good base to work from.

*Katrina* – We attended the women's picket outside Maghaberry

Prison on the Sunday. That in itself was a reason to go to Northern Ireland. Yellow Gate women throughout the years at Greenham have been in prison time and time again. Maghaberry is one of the most infamous prisons in Europe. It was important to go and support the Republican women incarcerated there. It's a very top security prison, built at great cost, and built at a great distance form Belfast. It is an horrific prison and I can't imagine what it is like to be in it. Maghaberry is like a big factory complex, miles from anywhere and with TV cameras filming the outside. It is like a fortress and to be inside must be like being entombed. 100 women marched to the prison gates, which is like the first fence around the silos. Many of the women were relatives and friends of the women inside. A woman spoke who had been let out of the prison two weeks before, after four years inside.

*Sarah* − As we marched towards the prison it was a strong windy day, threatening rain. Women unfurled their banners and walked slowly forward. I felt and I know the other women did too, a sense of pride carrying the wonderful banner Katrina had painted. It was full of colour and full of hope and was a focus in the bleak surroundings. It depicted the women from Belfast and Yellow Gate reaching out to each other, joining in the struggle against strip searching, and acknowledging the work of both communities against the military. With a clear unambigious statement about getting the troops out of Northern Ireland. It was a great spirit lifter on a gloomy, windy day.

*Katrina* − Women shouted out the names of women inside. An ex-prisoner told us that they put all the generators on inside to drown out our voices of support.

*Sarah* − The choice of location has a sinister, psychological aspect to it. It's a way of distancing and reducing the women who are extremely committed to the Republican Movement. I agree with their aspirations, I don't agree with violent paths to these aspirations. We were there to make a communication with the women inside, who they were definitely trying to bury both sociologically and to minimise the importance of their struggle. Previously women were kept in Armagh Prison, which was in the centre of town, and women were able to keep in touch with their roots. Women still being part of the community presented a rallying point to the community and kept the focus of the struggle. Maghaberry represents the removal of women to a Siberian-like exile.

*Katrina* − I have done a six month prison sentence and smaller sentences in British prisons. Sarah has done months at a time, and many sentences. I looked at Maghaberry in relation to the prison I've done, and what the British State has done to me. The sentencing the Republican women get is awesome.

*Sarah* – I went to a workshop on 'Political Vetting'. A Republican woman was talking as a member of the Twinbrook Tenants Association. Their funding was cut off simply because she was a Sinn Fein woman. Anyone who organised their community, and we are not talking about organising to take up arms, but organising the community to get the most for everyone, seems to be suspect. There is a vested interest in keeping people powerless in bad housing, without rights, without hope, without any future. Anyone who has a vision to see a non-violent way of bringing that situation into hope is going to be regarded as a bad influence, and a front for the IRA. It is not true on any level. When this woman was explaining how this worked bells were ringing in my head. I had been in Camden when Camden Council cut the grant to the King's Cross Women's Centre.

I said I was interested in political vetting and that it reminded me of what was happening in the women's movement. I said that since we'd been to Moscow, we were being dealt with in the same kind of way by the women's network. I said these techniques that the state uses are being used by women who are supposed to be on your side.

Margaretta had also arranged for me to meet Des Wilson, who says Mass from his own home. There is a community of people around him who avoid the official Catholic Church, and come together for spiritual nourishment. He had his church taken away form him because he was seen to be too closely working with the people. It started with a woman in her late 30's who said she wanted to read and write. He said, 'No problem, I can help you' – he took her on as a pupil and other people wanted to go. Then nuns came in to help. Des Wilson was making clear cut statements about Justice in his church. He's now freelance, and happy about that. He practises what is practised in Brazil, 'Liberation Theology'. The more people know about themselves the more they will feel liberated.

*Katrina* – When we were there the news of the three Republicans murdered in Gibraltar had just come through. You could see how the murders were a huge blow to the Catholic community. The community was in mourning, and it was obvious that Mairead Farrell had been a strong woman. On the afternoon she was killed we were outside Maghaberry Prison. Mairead Farrell had spent ten years in Armagh Prison. She had only been released about 1½ years before she was murdered. She was a woman who believed in an armed struggle, we believe in non-violent direct action. We have a real connection with her as a woman of great strength who resisted the British state. The injustice that motivated her, and brought out great skills, determination and strength, we can identify with as women up against the viciousness of the British state. She was on hunger strike, she was on the 'no wash' protest in prisonÛhappens to women who achieve a certain level of resistance that is too much for the state to control. The state then reacts with great brutality.

We are always aware that the eye of the state is on us. They make decisions to put us in prison under the pretext of criminal charges. Because we are political and won't stop, they put us in prison, harass us, intimidate us – we have the whole state against us. There is a strong connnection running through our work and the work of Mairead Farrell, for which they killed her.

*Sarah* – Ann Marie was very shaken and upset. It seemed so awful for her because when Mairead Farrell came out of prison she came to see Ann Marie and was very anxious to see how she was. So there was a connection between the families. Ann Marie kept crying, saying, 'She was so lovely, and she's dead now.'³

**MARCH 9th, 1988:** cruise missile convoy support vehicles out during the day, double convoy out at midnight from the Main Gate – both resisted non-violently at Yellow Gate.

**MARCH 17th, 1988**, Newbury Magistrates Court: trial of 5 women for Criminal Damage charges brought against them on August 13th 1987, during convoy exercise in period of tension in the Gulf.

*Aniko Jones* – We had promised each other to see the action all the way to the end. This meant all eight turning up to Court and facing prison. Two women did not turn up for court, withdrawing their support from the women with whom they'd done the action. The women who turned up were: Sarah Hipperson, Jean Hutchinson, Joan Hayman and myself from Yellow Gate, and Jane Gregory from Blue Gate.

We had a Stipendiary magistrate. He refused to listen to any arguments put forward for an adjournment. The case was Criminal Damage as far as he was concerned and not connected with the Byelaws case.

The prosecutor called his first witness. He was no other than 'Thumper' from RAF/USAF Welford: a USAF airman who had threatened to 'thump' two of us who had broken into Welford, each time we stood up while being held in detention. 'Tonight I'm Adolf Hilter' he informed us, 'I'm the dictator, and you do as I say...' I had been thumped in the chest as a result of standing up.

Thumper's job is to protect resources and personnel – he had however never been in Hangar 303 and was unaware of its use. He was challenged on his violent behaviour at Welford. He said he did not recall behaving in such a manner.

The second and third witnesses were Ministry of Defence Police officers, to give evidence as eye-witnesses to us painting. All three witnesses could not remember the convoy of the night before.

The fourth witness worked for the Property Service Agency, contracted to the Department of the Environment. His job was the maintenance and repair of the buildings at Greenham. He said he received orders from a Commander to do a quick job on the hangars because they were having a parade on Monday. The base RAF Commander had, on a previous occasion, stated in court that only he could give permission for work to be done on the base, for he was the 'Landlord'. This man received orders from the USAF Commander and used British taxpayers money, allocated from the Department of the Environment, for the repair and maintenance of the USAF buildings.

The fifth witness was to give evidence on the Sherpa van and the RAF van. As with the previous witness, he produced no photographs or receipts to prove that the damage had be done or the cost of the repairs. It came out from questioning that the cost of labour (the most expensive item) was a mere estimate. The men doing the labour were army men and would not get paid extra for cleaning the vehicles. They already received a daily wage regardless of the work they did.

From questioning the sixth witness, a Policeman, we were able to bring out in Court how we were treated while in custody. We were arrested at 8.00pm. When questioned in the portakabins we were refused a seat. At 1.00am on the 14th August we were taken to Newbury Police Station. It had gone 4.00am before we were formally charged. During this time, we were refused the right to have anyone informed of our detention. We were also refused bail. The next morning we were facing a possible remand. It was quite possible for us to have been remanded without anyone knowing.

Sarah began her evidence with the day before, the 12th August. She told of the unscheduled convoy leaving Greenham Common at the same time as an unscheduled convoy leaving Comiso, another cruise missile base in Europe. The last time this scenario happened was two or three days before the bombing of Libya. This time we were facing an escalation in the Gulf crisis. Cruise missiles are first strike weapons; there was every reason to believe these missiles were going to be used. We tried to contact the Press to inform them. The women from Yellow Gate signed a letter and gave it to the MoD on the Gate. Sarah read it out: 'To all ranks, Ministry of Defence: tonight there will be a convoy leaving the base. Today you will help them bring out the support vehicles to this convoy. We believe there will be live warheads on the convoy. Go home to your families – it may be your last chance.'

Sarah described the struggle and protest the women put up the night of the convoy. Two hugh fires and a tug-of -war with hosepipes – they called in reinforcements. Our action was a daylight action to show our visible contempt and our refusal to participate in their madness. It showed their moral corruption to charge us with an illegal act. Sarah then said it was she who painted ILLEGAL, IMMORAL, INSANE on the Hangers and Portakabin.

Jean was next. She explained why Hangar 303 was the one to be painted. It was because it contained the vehicles used for the nuclear convoy. The convoy was unscheduled; convoys do not leave in August unless it is an emergency. Jean also spotted a new vehicle in the convoy with steam or smoke coming from it. The speed was unusually slow.

Jean addressed the question of guilt. The prosecutors had to prove guilt in the mind as well as in action. She felt no guilt nor did any of the other women.

Janet was called as a witness; with great clarity she described the unscheduled convoy, and the abnormally slow speed of the convoy. She told of the expressions on the faces of the drivers when she and Jean got in front of the vehicles. They showed fear and fright, not the usual arrogance. She spoke of the fear we felt of another similar incident to the bombing of Libya. The atmosphere of the court room was becoming electric. What had begun with a Criminal Damage charge was becoming an arena where good and evil were being tested.

Joan's evidence was about how people throughout the ages had protested by writing on walls. She quoted from the bible and from incidents in Argentina. It was the only protest open to us.

Jane from Blue Gate then gave her evidence. She refused to explain her actions because, she said, the magistrate and she lived in two different worlds – there was no point, as he would not understand.

It was then my turn to give evidence. I spoke of my fear of a repeat escalation leading to the loss of life or nuclear war. I said I deliberately painted the hangars, portakabin and a Sherpa van. I also said we had to stand up and show these people the evil they were committing, in a non-violent way, every chance we could.

The court was adjourned until the next day.

We were then to give our statements. Sarah spoke first:

'To say that nuclear weapons will be used is to break every law agreed by God and humanity. To express the hope that they will never be used is to agree with us and therefore we should be found Not Guilty.

'Because of apathy around us, the lack of concern for the planet and continuation of creation, we are forced to do what we do. The witnesses against us have been brutalised. All of those people who work with and around the cruise convoy, and, to a certain extent everyone who is involved in the law being used against us, is having their humanity trained out of them.

'Some of us have refused to enter into this corruption – someone has to give hope to the poor and starving people of this planet. I hope that we do so.'

Jean then spoke. She built on the momentum Sarah had begun. She too spoke with power – her strength and conviction flowed and helped the court room.

I spoke of how we had to stand against injustice – I was being tried for Criminal Damage when people were planning to wipe out whole nations. These murderers have no excuse that they did not know the consequences of their actions. We point it out every day at our camp, every convoy and every action. I will continue to protest against their every evil in a non-violent way every chance I get.

Joan spoke of her commitment to the struggle. She went on to describe the convoy, of the emotions we feel. They bring out those weapons – practicing for, waiting for the day they will be used. Joan could not continue – she stopped mid- sentence and had to sit down.

The magistrate and the court seemed a very inadequate setting to deal with this struggle.

Jane from Blue Gate repeated her statement of how the gap between the magistrate and herself was unbridgeable. Thus she did not want to give a statement. She also felt we should not pay extra charges for a rush job on the hangars. We should not go to prison.

The Stipendiary magistrate retired. Sarah was given 3 months imprisonment plus one month suspended for a year and ordered to pay £50.00 Compensation and £50.00 Costs. Jean was given 4 months imprisonment suspended for a year and ordered to pay the same Compensation and Costs, by the 25th April. I am to be sentenced in the Crown Court because I broke a Crown Court Conditional Discharge. Joan got one year's Conditional Discharge and was ordered to pay the same Costs and Compensation. Jane was similarily given one year's Conditional Discharge and ordered to pay the same Costs and Compensation.

The magistrate left as Joan demanded the same sentence as Jean and Sarah, saying she had done the same action .

However as Beth who had been there to support us said, we won, morally we won the case easily. Sarah Hipperson and Jean Hutchinson appealed their conviction.[4]

MARCH 18th, 1987, Newbury Magistrates Court: Sarah Hipperson, Katrina Howse and Beth Junor lay information before the court against Brian Thetford, Chief Executive of Newbury District Council, John Wilcox, Chief Crown Prosecutor, and Paul McMahon, Chief Executive Designate of Newbury District Council, that they had received gifts from the United States Airforce (Military Airlift Command), in the form of travel, visits, tours etc. to and within the United States of America, contrary to the Prevention of Corruption Acts

1889 to 1916.

**Beth Junor** – The process of getting the case to Court was to prove difficult, to put it mildly. Every step of the way a new hurdle was placed before us. For example, it was suggested that the matter should be referred to the Police, who would collect the evidence. Having been informed by a Newbury Community Policeman the previous year that 'there isn't anything that anyone could do to you lot, that we would consider criminal,' this did not seem to be a feasible option.

Sarah, Katrina and I set about collecting the necessary evidence ourselves. Through research and determination, affidavits were obtained and confirmation that gifts had been received was found. When at last we laid the information on oath before a Stipendiary magistrate, he said permission from the Attorney General was required before warrants for the arrest for these persons could be issued.

Subsequent correspondence with the Attorney General's Office revealed this had not been the case. Whenever one hurdle was removed, it was replaced by several others. The evidence requested by the Attorney General's office was sent to him and to this day, presumably remains in a file somewhere.

Legal challenges of this sort take place amidst endless camp chores, evictions, and continuing non-violent resistance to the military. The 'offices' we work from are our tents. We have neither a telephone nor photocopier nor computer systems at hand. Just preparing to begin your legal work can take hours, if you have to collect more wood, then water, and then heat the water to wash your hands, before you can begin handling the papers. If there is an eviction of the camp in the middle of this, you have to begin all over again. It is an achievement even to store all of your papers safely. This is why it's so exasperating when well-resourced government departments don't take on board the work which has been placed before them.

**MARCH 27th, 1988, Israel:** Mordechai Vanunu sentenced to 18 years imprisonment for selling details of the Israeli nuclear arms programme to the SUNDAY TIMES.

**APRIL 2nd-3rd, 1988:** five women from Yellow Gate enter Upper Heyford base – arrested inside an aircraft hangar and charged with Trespass.

**APRIL 19th, 1988:** Press Council adjudication on Morning Star article 'Greenham goes to Moscow' states the article was clearly partisan and selective, but was unlikely to mislead readers of that newspaper.

**APRIL 20th, 1988:** the GUARDIAN reports 'The Ministry of Defence has ordered its 144,000 civil servants to obtain official approval before accepting offers of free trips...from arms manufacturers, foreign governments . . .'[5]

APRIL 21st, 1988: cruise missile convoy support vehicles out yesterday during the day, main convoy out tonight. This unusual delay between support vehicles and main convoy was a result of the failure of Hampshire Police to turn up on the night of 20th April.

*Aniko Jones* recorded the resistance to the main convoy in the camp's September 1988 Newsletter – By 12 midnight there were five women from Yellow Gate waiting for the convoy to leave the silos.

Outside the Main Gate there were three or four women waiting, having to face a hundred police or more outside the base and forty or so on the inside of the Gate. There was also the USAF Commander and the UK Commander along with the sightseers. It is here the mask is dragged off revealing the stench of corruption on these men . . ..There they stand and salute the machinery coming from the base. This machinery has no other function than the Genocide of a race, to accomplish more thoroughly what Hitler could only imagine. We must not forget that similar preparations are being held in many countries. We must do whatever we can wherever we are.

Just after midnight, the police escort left the silos, followed slowly by the convoy. All the energy, resources, planning and time put in to get that convoy to run smoothly for death! The convoy drew level, we five got up and ran. The convoy was stopped. The monster had been halted. It waited for the police to show their active collaboration in this terror action.

Allison climbed one launcher vehicle and hung on. Beth, Katrina and Russell stood in front of another launcher. These women of life, relying on their strength and commitment to a society which values life, stood in front of men who have money, power, the media, the judicial system, the police and all the nuclear state's support, whose commitment is to fear, oppression and death.

I managed to get on the first vehicle unseen. I popped a potato down what I thought was an exhaust. The convoy moved on eventually, after the swarm of police finally cleared the runway.

As the convoy reached the Main Gate, I stood up and shouted, 'Non-violent women have stopped your convoy!' The convoy was stopped again. These men will always have to look over their shoulders – we can't rest while these people threaten our lives for their ego.

APRIL 25, 1988: three women arrested on Salisbury Plain, in a field of 30 cows near the convoy wood. Two of the women are dressed in a cow costume.

APRIL 27th, 1988: support vehicles return to the base through the Main Gate and are non-violently resisted at Yellow Gate. An MoD Policeman bangs one woman's head against the Gate.

The main convoy returns at 01:20 the following morning,

through the Main Gate. Four women protest down the A339 road, four women enter the convoy hangar after its return,

**APRIL 29th, 1988,** House of Commons, Written Answers:Michael McNair-Wilson – To ask the Secretary of State for Defence under what powers RAF Greenham Common was acquired and has been developed by his Department.Mr Freeman (Parliamentary Under-Secretary of State for the Armed Forces) –

'. . . Although the normal planning procedures applying to Crown Land have been scrupulously observed, no consents under the Law of Property Act 1925 from the Secretary of State for the Environment have been sought by the Ministry of Defence since the lapse of the wartime Defence Regulations. Consequently, doubts about the legal position have been raised.

Additional facilities at RAF Greenham Common will be needed in connection with the inspection arrangements under the agreed verification regime once the INF treaty is ratified. Steps therefore need to be taken to remove a legal obstacle to further construction which could impede this and other work.

It has therefore been decided that the appropriate course would be to negotiate fair compensation for the legal extinction of the commoners' rights which we propose to pursue under the provision of the Defence Act 1854.

This matter is legally quite distinct from the question of the legality of the byelaws at RAF Greenham Common which has arisen as a result of the recent decision by Reading Crown Court . . .'[6]

**MAY 4th, 1988,** Newbury Magistrates Court: Jean Hutchinson found Not Guilty of a charge under the Public Order Act which stated Jean 'used words or behaviour which is threatening, abusive or insulting or used disorderly behaviour within the hearing or sight of a person who is likely to be caused alarm or distress thereby . . .'

*Jean* – The lawyer passed to me the two precedents which she said were important. When I studied them I discovered one of them was an extremely unsavoury case about what had gone on in a male public toilet, so I immediately abandoned that, even if it was supposed to have good points about 'public place'. This is one of the disadvantages of instructing a barrister for Greenham cases! I used the other precedent when it came to my case, represented myself, as we usually do, and was successful in defeating the charge.

The legal moves I made, in brief were –

1.) At the material time (Yellow Gate, convoy time in the middle of the night) this was not a public place.

2.) It is a defence for the defendant to prove there was no person who was likely to be caused distress etc.

3.) I pointed out there have been no High Court decisions (since the 1986 Act) on 'harassing' or 'causing alarm or distress'.

4.) The police are not defenceless people who could fear harm to them -they are professional people. This point is clearly established in Marsh v Arscott.

5.) Breach of the peace being likely to be occasioned is something within the sights of the court. So it is necessary to refute it and moves can be made by means of the Marsh v Arscott case.

6.) The intention of the defendant is relevant whether the words 'with intent' are used or not. It is perfectly legitimate to discuss and show clearly, as women in Newbury court have done hundreds of times, the motives, the non-guilty mind – the *mens rea* of the situation.

MAY 5th, 1988: cruise missile convoy support vehicles out during the day, the main convoy out at night, both via the Main Gate and non-violently resisted by Yellow Gate women.

MAY 6th, 1988, Swindon Crown Court: Beth Junor, Katrina Howse, Janet Tavner and Aniko Jones appeal Trespass convictions arising from protests on Salisbury Plain. Despite women referring repeatedly throughout the hearing to the Genocide Act, the Judge dismisses the Appeals, and comments, 'Some people have these feelings, some don't.' The women are found Guilty again and ordered to pay £81.00 Costs.

MAY 7th, 1988, Salisbury Plain: six women Trespass and are arrested near the wire surrounding the convoy wood called Robin Hood Ball; this action stops the convoy working for at least 20 minutes.

MAY 8th, 1988: 04:30 am – van carrying the above 6 women back to the camp stopped just outside Tilshead village, by two Swindon police. One policeman examined the driver's papers, while the other went to the back of the van, ostensibly to check the tyres.

A couple hours after returning to the camp, one of the back tyres was completely flat.

MAY 9th, 1988: camp harrassed by vigilantes.

MAY 11th, 1988: vigilante attack on the camp.

MAY 12th, 1988: cruise missile convoy returns to the base, 01:40 am. Non-violently resisted by the women of the camp. US flags are burned at the Main Gate. The Gate is later locked by two women.

MAY 16th, 1988: approximately 01:00 – vigilante attack on the camp.

MAY 17th, 1988: coachload of Canadian visitors from VANA (Veterans Against Nuclear Arms) visits Yellow Gate.

21:30: vigilante attack on the peace camp.

MAY 24th, 1988: vehicles leave the base for a 'conventional' military exercise. Blockaded on their return; one woman has some liquid thrown into her eyes by a British soldier (not water, but stinging and smelling like petrol). The soldier tells the nearby laughing MoD policemen, 'It could be acid, next time.'

MAY 23rd – 27th, 1988: ratification of the INF Treaty. The Treaty was ratified unanimously on the 23rd of May by the two chambers of the Supreme Soviet, and by the US Senate by 93 votes to 5 (with 2 abstentions) on the 27th of May.

On the 27th, two women enter the base and write messages in coal about the ratification of the INF Treaty ('First the missiles – then the base', and others) and padlock a large gate in the Base. They are arrested and escorted off the base. The women re-enter to write more slogans on the hangar walls. They walk out of the Main Gate past two soliders, when finished their work.

At approximately 02:00am, MoD Police enter the sleeping clearing to arrest both the women on suspicion of Criminal Damage. They are taken away for interviews and processing, then released without charge.

MAY 29th, 1988: summit meeting in Moscow until June 2nd, between Gorbachev and Reagan, discussing arms control, human rights and other issues. The two leaders exchange and sign ratification documents for the INF Treaty.

JUNE 6th, 1988, Devizes Magistrates Court: Margaretta D'Arcy on trial for Trespassing on Salisbury Plain during nuclear convoy exercise. Found Guilty, fined £45.00 and ordered to pay £75.00 Costs.

JUNE 8th, 1988: international press gathering outside the base, to give publicity to the INF Treaty.

JUNE 9th – 10th, 1988, Madrid: NATO meeting welcomes the results of the Reagan-Gorbachev summit in Moscow, but agreed on the need to maintain current levels of military spending.2.

JUNE 13th, 1988: international support for the camp's work continues. Today a French Canadian woman visits Yellow Gate.

JUNE 14th, 1988, Salisbury Plain: In the early hours of the morning, Margaretta D'Arcy, Sarah Hipperson, Katrina Howse and Beth Junor enter Imber Village church within the Imber Ranges and take sanctuary there for 9 hours. All arrested in the church and charged with the Breach of the Imber Range military byelaws.

*Beth Junor* – With the help of two drivers, Kay from the King's Cross Women's Centre in London and Janet from Yellow Gate, plus the women who kept the camp going in our absence – Jean, Mia, Mary, Joan and Aniko – the action was a great success. We stopped the British Army's firing practice and strengthened our connection with women in West Belfast.

Imber is now a ghost village, which lies between Warminster

and Tilshead on Salisbury Plain. On 17th December 1943, the people of Imber were evacuated from their homes, so that the United States Forces could use the area as an artillery range.

Although it is recorded in the Domsesday Survey of 1086 under the name of Immerie, there had been many earlier settlements in the neighbourhood. It was an isolated community, on account of its situation, in the shelter of three valleys. It was completely self-sufficient: there was a blacksmith, carrier, carpenter, undertaker, miller, cobbler, grocer, baker, the church, and an Inn. Many cottages were thatched – it must have been a beautiful village.

When the villagers were removed, they were told they would be able to return when the War was over. But this promise has not been kept. It is said the blacksmith died of a broken heart.

The military are still in possession of Imber village, but now it is used by the British Army, for training in house-to-house combat – mock buildings of concrete blocks have been made to look like West Belfast streets; signs saying 'McBride's Upholstery' or 'Fruit and Veg' have been put up, to make this barren construction look like a Northern Irish community. The buildings are complete with the British Army's idea of Republican graffiti.

The cruise missile convoy from Greenham Commmon now also goes to Imber village to practise for genocide. We think that the convoy goes to Imber village when it has live warheads on it, since it is very difficult to reach and stop its exercises at this location. (Although we have managed to do this.)

Imber church nevertheless is opened once a year, for a service which the evacuees may attend. Some of the evacuees and their descendants have relations buried in the churchyard, and this is the only day in the year when these people can visit the graves. The church has a wire fence 'round it, topped with strands of barbed wire, as well as signs to the British Army saying OUT OF BOUNDS.

When Yellow Gate women were in West Belfast for International Women's Day 1988, they made a promise to the people of West Belfast that on their return to Britain, Yellow Gate would take non-violent direct action against the British Army's continual attempted destruction of their community. This action was taken to fulfill that promise. We couldn't have taken this action without Margaretta D'Arcy, who has taught us so much about the war in Northern Ireland, and introduced Yellow Gate women to West Belfast women.

The ghost village of Imber can only be reached by a military road. On either side of the road are fields containing unexploded bombs. Part of our non-violence is to take all measures to avoid injury not only to others but also to ourselves – so we could not leave the road on our approach to Imber. As we approached the village, we could see and hear Army manoevres on either side of us – this must have been between 1 and 2 o'clock in the morning. The military is always working, practising, rehearsing for war. That is why we have to put up a 24-hour-a-day resistance to the military.

Our passage from the entrance of Imber village to the church can only be described as nothing short of miraculous. We evaded tanks and Land Rovers, only to find we than had to walk right through an Army camp! We will never know whether we were seen, but not spoken of amongst the men for fear that each one would be derided for imagining things, or whether somehow we were able to pass through the middle of their camp invisibly. Their camp appeared to be at the bottom of Church Road – the likely way to the church was blocked. We continued through the village, passing in front of several Land Rovers with their engines still running, seemingly invisible to their occupants too. Still unable to see the church in the darkness, we were guided to a magnificent old oak tree, which seemed an inviting place to sit down for a drink of water and a rest. Here we also celebrated Margaretta's birthday! Katrina stood up after our break, and saw the tower of Imber church on the hillside opposite, its sandstone glowing now in the sunrise. We were delighted, and headed straight for it, but to evade the Army camp this time, we had to walk through the mock streets which they had constructed for their house-to-house fighting practice. This was a chilling experience. The Army were shouting, whether to us or each other, we didn't know or care – we kept our determination fixed on the church, believing that as soon we were within the church we would be safe. The OUT OF BOUNDS sign on the churchyard fence could only be meant for the Army – the only 'inhabitants' of the village in the present day.

We found a door which would open with just a turn of the handle, and we were in. I think we were all quite shocked to see the dilapidated state of the interior. I found bullet shells lying on top of a flagstone which marked the grave of an unnamed woman who had died in 1713, described only as 'the wife of Thomas...'. Sarah found a used flare outside in the graveyard. Parts of the exterior masonry were pitted with the Army's firing practices, and other parts were completely missing. Some of the tombstones has been broken up, their pieces stacked on the graves they had once marked.

We remained in and around the Church for 9 hours, then decided to make ourselves known by entering the churchyard and playing music. Margaretta and I played a recorder duet – a traditional Jewish folk song – which flushed the Army out of the concrete houses and brought them to the fence, directly adjacent to the OUT OF BOUNDS sign. A man in civilian clothes said they were just about to begin firing over the church. Margaretta asked the soldiers who were they firing at. They could make no reply. They were asked who they were trying to kill. Again they made no reply. We told them they shouldn't kill – this brought the immediate reply, 'Tell that to the IRA'. They were obviously practising for duties in Northern Ireland. We said we tell that to everyone – which returned them to their confused silence. Margaretta courageously revealed to them that she is an Irish woman.

As we were re-entering the church, the soldiers climbed over the fence into the churchyard, and tried to break down the door. Their 'discipline' had broken down completely – they had ceased to act only on orders and were now acting solely according to their own will. One of the soliders, who appeared to have some seniority, found a broken window, and tried to enter the church, saying, 'Where's that Irish woman?' We told him we would be calling him as a witness in our court case. When he saw Margaretta's tape recorder and our camera, he seemed to gain a bit more self-control. Then a younger soldier, obviously a new recruit, slid through the broken window into the church. He found the door by which we had entered, and opened it for the others to enter also. We had no idea how many Army were outside by this time – but it appeared to be no more than the original 5 or 6. The man in civilian clothes had disappeared. By sheer force of will and non-violent strength, we managed to keep control of the situation.

The MoD police arrived about half an hour later. We were arrested inside the church, all our belongings were grabbed by the police and the Army, and we were all subsequently charged with entering a Danger Area.

Whenever the military takes over a piece of land, they break their promises to return it, and even a church then becomes a Danger Area. Or does it? The court case in October will give a public airing to the issues raised by our occupation of Imber church.

JUNE 18th, 1988: two Australian women visit Yellow Gate.

JUNE 20th, 1988: new USAF base commander sworn in today – he is an ex-Vietnam bomber pilot.

JUNE 23rd, 1988: two visitors from New Zealand at Yellow Gate today.

*Beth Junor* – We see speaking with visitors as part of the work of the camp, and try our best with each one. We often give an impromptu workshop, to give some idea of the history of the camp and the situation we are in at the moment. Visitors can turn up at any time, although we ask men to visit only during daylight hours, which is safer for us. They have to accept the camp as they find it. Sometimes visitors can arrive at difficult times for us and then we are not always able to give them the time or consideration we would wish – it is quite something, after all, to have made the effort to find us and come out to the camp from sometimes very great distances.

One night we were expecting the convoy out at midnight. A group of us wanted to go into the base to stop it inside, but that meant the police's head-count would be low, and they would be searching for us inside the base beforehand – the police make regular counts of 'heads, tents and vehicles' at the camp in the hours before the convoy moves away from the silos. So on this night, we decided we would fool the police and protect ourselves inside the base, by making dummies of ourselves to sit 'round the fire. I got my winter coat out of the back of Gladys, my waterproof trousers and my wellies and stuffed them with blankets. I put the hood of the coat up, and sat my replica up on a chair at the fire. In the dark, it looked quite convincing. When we left to cut our way into the base, there was a good number of dummies sitting round the fire. We thought as many as possible of us should go into the base, as Sarah Hipperson said she would be alright and would distract the police by dressing up in a pink rabbit suit. We'd had the rabbit suit in Gladys, a leftover from an animal picnic held in the base many years previously, and might as well make use of it.

When we were released from our action, we were eager to hear from Sarah how things had gone outside the Main Gate. We were pleased to hear the convoy's exit had been considerably delayed. Sarah had also welcomed two male visitors from New Zealand who had turned up, with very unfortunate timing, at 11.30pm. They looked at the dummies sitting 'round the fire, and at Sarah dressed as a pink rabbit, and said, 'There's something strange going on here,' and, pointing to a dummy, 'look at her, she doesn't look human.' They left quickly, apparently.

So despite our efforts at hospitality, how visitors find us is entirely a matter of chance.

**JULY 1st, 1988:** a woman from Sweden, Ethel Carlsson, joins the camp for three weeks.

Sarah Hipperson is in Newbury Magistrates Court for a means test resulting from a £30.00 unpaid fine; sentenced to seven days imprisonment.

**JULY 2nd, 1988:** Spanish woman visits the camp.

**JULY 3rd, 1988:** US Navy shoots down a civilian Iranian plane, killing all 290 people aboard.

**JULY 18th, 1988:** Iran accepts UN Resolution 598, calling for a ceasefire in the Iran-Iraq war – to take effect on August 20th.

Iraq steps up its use of chemical weapons against Iranian troops and civilian targets.

JULY 19th, 1988: first Soviet military inspection at Greenham Common.

*Abigail Adams* – It was the second night of the Russian military team's stay at Greenham Common and probably their last, at least this time, we thought. Yellow Gate women had been in the base as their plane landed and had been in many times over the two days, despite the heavy security around the base. Thames Valley Police were driving around in riot vans, one van being stationed permanently at Yellow Gate. They were patrolling the fence and roads on foot as well, day and night. Extra Ministry of Defence police had been drafted in, and along with the USAF Security Forces and the RAF squaddies, were keeping a tight watch inside the base. This hadn't deterred the women so far, and it didn't this time, as Aniko and I decided to make one last try to reach the buildings where the Russian inspectors were staying and where their plane was waiting to take them out the next morning.

They were staying in the old school buildings near Violet Gate, which is in the north side. Aniko and I went in at the south-east of the base; there were a lot of police near the fence but we skirted around them and headed up a grassy stretch by the runway in the centre of the base. After a while we realised we were heading east instead of west, so we retraced our steps and headed towards Violet Gate. This worked to our advantage as it was late by the time we got close to the plane, and security was loosening as the Police thought us all asleep in our tents. We'd kept to the middle of the base, away from the fence, where most of the patrols were, and also approached Violet Gate from a direction they were least expecting.

To me the plane was a symbol of the reality of this so-called peace process. An Aeroflot plane, being guarded by USAF convoy vehicles and British MoD Police symbolised to me the collaboration of these three nuclear states in a fraud, to try and lull the world into a false sense of security. It also showed to me the importance of our non-aligned position: here were two states, supposedly sworn enemies, joining together in an operation to silence and block out what they both realise are their real enemies: non-violent, anti-racist women.

To get past the convoy Dodge and Texstar that were guarding the plane, which they'd floodlit for better vision with generator lights, we crawled on our hands and knees in the sodden grass. We even crawled across a stretch of tarmac – very painful to the knees and elbows! They didn't notice us, and so we reached the last streach of tarmac before the buildings. We'd decided to reach for these rather than the plane, as we wanted to be where the Russian military would hear us. Across this tarmac we ran, still unnoticed by the Dodge and Texstar drivers, but seen this time by the control tower which was watching the whole area.

He soon lost sight of us between the buildings, and sent the dog-handlers after us, who caught us quite soon, but not before we'd made quite a racket. 'NUCLEAR STATES COLLABORATE' we shouted 'BRITAIN, USA AND RUSSIA. THIS IS NOT A PEACE PROCESS, THIS IS A FRAUD; THE WAR- HEADS WILL REMAIN. WE DEMAND JUSTICE FOR THE PEOPLE OF THE WORLD. THERE CAN BE NO PEACE WITHOUT JUSTICE.'

The MoD dog-handlers went crazy, pulling us around and trying to shut us up. We got the impression a few embrassing questions would be asked of this maximum security. We felt, as they threw us roughly into the MoD van, and roughly out again at Wood Gate (5 miles walk home again), that we had made ourselves heard, and that their attempts to silence us had failed once again.

**JULY 19th, 20th, 21st, 25th and 26th, 1988**, High Court, London: Crown Prosecution Service appeal by case stated the Reading Crown Court judgement of 25th February.

**Jean Hutchinson** ‒ Georgina was represented by Beverley Lang and I represented myself. The Crown Prosecution lawyers were Mr Laws and Mr Panic. Their manoeuvring was skillfully desperate. They had to win because more was coming out of the Byelaws case than illegal byelaws, there was also an illegal fence, and illegal buildings and works. We had already begun a fence case by 1) cutting down the fence and 2) painting hangar 303 – these lawyers would have known that.

In what I've related earlier on the Byelaws, it would have seemed preposterous to include mention of our belief in an illegal fence. However, in our very first appearance in the Crown Court (2nd and 3rd April 1987), along with other points, we made a submission that the fence was illegal. We continued this all through the Byelaws case. I asked the question, 'The fence – what is its standing?' It probably sounded like a Greenham woman over the top, but we knew the fence to be illegal on at least two counts.

We knew from Halsburys Laws of England Vol. IV that the very worst thing to do to a Common is put a fence on it – Commoners are even allowed to abate fences (i.e. take them down).

The second count of fence illegality is even more exciting and comes under Section 194 (1) and (2) of the Law of Property Act 1925. Both these sections have always read like poetry to us. 194(1) involves asking the Minister of the Environment for permission to put up buildings, fences and works. 194(2) speaks of the means whereby the land will be *restored* – wonderful word! Did the Minister of the Environment give his permission? Could the Common be restored and the missiles swept away?

The judgement on this appeal was to come on 21st October.

To recap: the Ministry of Defence has a registered Common, a cruise missile base, illegal byelaws and illegal fences, buildings and works. Yellow Gate has a byelaws case, a fence case, a buildings and works case – no wonder they were in a panic!

The buildings, fences, gates and works did not have the consent of the Secretary of State for the *Environment*, as was revealed in Parliament on the 29th of April (see above).

**AUGUST 4th, 1988:** Sarah Hipperson, Katrina Howse, Jean Hutchinson and Beth Junor serve papers on the Secretary of State for Defence and the Property Services Agency (PSA), with the aim of injuncting a meeting called to deal with the issue of extinguishment of Commoners Rights on Greeenham Common.

**AUGUST 5th, 1988,** Newbury County Court: Jean Hutchinson and Katrina Howse apply for an injunction to stop meetings scheduled to take place on August 8th and 9th to deal with the proposed extinguishment of Commoners Rights.

*Katrina Howse* – Jean and I went into the hearing and sat on the right hand side of the front bench, the prosecution side, and the representative for the Secretary of Defence was for once in our usual place! Sarah Hipperson was the McKenzie friend for Jean and Beth Junor was mine. The hearing took a day, and it emerged the Judge was going to accept I had a valid claim. Jean argued strongly that the MoD's attempts to extinguish Common Rights should be put off until after the Byelaws judgement.

But it was in our argument against an 1854 Act (which the MoD claimed gave them power to extinguish, compulsorily, Commoners Rights) that we were successful. The 1854 Act gave them the power to hold meetings with the Commoners, and to form a Committee to negotiate compensation for the extinguishing of Commoners Rights. It did not give them the power to extinguish Commoners Rights under compulsion. The Defence Secretary's representative argued that the 1854 Act was an Enabling Act. The judge disagreed, he said the 1854 Act could not carry the weight being placed upon it.

The judge said no-one can injunct the Crown (very convenient), but although the meeting could go ahead it was rendered invalid. There was no legal compulsion for the Commoners to form a committee or sell their Rights.[7]

**AUGUST 6th,1988:** 43rd anniversary of the bombing of Hiroshima. Non-violent protests at Yellow Gate: road lined with candles and fire built in the slip-road leading to the base.

**AUGUST 8th and 9th, 1988:** two meetings in Newbury between the Ministry of Defence, Department of the Environment and Commoners to discuss extinguishment of Commoners Rights.

*Katrina Howse* — the MoD man from the County Court on August 5th was the man who led the meeting on Monday the 8th with the Commoners. Sarah, Beth and myself went to this evening meeting. He and the other government men present totally went against the judge's ruling, by telling the Commoners they had to form a Committee or have their rights compulsorily purchased. This he knew to be untrue, and the Commoners formed a Committee under this threat. I don't know how many of them knew they didn't have to. The Open Spaces Society man present knew they didn't have to. They all played straight into the MoD's hands, they formed a Committee. We were the only contingent who voted against it, and we were dismissed as not being Commoners.

I managed to confront this MoD man before he left. I told him he had acted illegally, without lawful authority. But the Committee was formed, and whatever the manipulations for power within and without that Committee I am glad we are so apart from it. The Commoners have already formed a pact with the MoD which they didn't have to, and the Open Spaces and other 'peace group' careerists knew they didn't have to.

We then instituted proceedings to take the PSA and the Secretary of State for Defence back to Court, where we shall produce evidence of the invalidity of that meeting, and where the MoD will have to find a valid law that can prove their right to take Commoners Rights.[8]

AUGUST 9th, 1988: 43rd anniversary of bombing of Nagasaki. Non-violent protests at Yellow Gate.

AUGUST 10th, 1988: despite a public announcement on television by the Defence Secretary that there would be no more cruise missile convoy dispersals form Greenham Common, convoy support vehicles leave the base during the day, the main convoy at midnight: the first since the ratification of the INF treaty. The convoy travels to Imber village for exercises.

AUGUST 12th, 1988, Imber village, Salisbury Plain: three Yellow Gate women arrested and charged with Trespass on Imber Ranges.

AUGUST 15th, 1988, Imber village, Salisbury Plain: another group of three women go to Imber village.

AUGUST 17th, 1988: cruise missile convoy returns to the base. Convoy stopped on the A339 road by four women, then on the Main Street in the base by two women, one of whom was consequently handcuffed; police very violent to both.

Soviet and US experts jointly monitor an experiment in which US test officials set off a large underground nuclear explosion in the Nevada test site. US experts monitor a similar Soviet test in September.

AUGUST 18th, 1988: convoy support vehicles return to the

base in the early hours, approximately 04:30. One woman is thrown into the path of a returning support vehicle by an MoD policeman and is knocked unconscious.

SEPTEMBER 3rd, 1988, Imber village: 'Open Day' for Imber Village church. Four women form Yellow Gate attend.

SEPTEMBER 5th, 1988: 7th Birthday of Yellow Gate. Katrina Howse sentenced to one month's imprisonment from Devizes Magistrates Court. She is sent to Pucklechurch Remand Centre, near Bristol.

SEPTEMBER 15th, 1988: second cruise missile convoy after the ratification of the INF Treaty begins to leave the Main Gate of the base in the afternoon. Every lot of support vehicles is stopped.

Double convoy (8 cruise missile launchers, 4 control vehicles) leaves at midnight. Police have to line the main road inside the base, as well as outside, this time, as women had previously stopped the main convoy inside.

SEPTEMBER 16th, 17th and 20th, 1988, Salisbury Plain: three groups of women trespass on Salisbury Plain to protest the convoy exercises on these three nights. The convoys are split between two woods, one called Blackball Firs, the other Robin Hood Ball. Three women get into Robin Hood Ball.

SEPTEMBER 26th, 1988, Devizes Magistrates Court: Janet Tavner sentenced to 28 days imprisonment for unpaid Trespass (Salisbury Plain) fines. Sent to Pucklechurch Remand Centre, held in solitary confinement.

Letter from *Janet Tavner* to the Board of Visitors, Pucklechurch Remand Centre, Pucklechurch, Bristol, Avon:

19th October 1988

On my arrival at the Remand Centre, I saw the prison nurse and answered two to three A4 pages of questions regarding my health. On my second day in custody, I saw the prison doctor. I explained that I had no objections to answering his questions, but since he was a male doctor, I would prefer not to be physically examined until I could see a female doctor. The doctor replied: 'Suit yourself, but that's going to be worse for you!'

Half an hour later, I was taken to a single cell where I was kept in solitary cellular confinement for the rest of my sentence. During the two weeks, I got no more than ten minutes exercise on one occasion, otherwise I was strictly confined to my cell.

When I questioned the prison officers about my conditions, they replied: 'You just stay where you are, until you see the doctor.' When I questioned the governor why I was being so excessively punished for not obeying one order she replied, 'You are not being punished, we are strictly acting on order from the medical officer.' When I questioned a prison nurse about this, she replied, 'You have to be kept in solitary confinement because of any infectious diseases you might have. That's why you have to see the doctor.' I replied I had already answered the questions about any infectious disease I might have had, at the prison nurse's examination. I was told I could have lied, and had to be physically examined by a medical officer.

This argument could carry some weight, if the routine physical examination did in any way detect infectious diseases. As it it, the doctor simply listens to your heart and lungs, no blood or other samples are taken.

Because of this, I claim it was not for medical reasons I was locked up for 24 hours a day, but rather for disciplinary reasons, since I would not submit to being examined by a male doctor when I was asked to do so.

While I was in custody I was told to use the same toilet, washbasin and bath as the other women, which strengthens my belief that I was being punished, rather than receiving special treatment.

And if a medical officer was seriously concerned about a woman's health, he should not keep her locked up 24 hours a day for two weeks!

As Pucklechurch Remand Centre has at least four wings with female prisoners, one of them being a hospital wing, I find it frightening that I could not get to see a female doctor for two weeks. I also find it frightening that I although I was supposedly being kept in solitary cellular confinement, due to medical reasons, I was given no further attention than any other prisoner.

I would like this letter to be considered by the Board, and I would like a response, since I am likely to serve more time in Pucklechurch Remand Centre in the future.

As three of my friends have also served time in PRC, and all refused the physical examination by a male doctor, without the repercussion of solitary confinement, I would like a full explanation of my treatment.

Yours faithfully,

Janet Tavner Copies to: British Medical Association, Mildred Gordon MP, Christine Crawley MEP.

Letter from the Board of Visitors, H.M.Remand Centre Pucklechurch, to Janet Tavner, Yellow Gate.

7th December 1988
Dear Miss Tavner,
Thank you for your letter to the Board. I am sorry for the delay

in my reply.

The points you raise have been considered and I understand these were explained to you at the time.

Yours sincerely,
[signed] M. Cooper
Chairman of BoV

Subsequently, all fines arising from trials in Devizes Magistrates Court were immediately transferred to Newbury Magistrates Court; the Newbury Court thus became responsible for the collection of the fines, and women were sent to Holloway Women's Prison in London for non-payment of fines arising from Salisbury Plain Trespasses.

SEPTEMBER 28th, 1988: the camp diary entry for today reads: 'Eviction a.m.

'Gale force winds, tents blown around the clearing, washing flying off the line, hair getting windswept (maybe the last comment isn't quite so important!). Abigail's jacket and trousers were unceremoniously cremated on the fire, by the wind. Allison's tent broke.'

SEPTEMBER 29th, 1988: the return visit of the Greenham-Zimbabwe exchange begins today with the arrival in London from Bulawayo of Edna Mhlanga and Busi Ncube.

*Mary Millington* – Wilmette Brown of Black Women for Wages for Housework was with us to meet them at Gatwick, and they started their visit with a week's stay at the camp, exchanging experiences and ideas. They then spent a busy week in Oxford, as guests of members of Oxford Anti-Apartheid, and finished with a fortnight in London, where they contributed to the Time Off for Women conference organised by the King's Cross Women's Centre, which was a huge success. Women from the Centre helped Busi get admitted to hospital when she was unfortunately taken ill at the end of her stay; as a Black 'foreign' woman she was in a very vulnerable position in this racist system.

OCTOBER 10th, 1988: Wilmette Brown, Sara Callaway and Margaret Prescod from Black Women for Wages for Housework bring Caesarina Makhoere to visit Yellow Gate. Caesarina Makhoere, a Black South African woman who continued to fight apartheid whilst jailed for more than five years in South Africa, describes her experiences in *No Child's Play*, published by the Women's Press.

*Beth Junor* – This visit was wonderful in itself. When Caesarina stepped onto the Common, she greeted each one of us in turn, with great warmth and acceptance. We shared a meal together around the fire, and spoke with each other.

In addition, this visit is another example of the generosity of

Wilmette Brown and Black Women for Wages for Housework in general. They have given us so much, have taught us so much. And I don't mean 'taught' in a pedantic way at all; I am referring to a generosity of spirit and intellect, a sharing with us. Such goodness never leaves the camp, it becomes part of the land on which we live and is always with us, just as the poplars, the sky and the earth are always with us. My whole perspective on situations has changed, through the 'education,' in the best sense of this word, I have received from women like this.

OCTOBER 15th, 1988, Swindon Crown Court: three charges made under the Larkhill Artillery Range Byelaws (Salisbury Plain) dropped on appeal by Katrina Howse, Beth Junor and Allison Lovell.

Appeals lodged by Katrina Howse, Beth Junor and Janet Tavner against convictions made under the Imber Range Byelaws are not upheld. The judge states that although there is no evidence against the defendants regarding the charge, 'common sense' leads him to infer they are Guilty. The MoD, prosecuting, argue that the Imber Ranges Byelaws differ from Larkhill Artillery Range Byelaws in that the Imber Ranges are all state-owned, and are always closed to the public – both statements untrue.

OCTOBER 19th,1988: UK Home Secretary, Douglas Hurd, announces that statements by representatives of banned organisations, for example Sinn Fein, the political wing of the IRA, cannot be broadcast.

OCTOBER 20th, 1988: Northern Ireland Secretary Tom King announces that the right to remain silent for suspects in both terrorism-related and other trials in Northern Ireland is being removed (a step which was revealed to be under consideration also for the rest of the UK). [4]

OCTOBER 21st, 1988, Divisional Court: the Reading Crown Court ruling which rendered the Greenham Common Byelaws invalid is overturned on appeal by the MoD.

*Jean Hutchinson* – Although it was agreed that the 1892 MLA Byelaws for Greenham Common were *ultra vires*, i.e. Heseltine went beyond his powers , it was also ruled that the part in which he had gone beyond could be excised, deleted, cut out or something! There was much talk of a curate's egg – good in parts. Also, they thought Heseltine had made an innocent mistake! By these means the Byelaws were declared valid.

When the Judgement was given by Justice Mann, we sang, 'It does not matter if you should jail us, for we are free and kept alive by hope,' a song from the South African freedom struggles. Justice Mann picked up the phone and then ran away; we have our methods for dealing with corrupt political decisions and we saw today it isn't only

Magistrates who run scared.

After this ruling the Byelaws were reinstated at 3.15 pm on the same day. Eight of us entered the base immediately on return to the camp, in two groups. The first four are in the base by 5.30; we were all charged with Trespass. The legal position was preposterous – Commoners could exercise their rights, but the rest of the world were kept out by the illegal Byelaws – we couldn't have that!

It will be obvious why the political machinations of the High Court did not distress us; they opened the way for our final non-violent assault on the Byelaw, and by implication, on the fence, the buildings and all the works, which of course took a part in getting rid of cruise missiles by shaking that USAF base to its foundations.

The second group of four women to enter the base this evening faced extreme police violence.

*Abigail Adams* made formal complaints against the officers involved – . . . I heard them call out for handcuffs for Catherine and saw two officers pin her down ready for handcuffs to be forced on...I shouted out, 'You will not handcuff that woman,' when I myself was grabbed and forced to the floor. I was face downwards and pressure, heavy pressure was applied to my body, particularly the back of my head, forcing my face into the floor, and the backs of my legs. I counted twelve officers altogether in the Portakabin immediately following the handcuffing of Catherine and myself.

The handcuffs had been put on too loosely so I wrenched my hand free . . . the officer who had the keys to the handcuffs was called back in to tighten them. He tightened them far too much, of which he must have been aware, as I called out in pain, but he left again, so I had to continue to complain and showed another officer my right wrist, which was swelling red with the pressure, while my hand was going white. Eventually this officer got the keys and loosened my right wrist.

In process, I demanded of the custody officer that before we proceeded the handcuffs should be removed. This he did, and I then demanded to know what had been the result of my request for a solicitor. The custody officer refused to answer me . . . I informed him that I considered the behaviour of the police at all levels to have been disgusting and that I was in no way cooperating with process...he sat two tables away from me, and at no time did he look at my wrists. He refused to write down on the Custody Record the statements I was making.

Some while later Allison was brought to the Gate . . . Allison told the police, 'Go back into your Belsen.' My arresting officer said, 'Don't talk to me about Belsen, my grandfather died at Belsen, falling out of the watchtower.' At this comment the other police at the Gate laughed uproariously. I regard this comment and the ensuing behaviour as a very serious incident.

On 25.10.88 I asked for a copy of my Custody Record. On my Custody Record there were several false and misleading statements by my Custody Officer. –

The outcome of the complaints laid against all of the officers involved was sent to Abigail in August 1990. The Deputy Chief Constable of the MoD Police considered the complaint of assault by PC Corby substantiated (one WPC admitted having seen Abigail hit the wall of the Portakabin), however, no disciplinary action could be taken as Corby had 'left the police service since the investigation for reasons unconnected with the complaint'. The investigation found no evidence to support the other complaints of violence. One officer was given formal advice on his 'unprofessional response' to remarks.

OCTOBER 24th, 1988: Time Off for Women day, organised by the International Wages for Housework Campaign, celebrated at Yellow Gate.

OCTOBER 25th, 1988: cruise missile convoy support vehicles leave the base in the early evening, main convoy vehicles leave the Main Gate at midnight. Both non-violently resisted at Yellow Gate.

OCTOBER 31st, 1988, Devizes Magistrates Court: trial for occupation of Imber village church begins; part-heard, then adjourned until November 22nd.

NOVEMBER 1st, 1988: group of Soviet inspectors and their entourage go through the Main Gate at 6.45pm, under heavy British police escort.

NOVEMBER 9th, 1988: this year's stream of international visitors to Yellow Gate continues, with the exchange of information and greetings between 2 visitors from Ottawa, Canada and women at Yellow Gate.

NOVEMBER 15th, 1988: cruise missile convoy support vehicles begin leaving the Main Gate of the base at approximately 08.35. Eviction of the camp in the afternoon, then the main convoy vehicles leave the Main Gate at midnight. Iron stakes are thrown from the main convoy vehicles.

Beth Junor's statement of complaint to Thames Valley Police:

. . . As a launcher vehicle passed Catherine Wenden, who was approximately 30 metres away from me, I heard a loud clanging noise.

The launchers in this convoy were labelled Cruisewatch Exterminator, The Bates Motel, Everyday Torture, amongst other things.

The vehicle which had produced the loud clanging noise continued on its way, swerving to the wrong side of the road.

. . . once all the convoy vehicles had gone past we approached

Catherine who told us that she was OK, but that something had been thrown at her, and that the police had thrown it on the grass verge . . . the three of us, in addition to the police, made a search of the grass verge, where Catherine found a 6-foot pointed iron stake.

. . . The iron stake is in our possession and can be produced in court as evidence.

NOVEMBER 16th, 1988, London: picket outside US Embassy, in protest against the violence of the previous night.

An Emergency Statement regarding the escalation in police and military violence is issued. As a result, letters are sent to the Chief Constable of Thames Valley Police, to the USAF Commander at Greenham Common and to the Chief Constable of the Ministry of Defence Police in London from our supporters all over the country and internationally. Emergency Statements sent to Newbury Quaker meeting, National CND, Spare Rib (feminist magazine) and several regional CND groups and Quaker meetings in Britain produce no response.

Seven months later, a reply from the Police Complaints Authority stated, 'Arising from the incident of the falling bars, you will wish to be aware that an American serviceman has been reported for the offence of an insecure load and particular attention will be paid to the secure attachment of loads. Additionally, the Investigating Officer has obtained an assurance from the base Commander that all slogans, of a nature which you consider to be offensive will be removed from vehicles and their use prohibited in future. The Authority have carefully studied all the papers contained in the report of the investigation and have decided that no disciplinary action should be taken.'

NOVEMBER 30th, 1988: morning eviction while cruise missile convoy support vehicles are leaving the Main Gate. Main convoy out at midnight. Both non-violently resisted.

DECEMBER 2nd, 1988: youth group from Norway is welcomed at Yellow Gate.

DECEMBER 10th-11th, 1988: workshops, an exhibition and non-violent direct action mark the ninth anniversary of the decision to site cruise missiles in Europe. The theme of the gathering this year is unrecognised wars, and the racism of the military's claim that nuclear weapons have brought peace.

A group of women enter the base with buckets and trowels to gather gravel from the Common for the repair of paths. The women take with them the following statement: 'Commoners rights over English commons have existed since 1159. These rights have included the rights to graze cattle, gather wood, gather gravel, etc . . . We claim today, and for the future, the ancient right and title to the gathering of gravel on

Greenham Common . . .' All are arrested and charged with Trespass.

**DECEMBER 17th, 1988:** nine women occupy Imber village church for 13 hours, on the 45th anniversary of the forced eviction of the Imber villagers. All are arrested, then later de-arrested and released without charge.

**DECEMBER 19th, 1988:** death of Irene Mkwayi, a Black South African woman who had been in correspondence with Sarah Hipperson and other Yellow Gate women.

*Sarah Hipperson* – It was with great sadness and regret that I received the news from Mrs Kotane that Irene Mkwayi had died on the 19th of December. Irene was in her 60's, she was a retired nurse and was in the struggle for the liberation of her country all her life. She leaves behind her husband who is still in prison on Robbin Island after more than 25 years. Their marriage was blessed only last year – they waited 20 years for permission from the state . . . We at Yellow Gate remain with the regret that we never had the privilege of meeting her when she was in England. May she rest in peace.

Mr Mkwayi was finally released from prison in October 1989.[9]

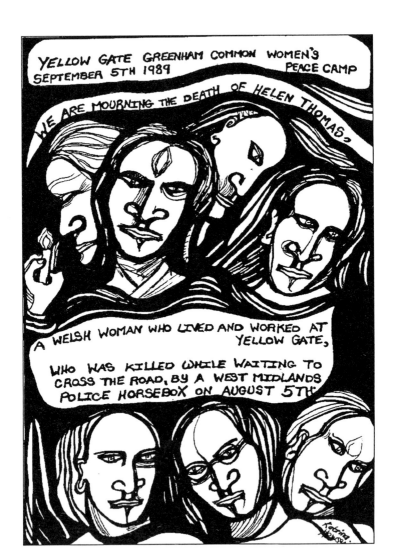

# 1989
## MAE'R YMGYRCH YN PARHAU

Each morning we wake innocently, not knowing whether the day will bring one of the sudden tragedies which few lives and certainly few political groups, particularly at this time in history, can escape. So the 5th of August 1989 began for the women of Yellow Gate and for the family of Helen Thomas in Wales.

Yellow Gate women began the day busily, with preparations for commemorations of Hiroshima (August 6th) and Nagasaki (August 9th) days. We had come together as a group the previous evening to plan an incursion into Imber church, as well as events at the Gate. It would be a special Hiroshima and Nagasaki gathering this year, with Sarah Hipperson representing the camp in Japan. We started the preparations early and were grateful for good weather – the sky clear blue and the air warm. One group of women went into town in Abigail's van for supplies for the church occupation and last minute messages. Others continued the preparations on the Common. A woman who had cycled from Oxford, Sarah Watts, came to visit Helen Thomas, a young Welsh woman living and working at Yellow Gate.

At 1 o'clock in the afternoon of August 5th 1989, Helen Thomas was killed immediately as she waited to cross the A339 road outside the Main Gate of the airbase, by a West Midlands Police horse-box.

All of the events of this year can only be seen in the light of what happened to Helen. Until that moment on the 5th of August when Helen's life was so suddenly extinguished, we had been proceeding with our work as we had always done – non-violently, wholeheartedly, often stretching ourselves to our very limits, and as always, *cautiously,* aware of the dangers we face in our protests and in our daily lives. We had not foreseen, though, the coincidence of the two fatal circumstances of August 5th: Helen standing at the side of the road on a sunny, warm afternoon, waiting to cross to post some letters, and the approach in conditions of good visibility of a West Midlands Police horse-box.

From that moment, all was changed. This chapter is the story of the events of the year which will be forever imprinted on our memories as 'the year Helen was killed' – now, in the distillation of memory that tragedy brings, 1989's events fall either into that part of the year which was with Helen, or that part of the year – as all following years would be – without Helen.

The year began with the visit to Yellow Gate of Helen Thomas.

*Sarah Hipperson* – As the old year of 1988 was finishing and just before the New Year of 1989 was about to begin, Helen Thomas

*Helen Thomas in Cardiff – Ceri's photo*

arrived at Yellow Gate. It was a very dull day. There were no buses running and she had hitched all the way from Cardiff, yet she was smiling and cheerful. Her hair was dyed bright orange, and she was wearing purple cotton trousers, a welcome contrast. I said something like, 'Do you know that this is Yellow Gate? Do you know there has been a split?'.

She said something to the effect that she did know and that was why she had come to Yellow Gate. She went on to say that she could not understand why so many women who had not been to Greenham were taking a position against us. She agreed with our stand on anti-racism, on non-violence, non-alignment and women's autonomy, and could not understand the reaction from the women's peace movement to us. She was determined that she would make others see that they were mistaken in their analysis and judgement of us.

Although she had originally intended staying a couple of nights she changed her plans and stayed for about a week. We were short of women because of the holiday period, with women having a break, and Helen stayed to fill the gap and help with the work.

She left to return to her work in the Cardiff Women's Aid refuge with Newsletters recording the work of the women of Yellow Gate. She intended placing them in the Peace Shop in Cardiff to make us visible and to counteract the prejudice against us. She made and fulfilled a commitment to the Yellow Gate women that when her contract ended at the end of March she would come to work and live at Yellow Gate.

Because there was difficulty in replacing her, she didn't arrive until the beginning of May.

**JANUARY 12th, 1989**: cruise missile convoy support vehicles begin leaving the Main Gate of the base at 07.20, for exercises on Salisbury Plain. Main convoy vehicles out at midnight. Both non-violently resisted at Yellow Gate.

Allison Lovell and Aniko Jones sentenced to 30 days imprisonment at Newbury Magistrates Court.

**JANUARY 16th, 1989**: Douglas Hurd, UK Home Secretary, orders the Court of Appeal to reconsider the cases of the Guildford Four, who had been convicted in 1975 of three pub bombings attributed to the IRA in 1974. A strong campaign had built up to alert the authorities to their innocence.

**JANUARY 18th, 1989**: Soviet inspectors visit Greenham Common air base. Cruise missile convoy expected to return tonight but was postponed – presumably to avoid embarassment during the visit of the Soviet military inspectors.

Viraj Mendis, 32, is seized by Police from his sanctuary in a church in Manchester. Home Secretary Douglas Hurd had claimed Viraj Mendis did not qualify for refugee status, despite Viraj's claim, supported by Amnesty International, that as a communist and as a supporter of the cause of Tamil separatism (although not himself a Tamil) his life would be in danger if he returned to Sri Lanka. Mendis sought and gained sanctuary at the Church of Ascension in the Hulme area of Manchester. He remained in the church until today when the Police cut the phone lines, broke into the Church and hauled him away. Negotiations with several other European countries, in particular Denmark, were under way immediately after Mendis's arrest with the aim of finding a third country that would accept him as a refugee. Hurd set a deadline of noon, January 20th, for any confirmed offers. An offer by the West German state of Bremen was reportedly received by the Home Office at 12:30 pm, but was soon followed by Viraj's Air Lanka flight to Colombo, Sri Lanka.

At the airport, a group of activists took non-violent direct action by reaching the tarmac where the plane was waiting, with paint to mark the plane and delay or prevent its departure. Among this group was Helen Thomas. Helen was arrested and charged for her actions.

**JANUARY 20th, 1989**, Reading Crown Court: Janet Tavner wins appeal against convinction under the 1986 Public Order Act.

George Bush is sworn into office as President of the United States.

**JANUARY 21st, 1989**: cruise missile convoy returns in the early

DATED the 27th day of JANUARY 1989

IN THE HIGH COURT OF JUSTICE

QUEEN'S BENCH DIVISION

DIVISIONAL COURT

Court CC2
Book DC1R
Folio 1 and 21
CO/1758/88
heard with
CO/1696/88

BEFORE THE RIGHT HONOURABLE LORD JUSTICE TAYLOR
and THE HONOURABLE MR JUSTICE HENRY

IN THE MATTER of an application by SARAH HIPPERSON BETH
JUNOR and KATRINA HOWSE for leave to apply for Judicial
Review

UPON HEARING the above named Applicants in person for
leave to issue a Notice of Motion for Judicial Review of the
decision of the Devizes Justices in respect of the Applicants
Conviction on November 22nd 1988 at Devizes Magistrates Court
under Section 3b of The Imber Range Byelaws 1963

Relief is sought

(1) to set aside the convictions that arose out of our
seeking and taking Sanctuary within a consecrated church

(2) An Order of Prohibition against the Crown Prosecution
Service restraining them from acting on the instructions of
the Ministry of Defence in applying these Imber Ranges Byelaws
1963 to gain criminjal convictions

(3) An Order of Prohibition against the Ministry of Defence
acting ultra vires and illegally in their making and use of
the Imber Ranges Byelaws 1963 and the Military Lands Act 1892

(4) A Writ of Mandamus is sought against Devizes Magistrates
Court to stop them from applying these Byelaws in spite of
prosecution admissions and defence evidence crucial to the
case

(5) Relief is sought to restore and return Imber Village
to its former inhatitants and to the descendants of its
former inhabitants therefore we seek a Judge to look at this
application

hours, 01:15. Three women enter the base and appear in front of the military personnel who have gathered around the sentry box at the Main Gate to salute the return of each vehicle. 'This is nothing to be proud of,' the women tell the military – all are arrested and charged with Trespass.

Nightime: Vigilante attack on camp.

JANUARY 27th, 1989: Katrina Howse, Beth Junor, Janet Tavner and Sarah Hipperson apply at the Court of Appeal for a Judicial Review into the uses of the Larkhill Artillery Range and Imber Ranges Byelaws. Applications refused.

JANUARY 30th, 1989, Devizes Magistrates Court: trial for Trespass on Salisbury Plain of 25th April 1988 when the women, disguised in a cow costume, were arrested in a field of cows adjacent to the convoy wood – the charges are dropped.

FEBRUARY 1st, 1989: camp at Woad Gate abandoned. By mid-February, both Orange and Woad Gate camps are abandoned, leaving only the Blue Gate camp (on the north side of the base, outside a base Gate which remains closed and out of use by the military) and Yellow Gate, outside the base's Main Gate.

FEBRUARY 15th, 1989: cruise missile convoy support vehicles begin to leave the Main Gate of the bases at 09:00. On duty at the Gate are several MoD Police who had previously been responsible for violence against women at Yellow Gate – their numbers are held up on a display board and women repeatedly challenge them on their violence – this restrains their behaviour, somewhat.

Main cruise missile convoy leaves the Main Gate at midnight – three women enter the base and are arrested for Trespass and under suspicion of Going Equipped to commit Criminal Damage – charged with Trespass and released.

FEBRUARY 17th, 1989, Imber village, Salisbury Plain: three women arrested for Trespass on Salibury Plain – the convoy is exercising in Imber Village.

FEBRUARY 20th, 1989, Imber village: despite intensive security, Katrina Howse, Aniko Jones and Allison Lovell manage to enter Imber village and are detained by two British soldiers, within yards of the working convoys.

*Katrina Howse* – I heard the click of safety catches being taken off rifles and saw two British soldiers standing up, aiming their rifles straight at us. I called out quickly, 'We are non-violent women' several times. By this time we had stopped walking. The taller soldier said, 'Don't move or I'll shoot.' He ordered us to sit down, which we did. I told him repeatedly we weren't going to move, we were going to do some shouting. We shouted and sang against the convoys, but all this time they still had their rifles trained on us. For what seemed like several minutes as we waited for the MoD Police, the taller soldier in particular had his rifle pointed at us as we sat singing on the ground. It was a dangerous and life-threatening situation. Later when we were charged with Trespass, I made a complaint about this use of guns against non-violent women.

Letter from the Wing Commander, Royal Air Force, Greenham Common, to Katrina Howse, 14 March 1989:

COMPLAINT – 20 FEBRUARY 1989

I am writing about the complaint which you made concerning an incident on Salisbury Plain on 20 Feb 89. Your statement to the MoD Police was forwarded to me and I have had the matter investigated by MoD Police here.

The 2 servicemen who apprehended you and your companions were involved in an exercise. That required them to take appropriate measures when encountering others whom they believe to be taking part in the exercise. Their encounter with you, during an exercise and at night, must be seen in that context. The actions which they took, bearing in mind that you are in an exercise area and were not immediately identifiable, were correct in those particular circumstances. As soon as they realised who you were, the servicemen stopped the action which was appropriate for simulated enemy personnel.

I am satisfied, therefore, that the servicemen committed no criminal offence or breach of military regulations.

Yours faithfully

(signed) S W KEYTE

Wg Cdr

RAF Cdr

Letter from Katrina Howse to RAF Commander Keyte, March 20th 1989:

To RAF Commander Keyte,

I am writing in response to your letter dated 14th March, and on behalf of Aniko Jones and Allison Lovell.

Yellow Gate women have been taking non-violent direct action involving walking to the cruise missile convoy deployment area nearly every monthly deployment . . . [since] the first cruise missile convoy was deployed from RAF Greenham Common. This non-violent action on Salisbury Plain has always involved Yellow Gate women taking action at night. This is well known to the Ministry of Defence Police, the military and to yourself, as it has happened consistently over 4 and a half years now.

At no time in the past four and half years have we seen soldiers attempting to get up to the convoy as a part of an exercise. British Army and RAF soldiers have always been clearly positioned at and in the deployment site. I contest that the soldiers who aimed rifles at us were involved in an exercise simulating aiming rifles to stop other soldiers. The point of my complaint is that the aiming of rifles at us was a real-life, life threatening situation which must be properly and independently investigated and must not happen again.

Your letter states that the aiming of rifles at non-violent women at night was correct action by those two soldiers. I reject such an assertion, which puts our lives under such a threat. We have reason to believe that these men were carrying 'live' ammunition. The step beyond taking 'safety' catches off rifles, aiming them at us and shouting, 'Don't move or I'll shoot' is shooting us. By saying these soldiers were right to be within a finger movement of shooting us you are paving the way to a future incident where soldiers might shoot us, with your approval. Quite clearly by your response you believe that because we take non-violent action at the night in the deployment area we would be 'asking for it' if we were shot. This is an attitude that puts the blame on the powerless and vulnerable in a situation where we meet the life threatening violence of the powerful armed forces of the state. It is the attitude of the rapist as well.

In this situation of facing such violence in Imber village we share solidarity with the people of West Belfast who for many years have been shot at on the streets, and with the children being killed on the streets by the British army. It is important also that Imber village has been used since 1971 as a training area for British soldiers occupying Northern Ireland. In Britain several years ago a boy of five years old was shot and killed in his bed by armed police; Mairead Farrell, Daniel McCann and Sean Savage were shot dead by the SAS in Gibraltar in March 1988. Again in Britain armed police have shot and paralysed a Black woman, Cherry Groce, in an armed raid on her home. Another Black woman, Cynthia Jarrett, died of a heart attack as a result of a police raid on her home. Such shootings and killings are the product of violent and racist targetting by the armed forces of the state.

We have seen ourselves under the threat of being shot at Greenham Common since Michael Heseltine's threat to us that we would be shot if we entered the silos area. Indeed we have had guns pointed at us when taking non-violent direct action inside USAF/RAF Greenham Common. Now the threat to us has increased on Salisbury Plain.

We are determined to get to the deployment site, and taking non-violent action we do so. The state has had the use of corrupt law to initially curtail each action, but the threat of guns has now carried this abuse of us further, to an immediate threat to our lives. We will continue our non-violent resistance against mass murder, and it is this resistance which is being targetted in the military's use of guns against us.

There are blatant untruths in your reply. I stated in my complaint as soon as I saw the soldiers I heard loud 'clicks' and saw two rifles pointing at us, I shouted several times, 'We are non-violent women'. The taller soldier's response was 'Don't move or I'll shoot'. They both continued to aim rifles at us for several minutes as we sat singing on the ground. The taller man in particular held his rifle on us longest.

We saw that West Down Army Camp was on 'Amber Alert' as we were being processed by the police. We believe this to mean that under this Alert soldiers carry 'live' ammunition. We want an independent inquiry to establish if these men were carrying 'live' ammunition, and if they loaded 'live' ammunition into the rifles aimed at us.

We are under no illusions about the use of violence against us, we know it is deliberate and escalating. We are doing all we can to non-violently safeguard our lives, and included in this is to let you know we want further steps to be taken in finding out the truth of that situation, and to stop it happening again.

(signed) Katrina Howse

Katrina worked to ensure that one of the riflemen would attend her trial for Trespass in Devizes Magistrates Court as a witness. During cross examination by Katrina, the soldier, who appeared in court in civilian clothes, stated that when he saw the three women, it went through his mind that they could have been (a) exercise intruders, (b) IRA terrorists or (c) peace women, in that order.

**FEBRUARY 22nd, 1988:** cruise missile convoy returns to the base at 01:30. Non-violently resisted by Yellow Gate women.

**FEBRUARY 23rd, 1989,** Newbury Magistrates Court: Aniko Jones found Not Guilty of offence under the 1986 Public Order Act.

High Court, London: Georgina Smith and Jean Hutchinson's petition to appeal to the House of Lords in their challenge to the validity of the Greenham Common Byelaws is accepted.

*Jean Hutchinson* – It was necessary for legal reasons to have an oral hearing prior to the full length hearing. We 'met' our five judges, one of whom was a home grown one from Newbury, Lord Goff of Chieveley. There was Lord Bridge, Lord Griffiths, Lord Oliver and Lord Lowry.

Initially, we seemed to have two for, and three against us. I thought, at first, they were trying to prevent a full hearing.

The question of 'buying out' the Commoners rights came up;

this had been hinted at by Roger Freeman in his answer to the Newbury MP's question of 29th April 1988, so I pointed out that should they think the problem of the Byelaws was a temporary one, it was not so simple. The buying out of the rights could not succeed because the laws from the 19th century which they were trying to use did not work. We do go for it at Yellow Gate – why go soft just because it is the House of Lords?

We got our full hearing.

MARCH 9th, 1989, Swindon Crown Court: appeal against conviction in Devizes Magistrates Court for Imber church occupation of June 14th 1988. Case part-held – Prosecution granted three weeks in which to prepare reply to our arguments. The case will continue on March 31st.

MARCH 13th, 1989: cruise missile convoy support vehicles out between noon and 13.30. Main convoy vehicles leave the Main Gate at midnight. Both non-violently resisted at Yellow Gate.

MARCH 15th, 1989, Salisbury Plain: convoy found at West Down Plantation. Katrina and Aniko Trespass twice, disrupting the convoy's exercises.

MARCH 16th, 1989: three more women travel to Salisbury Plain, trespass twice, disrupt the convoy's exercises.

MARCH 17th, 1989: another group of three women travel to Salisbury Plain. Allison and Beth walk up to West Down Plantation, only to find the wood now deserted. The convoy has been moved, presumably to a more 'secure' location.

MARCH 19th, 1989, Salisbury Plain: convoy found at Robin Hood Ball. Allison and Beth Trespass.

MARCH 20th, 1989: convoy due to return to the base. However, since it is the time of the Spring Equinox, a gathering is beginning to form at Stonehenge to mark this and there are insufficient numbers of police to both escort the cruise missile convoy back to Greenham Common and police the Stonehenge site. The convoy is taken into hangars at the nearby Boscombe Down base, where it remains until the next deployment to Salisbury Plain.

Today, only the convoy support vehicles return to the base at Greenham Common, from 13:00 onwards. Non-violently resisted at Yellow Gate.

MARCH 25th, 1989, Easter Eve, Imber village, Salisbury Plain: eight women occupy Imber village church, from 01:30 until 10:00, during which time they spring-clean the church. All arrested in the church, but not charged.

The decision not to charge the women is taken as an indication that, even if the women appealing the charge for occupying the church on June 14th 1988 is not allowed to succeed, the appeal has nevertheless had some effect.

MARCH 27th, 1989: Helen Thomas visits Yellow Gate, stays overnight.

MARCH 31st, 1989, Swindon Crown Court: continuation of Imber village church occupation appeal. Appeal dismissed; judge rules that the Imber Range Byelaws are valid and that the case against the four women charged with Trespass on June 14th '88 is proved.

APRIL 3rd, 1989: late at night, Abigail Adams, Aniko Jones and Janet Tavner travel to Boscombe Down base, where the cruise missile convoy is still being kept. Aniko and Janet enter the base and are charged with Going Equipped to commit Criminal Damage, having been found with a crowbar, a pair of boltcutters, and two buckets of paint.

APRIL 4th and 5th, 1989: snow falls on the Common.

APRIL 5th, 1989: official visit of Gorbachev to the UK.

APRIL 8th, 1989: visitors form the Basque region of Spain are welcomed at Yellow Gate.

APRIL 11th, 1989: cruise missile convoy returns to the base at 01:15.

APRIL 24th, 1989: cruise missile convoy support vehicles begin leaving the Main Gate, while the camp is being evicted.

Beijing, China: students at approximately thirty of the city's seventy colleges and universities begin a strike in support of their demands for the democratisation and reform of the country's political structure. The next day, small groups of students leave the campus to meet with members of the public in Beijing to discuss their movement and its aims.

APRIL 25th, 1989, High Court, London: Sarah Hipperson, Katrina Howse, Jean Hutchinson and Beth Junor attend an oral hearing to determine whether there can be a Judicial Review to look into the Ministry of Defence's process to extinguish Commoners Rights on Greenham Common. Judgement will be given the folowing day.

Two visitors from Canada, then two visitors from Japan welcomed at Yellow Gate.

APRIL 26th, 1989: Helen Thomas's trial for entering the runway area at Gatwick on January 20th 1989. Fines imposed.

High Court, London: Judicial Review application turned down. Mr Justice Roch rules that the application is out of time, and that all the points whcih the applicants wish to raise by way of Judicial Review can be raised in the Byelaws case, to be heard in the House of Lords, and in the County Court 'Removal of the Works' case.

**APRIL 29th, 1988:** Katrina Howse, Beth Junor and Mary Millington enter the base at Greenham Common, and are arrested under the Greenham Common Byelaws, but not charged – they are 'reported with a view to prosecution'.

It is discovered, however, that the processing Portakabin's windows have been bolted over with steel plates. The door has been steel plated. All the chairs have been removed and replaced by benches, one in each corner, consisting of wooden slats bolted to the floor. The only ventilation is provided by two small 'expelair' fans.

Beth writes to the Chief Constable of the Ministry of Defence Police in London, enquiring whether he is aware of the alterations, and why they were deemed necessary when the Portakabin is only ever used for the temporary detention of non-violent women. No reply received to date.

On a subsequent occasion (see May 18th, below) an MoD police officer responsible for detaining women in the Portakabin remarks, 'Now we'll shut the door and put the gas on.'

On the 31st May 1989 the GUARDIAN publishes a letter from Beth Junor, Katrina Howse and Sarah Hipperson, which makes reference to the alterations to the processing centre. On 13th June 1989, an MoD Inspector calls at Yellow Gate, and questions Beth about the letter to the GUARDIAN, holding a photocopy of the letter and a covering letter from the Ministry of Defence in London.

**MAY 4th, 1989:** an estimated 50,000 students, supported by large numbers of non-students, march from their campus in Beijing, China to Tiananmen Square, the city's centre. An encampment in the Square begins. All of the developments of the pro-democracy, non-violent demonstrations in Beijing are followed closely by the women at Yellow Gate.

**MAY 8th, 1989:** details are released of an incident in 1965 when the US Navy accidentally released a 1-megaton B-43 hydrogen bomb into Pacific waters, near Japan. Environmental and anti-nuclear groups in Japan demand an immediate retrieval of the bomb, saying the 33 pounds of plutonium contained in the weapon is a threat to the environment as it slowly deteriorates. The US Defence Department says the bomb poses 'no danger to anyone' and would be almost impossible to retrieve from the depth of 16,000 feet.

**MAY 15th, 1989:** cruise missile convoy support vehicles begin leaving the Main Gate of the base at 14.00. Main convoy out at midnight. Both non-violently restisted at Yellow Gate.

**MAY 17th , 1989:** Helen Thomas arrives at Yellow Gate, to stay.

*Mary Millington* - On my first meeting with Helen, I made the mistake of presuming that Welsh was a language she had learned at school. Very firmly, she stated, 'Everyone seems to think that,' and explained that her first language was Welsh. It was English she had had to learn.

I felt a great liking for a woman who could make clear, in a first conversation with someone, who she was and what she stood for, without either placating in any way, or causing offence.

She started me thinking: why are we in England not taught the language of the country next door? The answers go back into English colonialist history, and still continue today.

Vaclav Havel, playwright and human rights activist, is conditionally released from prison in Czechoslovakia, after serving four months of his eight month sentence for his part in non-violent demonstrations in Prague in mid-January.

**MAY 18th, 1989:** UK Labour Party publishes policy review entitled 'Make the Challenge, Meet the Change.' On nuclear disarmament, the unilateralist stance which the party had taken since 1980 is abandoned.

**MAY 18th, 1989:** convoy support vehicles return in the afternoon, main convoy at 01.15 on May 23rd. Abigail and Katrina enter the base for the convoy's return; when Abigail is released, and Katrina is detained on her own in the Portakabin, the MoD police officer on duty remarks,in a mock German accent, 'Now we'll shut the door, and turn the gas on.' Katrina immediately makes a formal Complaint.

Convoy's return strongly resisted at the Gate by Sarah, Beth and Helen.

MAY 20th, 1989, Beijing, China: martial law is declared, banning all demonstrations and strikes, prohibiting the distribution of leaflets and the spreading of rumours, and imposing restrictions on foreign and local journalists. The encampment remains.

MAY 26th, 1989: first anniversary of the ratification of the INF Treaty. Mary, Katrina and Beth enter the base and are arrested for Trespass.

Helen, Aniko and Allison enter the base and paint hangars 301, 302 and 303, as well as blast walls and the flight line. Held overnight in Newbury Police Station.

Aniko copied the following from notes written and prepared by *Helen:*

Report of Action – 26th-27th May 1989

1st Anniversary of Ratification of the INF Treaty

On May 26-27th 1989 six women from Yellow Gate went into the USAF/RAF base at Greenham Common, to expose the INF Treaty as a betrayal of people worldwide. It states that the signatories of the treaty are *committed* to world peace and they see the existence of these weapons as a threat to peace. This is a shift from the claim that nuclear weapons 'secured peace'.

This action was the first time I had been arrested and held within the base: whilst always being cautious of the police, especially in custody, discussions with the other women and their solidarity gave me confidence. Outside the base, this solidarity was also where the women were; working to keep the camp going during the night we were kept in Newbury Police cells. I realise from the little experience I had had of living at Greenham how much of a strain it can be on the women outside, when numbers are reduced.

I was surprised about how much the police seemed to want to treat us as equals on a superficial level; calling us by our first names, treating us in such a way which still leaves us space to be one of them. The police call you by your first name hoping to make you sociable, in order to avoid confrontation and to block the challenge to them that we represent. It also cushions them from the challenge we represent to them as individuals. To accept this, I think is to be wanted to be accepted by them and to distance yourself from other prisoners.

The first three women were arrested and reported with a 'view to being charged' by the MoD police in the base. I was one of the three who went in later. We painted the exterior of three hangars which house the cruise missile convoy, and the runway. At any time we could have been spotted and arrested but we were only found when all our paint had been used up in expressing our message. We wrote 'The treaty is a con – stop your killing' and finished up writing other messages which we felt needed to be written; about the oppression and theft of resources which makes the existence of these weapons possible.

These weapons are not only a constant threat of the final nuclear destruction of the Earth – they are being paid for through the profits gained by multi-national companies, through the pillaging of the Earth's resources, and the blood of those whose homelands are bulldozed and invaded, in order to test and mine for raw materials for these weapons.

This action was done in an atmosphere of continued censorship by the peace movement and the media in general, which makes us vulnerable to the police, military and other threats to our safety. The world press has also played a part in continuing the destruction of human lives, by working against and denying a voice to the oppressed and people in struggle against genocide in all its forms.

Helen Thomas

**MAY 30th, 1989,** Beijing: at midnight a 10-metre high Goddess of Democracy and Freedom statue is unveiled in Tiananmen Square.

**JUNE 4th, 1989, Tiananmen Square:** at 04.00 am the lights in the square are extinguished without warning and a large convoy of military vehicles moves in. At about 05.00 the remaining students in the Square vote to depart; they proceed to the south and are leaving Tiananmen when they are shot and crushed by tanks and personnel carriers. Many make non-violent direct actions to stop the massacre. Thousands of non-violent, unarmed students and other people are killed, according to Western journalists present.

*Sarah Hipperson* – On Sunday afternoon of June the 4th I was at Yellow Gate with Helen Thomas when the news of the massacre in Tiananmen Square came over the radio. We were stunned at the news – for weeks the women of Yellow Gate had kept tuned to the radio to keep in touch with events in China. Because the pro-democracy students and workers had defined their struggle as non-violent we felt an answering response to them and to their aspirations, through our own non-violent resistance to the military on Greenham Common.

Helen and I both felt the need to do something immediately. We took a blanket and with strong black pens wrote the message, 'Non-violent women of Yellow Gate Greenham Common Women's Peace Camp deplore the slaughter of our Chinese sisters and brothers.'

We hung the blanket where it could be seen by passing motorists and all who entered the base. We lit candles, had a silent vigil and paid our respects to all those who had lost their lives while being committed to non-violent resistance in Tiananmen Square.

Later when all the camp women came together we all felt the need to do something. Beth Junor gave us the lead when she said she wanted to be part of the picket at the Chinese Embassy. That night she and Katrina Howse went to London,stayed all night and waited there until Helen and I took over in the morning. In spite of the shortage of women (with women in court, women going to prison) we managed to keep two women, round the clock, at the picket all week. The women who did this work in solidarity with our non-violent Chinese sisters and brothers were Beth Junor, Katrina Howse, Helen Thomas, Sarah Hipperson, Aniko Jones, Janet Tavner, Abigail Adams and Mary Millington.

The following message was placed on the memorial shrine opposite the Chinese Embassy:

MESSAGE OF SYMPATHY, SUPPORT AND SOLIDARITY

We, the non-violent women of Yellow Gate, Greenham Common Women's Peace Camp, deplore and condemn the massacre of students for the movement for democracy and their supporters.

For weeks now we have been following the events of this non-violent struggle for dialogue with the Chinese state to further democracy and freedom, and have felt in solidarity with the encampment in Tiananmen Square, Peking. As women who have maintained an encampment for eight years now, non-stop, outside the Main Gate of the Greenham Common Airbase, we know how threatening persistent non-violence is to the military, and to all states who depend upon the military for 'order', to supress dissent.

As we continue our non-violent struggle at Greenham Common we always have in our thoughts all people who struggle for justice and peace. Particularly at this time we keep in our minds and hearts the people of the Chinese movement for democracy and their supporters – those who have been killed, and those surviving to bear that great loss and to continue the struggle.

We send you our sympathy, support and solidarity.

*A LUTA CONTINUA!* – The Struggle Continues!

– from Yellow Gate women

At the end of the week, there was a march from Soho to the Chinese Embassy. The Chinese Solidarity Campaign, who organised the picket, asked Yellow Gate women to steward the march, in recognition of our support. Aniko Jones did this and Mary Millington and I carried the blanket as a banner – the same blanket on which Helen and I had written and displayed at the Yellow Gate camp – it travelled on the first night to London with Beth and Katrina, had stayed at the picket and was clearly visible to all as a mark of support from the women of Yellow Gate to the students and workers in Tiananmen Square and to the Chinese Solidarity Campaign.

JUNE 5th, 1989: military exercise disrupted outside the Main Gate.

*Beth Junor* – On the Monday morning following the massacre in Tiananmen Square, it was business as usual for the military at Greenham Common. As I walked up to the Gate it was good to see Helen and Sarah's banner up. We spoke again about the massacre, then the bailiffs came. We evicted all the camp and left the banner up, which was over the road and not within the main area of the camp. Then the bailiffs went towards the banner, to take it down. This was intolerable. We went over to challenge them, and eventually they had to give in, and the banner stayed up.

We set up the camp again. There were military vehicles leaving the base, on some kind of exercise. This, too, was intolerable, particularly in light of what had happened in Tiananmen Square. I told the women at the Gate I would like to paint one of the military vehicles which comes out of the base – no military vehicles should have been seen on the roads that day. They supported the idea. I prepared the paint, and shortly afterwards, another USAF military vehicle exited with personnel in the back in full combat gear. It came to a halt on the slip road. Just at that moment, Helen and Sarah were returning from a water run. Sarah was carrying the water pipes and had seen me walking towards the military vehicle. She helpfully slowed down her pace just as she passed in front of the stationary vehicle, enabling me to take my time in pouring red paint over the side and rear of the vehicle, while its occupants pleaded with me not to do so.

The vehicle turned around on the slip road and went back inside the base. I returned to the camp and gathered some things, some paper and a pen, and waited for them to come and arrest me. I was taken to the processing centre and charged with Criminal Damage to United States Government property. I made a Voluntary Statement while in custody about the massacre in Tiananmen Square, asking why Thatcher had refused to meet the Dalai Lama of Tibet when he had visited Britain – '. . . Her refusal to meet with the Dalai Lama gave protection and comfort to the Chinese state while their Army was carrying out atrocities against the Tibetan people....Now another cruise missile convoy is being prepared, more men are being trained to commit a massacre greater even than yesterday's massacre in Peking . . . and [military states] won't admit that today's exercises are causing a massacre of the world's poor, AT THIS MOMENT . . .'

Some days later, another woman at the camp saw a tank travelling down the A34 road and a local woman standing at the side of the road holding her hands up to her face in horror as she watched it pass. This is how the military terrorizes people – massacres such as the one in Tiananmen Square instil in people an awareness that the military are not only there to fight the 'enemy', but can also be used against the country's own people, at any time.

**JUNE 17th, 1989**: visit of Edna Mhlanga of the Greenham-Zimbabwe exchange and others to Yellow Gate.

*Mary Millington* – Edna returned to Britain on a course at Birmingham, and brought two friends from the course to the camp: Lata Patel from India and Comfort Ntiamoa-Mensah from Ghana. Sarah Hipperson, Helen Thomas and I held a workshop with them at Yellow Gate, where we all shared our stories as women. Helen spoke of being a Welsh-speaking woman resisting oppression from English culture and language. Lata told us of a fast day Hindu women keep at full moon, to ensure they will be with their husbands in the life to come. Comfort, as a Christian woman, told of how she had been brought up with the figure of a goddess in her Grandmother's house, that she had been baptised by a woman minister in Ghana, that women in Ghana still had independent rights to the land they use to grow food.

All of us women of planet Earth, besides trying to weave our stories together, persisting in our struggles against the military, against racism and sexism, against poverty and injustice, continually creating in the face of the forces of destruction.

London: Janet and Aniko attend 'Time to Go' conference, organised to mark 20 years of British military occupation of Northern Ireland.

**JUNE 21st, 1989**: Abigail, Aniko and Katrina enter the base in protest to the execution of the non-violent demonstrators in Tiananmen Square.

**JUNE 23rd, 1989**, Newbury Magistrates Court: Janet Tavner sentenced to 28 days imprisonment and Jean Hutchinson to 21 days.

**JUNE 24th, 1989**: Abigail attends 'Women and Land' conference in London.

**JUNE 26th – 29th, 1989**: Yellow Gate women protest against Billy Graham (evangelist preacher) 'Live-Link' event being held inside the base.

**JULY 1st, 1989**, London: Helen and Abigail visit Janet in prison (Jean released by this date).

**JULY 4th, 1989**: visitors from Germany and Japan welcomed at Yellow Gate.

JULY 8th, 1989: visitor from Switzerland welcomed; two women from Germany arrive to stay a few days.

JULY 10th, 1989: Helen hitches to Wales and back to bring her typewriter to the camp for preparation of the 'Resist the Military' handbook.

JULY 17th, 1989, California, US: B-2 stealth bomber, the most expensive US military aircraft ever built, has its first flight. The bomber's cost: $530,000,000. The USAF plans to build 132 B-2s at an estimated total cost of over $70,000 million.

JULY 18th, 1989: cruise missile convoy support vehicles start leaving the Main Gate of the base at 18.15. Non-violently resisted at Yellow Gate: Janet, Helen, Frances, Rosy, Louise, Katrina and Beth at the camp.

JULY 19th, 1989: Main convoy leaves the Main Gate at 01.30. Jean and Aniko enter the base. Janet, Helen, Frances, Louise and Rosy resist the convoy's exit at the Gate, inspired by a workshop on circle-dancing.

*Louise Blakley* – I saw the convoy on my very first visit to Yellow Gate. Rosy, Frances and I had come to stay for a week. After a few days, the convoy support vehicles left the base during the day.

I have grown up around military vehicles, as my father was in the army. I've climbed over them, ridden inside them and have also seen them work.

The military vehicles that had the greatest impression on me at Yellow Gate were not the support vehicles but the launchers and control vehicles that left after midnight. My reactions to the main convoy took me by surprise. It was a disturbing experience. There is a difference between knowing nuclear weapons exist and seeing the vehicles that launch them. The reality that military men with these vehicles can commit genocide was overwhelming.

Evening: Helen, Katrina and Beth Trespass on Salisbury Plain. The convoy is found at West Down Plantation.

*Beth Junor* – Janet dropped us off, and we ran onto the Plain. Janet drove away immediately, and the silence and beauty of the Plain at night enveloped us. It also hid the convoy and other military manoevres, though, which it would be our night's work to expose. Rosy also contributed to the action by remaining in the vehicle with Janet, until our return. Frances, Louise, Jean and Aniko held the camp in our absence.

It didn't take us long to arrive at the convoy site. When we reached the summit of the last hill, West Down wood was in view, beyond a strip of very tall grass. The moon had been full just the day before and now the newly waning moon was showing her warm colour just above the horizon near the wood. She seemed to shine approvingly on us as we began shouting and singing to disrupt the military work going on inside the wood.

Four unkempt soldiers emerged from the tall grass – all Rambo lookalikes: one had a red bandana tied on his head; all were shirtless or wearing vests, and their trousers were rolled up to their knees or shins. It was as if a wave of violence had emerged form the woods – it was very frightening, and brought to mind images I'd seen of Vietnam.

We held our ground, hands joined, and continued our resistance until we were arrested and removed from the area by Ministry of Defence police.

This was the first time Helen had been on the Plain. In the processing centre she was dignified and admirable, and her conduct made a lasting impression on me.

While we were waiting together to be charged, an MoD police officer approached the doorway, holding Helen's Voluntary Statement, which she had written in her first language, Welsh. This officer began speaking to Helen in Welsh! This was the first time I'd heard Helen speaking Welsh.

Helen did not take the opportunity to enter into an extended conversation with this officer, despite her longing to speak in Welsh, but responded in a few words. It was as if she was signalling to him – 'You may speak Welsh but you're nevertheless still my oppressor in this situation.' He was uniformed and powerful, we were prisoners of the police force who is his employer. Thus Helen, in a dignified manner, forced this officer to confront his situation – whether he joined the MoD to escape unemployment or for whatever reason he held to, he would have to be part of the oppression of other Welsh-speaking people. Helen took two non-violent actions that night.

Once released, she told us what he had said: 'I can read your statement – this is very good Welsh.' He had added, 'Where are you from?' Not disarmed by his approach, Helen had refused to tell him. He also said he thought he'd seen Helen before somewhere, in such-and-such a place. Helen had laughed, and brushed this aside. As we walked down the hill out of West Down Army camp we laughed again, when Helen said that it was indeed possible that he'd seen her, when she was young! We joked about this, then jumped into the car again and told Janet and Rosy about the work on our way home.

Helen's reply when charged was 'MAE'R YMGYRCH YN PARHAU' – the struggle continues; written on Helen's charge sheet by the police, with corrections – you can almost hear Helen patiently and

determinedly instructing the officer to correct his first attempt at the language about which Helen intended to educate them. Helen intended conducting her court case in Welsh.

JULY 20th, 1989: Katrina and Helen enter the base to protest against military exercises.

*Katrina Howse* – On Thursday, 20th July, the convoy had been out since Tuesday night/ Wednesday morning. At 6.00am a general alert sounded in the base, 'Air attack, air attack'. The Yellow, Red, Black Alerts sounded all that hot day. As part of the military exercise they announced that the water was contaminated, that toxic gas was dispersing on the south side of building 800. All the USAF personnel were in padded battle fatigues, armed, with metal helmets. It was unbearable, the way the military tortures life and turns it all into killing.

At Yellow Gate I asked Helen if she wanted to go in, she said she did. We set off in the heat to a tree lined part of the fence. There was a man on top of a vehicle with a machine gun, at this section. We walked for a mile or so, sighting men with machine guns inside the fence. We were both determined to go in. We came to a spot in the fence free of military and went through, then up onto the road inside the base. A Texstar vehicle saw us and sped over to us. The man on top of it was behind a machine gun, inside was a driver and a young woman. For some five minutes or more this vehicle blocked our way; the machine gun was mounted and so it pointed straight at us. We stood in front of it, holding hands. Helen was calm and strong. Eventually the MoD police came, and with them two USAF personnel, who dismantled the machine gun and laid it on its side.

We were arrested and taken to the boiling hot MoD holding cabin, sealed on all sides now but for the open door. Helen had to sit in there patiently for some time as the MoD processed me first.

We walked back to the Sanctuary along the fence, talking over the disturbing incident. Later on after a complaint RAF Commander Keyte wrote saying, 'I can assure you that the weapon to which you referred was not loaded and represented no threat to you.' Helen saw this letter and was not assured, nor am I.

Helen was strong taking non-violent direct action; she strengthened this action. Helen always took on extra work in action. The MoD forms are all in English, and because Helen's first language is Welsh she would not sign them, except to sign for bail. Helen was principled on this. She did not sign that the MoD hadn't non-strip searched her. This meant she was subjected to a non-strip search.

The time Helen and I went in to oppose the 'Live Link' Billy Graham event in the base, we both didn't sign the non-strip search part of the forms and were therefore 'patted down' and had our footwear removed. On this Helen would not compromise, so she was singled out at West Down Processing Centre after taking action at the convoy deployment site and given a non-strip search.

Clear and strong, aware in all her dealings with the MoD police of her struggle for Welsh language and culture, Helen would not compromise.

The struggle at Yellow Gate is enriched by having Helen live with us and taking non-violent direct action with us. −

Janet, Aniko and Jean Trespass on Salisbury Plain at West Down Plantation, are arrested and charged with Trespass.

**JULY 21st, 1989:** Frances, Janet, Beth, Katrina and Aniko travel to Salisbury Plain. Katrina, Beth and Aniko walk up to West Down Plantation, but the convoy has been moved. Later the five women find the convoy at the Bulford Ranges. Jean, Rosy, Helen and Louise hold the camp.

**JULY 26th, 1989:** cruise missile convoy returns to the base. Non-violently resisted at Yellow Gate.

**JULY 27th, 1989,** Salisbury Crown Court: Beth, Abigail and Sarah appeal convictions under Larkhill Artillery Range Byelaws. Case part-heard, to be continued tomorrow, when the appeal is dismissed.

**JULY 28th, 1989,** Salisbury Magistrates' Court: Janet and Aniko on trial for Going Equipped to Commit Criminal Damage in Boscombe Down. Both are found Guilty, fined £75.00 each and ordered to pay costs of £50.00 each.

Devizes Magistrates Court: Katrina on trial for two Salisbury

Plain Trespass cases. Cases postponed.

JULY 29th, 1989: Sarah Hipperson leaves for Japan, to participate in a conference and memorial services on Hiroshima and Nagasaki days. Katrina and Beth, as well as some women from London, see Sarah off at the airport.

AUGUST 1st, 1989: a launcher and control vehicle are flown out of the base, amidst widespread publicity, in accordance with the INF Treaty. Katrina, Jean and Aniko enter the base.

AUGUST 3rd, 1989:

*Janet Tavner* – Helen and I have been in the Sanctuary these past two weeks. It has been two weeks of beautiful summer weather, sunshine and warmth. Helen and I worked side by side on the 'Resist the Military' booklet. She has been translating it into Welsh, and works very hard with it, from 9 o'clock in the morning until 8 o'clock at night. After that we spend a couple of hours watering the garden, with water from a nearby stream.

She and Aniko surprised me one evening with an apple crumble made with the first nearly-ripe apples from our apple tree. We enjoyed many more after that.

Helen also worked on a letter to the INDEPENDENT, which impressed me as she read it out to me before she sent it:

I'm writing in response to your article 'Greenham Women's Parting Shot to Missiles', written by Mike Prestage, 2nd August 1989.

Not only does the article trivialise the real issues involved in the 8 year struggle against the military at Yellow Gate, Greenham Common Women's Peace Camp, it also contains many inaccuracies. Before yesterday's flight there were 101 not 96 missiles inside the base.

Secondly, your treatment of the important issue of warheads is very ambiguous. We have found that the INF Treaty, signed two years ago this December, does not in fact cover the warheads at all – and we have no proof that these will leave the base.

The base is just as much a threat to life now as it has always been. The money stolen from the work of oppressed people throughout the world is still being misused to test more nuclear weapons in the Pacific and in Canada, raping the land of the indigenous people of those countries.

Your article takes no account of the real work going on at Yellow Gate to resist the military at Greenham Common, work which results in prison sentences for those who take non-violent direct action against the military.

The military's publicity exercise at Greenham Common on August 1st was not a 'moving moment' for us, but yet another reminder of the role of the British press in upholding the lies and propaganda of the military powers' preparation for Genocide.

We at Yellow Gate did not consider August 1st to be a 'great day' in any way. All that is leaving Greenham is the weapons casings, not the warheads. Every month cruise missile convoys still leave Greenham Common to practice Genocide on Salisbury Plain, and every month women are arrested for tracking and stopping it.

The article also claimed that the INF Treaty was aimed to scrap 'all US and Soviet land missile bases in Europe'. There are no such plans. The INF Treaty covers the missile casings alone, not the warheads, not the bases.

This Treaty was basically designed to lull people into thinking that the world is actually a safer place. It is a victory for us though, that the world is seen as more secure 'without' nuclear weapons, whereas before we heard about the need for the security of a nuclear deterrent.

Helen Thomas
Yellow Gate
Women's Peace Camp
Greenham Common
Newbury
Berks.

The next day, Helen told us how happy she was to be living and working at Greenham, and how much she wanted to be here.

Helen also wrote to her mother in Wales:

*Janet Thomas* – In her letters from Greenham Helen explained why she felt that she had to work for what she so strongly believed. I quote some of the things she said in her last letter to me; I regret that much of what she said loses its strength and meaning in the translation into English -

'I have decided that I want to work for peace and justice . . .

'You must not worry about me, after all there are thousands of people worse off than me; I'm fine . . .

'I can understand why you are concerned, and I know that you have more to worry about than other mothers whose daughters have gone to comfortable, 'respectable' jobs. But there is more to life, than earning 'money' and being 'respectable' . . .

'I just cannot understand how people can turn their backs on all the injustice that goes on in the world and pretend it has got nothing to do with them . . .

'You must come and visit us at Greenham and see for yourself how we live, and the work we are doing . . .

'We are ever so busy writing leaflets and newsletters for our

August gathering which will be around Hiroshima and Nagasaki days, 6th and 9th; there is a lot of work to do. I'm translating some of the work into Welsh and sending it to people in Wales . . .

'. . . Anyway I hope to be coming home soon; probably around my birthday and Louise's 'A' level results; I'll phone you sooner . . .

'. . . But I want to keep coming here to Greenham for some months of the year from now on, I find it very inspiring to be working alongside such brave and determined women . . .'

Helen ends her final letter to me by saying,

'Please try and understand why this work is so important to me . . .You are a strong and determined woman and you know you can pull through and be stronger and even more determined.'

AUGUST 4th, 1989: all week, women have been gathering at Yellow Gate for the actions planned for Hiroshima and Nagasaki days.

These actions had been planned and leaflets distributed far in advance. Helen translated the leaflet for these days into Welsh, and widely distributed these. She also drafted and translated a leaflet for the December demonstration, and had begun mailing it out to colleges and universities.

Now, Lise Lafleur arrives·from Montreal, Judith Walker from Germany, Margaretta D'Arcy from Ireland; Frances Vigay and Louise Blakley return to the camp, Bee Ring arrives from London. By this evening, there are 13 women gathered at Yellow Gate. A meeting is held to finalise practical arrangements for the following days.

AUGUST 5th, 1989: Helen Thomas is killed immediately at 1 o'clock noon, as she waits at the side of the road, by a West Midlands Police horse-box.

An MoD Police officer on duty at the Gate witnesses the tragedy, as do several women from the camp, their attention drawn to the road by the speed of the oncoming vehicle. All testify that Helen was standing at the side of the road, in the hatched area which vehicles are not to enter.

After some time the driver of the vehicle, who is in uniform, comes up to the camp and approaches the women. 'I know you don't think much of the police,' he begins, 'but I'm sorry.' When asked for his name, he replies, 'It doesn't matter who I am, I've come on behalf of the police.' Thus already, he was careful not to identify himself as an individual making an approach on a personal level, but as a representative of the West Midlands Police force.

*Abigail Adams* – Soon after Helen was killed a shrine was set up to her memory. Although at first no more than an upturned wooden pallet, with candles standing in their own wax, incense burning and flowers from the Common on the nearby pavement, it was an island of calm in the midst of that scene of overwhelming sadness. It was something we could do when we felt so powerless. The idea grew, and we covered a table with a white sheet, on which we placed some things of Helen's, and again candles, incense and flowers. A card with a short message in dedication to Helen was placed at the front.

We removed all the camp things into the back clearing and kept a silent vigil at the shrine, in the area by the road, from the day after Helen's death until her birth-date on August 16th. During those first hours we kept vigil at the hospital which held Helen's body, until Helen's parents came and kindly allowed some of us to pay our last respects to Helen on behalf of the camp.

Many friends of Helen visited the camp during that week and joined us on the vigil, and brought things that had a special connection to Helen for them to place on the table. It has been good to share memories of Helen's life and work with so many different people whom she knew, and who knew her. Also many people who had never met Helen were saddened nevertheless to hear of her death and joined us in mourning. On the day of her birthday, when Helen was to be 23, we were privileged to be joined by her parents, Janet and John Thomas. −

On the afternoon of the 5th, we found Helen's driving licence which recorded her address in Wales, and began the process of notifying her family. A film crew arrived at the camp, and were asked to leave.

Later, Katrina and Beth went into town in an attempt to get a message to Sarah in Japan.

**Sarah Hipperson** − I had said goodbye to Helen in the Sanctuary on July 29th, on my way to the airport. It was around midday on a gloriously warm and sunny day.

Janet and Helen were busy with their writings. Helen was seated at the typewriter in the tipi. I marvelled at the scene – it represented two contrasting impressions, first the industry and commitment to the work of producing Yellow Gate's important book on non-violence, *Resist the Military*, secondly the unusual dwelling place of the tipi where this work was being carried out. On each occasion I enter the Sanctuary, I am aware that it is spiritually inviting; it was no less on this day.

We had only a few moments together but it was important to see and speak with both Janet and Helen before undertaking the journey and the work for the camp. I gained great strength from them both, as I did from the other women.

It has always been a feature of Yellow Gate that when we leave to represent the camp or to take action that we travel with the goodwill of each other to strengthen us. This day was no different, apart from some unexplained uncertainty I felt – which was dispelled by the good wishes and loving embraces given and received.

As we said goodbye, Helen was in sparkling form, full of energy and much laughter. I will always carry that image of her with me.

On the morning of the 6th of August, I awoke with the sense that this was going to be a difficult day emotionally. I had met and spent some time with survivors of the Hiroshima bombing and listened to the harrowing accounts of their experiences. My presence in Hiroshima seemed a bit unreal to me at times. I think this had something to do with the knowledge that these people had lived through an experience that separated us, and seemed to leave me with a sense of embarrassment.

I attended the memorial ceremony at the Peace Park with other Europeans attending the conference. It was the most moving experience – intonements and music filled the air. We had been given flowers to carry when we entered the Peace Park and as I sat with them on my lap, I suddenly felt overcome with a heavy sense of sadness. I heard the sound of shuffling feet as survivors and relatives of the victims made their way slowly to place their flowers on the altar. I felt compelled to join them and left my seat to do so.

It was around 6.00pm that Isabel Strang of Newbury, a good friend to the women of Yellow Gate over the years, phoned to tell me of the tragedy of Helen's death. I was devastated and asked to be called again in 30 minutes to give an answer to the question, should I continue on to Nagasaki and complete the work of meeting with women who were also working against the military and nuclear weapons, and continue to meet with the survivors? After a while it was a sense of responsibility to the survivors that led me to decide to continue. To this day, I'm not sure if that was the best decision.

I spoke on the phone to Katrina, Beth and Mary. We were all brokenhearted and were unable to comfort each other.

Later that evening when I joined the survivors and friends, there was no longer a separation between us. The death of Helen had placed us together. This was the night when the dead are remembered and their lives are spoken of. I was in the company of very understanding people. I was able to share with them something of the part of Helen's life I knew, through Kazuko Kondo's interpretation. The invitation to come to Japan had come from Kazuko and she was very understanding and supportive at this time.

A survivor, always known to me as Mr Kondo (not related to Kazuko), took charge of the evening and shared his memories of the 6th of August 1945 with us during a trip through the Peace Park. I felt privileged to hear his own personal account, his history and a full explanation of every monument and mound of burial earth.

Later we went to the Motoyasu river where we joined others floating lanterns on the river in memory of the souls of loved ones. This custom is carried out each year on the night of the 6th of August. The lantern I floated carried the inscription, 'Helen Thomas – a brave woman from Greenham Common.'

The women of Yellow Gate will always feel the loss of Helen Thomas. At a time when we were censured by the 'peace movement' she payed us the compliment of joining us.

Helen was as respectful of her own life as she was of the lives of others. She was a woman of immense courage and understanding who committed herself unstintingly to the struggle for justice and peace for all people.

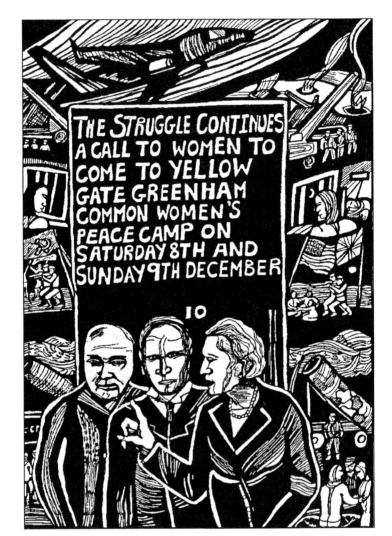

THE STRUGGLE CONTINUES A CALL TO WOMEN TO COME TO YELLOW GATE GREENHAM COMMON WOMEN'S PEACE CAMP ON SATURDAY 8TH AND SUNDAY 9TH DECEMBER

10

# *1990*
## *YOU CAN'T KILL THE SPIRIT*

In the hours and days following the killing of Helen, it was gradually revealed to us that she would be subjected, in her death, to many levels of injustice.

The very next day, the press, which had only recently prompted Helen to write and rectify their inaccurate and misleading account of the removal of military hardware from Greenham Common, printed inaccurate accounts of her death. It was said that she had been dancing in the middle of the road, a lie which fits the media image of a 'Greenham woman'. Accounts of her injuries were distorted, leaving the reader or listener with the most dehumanised image of Helen: it was said that Helen had been decapitated. This is untrue. Helen suffered massive head injuries as well as other injuries, but this media version is simply untrue. Many months later, the source of this report was traced: it had been the police who had given this misinformation to the media.

Women at the camp had to be vigilant, not only in a physical sense first at the hospital and then at the camp, but also mentally, to protect Helen's good character in her death. We knew from the time of the initial press reports that there would be a battle for the truth of what had happened. We had no idea then, however, of the extent of the injustice which was to come.

The state tried to deflect us in our attempts to tell the truth about the killing of Helen. This first became apparent when Helen's parents arrived at the hospital; the police informed Mr and Mrs Thomas they would be taken in the back entrance, as there were peace women holding vigil at the front. Mrs Thomas then insisted on going round to the front of the hospital to meet the women.

The pressure on the women at the camp increased. Our obvious period of mourning in the front area of the camp did not temper the hostility of the military, police, or the local residents which we – including Helen – had faced in the past. Rather, as the news spread, it seemed to have given them licence to be more openly hostile.

One taxi driver shouted abuse at the mourners each time he entered the base to pick up his fare, which was several times each day. Janet gave information about the driver to a PC Anderson on duty at the Gate; twice he stopped the taxi driver and held him at the Gate for some minutes, threatening to ban him from the base.

One military driver leaving the base shouted, 'One down, and eight to go.' There were eight remaining women committed to the camp on a full-time or part-time basis, at the time.

The MoD police officer who had been on duty at the Main Gate at the time of the tragedy, PC Conway, later resigned, and in a sworn affidavit written after the Inquest, he stated, '. . . I am concerned about the manner in which the original Inquest was conducted, and I am also concerned about the police investigation of the incident . . . I confirm that I remember very clearly that Helen Thomas did not step into the path of the vehicle which killed her . . . I regret to say it, but some of my colleagues made jokes about Helen Thomas' death which I found extremely distressing. The whole incident had a very profound effect on me, and indeed affected my health. I eventually left the Ministry of Defence Police Force and I am now working for a housing association.'[1]

The bailiffs tried to evict the simple shrine which had been created in the mourning area of the camp. Women managed to protect the shrine on the bailiffs' first attempt, but the bailiffs later succeeded in destroying and evicting it.

The pro-Soviet peace movement and women's movement network which had been bent on the destruction of Yellow Gate since 1987 issued a Newsletter in which a notice of Helen's death appeared. It read, 'Helen Thomas died in a road accident on the 7th of August outside Greenham Common. It was her first visit to the camp.'

AUGUST 7th, 1989: the Inquest into the death of Helen Thomas is formally opened. The full hearing is to take place on 12th September.

*Katrina Howse* – I have lived at Yellow Gate, Greenham Common Women's Peace Camp since August 1982, as a full time resident. In that time, I have experienced bias and prejudice against women who live at the camp. The camp has been attacked by a Newbury vigilante group. Women have been seriously beaten up by unknown assailants. We have been banned from some cafes and pubs, simply for being women who live at the camp. We have been refused rides in taxis by several taxi drivers. I am still treated as a temporary patient at the local doctor's surgery despite having lived at the camp for 8½ years. I have also seen numerous assaults on women at the camp by policemen, both Ministry of Defence Police, Thames Valley Police and other forces. I have been roughly and violently handled by policemen while being totally non-violent. I have seen women with bruises and cuts caused by policemen on many occasions. I have been at the camp when women have been knocked unconscious by policemen. No policeman has ever been prosecuted for assaults against women, despite the number and severity of incidents.

It is within this context of years of no protection for us when we have faced police violence, that I wish to express my disquiet about the circumstances of Helen's death.

Over the years Yellow Gate, Greenham Common Women's Peace Camp has been policed by forces from all over the country. Immediately after Helen was killed, it was totally relevant to us that it was a police horse-box that had killed Helen. Sergeant Dunn came up to the camp and said to us, 'I know you don't think much of the police but I'm sorry.' He did not reveal if he had been to the camp before, or what his attitude to us was.

The Ministry of Defence police who placed Helen into the ambulance showed a complete lack of respect to a dead woman. They were loud and noisy, and I thought I heard one of them laughing. This incident was so shameful that I would not look at them, but concentrated on standing close by and holding hands with two other women out of respect for Helen.

As the days passed up to the initial hearing our upset and distress increased. We were not told where the initial hearing was being held, as the police refused to tell us. When we turned up at the court PC Freemantle [the coroner's officer] told us we couldn't go in. This was plainly untrue, and eventually we were allowed in. The initial hearing was extremely short.

After the hearing on August 7th, we discovered that several tabloid newspapers were saying that Helen had been 'dancing in the road' and that Helen had been decapitated. Neither of these assertions were true, but I felt already an attempt was being made to blame Helen for her own death, and to dehumanise her in the eyes of the general public. This was public information which the Inquest jury could have read or heard.

PC Freemantle informed us that there wasn't going to be a jury; it was only when on Mrs Thomas's instruction, her solicitor contacted the court, that preparations were made to find a jury.

Women had been holding a vigil of respect outside the hospital, which was stopped after we felt we did not want to interfere with the running of the hospital. When Aniko Jones phoned the police to ask when Helen's body would be taken back to Wales, so we could pay our last respects, she was told, 'Oh, you're not going to cause a fuss are you?'

We were concerned initially that the Inquest was going to be in Newbury, and held by a Newbury coroner in front of a Newbury jury, because we felt that there was too much prejudice against us in the Newbury area.

Before the Inquest PC Freemantle had already told us Helen's death was being treated as a road accident. We had been informed that although an Inspector had originally investigated the case, it had been handed over to another Sergeant. The police and the court seemed already closed to the possibility that Helen being killed was anything other than 'a road accident'.[2]

AUGUST 8th, 1989: in the morning, the body of Helen Thomas is taken on its final journey back to Wales, accompanied by a rose not yet in full bloom from the Sanctuary, and other flowers from the Common.

Cruise missile convoy vehicles begin leaving the Main Gate later in the day; the full convoy leaves the Main Gate at midnight and travels to Imber village.

The feeling at the peace camp was that the military were taking the opportunity to, for once, have an uninterrupted exercise. The deployment was met with all the opposition we could muster.

*Aniko Jones* – The sorrow and bewilderment of Helen's death was magnified by the callous act of the military bringing out the ultimate symbol of death and lack of respect for life. It was with total disbelief I saw the Ministry of Defence police line the roads to allow the 'safe passage' of the cruise missile convoy vehicles past us. Women put themselves between the memorial shrine to Helen's memory and the military, maintaining the silent vigil and also being a witness to the genocidal crimes of the state.

Beth Junor and myself each took a container of white paint and walked across the slip-road, tipping the paint as we went, leaving behind us two white lines. This was done while no traffic was using the slip road to the base. We stood at the opposite side of the road looking across at the women holding hands, still protecting the memorial. Some Ministry of Defence police ran down and we were arrested and taken to the process centre in the base.

In the process centre Beth and I maintained our silent vigil, broken only to answer in reply to our charges. Beth said, 'I intended to commit Criminal Damage in respectful memory of Helen Thomas.' I said, 'I intended to do Criminal Damage to continue resistance against the military convoy in the same spirit as Helen.'

AUGUST 10th, 1989: Mary Millington, Aniko Jones and Katrina Howse attend Helen's funeral on behalf of all Yellow Gate women.

AUGUST 14th, 1989: Sarah Hipperson returns from Japan, and is met at the airport by Katrina and Beth, who drive her back to the camp, where the mourning area has been preserved just as it has been since August 5th, for her return.

AUGUST 15th – 16th, 1989: the convoy returns during the night and on the 16th, the period of mourning (a vigil has been kept day and night) ends; it is Helen's birth-date, and Helen's parents come to spend what would have been Helen's 23rd birthday at the camp.

In the evening, women leave the camp to occupy the church at Imber village, the action which Helen had been so much looking forward to, on August 5th.

*Jean Hutchinson* – We feel that Helen's joy and happiness at the prospect of the action led us and inspired us to do the action on her birthday.

Seven of us, Katrina, Sarah, Beth, Aniko, Henrietta, Lise and I successfully occupied the church. Abigail was the driver and became an efficient decoy! On the way in, just as we prepared to go into the church, a vehicle, which turned out to be an army vehicle, came along as we disappeared into the trees. The soldiers showed Abi a map, told her where she was and 'rescued' her – Abigail escorted them out!

In the church we rejoiced at a successfully carried out action and a fourth occupation. The golden summer sun had warmed the church and the warmth enveloped us as we went inside. We remembered and missed Helen; flowers and fruits of the Common had been brought to commemorate her memory. We heard music and settled down to rest during what was to be an 11- hour occupation.

Then, as if to remind us of our reasons for being there, if we need that, the army began firing. Our commemoration of Helen has a real objective, one she was ready to take part in when she died. We slept safely in the church on this special night when the moon was eclipsed, surrounded by the firing of the army.

In the morning, the army prepared to start firing again and we ate breakfast in bed! We noticed that the church was still clean from our cleaning during our last visit (March 25th). Our resistance to the military state is made real by our occupation of this church 4 miles into the beautiful country they call the Imber Ranges.

Due to our presence that morning the Ranges could not be used. When we had scattered flowers in the churchyard and taken our photographs we stood in the church remembering Helen. Our occupation ended, for the time being, when 3 vans of MoD police came.

**SEPTEMBER 12th, 1989:** Inquest into the death of Helen Thomas, in Newbury Magistrates Court.

In addition to the MoD police witness and the witnesses from the peace camp, all of whom clearly saw Helen standing at the side of the road, two USAF employees, Mr and Mrs Estus, attend to give evidence. In their evidence they say they were waiting to turn into the slip-road when the incident took place and that they saw Helen in front of the vehicle which killed her. The Newbury coroner emphasises this evidence in his summing up to the jury.

A booklet of Police photographs of the horse-box is produced; however, there is no photograph of the passenger side of the vehicle, the side nearest Helen Thomas.

The passenger in the vehicle is unable to attend the Inquest. It is said that he has broken ribs.

Sarah Hipperson is initially obstructed from submitting a character statement on Helen to the coroner, until intervention by Mrs Thomas ensures the statement is accepted; the statement is not read out in court.

The jury of 9 Newbury people hear the evidence of 11 witnesses in 1½ hours. The coroner directs the jury to return a verdict of Accidental Death, which they do.

A press release issued from the camp summarises many of the shortfalls of the Inquest:

The women of Yellow Gate believe there should have been an Open Verdict because:

1. There was no verifiable evidence of the speed of the police vehicle (horse-box). One witness, Mary Ring, testified that the vehicle was speeding. The driver of the vehicle, Sergeant Anthony Dunn of the West Midlands Police, admitted that a Tachograph is fitted to the vehicle, but added that 'the West Midlands Police don't use them.'

2. The driver testified that he first saw Helen Thomas from 75 yards away, and that he was travelling at approx. 40 mph, the speed limit for the vehicle, but he did not sound his horn, or make an emergency stop.

3. Sgt. Reid of Thames Valley Police, in charge of the investigation, admitted that the driver of the Police horse-box was not subjected to a breathalyser test, as is required by law.

And yet Helen Thomas's blood and urine were tested, and found to be free of any alcohol.

4. Several witnesses, including a Ministry of Defence Police officer, gave evidence that Helen had been standing in the cross-hatched safety area for pedestrians, adjacent to the traffic island.

5. The Coroner directed the Jury to the testimony of the weakest witness, who claimed that Helen Thomas had been in front of the approaching horse-box. Photographic evidence of damage to the horse-box conflicts with this statement.

We are quite clear in our minds that Helen Thomas was standing in a recognised safety zone when she was struck by the vehicle. We are also quite clear that there has been a cover-up. This inquest failed to thoroughly investigate all of the circumstances surrounding Helen

Thomas's death. At worst, there has been a deliberate intention to dismiss statements of competent witnesses; at best, there has been gross negligence.

*Katrina Howse* – The coroner also did not insist that Mr Leo Horton, the pathologist, be present at the Inquest. This meant no questioning could be done about how Helen's injuries had occurred. Mr Horton had said at the initial hearing that Helen's injuries had been consistent with the accident as described to him. Mr Horton not being there was a grave omission, particularly given the contradictory statements about where Helen was standing.

Throughout the Inquest, Helen was referred to as 'a peacewoman'. Although Helen had lived at the camp full time since May, I felt the term 'peacewoman' was being used to mask her individuality and uniqueness. The term 'peacewoman' has been used so derogatively that it made Helen seem an attachment to a group which is not liked by Newbury society at large.

The jury seemed energyless and lacklustre, and had no obvious enthusiasm for investigating the death of one of a group referred to as peacewomen. I felt they did not take on their responsibility as jurors to fully investigate.

The Inquest seemed to be a cover-up, that had tried to obliterate the truth, not an uncovering of the truth. The hardest thing to live with has been the cover-up of how Helen was killed. As long as the truth has not been uncovered, without bias or prejudice, we cannot rest. We will have to try to uncover the truth to the public, even if this could take years. A blight has been put on Helen which we are determined to clear.

We knew Helen to be careful and respectful of her own life and the lives of others. We feel under threat ourselves, that a killing could be made to look like an accident and not be properly investigated, and we know this could happen to any one of us.

We are angered by the disrespect the inadequate Inquest showed to Helen. We keenly feel the injustice, and cannot rest until justice has been done and the truth has been uncovered.[3] –

Mrs Thomas decided to take the Inquest verdict to Judicial Review.

When we returned to the camp, once again we spoke at length about what could have happened on the 5th of August – we asked over and over again, why did the passenger in the vehicle not appear at the inquest? Why was the inquest not adjourned until he could appear? Why were there no photographs of the passenger side of the vehicle? Could anyone remember the Estuses having been stopped and interviewed by the police on the 5th? How could the report of Helen's injuries tally with the Estuses, and the driver's reports? We would go down to measure the road again – the distance between the cross-hatched area and the path of vehicles is considerable. There is room also on the other side of the carriageway for vehicles to move to the right. We would speak about it again, at length. One evening, the realisation came to us at last: Helen was most likely killed by the wing mirror on the passenger side of the vehicle. We calculated the height of the wing mirror from the photograph of the driver's side of the horse-box parked in the bus-stop lay-by. We spoke of all the convoy drivers, police motorcycle outriders and other drivers who in the past had swerved towards us on the pavements. We say that these drivers 'buzz' us, or try to frighten us by doing so. We believe that Helen was killed by the wing mirror of the police horse-box as she stood where she believed she would be safe, at the side of the road, inside the cross-hatched area which vehicles should not enter. This is the explanation which seems to make sense of all that we know of the events of the 5th of August.

The bravery we saw in Janet Thomas, Helen's mother, as well as her ability to focus on justice and truth in the wake of her daughter's death, showed us that we too could carry on with our struggle.

There was some unfinished work of Helen's at the camp, which we were bound to complete for her: the *Resist the Military* handbook on non-violence which Helen had finished translating into Welsh just shortly before she was killed had still to be produced. In addition, the work Helen had put in to preparing for the actions at Imber and FIBUA (see January 27-28th 1990, below), and her preparations for the December demonstration had to be completed. A pile of more than a hundred envelopes addressed in Helen's handwriting to colleges and universities throughout Wales, Scotland, Ireland and England had still to be filled with her leaflets, some in Welsh, and posted out.

It was this work which we set about doing in the autumn of 1989, and which carried us through the first months at the camp after the killing of Helen.

Helen's mailing was posted out and the leaflet she, Abigail and Aniko had produced (translated into Welsh by Helen) for the December demonstration asking colleges, polytechnics and universities whether they would like a speaker from the camp to visit, drew a good response. In the three months before the December demonstration, Janet, Aniko, Abigail, Katrina and Beth each gave many talks about the camp's work in Ireland, Wales, Scotland and throughout England. The talks provided the opportunity to counter the media lies and expose the police's lack of investigation and cover-up of what had happened to Helen.

Convoy exercises continued and were non-violently resisted,

and the camp was kept going with depleted numbers of women. Several terms of imprisonment were also served during this period: Abigail was sentenced to 7 days on October 5th, Sarah to 7 days on October 10th; Katrina and Beth received 28 days each on October 6th. Janet was sentenced to 10 days imprisonment on October 25th, Mary to two weeks.

**NOVEMBER 7th, 1989:** Aniko and Abigail enter the base and disrupt the fuelling of a cruise missile convoy control vehicle.

**NOVEMBER 9th, 1989:** Janet and Katrina are arrested at the convoy deployment site – Imber. Katrina is held over on a Warrant, and is released the following day.

**NOVEMBER 10th, 1989:** Aniko and Abigail arrested at Imber.

**NOVEMBER 11th, 1989:** Janet and Katrina arrested at Imber.

**NOVEMBER 14th, 1989:** cruise missile convoy is moved from Imber to West Down plantation, Salisbury Plain.

The continuing convoy exercises from Greenham Common in the latter months of 1989 take place against a backdrop of sweeping changes throughout Eastern Europe: the 'enemies' the missiles were intended for were rapidly disappearing.

At the beginning of November 1989, it was announced in East Germany that in future people would be allowed to travel freely abroad, and over the weekend of November 10-11th around 2 million East German people flooded through breaches in the Berlin Wall. On November 17th, there was a march and non-violent demonstration of over 30,000 people in Prague, Czechoslovakia, against Communist rule – riot police reacted with violence to a sit-in in Wenceslas Square and many people were injured and detained.

**NOVEMBER 13th, 14th and 15th, 1989,** House of Lords: legal challenge to the validity of the Greenham Common Byelaws (1985) continues.

*Jean Hutchinson* – During the preparations, I remember thinking, this is a new ball game. I was told that only the best vellum paper is allowed to go to their Lordships, with files 'just so' and bound in red covers. The papers were definitely not to be like those we produced under extreme pressure at the camp.

I believe now, however, that the pomp and fuss is only meant to deter ordinary people from representing themselves in the highest court in the land. We'd been in this thing for over 3 years, had a full belief in our case, and were not likely to be deterred. Though I have to admit that the looming threat of £10,000.00 costs for each of us got me down sometimes, but Sarah Hipperson came out with a well-kent Scots quote for the occasion, 'Ye cannae tak the breeks off a Heely-man!' Georgina would have lost much more because she had put money in to keep the case going.

When we went to the House of Lords, Georgina Smith was represented by Beverley Lang who was able to work effectively and well to counter the legal points on severability which we had gained in the High Court.

I represented myself, using all the previously mentioned points, knowing now that the case did not need to be embroidered unduly. I did my best to convey the atmosphere of our work, our discovery of the proviso, what the criminalising of women meant for us. Also not forgetting the illegal fence, buildings, works, etc. plus one large item which came into my hands: I have referred to the fact that we were not sure whether there was carelessness or lawlessness on the part of the Secretary of State for Defence, Michael Heseltine. We were not surprised to have our suspicions confirmed and we now publish the relevant passage from a Defence Committee report of 16 May 1984:

(Mr Ward) I had promised to say a little more about bylaws, in closed session. There is not a lot to say, but one problem with the application of bylaws under the Military Lands Act is that the process of public consultation that is required can give rise to greater knowledge about little-known commoners' rights and rights of way across Ministry of Defence establishments, which do seem to exist, for reasons which I do not fully understand. They are very long in history, and some such rights are very hard to extinguish, but as the commoners die then perhaps the commoners' rights die.

1247. I am sure that is not the case.

(Mr Ward) I do not know. Either that, or they are passed on to the successor householder. * * * [a section of the report is deleted here] There is very little known about them. The process of consulting about bylaws runs the risk of spreading the knowledge about their existence. This is a fact that has to be taken into account sometimes.[4]

Spreading the knowledge about commoners and the byelaws runs a risk . . . it certainly does! Lord Justice Mann and Justice Shiemann had been wrong, when pointing to Heseltine's 'mistake'. The MoD simply hoped no one would notice the byelaws were invalid.

We had to wait until the 12 July, 1990 for the judgement. In the judgement, two of the Law Lords wrote words which show the importance of the Defence Committee information. Lord Bridge: 'The draftsman of the byelaws cannot possibly have been in ignorance of the terms and effect of the proviso to section 14(1) of the Act of 1892 and the theory of an inadvertent omission appears the less plausible since five sets of byelaws in relation to Common lands used for military purposes which were made by the Secretary of State for Defence under section 14 of the Act of 1892 in the years 1976 to 1980 all contain careful express provisions to safeguard rights of common.'

From Lord Lowry: 'It is up to the law-maker to keep within his powers and it is in the public interest that he should take care, in order that the public may be able to rely on the written word as representing the law. Further enlargement of the court's power to validate what is partially invalid will encourage the law-maker to enact what he pleases, or at least to enact what may or may not be valid, without having to fear any worse result than merely being brought back 'within bounds'.

When Lord Bridge had unpacked the piece of nonsense called the Greenham Common Byelaws, the commoners allowed to exercise their rights on a cruise missile base with the 'rest of the world' kept out, etc. etc., he came to the conclusion which Judge Lait came to and the words are music to our ears: 'For these reasons I conclude that the invalidity of the byelaw 2(b) cannot be cured by severance. It follows that the appellants were wrongly convicted and I would allow their appeals. Set aside the order of the Divisional Court and restore the order of the Crown Court at Reading.'

Through 15 court appearances in over 4 years we had struggled to get justice and the truth recognised. The judgement was given in writing and confirmed verbally in the chamber of the House of Lords. I don't believe one of our lawyers who was present understood what happened next. We were not required to speak but Sarah Hipperson's voice from the gallery called, 'Well done women!' Georgina and I protested the time it had taken and the political manoeuvrings – we were shown out.

The lawyer felt we should be grateful for the judgement and winning through in the end. There is a sense in which this is true, but time and political judgements had caused us to have to struggle. I think we were supposed to give up after the High Court stage.

We were sustained by the facts (1) the criminalising of thousands of women who were protesting about the genocidal weapons of cruise missiles (2)the Byelaws case had opened up an inferno of illegality which was the main feature of USAF Greenham Common.

The illegal fence, buildings and works were still needing to be worked on. Though our victory over the byelaws was complete, we needed to build on that foundation.

NOVEMBER 22nd, 1989: the Brandenburg Gate in the Berlin Wall is opened. At the camp, we feel that the encampment of non-violent pro-democracy demonstrators in Tiananmen Square had had a great influence upon people worldwide; we regretted that Helen, who had put so much into protesting against the massacre in Tiananmen Square, had not lived to see the changes in Eastern Europe.

Aniko is sentenced to 14 days imprisonment.

Meanwhile, the last few talks at colleges around the country take place.

The military take the convoy out on exercise once more before the December demonstration. Support vehicles begin leaving the Main Gate on the morning of November 30th; the launcher and control vehicles leave at 12.30 midnight – both are non-violently resisted by Yellow Gate women.

**DECEMBER 3rd, 1989:** Beth, Janet and Katrina go into the base and get inside hangar 302. All are arrested.

**DECEMBER 4th, 1989:** Aniko and Abigail go into the base during a nuclear 'black alert' exercise. They get up to the Command Centre in the midst of soldiers in full combat uniform including gas masks. Both arrested.

**DECEMBER 5th, 1989,** Newbury County Court: Katrina and Beth attend a pre-trial hearing regarding their application for the removal of the works on the base on Greenham Common.

*Beth Junor* – This case arose from the legal challenges to the Greenham Common Byelaws.

We wished to argue that we fell within the categories of people entitled to invoke the jurisdiction of the County Court, as 'persons interested in the Common'. Section 194 of the Property Act 1925 states, '(2) Where any building or fence is erected, or any other work constructed without such consent as is required by this section, the County Court within whose jurisdiction the land is situated, shall, on application being made by the council of any county or borough or district concerned, or by the lord of the manor or any other person interested in the common, have power to make an order for the removal of the work, and the restoration of the land to the condition in which it was before the work was erected or constructed . . .'

We claimed an interest in the Common on the basis that Katrina is a Trustee of land which was purchased for the benefit of women living permanently at the peace camp and which is completely surrounded by Common.

The Ministry of Defence argued (it was more of a casual suggestion, actually) that the correct interpretation of the Property Act Section 194 (2) is that only those with registered commoners rights can be said to have an interest in the Common. The Registrar leapt at the suggestion, and ruled as follows: 'The Plaintiffs' claim is in two parts – the second part is for an Injunction, and the Plaintiffs concede, as they are bound to do, that under Section 21 of the Crown Proceedings Act they are not entitled to take an Injunction against the Crown. The other part of their claim is under Section 194 of the Law of Property Act where they are 'persons interested in the Common' on the basis that they own land abutting the Common. The question is whether the mere fact that they own land abutting the Common, the transfer of which concerned certain rights, gives them an 'interest' in the Law of Property Act 1925. Having heard from the Defendants, I take the view that persons interested are only those persons whose rights of common were registered under the 1965 Commons Registration Act, passed to rationalise the land upon commons, and that the Plaintiffs therefore have no legal interest for the purpose of these proceedings more than any other member of the public at large . . . The action is struck out, on grounds of no *locus standi*.'

All day on the 5th the base is on exercise, with machine gunning and heavier firing heard from the camp. The convoy remains on Salisbury Plain.

DECEMBER 8th, 1989: convoy returns at 01.00am. Then, at last, the weekend of the December demonstration had arrived.Press Release: This year the annual December demonstration at Yellow Gate, Greenham Common Women's Peace Camp fell on the 10th anniversary of the decision to site cruise missiles in Europe, and the 2nd anniversary of the decision to remove them. The theme of the weekend was 'RESIST THE MILITARY'.

The international gathering of women over this weekend was as a living tribute to Helen Thomas, a Welsh woman living at Yellow Gate who was killed on the 5th August 1989 by a Police horse-box, while waiting to cross the road.

A workshop was held on the Saturday in Welsh and English. Women from Cymdeithas yr Iaith Gymraeg (Welsh Language Society) and other women who had worked with Helen in Wales and at the camp, spoke of how Helen connected the struggle for equal civil status for Welsh speakers and the struggle against the military at Yellow Gate.

Following the workshop, non-violent direct action was taken. 15 women went into the base and walked down the runway towards the silos area. As they lit candles and formed a circle, singing, they were arrested by Ministry of Defence police for Trespass under the Greenham Common Byelaws. They were reported with a view to prosecution, except one woman who was de-arrested. The action was taken to show the continuing resistance to the military at Greenham Common, and to carry on the work that Helen Thomas came here to do.[5]

DECEMBER 25th, 1989: Abigail, Beth and Morgreen enter the

base and light candles for those who had been killed in the uprising in Romania. They are arrested for Trespassing on Common land.

During 1990, there are 6 more cruise missile convoy deployment exercises, each one vigorously and non-violently opposed by the women at Yellow Gate. Convoy deployments continue regularly right up until July 1990; numerous court cases and prison sentences follow, the consequence of that resistance.

The first convoy exercise of the year begins at half-past midnight January 10-11th, and results in 13 arrests for Trespass on Bulford Ranges, Salisbury Plain.

JANUARY 16th, 1990, Devizes Magistrates Court: Katrina and Beth appear for trial for the Trespass action taken with Helen Thomas during the July 1989 convoy deployment.

*Katrina* − The case was dismissed on the basis that the soldier who could give evidence about firing (essential for a conviction) was not available. We had not been informed of this beforehand.

We both felt that this was a planned move by the state to stop a case where Helen had taken non-violent direct action with us, and to stop Helen's statement being read out in court.

Three of Helen's friends from Wales: Joe, Caroline and Cathy were in the court. The Magistrates, despite our protests, dismissed the case and left the court. At that point Caroline stepped forward and read out Helen's statement, which was written in Welsh.

It was a sad day for us, but Helen's words were read out despite the legal manoeuvre.

JANUARY 27-28th, 1990: three women from Yellow Gate − Aniko, Abigail and Morgreen Linder together with three women from London − Carolyn Halcrow, Catherine Crabtree and Alison Renouf trespass in an £8 million mock German village being built for the Army on Salisbury Plain, called FIBUA (Fighting In Built Up Areas). After a warning the women are released. They return to the village and are arrested a second time. The women hang banners from the mock church tower, HOMES FOR THE HOMELESS and VILLAGE RECLAIMED.

*Abigail Adams* − The three women from London had been working in the US at a community providing shelter for the homeless and also taking non-violent direct action on issues surrounding homelessness.

The action was also taken in memory of Helen Thomas, who was preparing to take action at this village, before her death.

FIBUA is a frightening escalation in military training, to desensitize troops to war against civilians.

The mock West Belfast streets in Imber village are just block shells. At FIBUA they are building real houses; with gardens, a mock petrol station, and most horrifying of all, the church with its blank gravestones. So that, for these soldiers, there is no place that is 'taboo' for their killing. Just like nuclear weapons, FIBUA is not about a war between armies, but a war against the people.

Since taking this action we have received messages of support from Southwark Homeless Information Project and the Advisory Service for Squatters.

**FEBRUARY 2nd, 1990,** Devizes Magistrates Court: a truly international court case, in which four women are tried for Trespass, one of whom had travelled from Montreal, Canada to attend. The defendants are Janet Tavner, Katrina Howse, Judith Walker and Lise Lafleur.

*Judith Walker* − We were on trial for a Trespass committed under the Imber Ranges Byelaws on the 12th of August 1989 when we resisted the nuclear convoy.

One important part of taking non-violent direct action is not to run away after you have committed an offence, but there is a difference between getting arrested and going to court.

It is a very good feeling to be the very same group in the dock as in the action. In our case it was an especially powerful impression, for Lise had come from Canada.

In the trial events and people as well as bits and pieces of the action were named and together gave a portrait of our reasons and ideals and reference points which had led to our 'being without permission upon the Danger Area...Contrary to Byelaw 3(b) . . .'

The experience of the Court case made clear to me that the action would have been incomplete without attending. Being in court is not only or merely taking the consequences but it is a renewal of the challenge and the reproach raised against the state by the action in the first place. −

Judith and Lise each received one year's Conditional Discharge and were ordered to pay £26.00 Costs; Janet and Katrina were each fined £100.00 and ordered to pay £26.00 Costs.

The February convoy exercise again resulted in 13 arrests for Trespass on Salisbury Plain, with an additional 2 arrests inside the base − a fine record of resistance for a small group of women.

Evictions continued to be regular. Storms returned in late February, after the land was beginning to recover from the devastation caused by the severe storm of January 25th.

**MARCH 13th, 1990:** Aniko and Katrina enter the base during the day.

*Katrina Howse* – We went into Building 153, the Communications Squadron Building. I knew from past non-violent action that this building had many important files in it.

We walked in openly, not to take documents, but to assert our right to look at information that is preparing for mass murder, now and in the future. We walked into a room and opened the filing cabinet. A man in the room said, 'Can I help you?'

I said, 'Maybe.' Then, as he was closing the cabinet, Aniko and I walked into another room. We took out a file that was about cruise missile exercises. It seemed to be about the operation of different 'keys'; this I took to be about the sequence of firing keys that would launch the missiles.

We didn't have long to look because a USAF man came in, told us to put the file down and leave the room. This we did, but not before we had a chance to look around. On the noticeboard was a notice saying 'Nuclear Exercise March 14th'.

We stood in the hall. People started reacting to our presence. A small group of USAF men filed silently away from us, a group of people stared at us, and a uniformed photographer took pictures of us.

Then we were arrested by the MoD police. At the processing centre it became clear that our action of looking was being taken very seriously. We were informed we would be interviewed by the CID with a view to charges of Burglary.

I managed to get a solicitor to come and see me before I went in to be interviewed. This I felt gave us both more power in the situation. The solicitor, Mrs Murdoch, and her assistant were a big help as they told me they didn't think the charge was applicable.

After giving a full statement in an hour-long interview with the CID, Aniko and I were released.

The non-violent action was strong, and asserted our right to look at information that holds all our lives to ransom. –

The charges laid against Aniko and Katrina were later dropped.

**MARCH 14th, 1990:** as expected, convoy support vehicles begin leaving the base, but not before Janet and Abigail disrupt the preparation of the vehicles by entering hangar 301.

The launchers and control vehicles leave the Main Gate at 12.30 midnight, under heavy police escort, as always.

The convoy's exercises on Salisbury Plain are constantly disrupted; 19 arrests for Trespass are made of Yellow Gate women.

Neither was the April convoy permitted an uninterrupted exercise on the Plain – 10 more arrests for Trespass are made, as a result of four disruptions during the six-day exercise.

APRIL 15th, 1990, Easter Sunday: Imber village church is opened and occupied by Frances Vigay, Morgreen, Janet and Katrina.

Approximately 40 people wander in and out of the church and graveyard during the day, the road through the village having been opened by the military.

APRIL 30th, 1990: amidst a spate of court cases, Yellow Gate's campaign against strip-searching in prisons is begun by Margaretta D'Arcy. Margaretta wrote the following Statement for the camp's December 1990 newsletter:

'On Monday 30 April 1990 I attended Newbury Magistrates Court (no. 2) to be sentenced to seven days in gaol for non-payment of a fine of £65. The fine had been imposed for a breach of the byelaws in June 1988, i.e. the occupation of Imber church, Salisbury Plain, to protest (with three other women from Yellow Gate, Greenham) against the assassination of Mairead Farrell by the SAS. A warrant had been made out for my arrest for non-payment of the fine, but it had not been issued. I rang up the Clerk of the Court from my home in the west of Ireland to arrange for the non-payment of the fine to be dealt with in court on 30 April.

'When my sentence was imposed I declared to the magistrate that I would not be cooperating with my own imprisonment or my own strip-searching because strip-searching is akin to rape. When I was asked to leave the dock I explained that it was up to them to remove my body for imprisonment. Two police, a woman and a man, dragged me downstairs and threw me in a cell. The sergeant came to the cell and pulled the mattress from under me, tossing me onto the concrete floor of the cell. He then asked me to sign permission for him to search my bag of personal effects before I took it to Holloway. I refused to sign. He said that the bag must therefore stay in Newbury because 'it might contain bombs' which he would not be willing to send on to Holloway. He said he was quite happy to have my unsearched bag (perhaps with bombs in it) in the Newbury courthouse.

'Later in the day I was dragged and pushed into a police car and taken to Holloway, without my bag of personal effects. At no time were any of my pockets searched. At Holloway I was put into a single cell, carrying on my non-cooperation. After a time I was dragged upstairs by four prison officers and put on a bed in another cell. I was asked to cooperate with my strip-search. I refused, and was thrown onto the cell floor and pounced on by the four POs. They dragged my clothes off, and then left me naked. I stayed naked until my release, saying that as they had taken my clothes off, they should therefore put them on me again.

'The following morning (Tuesday) I was asked to get up. I said

185

that was up to them. That evening a PO came and told me I was to be reported to the governor.

'On Wednesday morning a blanket was put round me and I was dragged off to the punishment block. I was asked to go to the governor, and I refused. I was handed a booklet *Information for Female Prisoners*. Later on, my mattress and blankets were removed; and my clothes left with me in a paper bag. Later on on Wednesday, also, the prison doctor came to see me: he warned me that he was there to assess if I should be put into the psychiatric wing. I informed him that I had already informed the press about my non-cooperation policy due to the strip-searching. On Wednesday night my mattress and blankets were returned.

'On Thursday morning the mattress was again removed and I was left with one blanket. The doctor came in during the day and advised me on the importance of drinking liquids, as I had not eaten since Monday. They had asked me if I wanted food and I had said no.

'On Friday, they asked me was I ready to be released? I said yes. They told me I could not be released if I was naked. I repeated that it was up to them to put my clothes on as they had taken them off. They came back later and said that if they released me naked I would be arrested immediately outside the gaol and brought back in again. I said that if this was so there would be no reason to strip-search me again. They put a blanket round me and put my shoes on me. They brought me down to reception. I insisted on being searched, so that they would not be able to put my clothes on me only to order me to take them off again for another search. I put my dress on, signed for my watch, and left the gaol.

'To sum up my experience of non-cooperation: at no time did I resist or struggle against them. There seemed no understanding of my position. Instead, in the court-house, through a sequence of rough handling, banging me downstairs, banging me against corners, banging me against doors, they hoped to break my resolve and force me to cooperate. In Holloway, even though in *Information for Female Prisoners* it says, 'If you wish to see a copy of the rules, ask your landing- or wing-officer,' and I constantly asked for a copy, I never received one.

'Incidentally, in the appendix to the booklet (page 16, 'Discipline Rules') the female prisoner is referred to as 'he' all the time.

'The questions I would like to ask -

'What are the minimum rights that prisoners have? And how far do such rights extend to prisoners who take conscientious stands upon (as in my case) such contentious matters as strip-searching? Strip-searching seems to be imposed simply to avoid the cost of metal-detectors etc., and – far from being a genuine security measure – is most frequently employed to humiliate and degrade. At no time did anyone, for example, examine my eyes or skin or urine for signs of drugs; neither were my bodily orifices probed.

'Is the gaoling of a person in fact a mutual contract between herself and the state whereby the state undertakes a humane care of the prisoner provided that the prisoner agrees to cooperate. If the prisoner refuses to agree, how far may the state refuse the humane care, food, clothes, etc.?

'In the case of non-payment of a fine, what is the actual purpose of imprisonment? Is the non-payer being punished for non-payment; or is her body simply being taken by the state for a specified period of time in lieu of money (on the analogy of a pawnshop)? The subsequent relationship between prisoner and prison authorities would seem to depend upon the answer to this question. And how far is this question understood by the magistrates who impose the sentence?

'The arbitrary inconsistencies that I have outlined above have their effect upon the psychology of the POs. They themselves can be perfectly pleasant in their manner only to become completely confused and hysterically violent when meeting a sudden obstacle to their authority. They don't know what to do, because they do not understand the situation that they have been placed in. So they swing between wanting to be liked and wanting to be feared and they feel guilty about the whole business.

'In the long run, I suggest, the relationship between the courts and the prison should be stated in court for the public to hear and understand; for after all, it is the public that pays for court and prison and for whatever philosophy may be thought to lie behind them both.'

**MAY 4th, 1990**, Devizes Magistrates Court: Katrina on trial for Trespassing on Salisbury Plain. Fined £100.00 and ordered to pay £35.00 Costs.

**MAY 15th, 1990**, Newbury Magistrates Court: Beth sentenced to 14 days.

*Beth Junor* – I appeared in court for a Means Enquiry – an enquiry into my finances as a result of un-paid fines. Two convictions were read out: one Criminal Damage offence of painting a USAF vehicle on June 5th '89, after we had learned of the Tiananmen Square massacre (this vehicle, which was on exercise, was forced to return to the base, and was out of commission for several weeks, until the red paint was removed); the other also a Criminal Damage offence resulting from pouring a line of white paint across the slip-road from the Main Gate of the base on August 8th '89, to try to stop cruise missile convoy support vehicles from leaving the base during our period of mourning for Helen Thomas.

For the latter charge, my co-defendant Aniko Jones and myself were both given a Conditional Discharge by Newbury Magistrates on 3rd January '90. We were ordered to pay £200.00 Compensation and £20.00 Costs. When Aniko appeared for her Means Enquiry, she was told by the Clerk of the Court that she couldn't be imprisoned for non-payment of Compensation and Costs – the Ministry of Defence would have to apply to the County Court if they wanted to retrieve these.

For the June 5th offence, I'd been fined £50.00 plus ordered to pay Compensation to the USAF plus Costs, totalling £219.00. So the total of unpaid fines for which I was appearing was £50.00, and I was expecting a day in the police cells, or 7 days at the most.

In fact I was sentenced to 14 days for each conviction, but to be served concurrently. This is yet another example of how unclear the courts are about what they're supposed to be doing.

I was taken down to Newbury Police cells to await transportation to Holloway. I was driven to Holloway in a police car which travelled on average over 80 mph, in the third and fastest lane of the motorway. We passed through a restricted speed zone where the speed limit was 50 mph, and here we 'slowed down' to 70 mph. I didn't dare speak to the driver, as he was driving so fast that any break in concentration would have endangered others and all of us. He obviously believed he could drive however he pleased, because he was in his police uniform and in a police car. But if we'd been in an accident, would he say in court that he'd been driving at the speed limit, just like the driver of the West Midlands Police vehicle which killed Helen Thomas? The fact is police drivers think that they don't have to obey traffic laws, and this experience of being driven to Holloway at such dangerous speed confirms this to me.

In the Reception area of the prison, the conversation turned to strip-searching, as it always has done whenever I've been in. Women who have been in court that day are returning to the prison – they were strip-searched before leaving in the morning, have been accompanied by a prison officer throughout the day, then on return to the prison they are strip-searched again. Everyone talks about how pointless this is.

I was determined to continue the non-violent resistance to strip-searching which Margaretta had begun. When it was my turn to be processed I informed the officer dealing with me that I would not be cooperating with my strip-search, and that as I am non-violent, any violence that took place would be coming from them. As I left the room, she shouted to the others, 'She's not cooperating with the strip search!'

This seemed to set off a kind of panic in all the Reception officers – I was left to wait again and when I was eventually called in they were all in state of agitation. It was obvious there had been some discussion – or rather rationalising – after Margaretta had been in, because each officer had her own little speech to make about strip-searches. One of the officers nervously declared – 'The minute you walked in that door, you walked into a PRISON, and in the prison there are RULES, and you've got to OBEY the rules. Strip-searching is one of the rules, and if you don't cooperate you'll be punished!' -All as if I'd voluntarily walked in off the street!

I was forcibly stripped by a group of officers while one of them said that she was employed by the Home Office to do a job, she was paid a salary for that job, and so she would do whatever she was asked to do. That attitude is just the one in which torture flourishes. One asked whether it would be OK by me if someone got a knife into the prison, took it up to the wing, and stabbed me with it! I replied they never find anything on strip-searches, anyway [I think a small vial of perfume and a five-pound note are the only recorded finds]; metal detectors would find any kind of weapon like this, anyway. They were all shaking.

This non-violent resistance to strip-searching is the most dignified way to enter Holloway. The indignity lies with the state which carries out such practices. –

The next woman who went to prison and refused to cooperate with the strip-search was Katrina. She was sentenced to 14 days on 19th June. On her day of release, a group of Yellow Gate women went up to London and held a picket against strip searching outside Holloway.

The July convoy leaves the base at 12.30 midnight on the 11th, the eve of the House of Lords ruling that the Greenham Common Byelaws are invalid. The convoy was non-violently resisted by the women at Yellow Gate, thus the morale of the military was dealt a double blow, over these two days.

In response to a Parliamentary Written Question, it is revealed that women were escorted from RAF Greenham Common on 128 occasions between 12 an 22 July 1990. The Minister replying felt compelled to add, 'This figure does not refer to 128 different people as many individuals have been escorted from the base on more than one occasion.'[6]

Morale inside the base suffers another blow on July 24th, when Janet and Aniko enter the high security area of the silos and implant a white flag in the fence.

The July 1990 convoy was the last to leave the base at Greenham Common on exercise. The convoys had remained potentially operational long after the public believed cruise missiles had gone from bases in Britain. The level of activity within the base remained high, after July – an effort to sustain morale.

On August 2nd, Iraq invaded Kuwait, and the USAF presence in the Gulf region was stepped up; on August 8th, a USAF Galaxy transporter plane brought 36 cruise missiles into Greenham Common, under heavy police protection within the base. Police from Wittering and Hampshire had been drafted in to reinforce the MoD police. Nevertheless, women manage to enter the base in protest to this military activity which was clearly related to recent events in the Gulf. The arrival of these missiles was carefully documented in a series of photographs, and in notes made at the time of times, numbers, etc. but all attempts to bring this to public attention failed.

It wasn't until some months later that we fully understood the events of this day: when tens of thousands of Iraqi people had been killed with so-called conventional cruise missiles. The base at Greenham Common was being used as a supply base for the war in the Gulf.

The camp therefore marked its 9th birthday in an atmosphere of escalating international tension. ·

Throughout the autumn, the court cases continued, more prison sentences were served, the camp was protected from the evictions, and preparations began once more for the annual December demonstration.

International visitors continued to make their way to Yellow Gate – in 1990 we were privileged to receive visitors from Australia, Brazil, Canada, France, Germany, Greece, Holland, Ireland, New Zealand, South Africa, Sweden, Switzerland and the US.

On Saturday November 3rd, the SUN tabloid newspaper published a libellous article about Katrina Howse.

*Aniko Jones* – 'In October 1990, I was at Yellow Gate when a woman came up to me and asked for Katrina Howse by name. She said her name was Sarah Courtney and that she worked for a local news agency. When I asked why she wanted to speak to Katrina, she said she wanted to do an article on the peace camps of Greenham Common as it was coming to its 10th anniversary; she thought it important to talk to Katrina because she had resided at the peace camp longer than any other woman. Ms Courtney said she wanted to talk to Katrina about the changes she had seen over the years and of the important events in the history of the camp.

'I told Ms Courtney that Katrina was not at the camp at that moment, as the work of the camp means a lot of coming and going. I asked her to return in two days – this would give me time to pass on what she had said, and Katrina would be prepared for the interview.

'The impression Sarah Courtney gave was that she was genuinely interested in finding out what we thought were important events and achievements of the peace camp on Greenham Common. I remember telling her I doubted very much that her article would be printed, if it wrote about what we thought was important. She replied, 'We will see.'

'When Ms Courtney arrived for the interview, she brought with her a photographer. I was involved with the general housework of the camp and I did not hear the interview. I was present when Katrina was being asked if she minded having her photograph taken. The photographer asked Katrina to stand and pose. After this I heard Ms Courtney ask Katrina where she got her money from. I was quite surprised at the question. To prevent myself from interrupting the interview I had to walk away.

'The day of the publication of the article in the SUN, entitled 'Scram scrounger,' there was a demonstration at the Main Gate of Greenham Common. Katrina was not involved in the demonstration. The Ministry of Defence police who were on the other side of the Gate became very abusive. I particularly remember an MoD policeman asking when we were next going to sign on [for Social Security benefit]. I thought this was a strange question. This police sergeant then began to name each day of the week, asking if it was one of those. I asked why he wanted to know. He said we were all scroungers off the state and stole money from the people who needed it. He said we should all be put in prison and the key thrown away because we were all wasters. Of all the years of being involved with working against the military I had not experienced such questioning or insults about where I get my money from. I asked one MoD policeman who had remained quiet what was the cause for this. The MoD policeman asked me if we had read the SUN. I said we never read it. The police sergeant shouted out there was a really good article about Katrina in the SUN. I said, 'Oh, so you read the SUN.' He replied no, someone had photocopied the article and pinned up copies of it on the notice boards around the base.

'The next day I went to a local newsagent and bought a copy of the previous day's SUN. After I had read the offensive article I spent some time debating whether to show Katrina. The article was so horrible I knew it would hurt Katrina. In the end I knew I had to show it to her because she had a right to know what was written about her.

'After seeing the article, Katrina was very nervous about going into Newbury. From experience, we know there is a lot of prejudice against us, mainly because of lies printed in the press. Because of this article Katrina felt vulnerable to abuse or attacks from people, who through reading the article were given an excuse to express their prejudice. Katrina could not go into Newbury on her own for a long time, through fear of being recognised.

'I was present at the camp when Katrina opened a letter addressed to her. The letter called Katrina a scrounger and had a copy of the SUN article with it.

'I was shocked at the article. It was attacking the peace camp through Katrina. This made me angry, but it was the personal, hurtful and untruthful abuse of Katrina which made me decide I wanted to participate in taking non-violent direct action against the news agency, who had made money from such a despicable article. I along with Katrina painted the walls of the news agency responsible. Both Katrina and I took responsibility for the action and served prison sentences for it.'[7] A similar article appeared in the DAILY STAR. Katrina issued writs for libel against both papers, and was successful in each action.

On Saturday December 8th, our demonstration, 'The Struggle Continues' took place in a blizzard. Strong winds and snow prevented many women from travelling to the camp. By the afternoon, however, Ceri had braved the journey from Wales, Frances made a safe arrival from Cambridge as did Pauline from London. Women entered the base continuously, and 11 sections of perimeter fence came down. This was one of those days when the greatest achievement is holding the camp – everything else is a bonus!

Daily incursions into the base continue until December 17th, when 9 women travel to Imber village, to occupy the church on the 47th anniversary of the final eviction of the villagers.

On December 20th Rosy, Judith, Morgreen, Beth and Katrina are found Guilty by Devizes magistrates of having broken the Salisbury Plain byelaws during an occupation of FIBUA on Hiroshima Day.

The bailiffs appear for their pre-Christmas eviction on December 23rd. Tents come down again in the hurricane force winds and torrential rains of Christmas day. But by December 31st, we were still holding our ground, and the year ended with a sense of achievement.

19. Left to right: Janet Tavner, Judith Walker, Jean Huchinson, Mary Millington at Yellow Gate.

*20. Our water supply is across the A339 road. Lisa Medici (left) and Louise Blakley. Winter 1990.*

*21. The Sanctuary in winter. 1990.*

22. Ethel Carlsson, Sweden
and

23. Sue Frazer, Canada, two long-standing friends and
supporters of Yellow Gate's work.

24. *The watchtower, silos area.*

*25. Departure lounge, Heathrow airport.*
*11th September 1991.*

*26. Katrina Howse leaving Holloway Women's Prison, having served her 16th sentence.*
*March 1991.*

*27. December gathering, 1991, when over 2,000 feet of perimeter fence is removed from Greenham Common*

*28. The Yellow Gate, Hiroshima and Nagasaki Days Gathering, 1995.*
*Back row, left to right: Beth Junor, Mary Millington, Louise Blakley, Frances Vigay, Katrina Howse, Jean Hutchinson, Peggy Walford, Fiona Gillespie.*
*Front row, left to right: Aniko Jones, Rosy Bremer, Sarah Hipperson.*
*The banners quote the poem When Hiroshima is Spoken Of by Sadako Kurihara, translated by Miyao Ohara.*

29. Since July 1983, bolt-cutters have been an essential tool for removing fences and thereby the security behind which the military hide. Aldermaston Atomic Weapons Establishment, Hiroshima Day, 1995. Sarah Hipperson and Katrina Howse.

*30. Trident nuclear warheads leaving Burghfield Atomic Weapons Establishment, 1994.*

*31. Women entering Aldermaston AWE, Nagasaki Day 1995.*

# 1991
# TEN YEARS
## by Janet Tavner

The women at the camp started 1991 by first-footing the base under the full moon, with candles, twigs, a penny and salt (a Scottish tradition, embellished with our own international flavour). The weather was harsh; cold and wet. We were living in what abodes we could afford – and had the strength to carry during evictions; this meant poor to average quality tents at the Gate and two tipis in the Sanctuary. It was hard to keep the fire going with damp and wet wood, but the necessity of hot drinks and warm food made women dig out the extra reserve of energy needed to keep the fire fuelled and burning.

Apart from the continuous, weary work of keeping the camp going, with numerous evictions and vigilante attacks during the nights, the camp was in the midst of the build-up of the U.S./British attack on Iraq. USAF/RAF Greenham Common was heavily used during the whole build-up. Large American air-force planes kept landing in and taking off from the base. We believed the base was used as a transport base during the war, mainly because of its large runway, ample storage facilities and high security.

During the first week of January many vehicles – Dodges and Texstars – were taken out of the base on low-loaders. The vehicles had been used in the cruise missile convoys and were now most likely being taken to the Upper Heyford airbase to be re-painted beige (desert camouflage) and flown to the Gulf.

On the 7th of January, Aniko was up in Devizes Magistrates Court for a charge of Trespass on Salisbury Plain, dating back to when the cruise convoys were still going out. Aniko was found Guilty and fined.

We sent out a large mailing to women in Britain to come to the camp every Saturday after the break-out of the war in the Gulf. Katrina and Aniko brought the leaflets up to an anti-Gulf war march in London and shared them out as they marched. Katrina also took the opportunity to do a prison visit. She visited Adebayo, whom she had met inside during one of her many sentences.

The 14th of January was the day before the deadline set by the Allied Forces for the Iraqi withdrawal from Kuwait. We woke up with an endless queue of traffic running past the camp, waiting to get into the base. Up at the Main Gate, MoD Police had been replaced by armed US soldiers. Every vehicle going in through the Gate was minutely searched. The base was on full war alert.

Station ...... Newbury ......................................... Station Ref. ......... 107/91 ..........

FULL NAME ...... Katrina HOWSE ..................... Date of Birth ...... Refused ...............

Address ...... Yellow Gate, Greenham Common, Nr. Newbury, Berks. ...........

You are charged with the Offence(s) shown below.  You do not have to say anything unless you wish to do so, but what you say may be given in evidence.

CHARGE(S):

On the 17th day of January, 1991 at Greenham in the County of Berkshire,
being concerned together with Janet Marie TAVNER, damaged a building to
an amount at Present unknown, the property of the Ministry of Defence,
intending to destroy or damage property belonging to another or being
reckless as to whether property belonging to another would be destroyed
or damaged, contrary to Section 1 of the Criminal Damage Act, 1971.

Reply to Charge(s) ...... PULLED WIRE DOWN VIOLENTLY OVERTHROW
LOCAL MILITARY STATES. .............

Officer ACCEPTING THE CHARGE ...... Sgt.882 ......
(Signature, Rank & Number)

Person Charging ...... A. others ...... Pc F633 ...... which is true ...... P.C. 633 OFKANCE .........
(include Rank & Number)      Name, Rank & No. (In Block Capitals)

Time & date charged ...... 0129 ...... 18.1.91. ......

If dealing with PEACE ACT 1984, specify offence(s) being committed with full approval, quote date and Court of hearing.

---

BAIL RECORD (Criminal Cases)

I ...... Katrina HOWSE ......
acknowledge that I am under a duty to surrender to custody at the
Magistrates'/Crown COURT / Police Station
The Courthouse, Mill Lane, Newbury, Berks.
On the 15th FEBRUARY, 19.91 at 09.45 am/pm in
connection with the offence(s) shown hereon.

Signature ...... Katrina Haus ......

NB: FAILURE to surrender to custody is an offence punishable by imprisonment and/or a fine.

I ......
of ......

as SURETY acknowledge my obligation to pay the court the sum of £...... if the
above named fails to surrender to the custody of a Juvenile/Magistrates/Crown

COURT/Police Station at ......
...... am the ...... at ...... 19......
...... am/pm in connection with the offence(s) shown hereon. *(And that I
am required to attend the above Juvenile Court at the time and date shown.)

Signature ......

SECURITY in the sum of ...... has been received from ......
of ...... by ......

TAKEN and acknowledged at 01.30 am/pm on 18th JANUARY, 19.91 by ...... Signature

IN BLOCK CAPITALS - FULL name and Rank of Officer taking bail ...... Raymond COX ...... Sgt.882 ......

---

BAIL RECOGNIZANCE (Civil Cases)

I ......
acknowledge my obligation to pay the Court the sum of £......
I'll fail to appear before the ...... Court at
...... on the ...... 19...... at ...... *am/pm *(unless the
sum(s) of £...... being the amount outstanding on the warrant(s) be sooner paid.

Signature ......

I ......
of ......
as SURETY acknowledge my obligation to pay the Court the sum of £......
of ......
fail to appear before the ...... Court at
on the ...... 19...... at ...... *am/pm *(unless the sum(s)
of £...... being the amount outstanding on the warrant(s) be sooner paid.

Signature ......

I acknowledge that I have received a written copy of the Charge(s), *Bail Record, *Legal Aid, *Notice to Indicate Plea, *Statement notification of Advance Disclosure Entitlement.

...... Katrina Haus ...... Signature

PAC 41A (7/87)      *Delete as appropriate

In the middle of all this, Abigail and I have to drive the 40 miles to Devizes to defend ourselves in the Magistrates Court for charges from Salisbury Plain. Abigail's case is adjourned, I am found guilty and fined.

That same afternoon, RAF Commander Brookes came down to the camp in full uniform, with a police escort. He asks what we intend to do after January 15th. He explains the base is now on war alert and that if we enter the base we could be mistaken for terrorists and shot. He tells us we 'won't meet President Bush in there; it will be a 21 year old with his finger on the trigger. The situation in the base has changed.' We ask what authority the military has to place arms with live ammunition in the hands of 21 year-olds they have talked into such a state they may indiscriminately shoot any living human being in their vicinity. We also ask about internment as we all feel the threat hanging over our heads. The Commander gives no reply.

We affirm strongly that we will continue to take non-violent direct action against all military activities going on inside the base, and that we will do everything we possibly can to stop the war. We're all worried but do not feel we have the choice to comply with the preparations for war through our silent consent. Too many lives are at stake.

Journalists come up to the camp, but interviews with us are broadcast heavily edited to fit in with the continuous war propaganda. There have been announcements from the British government confessing that the media will be censored on the issue of the Gulf War.

We drive around to tell the camp on the north side about Commander Brookes' warning. They knew already.

Midnight on the 15th January was the deadline set by the allied forces for the start of the war. It is dark of moon and no bombing takes place tonight. In the morning the whole camp gets evicted. We work throughout the day to publicise the threat made to us and to try, and try again to get an incentive out to *resist* the planned attack on Iraqi people.

On the 16th/17th the attacks on Iraq start. Hardly any reports come through on the radio, apart from to say that the attack had started. Katrina and I go into the base and walk into the Commander's office. In there we manage to find a paper called *Home Defence Plan*. Section 5.2 instructs that, in the shooting of terrorists, one should use 'only as many bullets as are necessary' to ensure the person is dead; they are not to use any more ammunition than is necessary to kill. In a letter to the Editor of Republican News, Beth suggests 'this is the British state's response to the realisation that it is 'bad public relations' to put as many bullets into Mairead Farrell, Daniel McCann and Sean Savage as they had done when these three people were summarily executed in Gibraltar....Their definition of 'terrorists' was publicly widened when the RAF Commander visited the peace camp in person to say that if the women entered the base at night, they 'may be mistaken for terrorists'.

We continued to take action after action. Katrina wrote about some of our actions in our September 1991 newsletter:

'After one day of the air bombardment of Baghdad, Janet and I felt the need to express our horror and revulsion at the mass killing by the US, British and other air forces. We decided on Building 92, which held offices for both the RAF Commander and the USAF Commander. Looking back months afterwards, we knew thousands upon thousands of Iraqi people were being killed; we didn't know that at the end of the war the figure of 300,000 people murdered would be estimated. More women were coming down as a result of Beth's emergency statement, 'In the event of war . . .', particularly every Saturday. We were going in the base as much as we could, and on one of the Saturdays a large group of women was taken to Newbury Police Station under the Public Order Act for shouting and singing in the base against the Gulf War. A second group went in, and deliberately sang and danced against the Gulf war in the Recreation Centre. We were also taken to Newbury Police Station, but all of us were held and released several hours later without charge. Janet and I felt the need to go in at night and spray paint the Commander's office.

'We were mindful of Commander Brookes' threat to us that we could be shot, particularly if we took action at night. All the security police carried their machine guns during the Gulf War. We felt we weren't going to be prevented from taking much needed action, we would walk openly and if challenged identify ourselves quickly. The Commander's office is very close to the Main Gate so we got there very quickly. It wasn't guarded, so we had a clear ten minutes plus to spray paint the whole building (a small bungalow type). We had already decided we were going to paint until we were caught, so that the non-violent resistance was recorded and the police would have to deal with us. I painted, BUSH BUILDS FASCISM ON THE BONES OF IRAQI PEOPLE. Janet painted STOP YOUR KILLING. Eventually USAF Security Police stopped us, but not before we had covered all the walls, but the back one. I took action against all the killing of Iraqi people; I also knew that Hussein had threatened that if Iraq was bombed he would bomb Israel. I kept thinking of my sister, her husband and two children who live near Tel Aviv. I spoke about this to the security policeman, who looked at me in a kind of exultant, nasty way and said something like, 'It's probably already begun!' I said to him, 'If it has, the USAF and RAF pushed it to that situation.' I knew that with such a large bombardment killing Iraqi people, the Iraqi military would hit out at Israel.

'In the police cells, before and after being interviewed, I kept thinking of the two children I had a family connection with, and feeling sure they had had gas masks put on them. They were facing a chemical weapons attack, while children in Iraq were being massacred by bombs. After being charged, we were released and met by women outside the police station. They said there had been a missile attack on Israel by the Iraqi military, that they had fallen in the Tel Aviv area, but were believed not to be chemical weapons. I knew my sister must be going through so much worry and fear. Luckily they were alright, although a number of Israeli people were killed. If a limited number of missiles caused people to be killed, and caused such damage, I could only imagine what amount of killing a continuous bombardment was doing.

'The facts of the killing were kept from us by the media, as they are today. We knew it was mass killing, and I believe the estimate of 300,000 people killed. These people were termed 'the enemy' by the USAF and RAF killers who murdered them, and we could all hear on the radio the way they carried out their mass murder. They were exultant, just like the security policeman we met. They are branded men, and will carry that murder with them for the rest of their lives.'

Women came to the camp in response to the mailing and in response to their own revulsion at the situation. In the same 1991 newsletter, Jan Dodd wrote about the time she spent at the camp:

'The Tuesday night vigils for peace in the Gulf, held in Dundee's City Square, had not been enough. On the morning of Thursday 17th January when the Allies began bombing misions on Iraq, I felt powerless and merely eaten up by my own distress at the situation. I felt I would have to do something more to be absolutely clear for myself and the world that this war was not in my name. And so, that night I set off for the eighth time in the past six years to Greenham – still an active focus for work against the military thanks to the long term commitment and dedication of a few women.

'. . . Immediately empowered and no longer silenced in solitary resistance to the war, I joined in three weeks of non-violent direct action against the military.

'Such atrocities take place without our consent but they cannot ignore our active dissent.'

During the whole of January and February it is very cold at the camp. With the wind-chill factor it goes down to as low as -19C. We all get ill at various points.

During this time, we manage to get hold of a second-hand

mobile home 'though, with an old gas heater in it which makes life a bit easier. With a great struggle, we place the mobile home on the Sanctuary land.

On the 31st January Katrina and Aniko are on trial at Newbury Magistrates Court for painting Wessex News Agency's office. They are both found guilty and ordered to pay £350.00 Compensation each.

On the 12th February it is -14C and snowing as Katrina got up from her tent on the Common, went down to Newbury Magistrates Court and was sentenced to 28 days imprisonment for refusing to pay fines.

After a month of air raids on Iraqi people, the allies send in the ground force offensive on the 24th of February. We keep breaking into the base, interrupting military activities and causing as much disturbance as we can.

Aniko had to do yet another journey to Devizes to stand trial for Salisbury Plain charges. She is found Guilty, fined £100.00 and ordered to pay £40.00 Compensation.

One of the main British bases used in the war was Fairford. On March 3rd, Beth, Aniko and Polly go there to throw white paint on the B52 bombers used for huge aerial bombardments which killed thousands of people. Beth is arrested outside Fairford under the Official Secrets Act and Aniko and Polly are arrested for Going Equipped to cause Criminal Damage before they get a chance to paint the planes. All charges are dropped within two months.

The very next day Beth has to get up in the dark to go with Katrina to Devizes to stand trial for Trespass charges from Salisbury Plain. Both are fined £100 and ordered to pay £40 Costs.

On the 5th of March, the camp is invaded by various press representatives as this, apparently, is to be the day when the last of the missiles are being flown back to America. The GUARDIAN later carries the headline, FAREWELL TO CRUISE LEAVES PEACE WOMEN UNMOVED. Katrina is quoted as saying, 'We can't celebrate this when there is still so much weaponry and so much killing. Nothing less than the dismantling of the whole military machine will satisfy us . . . It is crucial to keep this camp as a focus for women's non-violent, direct action protests.'

Three days later Aniko is up in Newbury Magistrates Court for causing Criminal Damage to a US flag, the stars and stripes. She is found Guilty and fined. Four days later she's in court for a number of unpaid fines and is sentenced to prison for 14 days.

In Mid-March the first daffodils dare to come out and there is a general feeling that the very harsh winter has lost its frightening grip.

The Birmingham Six are released on the 14th March after spending 16 years in prison for a crime they never committed, found Guilty on the evidence given by lying policemen. Their appeal had been turned down three years before, with the revealing comment from Lord Denning that he would prefer to set aside the cases of injustice raised by television rather than call into question the reputation of the British system of criminal justice. It felt very good that the persistent, long, grassroots struggle to bring justice into what happened to the Birmingham Six gained some victory. When we went into court again, we spoke about how the British legal system had been shown up and most of the court officials looked down.

In keeping with our 'The Base Must Go' motto, adopted for this year's December gathering, dozens of sections of perimeter fence around the base were cut down by women during March.

Abigail went to Devizes for yet another Salisbury Plain charge, on the 18th March. She is found Guilty and fined. The next day, I am called to Newbury court for non-payment of fines and sentenced to 14 days imprisonment.

The rest of March is mainly wet and cold. Women take action on a daily basis, and spend time planting peas, beans and parsnips. Evictions have to be coped with on a weekly basis.

The first two weeks of April go by as we cut even more fence down around the base, do prison visits and try to get a deer poacher arrested. We also have to deal with yet another attack by men at the camp who spray paint our Ford transit van.

We also work together with Mrs Thomas for the hearing in the High Court on April 23rd.

### PRESS RELEASE

Yesterday a judicial review was held in the High Court, London, to determine whether there should be a fresh inquest into the killing of Helen Wynne Thomas.

. . . Lord Justice Bingham and Mr Justice Hodgson ruled that, despite the irregularities in the procedure of the initial inquest, there would be no fresh inquest into the killing.

Mrs Janet Thomas, Helen's mother, said yesterday at the High Court: 'I am of course disappointed at the court's decision. I do not believe that the whole truth about Helen's death came out at the inquest and the hearing today has now deprived me and my family of the opportunity to have a fresh inquest to get at the truth.

'I am pleased that this court recognised there were inadequacies in the way the coroner handled the inquest. One of the main reasons I made the application was that I felt justice had neither been done nor seen to be done at the original inquest. I wanted to ensure that no-one else would feel like that in the future.

'I am a Justice of the Peace and seeing that a hearing is fair and full is particularly important to me.

'I can't help feeling that much of what happened after Helen's death is related to the fact she was living at Greenham Common Peace Camp.'

We were all very disappointed with the ruling from the High Court. We felt the judges were prejudiced against us, whether we were dead or alive. Lord Justice Bingham, who was the most authoritative judge in giving the ruling, was shortly after made Master of the Rolls.

Mrs Thomas, who had been working so hard to truly make clear exactly how Helen died, went back to Wales to consider what to do next. We went back to the camp feeling dejected but knowing we have to rise and continue the struggle.

Three days after the Judicial Review hearing, two Newbury District Council officials arrive at our old mobile home and threaten us with having to move it, as we have neither a site certificate nor planning permission. They threaten that if we don't move it they will cut it up and remove it piece by piece (it is stuck in the woods). We remind them there is such a thing as Human Rights. The mobile home is the only stable shelter we have and everyone does have the right to shelter and enough heat as you need to survive. The men walk away, repeating their threats. We are determined not to let them get away with ignoring Human Rights.

On the last day of April Aniko and I are called to Swindon Crown Court, for an appeal of the Salisbury Plain Byelaws, which we have been convicted under so many times. We represent ourselves and argue well, but although it is clear that the MoD had been using the law beyond its powers, the appeal was not upheld.

During the first three weeks of May women keep breaking into the base over and over again, in large and small groups. We disrupt the military on a consistent basis. We also work on the fence to prepare it for the December demonstration. Section by section we cut the fence loose from its attachment to the ground, only leaving a few strands to snip on the actual day of action.

On the May full moon we hear a heavy plane land in the base. The Russians were back again for another 24-hour inspection of the silos. They fly in over the heads of the people, just as communication between the two super-powers went on over the heads of the people. Women go into the base and make our voices heard amongst all the military men.

Two days later, a message is given to the camp: the MoD would drive down from London in an armoured car, filled with cash to be paid to the commoners to enable the MoD to extinguish Commoners Rights on Greenham Common. No armoured car appeared, but the MoD are definitely in the process of extinguishing the ancient Rights on Greenham Common.

The MoD's move is directly connected with the court case which starts the day after we receive the message about the armoured car and the cash, on 3rd June. Jean Hutchinson, Sarah Hipperson and Georgina Smith had appealed convictions for cutting fence down in June 1987. The appeal is now being heard in Reading Crown Court. On the same day Katrina is in the same court to have her Byelaws convictions quashed.

The appeal case continues the next day as well, and after having attended the case, Katrina and I come back to the camp and carry out a long longed for action. We cut through several layers of superfence and occupy one of the silos for over an hour. We are arrested, taken down to Newbury Police station and charged with Criminal Damage to the fence. Katrina wrote in our Newsletter, 'It was a wonderful feeling to cut through four fences, and stay on top of the silos for nearly an hour. A real reclamation. The superfence was hard work to get through and took several minutes of cutting with the boltcutters . . . It was a very strong non-violent direct action against the base, and for the restoration of Common land.'

Women continue to break into the base and on 11th June Abigail is called to Newbury court for non-payment of fines. She refuses to pay the fines and is given 7 days imprisonment. She's released on the 14th, but on the 18th Rosy, Beth, and Claire Downs are called to court for non-payment. Beth gets 28 days, Claire and Rosy get 7 days.

Amidst evictions and administrative court appearances, Katrina and Aniko drive up to London to visit Beth. The weather is now kinder, but the extra energy and light hours that come with it also bring a demand for more work to be done while it is possible. We're preparing for Helen's memorial in August, and for Hiroshima and Nagasaki days. At the same time we never cease breaking into the base to disrupt and stop the war preparations.

First of July Beth is released from prison and the same day the Reading Crown Court appeal starts up again and goes on for a week. We send women up to support the case the whole week. During the evenings and nights we take action. Aniko is arrested and charged with criminal damage to another USAF/RAF flag.

The next week, with no court to attend, we seriously work on the fence. We want it to be cut as loose as possible for the December action without it looking suspicious to the MoD.

On the 16th July Katrina has a means enquiry and is sentenced to seven days imprisonment. The day after her release, she, Ethel and I go to RAF Fairford. Ethel recorded our actions in our Newsletter:

'In Fairford on Saturday 20th and Sunday 21st there was a tattoo in the air base with lots of war aeroplanes playing circus tricks to honour the Gulf war. Both Katrina and Janet had seen the advertising and wanted to take action. I dreamed of how nice it would have been to get to a microphone and start to tell people some truth. But to get to one would have been too difficult. We three dressed up nicely in skirts and carried handbags, one containing the banner of the camp, saying BLOOD ON YOUR HANDS to the leaders of that war.

'We went away in the camp car with Janet driving, time already past three o'clock pm but in hot weather. We could not get near the tattoo base at all in the car, as all roads were blocked in that direction now by policemen. Well, after lots of driving and after having seen a fox we were at the end of a path, among fields and bushes. Janet parked the car and we went off. We passed along fields, found a new path, walked one mile, two miles, three . . . crossed some barbed wire, followed a ditch, crossed more barbed wire and so on.

'We often saw aeroplanes starting in the distance, letting out coloured smoke and once dropping parachutists. Katrina kept encouraging us by saying, 'probably only three more fields now.' We crossed a farm and a big field where a tractor driver was bringing in the last hay. He just stared at us, three tidy women with handbags rushing over his field. More barbed wire. A very big, roaring plane, a Vulcan, came low over us now and then. Suddenly Janet said, 'There's a river in front of us!' Yes, River Thames, with a beautiful swan on it but already broad and deep. We turned right and followed it as we saw a bridge far away. We had to cross some gardens to get close. Very embarrasing. And to get up to the road to the bridge we had to climb a six foot high brick wall out of a garden. We crossed the bridge and went on between a wheat field and some bushes. We could see tails of parked aeroplanes between treetops now. An hour and a half after we had left the car we were at the fence.

'Somehow we came in close to a lot of parked planes. We saw a huge B52, pink desert coloured and two other planes within ropes. When we came to them we also met hundreds of people on their way out from the tattoo. Then we brought out our banner and carried it amongst the people, loudly saying '300 thousand murdered! An increasing lot of children dying there now!' Rather many took photos of us. Soon somebody followed us, describing us into a walkie-talkie. A military van came along. Then a police van stopped us. We were put in and taken to a big police area in the base. On the way we shouted SHAME ON THE RAF, SHAME ON THE MILITARY! People heard us and turned around. We got put in a riot van, everyone in a small box each. We sang peace songs. It was the first time I was in a riot van. I felt proud and enjoyed the songs and the fact that I could see and hear Katrina and Janet and was relieved that we had been able to get to a good place for the action. Surprise: two other women were brought in who had got in somewhere else at the base with a banner. I could later see two policemen looking at that banner. It said MURDERERS in red on white.

'We were taken to Cirencester police station. There we were not bad handled. We got questioned and searched and put into cells, but offered blankets, coffee and food. In the middle of the night when we were let out, one at a time, an MoD officer from the base on Greenham Common arrived and accused me of having broken the peace! Did I have something to say? It could be used against me in court. I said again that I had just tried to tell some truth and had not broken any peace. But you can say, I said, that the war planes have broken the peace with their noise and by using up so much tax money for petrol this day, to say nothing about the killing some of them have done. He did not take down any notes.

'A police car took us back to our car. Back at the camp Aniko was still looking after the fire and had cooked for us. We do not know if we will be taken to court for telling the truth in Britain or not. I do hope I will not be in prison when I am supposed to work in Sweden, as that can cost me my job. The military uses up so much tax money everywhere, while children are starving to death.'

On the last day of July the Reading Crown Court case starts up again to go on for another week. Again, women keep getting up at early hours to be in court to support.

We were now in the very last stages of organising for the Reclaim The Plain walk which will start from the camp on Hiroshima day, August 6th. The walk would be performed to mark the nuclear bombings of Hiroshima and Nagasaki. We also wanted to revisit, cleanse and purify the sites on the Plain that had been used over the years as deployment sites for the cruise missile convoys. We were all prepared for a number of non-violent direct actions against military strongholds on the Plain.

On the 4th August, eleven women go into the base and carry out a strong and beautiful circle dance, to focus and strengthen the camp. On the 5th, we hold a silent vigil at the Gate in memory of Helen. Many women gather and show their respect for Helen and her work. In the evening we move into the back of the camp and hold a last meeting in preparation for the march. We all have a short night's sleep and set off in two cars in the early hours next morning.

On the walk are: Janet, Katrina, Beth, Aniko, Abigail, Claire, Frances, Raylene, Emma, Polly, Lisa and Rosy. The women who held the camp over the week were Judith, Jan and Andrea.

The first part of our walk takes us from Redhorn Hill to the Bustard Vedette near the old convoy site at Blackball Firs. Five women go inside the wood and cleanse the site by burning sage and sprinkling water from the Sanctuary. The next morning we walk from our camp site near Stonehenge back to the Bustard and from there to Robin Hood Ball, another ex-convoy wood. Again, we cleanse the site. We then walk for three miles on public roads to West Down Camp and on the way we visit another convoy wood – West Down Plantation. As we march into West Down Camp an MoD car joins us and follows us for the rest of the day, even when we stop for a cup of tea in Tilshead. We're chased from our next camp site at 10.00pm when the police manage to get a huge prison bus up onto the sacred site of White Barrow. At approximately 11.30pm we arrive at Imber church to stay the night. We occupy the church for a good 12 hours before we are arrested and taken to Larkhill police station. All the women, apart from myself, are released without charge. Beth recorded what happened next:

'Although 8 women occupied the church on the night of August 7th/8th, Katrina, Polly and I left early in the morning of the 8th, drove out of the village unseen, and on to Newbury. We dropped Polly off and drove back to the Plain a few hours later, with Aniko, and searched for the women who we assumed would by that time, have been arrested and removed from Imber church by the police.

'We arrived at Larkhill MoD police station just in time to see Janet being brought out of the building, accompanied by an Inspector and another MoD Police Constable – both male. Janet said 'They're taking me out – they haven't even asked my name!' It then became clear Janet was going to be bundled into a waiting police car. We began asking where Janet was being taken. The inspector said 'I've got nothing to say.' We said he MUST tell us where they were taking Janet, and if he didn't, we would issue a writ of Habeas Corpus. He then said 'Amesbury.'

'Katrina asked 'Is there a police station at Amesbury?' since this sounded like a very dubious answer and we were beginning to worry about Janet's safety. The police were trying to get Janet into the car as quickly as possible – preferably with no questions asked. We continued asking questions. Janet asked for a WPC (woman police constable), saying she wasn't happy about just being driven off in a car by two male officers. This reasonable request was dismissed, and Janet said 'Follow me...' before she got in the car and was driven off. Aniko followed in the Princess, the camp car.

'Whenever the police appeared at Larkhill we asked why Janet had been taken away. 'A Byelaws offence,' they said.

'Aniko returned some hours later to report Janet was being detained at Salisbury police station, under the Immigration Act. The Salisbury police hadn't given Aniko any information, she had found this out by going round to the back of the station and shouting to Janet through the window of her cell.'

When the women get back to the camp, all slightly shocked about what's happened to me, they find out about yet another attack on the camp. Jan has been subjected to a man's indecent exposure attack on her while she is on her own. Jan was shocked and upset, but reported the incident to the police and gave a good description to all of us.

As the days go by, it becomes clear I am fighting against a deportation and banning from the U.K. As an international woman I had always been perfectly aware and had to fight about this silent, invisible threat hanging over me like a guillotine that could at any minute separate me from the body of the camp. Now the threat became visible, even to the uninitiated. After a few days in police cells, I was taken to Pucklechurch prison, outside Bristol, where I was kept and questioned for five weeks.

During those five weeks, women work hard to do what they can to halt the deportation process and to support me. Women kept driving to Pucklechurch to visit me as often as it could be afforded and as often as there was the time and women for it. At the same time women do everything they can to highlight and expose what is happening. Letters are sent to the Home Office, questions asked through MPs, and a large petition is organised and sent to Her Majesty's Immigration Office. A full campaign to try and stop my deportation was being organised from the camp.

At the same time, the work at the camp had to go on. Women keep breaking into the base, and working on the fence during the night. On the 13th August, Judith Walker was sentenced to seven days imprisonment for non-payment.

On the 20th August, during the night, Rosy and Lisa went in the base and painted a plaque dedicated to the 501st squadron – the squadron which operated the cruise convoys. They manage to get out unseen, but the next morning brought it all back to them. The day started with an eviction, then women set off to support the women in the Reading Crown Court appeal which was finally coming to an end. Police arrive at the camp, and Rosy and Lisa are arrested for Criminal Damage.

The next day, women set off to Reading again at the same time as Aniko had to appear in Newbury Court to answer a charge of Criminal Damage to yet another military flag.

On the 28th, some slogans I had painted on the large hangars some time ago reappear during the night, on top of the paint the MOD had covered the originals with!

10 years!! Against all the odds, the camp holds its tenth birthday on the 5th September 1991. Although it's done while I am still in prison and we all feel this shadow, it does not make the feeling of achievement less. Aniko Jones writes about the 10th birthday: 'In our 10th year we can look back with pride over our achievements. Now we have to look to our future. The missiles have gone but not the military. The building on the Common is still continuing and there is constant preparation for war on Salisbury Plain. We have shown how consistent non-violent resistance works. We still have our work to do; we ask you to join us.'

During the following weekend Katrina holds an exhibition of her paintings at the camp which visitors and press attend. On the Monday three Japanese women who had come all the way from Japan to visit the camp on the tenth birthday, are brought to Pucklechurch to visit me. All parties, Kazuko, Chieko, Fu and I receive inspiration from the visit.

I manage to get a message out from the prison – I am to be deported in a few days time. I will be physically removed from the camp where I have lived and worked, and banned from returning. It all seemed unbelievable. Three years after Helen had been killed another woman was going to be taken from the camp – but at least I would have my life as a resource to fight back with.

### PRESS RELEASE

Janet Tavner of Yellow Gate Greenham Common Women's Peace Camp was deported on the 11th of September to Stockholm, after 5 yrs full time living at the camp. 12 women from Yellow Gate held a vigil at the Departure Terminal, Heathrow. A group of 5 women walked into the Departure Lounge before being stopped by the police, transported to the Airport's boundary and dumped there. A sixth woman managed to get up to the Departure Gate, before being handcuffed by the police, and later dumped with another woman at the Airport boundary.

In a letter from Stockholm of 12th September, Janet writes: 'At 5pm I was taken out, handcuffed to the WPC, put in a Metropolitan Sherpa police van with the Sergeant and three Police Officers. We drove madly with flashing lights up to the landing strip. I was taken into a small area under severe surveillance, with customs officers on full alert looking maniacally around all the time, talking in their walkie-talkies. I was thoroughly searched from head to toe, while everyone expected an attack any second. Everything was done in a MAD frenzy! I was rushed out back into the Sherpa (all the time attached to the WPC) and driven out to a small waiting area where we sat for a few minutes while the 3 PCs checked everything was clear. They stalked around looking prepared for a gun attack from every corner. The plane and surrounding area was checked. I was rushed back out into the Sherpa (flashing blue lights) driven speedily out to the plane, rushed up the steps and put in between the Sergeant and the WPC on the last three seats. The plane was surrounded by the three PCs and airport officials with walkie-talkies. The Sherpa stood ready with its lights on outside. All the other passengers were boarded, and we started taxiing, followed still by the Sherpa with its lights on. (At one point someone told us 'The pilot lives on Greenham Common and is well cheered up.') As we had taken off and were up in the air the WPC took the handcuffs off and after a while they both started talking to me a bit. They said they had never done this before, they were going to stay in Stockholm, have a look around the next morning and then fly back. I asked why they had to come all the way. The Sergeant looked to the side and said 'Well it's a bit of a special case.' I asked why. He said, 'It was believed you wouldn't leave voluntarily.' Damn right they are!

'I want to thank you, for talking to me about the strip protest and about standing on the seat, thus preventing take-off. These were exactly what my thoughts were as we boarded. It proved impossible though with the handcuffs and being jammed in between the two of them.'

Women keep speaking out, speaking out and making public the way in which I had been attacked. As well as being an immense attack on one single woman, it was also an attack on the camp, and the work I and other women stand for. We feel there are serious moves to try and close the camp down. The state has removed what they thought was the focus of the camp – the cruise missiles – it's now moving in on the camp itself. I respond to an article in a local newspaper:

'I am writing from the depths of Salisbury police station's holding cells, where I was handed a Newbury Weekly News by my friends.

'I am responding to last week's article placed smack-bang in the middle of the front page headed with fat, bold letters 'Peace women cost £1/2 million a year – claim'. The rest of the article is largely taken up by one man's inane personal opinions of the Women's Peace Camp. On NWN's own admission his opinions amount to 'an outspoken attack on women...'

'Why is one man's personal opinion given headlines and space on the front page? And why were the direct victims only allowed one sentence in a three column article to defend themselves?

'So far I have seen this tactic in the tabloid papers, but not as much in local papers. Furthermore the outspoken attack took place a mere three days after we sadly held our second memorial to Helen Wynne Thomas, a Yellow Gate woman who was killed by a West Midlands police horse-box as she was waiting to cross the road outside the Main Gate. It is *dangerous* to allow and highlight untruthful, prejudicial personal opinions against an already targetted group.

'. . . What is worth considering in the article is that the MoD is pumping thousands of pounds of tax-payers money into the base. Why don't all tax payers of Newbury refuse to pay their part to the MoD? Then the base occupying Greenham Common as an eyesore and blight on the area will be undermined and hopefully removed, and the Common will be rid of its worst harridan and violent squatter.'

At the camp, Beth reflected on the situation, 'While Janet was being held under the Immigration Act her solicitor managed to find out that her Home Office file dated from the time of the Fence Case – that is, our trial in Newbury Magistrates Court on October 5th, 6th and 7th 1987, resulting from eleven women having cut down the perimeter fence on 18 June 1987. Looking back, several things which were happening then now fall into place.

'This trial was heard by a Stipendiary magistrate. When the state wants to have a direct hand in what the courts do at this level, they always put in a Stipendiary magistrate. Normally there are 3 lay magistrates – the idea being that you will be tried by members of your community. A stipe is a barrister or solicitor who is paid a fee or Stipend for sitting in the court. Recently a stipe in a London court ruled that there would be no prosecutions brought against the police officers who had been involved in the beatings and frame-up of the Guildford Four. This stipe banned the press from reporting his reasons for having dismissed the charges against 3 Surrey policemen accused of perverting the course of justice in the Guildford Four case.

'So it was when we entered Newbury Magistrates court on October 5th 1987. A heavy-handed stipe sat in control of the court. He had been sent in to punish the activists at Greenham Common. This is when the Home Office began their file on Janet, with the Social Enquiry Reports on five Yellow Gate women. From this date on, Janet was being watched by the Home Office.

'The 1987 trial took place in the context of a witch-hunt against Yellow Gate women and women from the King's Cross Women's Centre in London, by the other Gates around Greenham Common at that time, who were wholeheartedly backed up by the mainstream peace movement. Thus the State could work in synchrony with this hostility – so much so that it is impossible to detect where the initial interest in Janet stemmed from. Rumours were circulating at the time that Janet and I were CIA agents, and threats were made to Yellow Gate women by those at, or associated with, the other Gates about our 'Nationality'. Lies like these were part of the the the witch-hunt – professed evidence was never forthcoming, just like the state couldn't come up with the evidence for Janet's removal, in the end, either.

'Time is gradually revealing who was and is sincerely resisting the military state and who is protecting and propping up that state by undermining the activists on Greenham Common.'

This was a time for analysing, for consolidation, for re-affirmation, but most of all, a time for continuing the struggle. We needed to support each other and to feed inspiration and motivation into each other.

Claire Pearson and Clare Downs decided that some sort of mark needed to be made to show anger at the situation the state had placed their friend and colleague in. They entered the base with specific targets in mind. The first was an MoD police prison bus inside the vehicle compound. They paint the bus with slogans such as: 'Women are angry at the deportation of Janet Tavner,' 'Justice is not law is not justice,' 'Women work in solidarity with Janet Tavner, 'Women continue the struggle against injustice.' They then move on to cover six walls of the HQ building with slogans protesting my deportation. Claire and Clare were both taken to Newbury police station and charged with Criminal Damage.

The work of the camp had to continue, to carry everyone forward. I sent a message from Stockholm that I was safe and had found lodgings. Women kept writing, calling and doing what they can for me from the camp.

In the meantime the fence preparation for the December action went ahead. There are more evictions, and vigilante attacks during the nights. The window on the camp van is smashed one night. Towards the end of October, the camp bought a tiny little caravan for the camp outside the Gate, as the van which stores all our belongings will not last much longer. The caravan is small enough for one or two women to pull off the camp area by hand in an eviction without a vehicle, and provides invaluable shelter during the pending winter storms and blizzards. The camp is being prepared for yet another winter.

On the 29th October, Katrina, Ethel and I are meant to be answering charges in Cirencester Magistrates court. Only Katrina could attend, to be told that the charges were all dropped.

On the 1st November, the funeral of Janet Cross is held in Salisbury. As Beth writes, 'we knew Janet as a friend and colleague in struggle for peace and justice. Janet's home in Tilshead was an oasis in the militarised area of Salisbury Plain. It was Janet who told us about the annual church service in Imber and sparked our interest in the history of Imber village. When we were regularly going to Salisbury Plain in resisting the Cruise missile deployments, Janet's home was always open to us, and gave protection to our drivers while they waited for the trespassers to return. In 1987 during the witch-hunts of Yellow Gate in the peace movement Janet remained openhearted and kind towards us, as she had always been.'

Time was now rapidly approaching the December weekend of action. Just a few days before, women drove to Wales to speak to Mrs Thomas about the continuation of the work to make clear how Helen was killed. Mrs Thomas expained she was considering taking private action against the police, but had not yet taken a decision. Her determination and will to struggle for justice was brought back to the camp and into The Base Must Go gathering and action.

### PRESS RELEASE

On the 14th and 15th December 1991 Yellow Gate called women to The Base Must Go weekend.

Women removed over 2000 feet of fence and proved conclusively the USAF/RAF base is a nonviable and criminal waste of taxpayers money.

At the moment there are severe cutbacks on public spending. The youth are the most affected and are prevented from taking their equal share and equal right to develop their potential, so we state once again the land and excellent facilities must be returned to the people.

Greenham Common belongs to all the people and all the people must have an opportunity to use all the Common.

The action was a complete success! The military and the police were stunned. The fence was still down a week later. A form of surrender.

But as the year of 1991, with all its sadness, its beauty, its hardships and its goodness was drawing to a close, women re-charged themselves and another strong action took place.

### PRESS RELEASE

. . . This year on the 48th anniversary of the eviction [of the Imber villagers from their homes], seven women from Yellow Gate Greenham Common Women's Peace Camp occupied the mock West Belfast streets. They lit a fire in the road and disrupted a live firing exercise. All were arrested and charged with trespassing on Military Land.

On Christmas Day, three Yellow Gate women entered the mock FIBUA (Fighting In Built Up Areas) village and wrote the names of all the children, women and men killed by plastic bullets on the mock headstones in the mock graveyard used as part of the training area for British and NATO troops. The three were arrested and charged with causing Criminal Damage to 43 headstones belonging to the Ministry of Defence.

In the very last days of the year, an oil leak is discovered on the Common. One of the USAF's vehicle fuel tanks had leaked 12,000 gallons of diesel oil onto the soil of Greenham Common. An extensive clean-up operation is put into action, but no-one knows how much of the oil is still on the ground.

1991 had now finally come to an end. The camp had seen another major war, Desert Storm, in which 300,000 Iraqi people were slaughtered, half of them civilians, 60% of them children. We had seen the courageous fight of Mrs Thomas in the High Court for the killing of her daughter to be given full examination. I had been imprisoned and exiled. But the struggle continued; the actions over the year had been powerful and strong, the politics getting clearer and clearer, the insights and understanding greater. Together, our determination, dedication and love of life took us into 1992.

# 1992
# LIVING ON THE EDGE
## by Katrina Howse

As the transition took place from '91 to '92 the reality of what had been done to Janet sunk in. The women living at the Camp were the shock absorbers. Faced with a public largely indifferent or lacking in information about us, the pressure to carry on was not from outside, but from within. The state had passed through with active malevolence and deported Janet; the public indifference felt like salt in the wound. We all felt bereft and angry, more so that Janet was deported at the time of our tenth anniversary. It was left to a few centred around the Camp and a few women internationally to raise an outcry about the exiling of Janet.

There was the important question that sometimes came out: do you think the Camp can survive? When I asked it once, I had already thought of it a hundred times. Facing January was a bleak prospect. We decided we would survive each day as we could, and continue. The Camp had to continue. Those whom we often compared to gold dust (sifted through and rare to find) were truly worth their weight in gold. Another battle for the survival of the Camp was on.

We felt bereaved by the exiling of Janet. This brought back the awful bereavement we felt when Helen was killed. Janet was one of the full-time Camp members. Beth wrote a communication asking women to put in what time they could over January, February and March. The women who supported Janet over her deportation sent in precious pledges of time. Days or weeks, it all adds to our determination to keep the Camp going.

The base infrastructure started to break up. The diesel oil which had leaked out of the fuel tanks in the Base, above our Sanctuary land, seemed to set the seal on a new, contaminated year. All of January, lorries go out of the Main Gate with contaminated soil, from excavations dug down deep into the earth – 16 on one day alone. We are sceptical that they are digging up all the contaminated soil. An equivalent amount of 'clean' soil is driven in, to replace it.

Labour announced its policy to retain 3 Trident submarines, already under construction. Mr Tom King, Defence Secretary, asks scornfully of Labour whether they would order a fourth submarine or not. In a Defence 'debate' a Tory MP says no party opposes nuclear weapons. Labour's Michael Mates MP says, 'We will retain nuclear weapons as long as other countries do while taking active steps to involve countries in the Non-Proliferation Treaty.' The year is contaminated by Trident – this is cut and dried for all the accepting MPs.

Rumours came to us that the USAF Base would close down soon.

On the 7th of January Aniko is sentenced to 7 days imprisonment for non-payment of a fine of £109.

We are getting no real information about what is going to happen to the base. We restart our continuous campaign of breaking into the base, making our way to the Commander's offices and asking, 'What is going to happen to this base?' The exchanges end at best with us being escorted out; at other times USAF men and MoD police roughly push us out. Just to go into these buildings is to encounter violent men, yet we feel we must find out what is going to happen.

It is cold winter weather. In the words of an '86 Greenham badge, KEEP WARM THIS WINTER, TAKE NON-VIOLENT DIRECT ACTION! In 20 days of freezing cold temperatures, night-time as low as minus 10 at the end of January and into February, we have two full evictions. Lisa does the latter eviction on her own, and writes in triumph in the diary, 'They left after about 20 minutes. I think I bored them by doing everything so slowly. They didn't even evict the tent or the caravan.' It's taken 11 years to reach the stage where any of our shelters would be left standing. Always we were made to 'move that tent,' 'move that plastic,' to the bitter and exhausting end.

The urgent questioning of the USAF continues. Abigail and I question Commander Neuvieux in his office. Despite security around Building 92, we get in, as do Aniko, Katharina, Emma and Lisa. It's under non-violent siege.

JANUARY 17th, 1992: first anniversary of the Gulf War. On the 15th, official US estimates of Iraqi military deaths are readjusted from 100,000 to 10,000.

On January 28th, President Bush gives his State of the Union address to the US people declaring an intent to reduce nuclear weapons and to stop new nuclear programmes, such as the Peace-keeper missiles. It's impossible to believe given his past warmongering track record.

JANUARY 22nd 1992: US Supreme Court rules that people fleeing from countries where rebel forces had tried to coerce them into military service are not entitled to political asylum.

JANUARY 25th 1992, Paris: more than 100,000 people march against the rise of right-wing extremism and racism in France and elsewhere in Europe. Many of the banners are aimed at the anti-immigration policies advocated by the National Front.

The February 4th new moon shows the British state's fixation with Trident. An announcement is made in parliament that the 4th order for Trident submarines has been placed.

On the same day Newbury MP Michael McNair Wilson has a 10 minute rule Bill passed, designed to deal with travellers and 'peace people'. It is intended to make one authorised site in the local authority's area, and those who don't go to it will be fined. Obviously they want to aim this at us. I don't know what chance this piece of fascism has of becoming law, but hearing it at the same time as the announcement for the 4th Trident submarine makes me feel uneasy. It's ominous, and it was totally unopposed.

The camp car has completely broken down, irreparable. Chris and Ralph at the garage suggest a 'new' secondhand car, and will do repairs needed on it.

The siege of Building 92 and the Commander's office continues. Aniko and I go in twice on February 14th, and interview the Base Commander about whether Trident will come to the Base. Neuvieux starts to talk from behind his Commander's desk. He says Trident is a Navy weapon, and no armament could be held in the ex-cruise missile silos. Then he says he doesn't know what the future will be.

The second time in, we see a written agenda for a meeting in a USAF office. It states dolefully that in December '91, 'Greenham women had successfully cut down the perimeter fence. The MoD had not been successful in apprehending them.' No USAF to back up the RAF, no MoD to back up the USAF.

The 'new' secondhand car arrives, thanks to Chris and Ralph – a W reg. green Ford Cortina. Immediately she gets named 'Imby' after the Pagan spring festival of Imbolc.

On February 18th Clare Downs and Claire Pearson get called in to Newbury Magistrates Court for their Means Enquiry into payment of £295.00 Compensation each for painting the MoD police prison bus with slogans against Janet's deportation.

They wrote of the Means Enquiry: 'We were given a 14 day prison sentence each for non-payment of Compensation. We felt then and still now that we were the only ones to leave that court with any integrity or self-respect. The case for the prosecution was made up of lies, manipulators and the manipulated. The magistrates again showed that the law is an ass and that they personally wouldn't know discretion or justice if it leapt up and bit them.

'To us the most important part of our defence was the affidavit of Janet Tavner which explained how she was denied human rights of the United Nations Declaration, and how we were attempting to defend her rights. It was 'heard before the court,' but not heard at all!

'The corrupt state thinks it won by finding us 'Guilty' but it lost severely by allowing its corruption to be so exposed.

'Thanks to Aniko Jones for support in court and especially to Janet Tavner, whose support and writings made it all worthwhile.'

Another blow the next day: Lisa is in the Sanctuary when two male Council officials come down the steep path onto our land and survey the mobile home.

Lisa notes, 'Two men came to the Sanctuary to serve notice to remove the mobile home. One of them I recognised as coming down when Janet and I were in the Sanctuary. We can apply for temporary permission, but it is very unlikely that it'll be granted. It just slows down the process. We can appeal against the notice to remove the mobile home. All in all it might take a whole year until, if we do not remove it, they will destroy it.'

Two harsh days, relieved a bit by Beth and I going to dinner at Lisa Gray and her husband Joe's cottage, Deepnell House, two miles away. After two tough days it is acts of hospitality like this that restore some sparkle, but more pressure follows.

When Beth and I are holding a camp depleted by two women in prison, there is a major attack on Saturday 22nd February, when at 3.30 am six drunk men coming out of the disco held in the Base throw stones at the caravan in which we are sleeping. They smash the large window.

We run out, afraid they are going to try and get in. Beth runs up to the Gate and commandeers the MoD police van, where police are standing watching – she ignores the police when they say 'Get out,' and insists they get down and arrest the men. She turns up with the police while I am talking to the men.

All six are arrested and taken to Newbury Police Station. Beth goes down and makes statements there. We don't know if they are charged or not. Beth comes back at 6.00 am, but has to leave at 8.00 am to catch a coach back to Edinburgh.

Bee arrives. That evening, Vanette, a Brazilian woman, Sarah, a Portuguese woman, and Maria arrive for dinner at 7.00 pm. Vanette speaks with real love and fervour of demonstrations of thousands of people organising tent cities. We recognise a similar passion to ours. She leaves a solidarity message and two books about rural women workers in Brazil.

Clare and Claire get out of prison on the 24th. Bee and I try to go to the Base Commissary (supermarket), but are not allowed in.

The decision to transfer our non-violent direct action intensively to Atomic Weapons Establishments Aldermaston and Burghfield was not made lightly.

Aldermaston makes the Trident nuclear warheads. Burghfield finishes them and then is the centre for transporting them by road, on a three day journey to Faslane naval base on the west coast of Scotland.

By Spring of 1992 the situation at the camp after Janet's deportation was strengthened enough to make this important step.

The Gulf War had meant a huge backlog of court cases, so we hadn't managed to complete this transition in '91, the year the last cruise missiles left. We were all aware of the need to start an intensive focus of opposition on Trident, but we were determined that it would be done well and thoroughly, step by step, as has all our resistance work.

As always the camp itself was the foundation for non-violent direct action. It needed holding, nurturing and strengthening. It was also unacceptable to us that we keep the camp going without resisting with all our strength the Trident nuclear programme, which was a five-fold increase in nuclear weapons compared with cruise missiles.

Prison gates yawned open to us again. We positively struggled to keep the camp to monitor Greenham's future use and as a base for non-violent direct action against Trident. What a decision, though, a commitment made to do what we had done to cruise missiles and the USAF Base! No lightening of the load, instead a commitment to carve out many more years of non-violent direct action work: more arrests, dangers and prison. We had no choice, but to ensure that the work was done properly. If the idea of a lessening of the load, and no more of facing guns, police and prison had seemed attractive, it was only a fantasy. The reality was that Trident needed to be stopped and being in struggle against it was always better than passively accepting it or not doing anything.

We passed over the chasm that many issue based groups fall into, but only with a tremendous commitment from a few women, and the knowledge that we were facing the successor to cruise missiles.

Rosy didn't flinch in her 'Introduction to Trident' which appeared in our next Newsletter -

'The world is not a significantly safer place now that cruise missiles have left Greenham Common. Trident missiles are now being manufactured at AWE Aldermaston, for use on submarines stationed at Faslane.

'The first submarine has been launched and the first convoy of missiles left Burghfield recently. There will be four submarines, each four football pitches long and two football pitches high.

'Each missile will have a firepower eight times more destructive than the Hiroshima bomb. At any one time, one missile can destroy 224 cities, and render them eternally uninhabitable. It is quite difficult to understand just how threatening these weapons are, but as Jim Douglas of the Ground Zero Centre for Nonviolent Action says, 'Trident is the end of the world.'

'To my mind, this is a madness which must be stopped. There must be no more Hiroshimas, and no more bombs. The plutonium which goes into the Trident weapons has a radioactive life of two hundred and fifty thousand years. The world would not recover from a Trident bomb, ever.'

We were understanding more and more what an enemy Trident was, and taking the first steps to oppose it. Aniko wrote in the Newsletter:

'On March 3rd, 1992 Erica Wilson, Katrina and I took non-violent direct action at AWE Aldermaston. As we walked through the fence an MoD man spotted us; he was unable to stop us because he was behind a second, superfence.

'We walked between the two fences, noting the sensor wires on the superfence, through a gate open in the inner fence, across a construction yard and towards the Main Street. As we were not wearing an identity tag, this led to a challenge from a worker. The worker, satisfied we had no 'right' to be there, sped off in a car to warn the police.

'We were arrested and spent three hours in custody before being released. We were reported with a view to prosecution for Criminal Damage; no charge was ever brought.

'To enter a Base known to be in the process of making one of the world's most destructive weapons systems is frightening. To come into contact with people who are so dehumanised as to work in a place of a 'final solution' to all 'enemies' is frightening. To be classed by the state who controls these weapons as an enemy is terrifying.

'We have to move beyond the state-inspired fear of the consequences of resisting, because nothing is more terrifying and life-threatening than weapons in the hands of the state. We have no security while the state continues to value the power of destruction over life. Too many people have been crushed or killed while keeping their head low and being respectable. Having a job and no criminal record will not get you a hospital bed or protect you from radiation. We have to depower the state by reclaiming our strength . . .'

There was still work to do at Greenham, also. On the 11th March the silos doors are opened. Even now that the silos are empty, the sound of them opening brings back sharp memories of fear and anger. At the same time, an air exercise involving high-powered jets shoots over the base airspace. This is a frequent occurence.

The next day, Aniko and I get into the Commander's office block again. This time they become violent in response. Aniko is pushed against a closed door by a 'new' MoD policeman.

Katharina arrives and will stay for 4 weeks. Hurrah! An extended stay from a woman is always appreciated enormously.

MARCH 19th, 1992: treasury figures reveal that the Trident nuclear submarine base on the Clyde has gone £539 million over budget due to long delays and late design changes.

A patchwork of work is stitched together, this March: another eviction survived, together with driving around Aldermaston to get more familiar with it, and myself going to London to discuss Janet's forthcoming Immigration Appeal with her solicitor, Wesley Gryk.

As Janet is now exiled in Sweden, there can be no Legal Aid to pay for legal representation. I will be Janet's advocate at the appeal, with many women called as witnesses.

Sarah brings the news that Mrs Thomas is considering taking a civil claim against the police. After the hearing at the High Court when Mr and Mrs Thomas's application for a fresh Inquest was turned down by Judge Bingham, they had striven to find ways of getting the case reopened in some way.

Beth and I are struggling to write the libel case and then have it accepted by the High Court. Beth wrote out a brilliant 'Statement of Claim' describing how I had been defamed, and suing for damages. The case is being conducted in a general atmosphere of censorship by the state of our work. Aniko and I had already pursued a Press Council complaint when Greenham was misrepresented on Woman's Hour – we had been erased on the 'Greenham Women, Greenham Men' programme on Radio 4 last summer. The libellous articles in the Sun and Daily Star tabloids were more than an attack on me, they were an attack on everything Yellow Gate stands for. It was a big case, and frightening to face, but Lisa and Aniko provided strong support at the camp for me.

APRIL 9th, 1992: General Election in Britain. For the 1987 election, Labour's defence policy had been centred on Britain's membership of NATO, in which context Britain's 'most useful possible contribution' would be through concentrating resources on its non-nuclear forces. A Labour government would therefore decommission the obsolescent Polaris system, cancel the Trident programme and use the money saved to strengthen Britain's conventional defences, the manifesto claimed.

For the 1992 election, the Labour manifesto released on Thursday March 19th states Labour would retain nuclear capability until other countries' nuclear stocks are eliminated, and provide 'whatever resources are needed for effective defence.' Labour would retain the Trident nuclear submarines, although there is some confusion as to whether this means three or four subs.

Despite the faint hope that the Conservative dictatorship might be overthrown, we all really knew that it wouldn't be, and had prepared ourselves accordingly. We had survived 11 years of Conservative rule at the camp. To say that this is like being tightrope walkers on the high wire would be an understatement! We know from history and from other struggles that long feats of endurance in struggle were done, and are being done continually. The South African struggle of Black people against apartheid showed us it could be done over a long period of many years.

General Election day is also the day of Janet's Immigration Appeal, to be held at Harmondsworth, London. Janet described her deportation and the appeal in an article sent from Stockholm:

'At the end of five weeks in Pucklechurch Prison; after many interrogations; after my life had been entirely turned upside down and I was left not knowing what would happen from one hour to the next, my removal from the UK was ordered.

'Once the decision had been taken the Home Office moved very quickly. On the 11th September I was flown to Stockholm in handcuffs with a police escort. On the other side of customs at Stockholm Airport, I was released and left.

'I have now, nine months later, managed to build up some form of life in Stockholm, very much thanks to good women in Stockholm and with the persistent help and support from the women at the camp. As well as taking care of me, the women at the camp picked up the work of carrying out an appeal of the decision to remove me. As I was not allowed to attend, Katrina Howse represented me, and did it well, and six women from the camp acted as witnesses, and did this well too. On the 16th April the determination of the appeal, by the Adjudicator, unexpectantly and surprisingly told us that the appeal was upheld. The Adjudicator ruled correctly and authoritatively too: 'On the totality of the evidence I find that the respondent has failed by a wide margin to satisfy me to the requisite degree of probability that the appellant obtained leave to enter in March 1988 by perpetrating a deception which constituted an offence under section 26(1)(c) of the Immigration Act 1971. I therefore find that she was not an illegal entrant and I allow her appeal.' The adjudicator then finds it 'appropriate to draw the attention of the Secretary of State to the fact that . . . the power to declare a person an illegal entrant – a much more Draconian provision which carries no right of appeal before removal – can apparently be exercised by an Immigration Officer subject only to the the concurrence of a Chief Immigration Officer.' The adjudicator says of the allegation of being an illegal entrant '. . . no more than hearsay upon hearsay. Indeed I entertain much doubt as to whether there was anything more positive than this before the Immigration Officer at the time he concluded the appellant was an illegal entrant.'

'The success of the appeal will make it easier for me to return, but the Home Office is trying to impede my moves. They have handed in an application to appeal the determination of the hearing.

'I wish to take this opportunity to thank every person who has worked to support me during this time. Having been the target for the Home Office's attack, I am now firmly and clearly convinced that it was the work of those who supported me that not only prepared the ground for a successful appeal, but also made it possible for me to go through the whole ordeal with a faint sense of hope and strength. Many times I could nearly visually perceive the good energy flowing through the letters sent to me while I was kept in custody.

'The last few months have clearly shown me of what vital importance accountable support is, to counteract attacks of these kinds. The Home Office counted on singling out one woman from the camp, accusing her of crimes that the British enjoy immunity from, so that it would be seen as a problem on an individual level. This never happened on a political level at the camp though. The women saw the attack for what it was, an attack on the camp, and upfront and openly fought back with me, thus taking some of the focus off me, which gave me a sense of security.'

It was a victory, as much as could be achieved with Janet still unable to come back. I felt it was the biggest court case of my life. Janet's whole future was at stake. The whole weight of the Immigration Office was against her, and us.

The Conservatives got in again – we were facing another five years of them. One infinitely small consolation was that a Liberal Democrat, David Rendel, got in as the Newbury MP, replacing the Conservative MP.

The next day, we took action against Aldermaston. Rosy described the actions with a gutsy strength:

'It felt like an important time to highlight and protest against the commitment of the state to manufacturing the most deadly weapons that men have ever invented: the Trident weapons system. Trident missiles are long-range missiles, capable of reaching and destroying any city in the world.

'The facts and figures about these weapons are deeply

disturbing, and it's equally disturbing that the state is so completely unaccountable for its life-threatening actions. The only reason the state builds such weapons and the death factories to make them is in fact not a reason at all, it's greed. All governments are greedy for power and wealth, either one of these perpetuating the other in a vicious circle of death and destruction.

'Because the state abuses its power and wealth like this, and because it pretends to be doing it to protect us, the six of us – Claire Pearson, Aniko Jones, Abigail Adams, Katrina Howse, Abi (a woman from Liverpool) and I – decided to expose its hypocrisy and brutality by undermining the killing work that is done in the name of democracy. We went in at about ten in the morning, and were inside for about a quarter of an hour, in what looked like an industrial wasteland, before we were spotted. The MoD police soon arrived, with dogs and vans. They had a bit of trouble getting us into the vans, as we weren't willing to make things easy for them. Once inside the vans, however, we got quite a good view of the genocide factory and noticed that the police were carrying guns; protecting fire with fire, bombs with bullets.

'We arrived at the processing centre, a flimsy plastic construction, and after being processed, we were left in our cells for a couple of hours. None of the police seemed to know whether we were to be charged or not, or why we were being held, and appeared to be working in a state of ignorance. We were eventually released without charge, even though we had contravened a byelaw. The rationale behind this treatment was, I think, that it's easier to cope with us if we don't get anywhere near the court to speak out against injustice.

'We refuse to be placated, because there is no room for compromise with a state that plans to annihilate the world. Four of us made the decision to trespass again, to test the state's reaction. Abigail drove Katrina, Claire, Aniko and I around the site, to look for somewhere to go in. After a while, it dawned on us that the easiest way to get in is through a gate, guarded by a lone MoD policeman in a box. We split into two groups of two, and walked past the box, closing a set of gates behind us. We were walking for quite a while down what is called the contractors' corridor, before the MoD police arrived, again with a large quantity of dogs and vans. One MoD even threatened to put Claire and Aniko in a van full of dogs.

'For the second time in a day we were processed and locked up in their cells, and again no one seemed to know if we were going to be charged with trespass, or released without charge. We were left for ages and ages whilst various MoD police took lengthy tea-breaks. The police did seem a bit baffled by our persistence and tried to account for it by explaining that it was some special occasion. At about seven in the evening, we were charged with trespass and bailed to appear in court on Monday morning.

'Aniko went in to plead Not Guilty and to hand in our Not Guilty pleas. Aniko had to agree not to go within a mile of AWE Aldermaston or Burghfield for a month and she came back with the news that there were warrants out for our arrests.

'This action, then, prompted a whole range of state responses. We were fined £20.00 at the end of a court case in which an MoD policeman stated we were a threat to national security.

'None of the state's tactics worked, really, because the day after the court case, Katrina, Aniko, Lisa Medici and I breached security once more and entered Aldermaston again. Lisa and Katrina went in in the morning, Aniko and I in the afternoon. We were all charged this time, and Katrina, Aniko and Lisa were banned from the village of Aldermaston the following weekend. So much for freedom of movement!

The struggle most definitely continues!'

1992 was a year, as all others had been, to oppose press misrepresentation, attacks and denial of us. Aniko and I went to the Broadcasting Complaints Commission to attend a hearing about my complaint against a Radio 4 programme. The Commission's response was a mixed one, but some exposure of the constant censorship we face had been achieved.

### *Greenham Women, Greenham Men*
### BBC RADIO 4

### COMPLAINT FROM
### YELLOW GATE WOMEN'S PEACE CAMP

Last autumn BBC Radio 4 broadcast *Greenham Women, Greenham Men*, a documentary about the Greenham Common women's peace movement. One of the two peace camps currently at the air base, Yellow Gate, complained to the Broadcasting Complaints Commission that the programme had unfairly represented the movement and their own part in it.

In one respect the Commission find the complaint justified. Since Yellow Gate is the only peace camp to have had a continuous presence at Greenham Common since the start of the movement, the Commission find it unfair to that camp that the programme gave no indication of its part in the movement.

Other aspects of the complaint, however, are not upheld.

Recognising that the programme was an insight into the Greenham Common peace movement through the personal recollections of some of the people involved, the Commission do not consider it unfairly concentrated on three protesters or that certain remarks were prejudicial to any particular group. The Commission also do not find unfairness to Yellow Gate camp in the programme's emphasis on particular events or aspects of the movement and the omission of others, including the death of Helen Thomas, one of the Yellow Gate demonstrators.

On another point we were reassured by the reason given for our omission from these radio or TV lightweight documentaries ('obscumentaries' would be a better word for them) – the explanation given by the BBC editor of this documentary for not including the interviews with Yellow Gate women was that they were too political. Beth and I had made a point in the interviewing of speaking about Helen being killed, and about Janet going to be deported. This wasn't what the BBC wanted to report.

Rosy got 7 days in prison for obstruction of a British Army Arms Fair at Whale Island, near Portsmouth. She gets good news on her release – on a routine incursion into the Commander's office, she reads on the desk top diary under September 30th, 'BASE CLOSED'. We can hardly believe it! Rosy and Aniko break into the base four times that day to express our joy at the news. (Multiple goings-in was a long established part of our repertoire.) This news was what we had worked for. Over these past few years we had said over and over again, if only the base would close finally we could put all our focus into opposing the making of Trident nuclear warheads at Aldermaston and Burghfield. It was going to be, that which we had hunted down for 11 years: a base of one of the biggest military powers in the world closed down.

There was also a financial crisis in the States. The billions squandered in the Gulf War were now sorely missed. Poor people in Los Angeles rioted against racism and poverty. Large scale rebellion at home made the military empire draw back, and the grip the USAF had held on Greenham Common for 50 years was broken.

Newbury District Council hoisted up the flag of No Surrender, as the USAF were about to take their's down for good. On the eviction of the 13th May, we notice the bailiffs have a new dark green van. No retreat for them! Did they know the USAF were about to desert them and their new green van? We know how much the local persecutors saw the USAF as their demi-gods. The Liberal Democrats were taking over the Council. The new green van was not such a jaunty symbol of eviction persecution as the new red muncher of the early '80's had been.

Still, the NDC orders were given and the bailiff army still marched, ritually evicting our tents while we ever stayed on in the open air, keeping the camp. Our studied disregard of the bailiffs and polite indifference sometimes made it seem as though they had come to watch us evict ourselves. The bad evictions were always the ones in which they made us angry through tiredness. Mostly the evictions were as much a test of mental endurance as physical. If you engaged with 3 or 4 bailiffs and 2 police in a furious exchange, they had you. They had it all, the game worked out, perfected over the years. Evict, evict and evict again. In these evictions we were made to move the small caravan that had taken 10 years to achieve placing at our camp. So, although 'only' two evictions in May and June, there it still was. The work of the eviction, the polite indifference that said more than anger could, 'You have never broken our spirits with the evictions, never.' Yes, they could make us evict, just as they could send us to prison. There is no point beating against prison doors nor evictions. They could not crack the enduring power within us that kept us outside the Main Gate of Greenham Common.

The MoD police army still marched on, occupying the base, but they also knew that without the USAF they couldn't stay on long. What a double act that had been, alternately sniping at each other over the years but basically buddies in the business of mutually assured destruction. Still territorial, they prowled their patch. When Abigail and I made one of many incursions into the empty silos, they vastly over-reacted with 5 MoD police, 2 dog handlers and dogs. All they can do now is escort us out.

On May 18th the state's verdict on the legality of the fence at Greenham Common was given at Oxford Crown Court, in response to the appeals of Sarah Hipperson, Jean Hutchinson and Georgina Smith.

One of the major legal arguments used was based on our right, indeed our responsibility, to take action to prevent genocide. The Genocide Act was ratified by the United Nations in 1948, and became British law in 1969. This act was a direct response to the genocide of 6 million Jewish people during the 2nd World War. The point of the Genocide Act is to prevent genocide being committed ever again, through the apprehension of those planning or committing it. We had used this law many times before, always aware of the horror of the Holocaust. It was obvious to us that genocide was being planned in the aiming of cruise missiles at the Soviet Union. The Act specifically deals with the planning of genocide.

Judge Lait accepted there is a right to take preventive action under the Genocide Act; however, nuclear weapons, he rules, are not genocidal weapons. He tries to make sense of that statement by saying nuclear weapons are not aimed at a specific group of people because they are that group. Therefore the women who cut the fence in June 1987 had no right under the Genocide Act to do so. Judge Lait agrees that the erection of the fence on Greenham Common was illegal. The fence is under the ownership of the Crown and the Crown cannot be prosecuted for breaking the law. The fence being illegal is no defence. He made it very clear that women on the Common had no rights of Common: Jean Hutchinson and Georgina Smith knew they had no rights of Common, but Sarah Hipperson had a mistaken belief she did have Commoners rights to cut down an illegal fence around the Common. A mistaken belief is a defence. Judge Lait allowed Sarah Hipperson's appeal but not Jean Hutchinson's nor Georgina Smith's. Jean had her 2-month sentence reduced to the day she had spent in the police cells. Georgina Smith had her 3-month sentence reduced to the 8 days she spent in Holloway in 1987.

The day of the judgement, new fence posts were brought into the base. It seemed the state would always move the goal posts, never the fence posts!

The Aldermaston Byelaws cases were heard in Newbury Magistrates Court, scene of all the Greenham Byelaws cases. On the 22nd May, Rosy, Claire, Aniko and I are up. The Crown Prosecutor tells the court there is no defence for breaking the Byelaws, a concept the Magistrates accept. The court case is reduced to a mere formality. Before the Magistrates deliver their verdict, we're allowed to sum up our evidence. Claire Pearson's summing up did what it always did, transform the case into a living, breathing act of resistance:

'I entered AWE Aldermaston because I feel that it is my right to know what goes on in there. It is my belief the Trident warheads are manufactured there and I wished to confirm my belief. When I pay taxes some of that money is spent on the military and in establishments such as Aldermaston. I have no say in how this money is spent and the information is not made public. I do not ask it to be spent on the military. The military and its weapons are referred to as existing for our defence, yet when I try to find out what the role of places like Aldermaston is I am treated as the enemy. I was in Aldermaston as a nonviolent woman, as were my colleagues, yet I was met with violence by the police.

'I have heard of figures running into millions of pounds being spent on Trident every day. This money should be spent on saving the lives of those people dying because of starvation or killer diseases, such as Aids. As a nuclear weapon, Trident poses a terrible threat not only to humans but to the environment. At a time when world leaders are about to hold a conference on how to save the environment it seem ludicrous to me that so much money is still being pumped into weapons such as Trident, which have the capacity to destroy the environment entirely.

'I deplore the way that this money is being spent on preparations for Genocide . . . I do not feel that by simply trying to find out what atrocities go on inside Aldermaston I have committed any offence. I was in the base as a nonviolent woman and harmed nobody, yet those people who are preparing for Genocide are protected from me and I am the one who is in court today, not these murderers.'

The following day we are back at AWE Aldermaston. Lisa notes: 'Women trespass in Aldermaston! 2 groups of women go in and get arrested & charged with trespass. Plea dates – 6th July.' It's a hot week. Aldermaston has a poignancy in such weather. The Earth breathes even there, the scent of the pine trees meets us as we make our way through two sets of fences. There are little muslin 'catchers' on posts, to catch radioactive dust and measure radioactivity levels. A 19th century device!

It's time to start taking on AWE Burghfield. Aniko comments, 'Lisa and I went to have a good look around Burghfield, and were tailed after we had gone halfway around the base. It has wires inside the fence similar to Aldermaston. No silo-type fencing, looks as if security not as good as Aldermaston. There is only one way to find out.'

Despite the courage women show in actions, these two places are frightening to enter. We know radioactivity is unseen, all around us, in the air, in the Earth and water at Aldermaston and Burghfield. However careful we are, we know we are closer to the contamination inside. The contamination doesn't just stop at the fence, it spills out, into the winds, rivers, the Earth. It is already in our cells and bones from all the atomic bomb tests, nuclear power and nuclear bomb production. We are the contaminated generations, that was our fate. We could, though, and can, stop it so that not everyone and everything is poisoned and destroyed.

We also have a responsibility to the people of the Pacific region, to Aboriginal Australian people and to Native American people who have been inflicted with the brunt of nuclear contamination. It is the genocidal colonialism of the British, American and French states that has poisoned their land and people to a much greater extent than we have had to face.

So, no choice again, but to go in and try to stop it, do what you can! We walk in Aldermaston aware of our double helix genes, wondering how much they are being damaged, what radioactive load our thyroids are picking up, what is settling in our bones, damaging our cells. We are conscious of what we are forced to be conscious of, the radioactive contamination that makes the Aldermaston area a childhood leukaemia and cancer cluster area. We are conscious of the workers who have died, a tiny splinter of plutonium in the finger, in the end the death of a man.

Now going into the base at Greenham Common when the security is no longer so intense seems so much simpler than straining our senses in contaminated Aldermaston and Burghfield.

Also, like the USAF at Greenham, the MoD police are armed with pistols and huge sub-machine guns. They are armed at the main gates of AWEs Aldermaston and Burghfield, and also patrolling inside. They tote their machine guns as though in their patriarchal minds they are an extension of their bodies. We feel a deep revulsion and fear when we look at these police. The unbroken threat of guns is going to continue.

Then, we are brought back to '85, '86, '87, when going into the base at Greenham Common meant arrests under their Byelaws, and eventual prison. We apply for a Judicial Review in my name, to try to get Compensation for all the prison we have done under Heseltine's Byelaws. There was a team of us eyeing up the High Court on the 12th June: Margaretta D'Arcy and John Arden from Ireland, Sarah and I from the camp, and Laura Logan, Kay Chapman and Sian Evans from the King's Cross Women's Centre. The application to have the Judicial Review is granted and we are over the first hurdle.

Claire has her Means test for her £20.00 fine under the Aldermaston Byelaws. She gets 5 days in Holloway, the first woman to go to prison under these Byelaws.

New beginnings, but also endings. On June 21st we pay our last visit to Harriet Smith of Newbury. On June 29th Harriet died aged 82 years old. Harriet was a true friend to me, and to women living on Greenham Common.

I remember going into the Rokeby Arms pub in the autumn of 1982, when the camp had had a major eviction and we were learning to live in makeshift shelters, during a constant rain downpour that seemed to last a mythic 30 days and 30 nights. Every day we got soaked, but during the evenings different groups of women would go to the Rokeby. There we would dry out, and there we met Harriet.

Harriet made it clear right from the start that she was with us, and soon became a friend. Harriet would always speak up for 'the girls,' and many of us must have seemed very young in our late teens or early twenties. In friendships with older and young women Harriet treated us with kindness and understanding. Harriet understood people, she could assess character very quickly and wisely, but never unfairly. This made Harriet such a strong supporter of the camp – she knew the different reactions for and against us in the surrounding community. Harriet introduced us to people, and this broke down the hostility to us.

The kindness of the landlord and his wife who left a mysterious hamper of goodies by our van door Christmas '82 in the Rokeby car park, was also to do with Harriet. Harriet wore a white dove of peace brooch on the lapel of her blouse every night she was in the Rokeby.

Harriet was born in Ireland, the landlord and his wife were Irish people, and the Rokeby was one of the pubs used by the Irish community in Newbury. The 'crack' was the sparkle of conversation, the humour, everything that was going on, and Harriet enjoyed knowing what the crack was.

Harriet had worked as a nurse in the Sandleford Hospital across the road from the Rokeby from the late 1920's until her retirement. From 1987 onwards Harriet became housebound in her bungalow, after a very serious illness. Several of us visited Harriet in her new home. Despite going through asthma attacks, Harriet would be alert and interested in what was happening at the camp.

In November '91 Harriet fell and broke her pelvis. She couldn't have an operation because of her lung condition so for months she was weighted down by traction. Miraculously her pelvis healed, and with great courage she refused to take pain killers or sleeping pills.

For five and a half years Harriet's son Jimmy looked after Harriet at home. Jimmy was a strong support for Harriet.

In our last visit Harriet told us she always knew we would get rid of cruise missiles. Being strong, and believing you must do what is right, Harriet could always see the strength of our position.

In the last years I admired her courage more and more. From being housebound she became confined to her bed, but she always retained her intelligence, understanding and courage.

Harriet's death is a sad loss for her sons, grandchildren and great-grandchild.

We will miss her wisdom, courage and support. Harriet told us we were put here to help one another, that's what she believed and that's what she did.

On the 25th the Immigration Department withdraw their appeal against the successful ruling Janet had received.

The last American Day of Independence celebrations are held in the base on the 4th July. Ethel Carlsson, who regularly each summer spends weeks with us at the camp, wrote to a friend in Sweden:

'The days are going so quick in this camp. It is good to have the caravan with a gas ring inside. We are being evicted once a week, but the caravan does not have to be moved every time. I have a new tent I bought in Sweden and luckily it is waterproof. After breakfast I wash, maybe go wooding, fetch water, wash up, wash some of my own clothes, talk with other women or read for a while. The others work part time, so often somebody has to go off for work, some of the others for a court case or for an action or for preparing those things or just shopping, but there always has to be at least one woman holding the camp, so I feel useful. We have visitors of different kinds now and then.

'The Americans are leaving Greenham Common Airbase now . . . On the 4th of July Lisa and I went in with banners and showed them to about a hundred persons on a feastplace inside Greenham base. My banner said WEAPONS RISK ALL LIVES, PROTECT NONE and Lisa's said WOMEN SAY NO TO MEN'S THREAT TO AND DESTRUCTION OF LIFE. Aniko had helped us to find the right place to walk in. She had also helped me to be able to press the alarm button of the sentry box just inside the Main Gate the evening before on our way out after a reconnaissance.

'Other times when we went into the base this summer we have walked out through the guarded gate, undisturbed and not until we wanted to, but this day they took us out in a van and asked for our names. But that was all that happened. We were not arrested. A court has settled that the fence around this base is illegal, but the state cannot be prosecuted and activists are not allowed to take down illegal fence.

Because I feel uncertain about my job in Sweden I am not going to take actions against Aldermaston or Burghfield myself, at least not this year, but I do admire the women who do. They deserve all support we can give them!

Best wishes, Ethel.'

The court work continues in its cycle, placing stronger restrictions on our individual political freedoms. At the plea date for more Aldermaston Byelaws charges at Newbury Magistrates court, harsh bail conditions are placed on Lisa, Rosy, Aniko and I not to go within one mile of AWE Aldermaston up until the court case. It's hard to agree, but it means instant prison to disagree, and the camp needs holding.

Back to London to the High Court again, this time to accept a minimal amount of Costs and an apology in open court from the Daily Star, as a result of the libel action I had taken against them. This leaves us to prepare for the full case against the SUN with a narrower and stronger focus.

The summer is passing, as it always does, with sustained work.

The programme of non-violent direct action, court cases and camp work sets our pace. I have never known a summer not to be a working summer, months of a rigorous, mind challenging programme which unfolds itself. We are always strengthened by the Common, the wildlife and our gardens.

Mr and Mrs Thomas are told by a London solicitor that it would cost as much as £30,000.00 to sue the police for Helen's death. Also, because Helen had no 'dependants' in the form of children, she was seen in the eyes of the state and courts not to be of high monetary value! This just summed up the brutality and sexism of this state. This brought inevitably more sadness and anger. We had had a hope that one day Helen being killed by a policeman would be exposed in the courts, and justice would be done. We now knew this would never happen in a court in Britain.

In the middle of July the first convoy of Trident warheads is taken by road on a three day journey from Burghfield to Faslane, Scotland. We knew we would have to start watching for these convoys, and non-violently resisting them.

We try when we can to get to Silbury Hill, Avebury stone circle and West Kennet Long Barrow, ancient matriarchal sacred sites. To go there is to be refreshed spiritually in the struggle against the patriarchy and its militarism. Ethel and Aniko partake of a refreshing trip, and then Ethel leaves 'til next year.

It is Lammas time, August 1st, a first fruits festival, and one of the eight major pagan festivals of the year. It is a quarter day, one of the four festivals between the Solstices and the Equinoxes. Court cases are the fruits of our non-violent direct actions. We have always seen the fruit of our work and been pleased with its integrity. On August 3rd, Judith and Beth attended Devizes Magistrates court for their Criminal Damage trial resulting from having painted 45 headstones belonging to the MoD in the mock FIBUA village. Both are arrested on arrival at the court. The police say they have some paperwork to clear up, and for some reason they can only do their paperwork while Judith and Beth are locked up. They are transferred from a holding cell in the court to Devizes police station at lunch time, given something to eat in their cell there, then taken back to the court and held again until the end of the court day. When they're brought up in court, the prosecution produce a book of photographs of the painted mock headstones and say, 'These speak for themselves.' They ask for £306.00 Compensation plus £100.00 Costs from each. Judith and Beth both say that they had done the painting, and explain why. They're not fined.

On the same day, the Imber case is heard. A full complement of women defend themselves: Honor, Emma, Lisa, Claire, Clare, Margaretta and I. We're all found Guilty, as usual, and fines range from £100.00 to £40.00, with 28 days to pay. A busy day – the Newsletter is taken to the printers, as well.

Janet Thomas visits the following day, having travelled all the way from Newcastle Emlyn, Dyfed, Cymru. This is a very precious visit for us all, the day before Helen's memorial day. We regard it as a great honour that Helen's mother wishes to visit and spend time with us, over the time of year when Helen was killed. Abigail recorded in our Newsletter, '. . . in the days preceding August 5th 1992, Janet Thomas had written to Sergeant Dunn, the driver of the West Midlands Police horsebox that had killed her daughter. She showed us the letter: it was a calm request from the heart, saying that although she did not intend to bring Dunn to court, and soon it would be beyond her power to do so, that did not lessen the need in her to know the final seconds of Helen's life; that she did not directly accuse him of responsibility, but that the obvious discrepancies at the inquest and the unsatisfactory nature of the verdict left her with the question: Why? As he was in fact the only person in the world who knew the answer to this question, she asked him to tell her. She then showed us the reply Dunn had sent her: it was a cold and calculated letter, which in its very manner, given the nature of her request, insulted the honesty and sincerity of what she had written. He apologized for the delay in responding, pleading an excess of work, and said there was nothing he could add to what had been said at the inquest. Then, in a final insult, he added that it would be best for all concerned that the matter be put behind them! Janet's letter was several pages long – his reply barely covered one side . . .'

The memorial day, August 5th, is always a day different to any other. As women gather, it is as though a loving hush falls over the camp. To spend this day together in quiet reflection and focused anger is absolutely necessary for all of us. Judith Walker wrote about this year's memorial in our Newsletter: 'All the camp had been moved into the clearing, a shrine was set up for the day with flowers and candles. We sat underneath the poplar trees in a silent vigil and held hands in a circle around one o'clock which is the time when Helen died . . . In 1992 the situation was different. Aniko explained that it had not been possible to have the verdict changed and that now, exactly three years after Helen's death, no further claims to the legal system can be made. In other words, there is no official way left to bring out the truth.

'We talked this over and found that since the state had absented itself from the demand for justice, the work to publicize the truth remains within the camp. If Helen had survived, she herself could make clear what happened when the horse van hit her. We cannot come to terms with her having been killed, and we will speak up for her who lost her life and her voice.

'Similar things have happened in other countries where political activists died under suspicious circumstances which the authorities were reluctant to inquire into. Not only the armies, but also the police forces, officially have an ultimate option to kill 'in emergencies.' This attitude towards violence does have an effect on policemen, its 'milder' consequences can be experienced at once when someone resists the state.

'Those of us who know Helen will not forget her, all of us who know about her will not forget her death and the events following it. It is sat to be constantly reminded and at times it is hard to tell the story to visitors who are seldom prepared. But there is no choice. Apart from some contacts with the alternative network and through taking non-violent direct action, the camp has no access to the media. So in the afternoon of the 5th of August we decided to hold a vigil outside Newbury Police Station, where the cover-up started. Later in the evening women walked down the High Street of the air base carrying the banner used in the afternoon and singing against the military for whose sake the cover-up has been committed.'

The next days are Hiroshima and Nagasaki days, and time to take non-violent direct action. This year, six women take action at AWE Burghfield. One woman is released without charge, and the remaining five are taken to Reading police station for charging. On Nagasaki day, five of us take action at AWE Aldermaston. Rosy said in the Newsletter, 'Non-violent direct action to stop the production of Trident nuclear warheads is one of the very few ways I've encountered so far to break the silence of consent surrounding these weapons. When the peace camp was first set up, everyone knew about cruise missiles and everyone knew that the 101 missiles lodged in the silos had a profound effect on the whole population; pro or anti-military. Ten years later, there's no cruise, but five times the amount of nuclear missiles are being made in a Reading suburb, and everyone is congratulating themselves and feeling safe in a post cold-war world. This is madness. Even if Trident warheads are never exploded, the production process alone is enough to wreck the immune system of every living thing that ever steps out of doors, through absorbing drastically increased amounts of atmospheric radiation.'

August 16th, Helen's birth date, passes quietly and remembered by us.

Warmongering continues unabated as Prime Minister Major

sends 6 Tornado planes to patrol Iraq.

Then to remind us that routines are back to normal, there is an eviction on the 19th.

A huge part of the work is balancing the camp back into our normal routines, covering our daily commitments and preparing for new moral challenges to Trident nuclear weapons. This last challenge takes us to Reading Magistrates court on September 4th to plea to the charges laid against us in August. We all enter pleas of Not Guilty and the dates for the two court cases are set for the 1st and 7th of December. More bail conditions are imposed: we are not to go within a quarter of a mile of either Aldermaston or Burghfield. We apply to the High Court for the bannings to be lifted. Aniko describes her visit to London: 'It was in early October when I had to go up for the hearing. We have to challenge every restriction the MoD put on our movements; this meant challenging the bannings. I believe every push against the state weakens it. In one of the many small rooms at the High Court, there sat myself, Sarah Hipperson who came to support me, the MoD solicitor and the High Court judge. The MoD solicitor argued that because my motives were political my actions were more dangerous. He produced my Criminal Record to show how active I had been against the military and that this was not a one off incident. I wanted to make it clear that I was not a member of a political party, as well as making the point that I have a democratic right to protest and that being outside military bases is not a crime. My actions were motivated by a belief that if the military are not stopped then there would be no future. The judge said he did not doubt my beliefs but he accepted the MoD solicitor's argument. Later this month Katrina and Lisa received the same treatment at the High Court. Abigail, who had not been charged with any offence to do with AWE Aldermaston yet had been banned from there as well as from AWE Burghfield, did not even receive a reply from the High Court.'

We were well aware we were banned from both Atomic Weapons Establishments at a time when the transportation of Trident nuclear warheads had begun.

September 5th arrives and Yellow Gate Greenham Common Women's Peace Camp is 11 years old. This is a proud day for us! The sense of our history of struggle seems to lie all around us, rustling in the leaves of the historic poplar trees, speaking in the stones and pebbles at our feet, living in the fire that crackles on Greenham Common. We are proud, we have stood against everything that the state could hurl at us.

Back to court on the 8th, for more Means enquiries. Honor, Rosy and I are sent to prison for 5 days, 5 days and 7 days respectively. We had made sure the court understood that 7 days is a shorter sentence than 5 days. As Honor is pregnant she is sent to the mother and baby wing, Rosy and I are kept together. I end up getting out on the Friday because 7 days prison means you are eligible for remission, which brings it to 4 days, but 5 days means 5 days so Rosy and Honor stay in until Saturday.

We are challenging the validity of the Aldermaston and Burghfield Byelaws, and doing legal research to back up our claim. Just by offering evidence before the next trials and making the challenge, the Crown Prosecution Service are put into such uncertainty about the Byelaws that they drop the cases, rather than have the Byelaws proved invalid. From this date on, we are never charged under the Aldermaston or Burghfield Byelaws again! The prison they had inflicted on us hadn't stopped us, and the Byelaws came tumbling down. The Aldermaston trespass cases are formally dropped on September 16th, the Burghfield ones on September 21st.

Persistent non-violent direct action backed up with legal challenges had advanced us a step further. We can now go through the odd open Gate at Aldermaston without being charged under the Byelaws. Burghfield is different – we have to cut the fence to get into Burghfield. From now on the MoD police were to try to get us under Criminal Damage charges.

It is a month of court cases. On 18th September I plead Not Guilty to Criminal Damage of Building 92, USAF headquarters, during the Gulf war. At the same time the case of Criminal Damage to the silos fence is dropped. Both actions were carried out with Janet, but only the Gulf war case against me will proceed. If this court case scenario appears confusing, imagine living it! The legal arguments prepared, expectation of the court battle and mentally working yourself up to that, then . . . case dropped. Whenever this happened, we realised even more that charging us had been a battle to make us stop taking non-violent direct action. Well, cases dropped meant a space in our programmes which could be filled with another strong moral challenge. Room for another court case! There is a group of us who are never off bail, or continually waiting on fines, non-payment of which always leads to prison.

As if all the September court isn't enough, on the 29th an eviction is thrown in by Newbury District Council. All the separate persecuting authorities like to 'keep their hand in.' Now this was a sad eviction, for the historic pram of so many Greenham photos, that held tins and other food containers, is consigned to the rubbish van, and finally driven away.

On the 30th September 1992 the USAF base closes down. It is returned to the Ministry of Defence and the Main Gate is padlocked and left. As this blocks entrance to the Common land, women repeatedly take the padlocks off. The MoD police whitemail us – if we don't stop taking the padlocks off, they'll put concrete blocks up, and in the event of a road accident on the A339, they won't be able to get out and help and it will be ALL OUR FAULT.

It is strange to walk through the ex-base. The land is very dear to us, especially as it is the land of so much struggle. The United States Air Force have finally gone, leaving their buildings. Thousands and thousands of people had been put here for military strategy, then taken away to fulfill another military strategy. Their bewilderment still hangs in the air. We were the only ones in the 1990's who knew what our mission was. Their mission could only have been successful if cruise missiles had exploded in a nuclear war! The end of all Life. There it is, the bewilderment, also the patriarchal disappointment. It is with profound relief and gratitude that we walk through the ex-base.

What is left are memories of the military encountered when we had to break the mission of the base. Airmen with submachine guns, who shook when they grabbed our arms. Black American people as a distinct group, oppressed within the military, who joined the military as a way out of the ghettoes, the racism, the enforced poverty. With us it was never 'Yanks Go Home,' the complexity of all the issues and the racism in Britain and the United States could never allow that.

Summer is over. The 15th October eviction is at 9.15am. Lisa has an interview at Newbury District Council offices to try and find out why we are the only camp to be evicted. They promise a written answer.

Safety and security at the camp again becomes a problem. On November 7th, an attacker attempts to rape a woman visiting Green Gate. He broke into her tent as she put her candle out at 03.00am. She bravely fought him off, and he ran away. The Sanctuary is close to Green Gate and as Green Gate packs up in response, an air of danger permeates the area. We become furious, ready to challenge and fight any time of the day or night.

The libel case is set for an opening of November 23rd, but is in fact settled at the eleventh hour, before the trial begins. So much work went into this case. Beth Junor did tireless research on how to proceed with each stage, as well as endless writing for the Statement of Claim and other areas of the case. We didn't know how to proceed with the case, it was a question of research and trial and error. I got used to having my forms sent back by the High Court. Each time, I would think, third time lucky!

Aniko Jones and Lisa Medici were tireless too, advising and helping with the casework, also driving me to the phone, to case hearings in London and to town.

Legal Action for Women from the King's Cross Women's Centre attended hearings, contributed a major bundle in the case, and prepared a witness statement with my expert witness on unwaged work, Selma James.

Many political activists, writers and artists wrote excellent witness statements, which were bound in their own court bundle in purple, green and white ribbon and which played an important part in pushing the SUN back. These people were: Aniko Jones, Janet Tavner, Lisa Gray, Isabel Strang, Jean Hutchinson, Sarah Hipperson, Abigail Adams, Margaretta D'Arcy (Ireland), John Arden (Ireland), Susanna Frazer (Canada), Meryl Olsen (Canada), Ethel Carlsson (Sweden), William Ash, Janus Avivson, Ute Henjes (Germany), Adrian Mitchell and Selma James.

I made the following Statement in Open Court on the settlement of the action:

'This is an action for damages for libel, brought by me, Katrina Howse, against News Group Newspapers in respect of the SUN of November 3rd 1990.

The Defendant alleged in that article that I was a 'Scrounger' who had received '8 years of handouts,' who was 'refusing to get a job' and 'refusing to pay poll tax.'

. . . I am a recognised professional mural artist – I run my own business and have set up an artistic workshop on Greenham Common. I am an artist who exhibits in London and have exhibited at venues nationally and internationally.

I have never refused to get a job, and I am not liable to pay poll tax because of the basic facilities and the situation of Yellow Gate Greenham Common Women's Peace Camp.

In fact I do a huge amount of unwaged work, non-violently opposing cruise missiles and Trident warheads: unpaid work which my conscience compels me to do, and which has led me to spend 8 months in prison and 10 years of my life living at Yellow Gate.

My hurt was compounded by the fact that the article not only refused to recognise the validity of all the unpaid work I have done, but also attacked me for that work.

Being poor and in a vulnerable situation, I had no buffer between myself and the article.

The Defendant now realises that there was not the slightest foundation for any of these allegations, and is here today by their counsel to apologise to me for having made them and to withdraw unreservedly all imputations upon me.

The Defendant has also agreed to pay a sum by way of damages and to pay my costs.

As I brought these proceedings with the sole object of clearing my name, I am content now to let the matter rest.

It only remains for me to ask leave that the money paid into the court by the Defendant [as an initial offer, which I refused] and the interest thereon be paid out to the Defendant, and for leave to withdraw the record.'

We have a Burghfield court case on December 1st and an Aldermaston case on December 7th. The Burghfield case for cutting the fence and going into AWE Burghfield on Hiroshima Day is defended by Abigail, Rosy, Lisa, Aniko and myself. We are judged by a Stipendiary magistrate, who was brought in for the case. Everyone is eloquent and strong in explaining the reasons we took the action.

The Aldermaston case is tough going because the second Stipendiary magistrate brought in to deal with us is determined to stop us expressing the reasons why we took this action. I am taken down to the cells for lunchtime (with no lunch) for refusing to be shut up. I preferred to be in the cells than constantly interrupted by him. Rosy is taken to the cells, after I've been brought back up. The court was filling up with police. It's hard to have a public trial when the media dutifully keep silent. There was one reporter in the court from the Reading Evening Post, but his report didn't convey how oppressive the court case was. The fines and costs were about £75.00 each. So was that it? No, he was determined to separate us on our Criminal Records, the only way that he could separate us. He demands that I agree to be bound over to keep the peace. I refuse and I'm sent to prison for 28 days. He then demands the same of Aniko, she refuses, and is sent to prison for 28 days. In their prison visits Abigail, Lisa and Rosy are strongly behind us not agreeing to be bound over. Three and a half weeks later on New Year's Eve we're released from Holloway. Lisa was there to meet us. It was a victory all round!

The symbolism of being released on New Year's Eve didn't escape us. For us all, it was a release and a coming together again to continue the struggle in 1993. We asked for good strength to face a New Year, not for good luck or good fortune – each of these is arbitrary; we had to make our struggle anew, year by year.

# 1993
# BRANCHING OUT
## by Rosy Bremer

Received military wisdom has it that it is a disaster to commit yourself on two fronts. Non-violent activists have a different experience. Our struggle is always branching out enormously; staying rooted on the Common, nurtured by the power of this land, we encompass AWE Aldermaston, AWE Burghfield, RAF Wittering in Cambridgeshire, as well as bases in East Anglia into our daily routine of resistance.

In 1993 we learnt a lot more about the convoys of nuclear warheads travelling from Burghfield to Faslane through checking and tracking them. The transition time was over, now it was time for consistent work against Trident. It was also the state's time for lashing back, with all the power available to it.

Heavy prison sentences ran throughout the year for women taking action against the convoys of Trident warheads on the roads. Claire got 56 days, as did Aniko. Aniko received an additional 2 months, for actions against AWE Burghfield. These sentences were later reduced on appeal. Katrina served her 18th prison sentence. I was held on remand for a week, and was then in and out of prison.

The military hit back directly, when a soldier threatened to shoot Katrina, Lisa and Melanie, when they were in a field outside the fence at RAF Wittering, opposing the convoy on an overnight stop.

We saw an increasingly wider interest in Aldermaston, with the likes of Greenpeace holding a public meeting. Interest in the Common itself also gathered momentum. Speculation in the media was rife; Newbury District Council stepped up its input, producing and publicising proposals for the Common, and the Defence Land Agent's chosen estate agents, Vail Williams, enticed the first few small businesses onto the Common.

For our part, we stepped up our tenacity in holding onto the the camp and lodged an application for a Judicial Review of Newbury District Council's eviction notice.

We were greatly boosted by having Peggy Walford strengthen her connection with the camp this year. Peggy is in her 70's, and after having been on the original Aldermaston marches is still on the frontline of non-violent resistance. She is proud to have been born on the same day as Nelson Mandela, two years later.

Aniko and Katrina's release from Holloway marks the start of the year. Aniko describes the sentence in our 1993 Newsletter: '. . . The symbol of what I experienced during my sentence was – food. This was the longest sentence I had ever done and my life became dominated by food.

'The tedium of the prison system was broken up by the meal times. Women have so little control over how they spend their time it engenders boredom. Women who are serving long prison sentences do have jobs in Holloway. I have no experience of having a paid job but I do know their wages are pitifully low, a good wage being £8.00 a week for working from 9.00 to 5.00. These wages make life more bearable.

'The food is atrocious, reinforcing the attitude of the establishment to women. Little effort goes into preparing the food or providing any variety. You can very quickly learn to predict what the next meal will be, and without exception it will be bland and unappetizing. One is made to realise how fundamental food is to one's life. To have control of this important element for life taken away, means having control of your existence taken away. This has a powerful effect on your psyche. This control is enforced in many ways. You cannot say what you need or like or at what time you want to eat. Breakfast is at 8.00am, lunch at 11.15am, tea at 3.15pm and at 7.00pm you could have tea and a biscuit. This regime is imposed on women without any regard to their need or wishes.

'After a while under this regime you begin to notice the effect the lack of a varied and balanced diet has on your health. This is exacerbated by the oppressive and unhealthy atmosphere of the prison. Women are often constipated because of the stodgy food. Stodgy food gives the illusion of filling you up without providing nourishment. Again symbolic of the illusion of a constructive and fair prison system.

'Any attempt to alter your diet because of a specific health reason, politics or religion is met with a slow infuriating bureaucracy. To fight just for a balanced diet is a demoralising energy-consuming exercise, reinforcing the fact your well-being is not important nor respected. While I was there three women risked their Christmas home leave to pick up food thrown over the prison wall. They were discovered and put in the punishment block, losing their 'privilege' of spending a few days with their family for Christmas.

'It was a long time before I could face eating some types of food which reminded me of Holloway. It was when I could face baked beans again I knew I had recovered from the last prison experience. An experience I will face again, but with a strong peace camp and good support from women I know, it is survivable.'

19 days after their release from prison, Aniko and Katrina are threatened with another Means Enquiry. Both had asked for their fines

244

to be dealt with whilst they were in prison. Newbury Magistrates court sat on this request for prompt action, and duly hauled the women in on the 19th.

Katrina explains to the court that they had requested they deal with the fines earlier and that they had not done so. She argues this is not normal practice. Both women state their intention to appeal the magistrates decision. This is enough to put the magistrates off imposing a sentence of several days, but keen as ever to be seen to uphold the rule of law, they sentence Aniko and Katrina to a day in the cells. The women are released at 4 o'clock in the afternoon, and make it back to a welcoming camp.

On the 26th January Newbury magistrates give Clare Downs a similar sentence, with an added half hour, when she attends her Means Enquiry.

We resume watching Burghfield for the Trident convoys in February. On February 2nd, the festival of Imbolc, women drive to AWE Burghfield, and this routine carries on for 10 days. It means you're up early in the morning, into the car, and away to Burghfield. If there's no convoy in, you're back again within a couple of hours. If a convoy is in the vehicle compound (and incidentally, there's no mistaking the huge 48 ton military green foden warhead carriers), you sit and you wait and wait and wait for any signs of the convoy drivers and personnel. You can tell if it's getting ready to leave, as there's a sudden influx of military personnel into the vehicle compound and there is a perceptible change of atmosphere. The personnel are highly charged, hyped-up, and very aware of their duties to protect and transport Great Britain's nuclear warheads. They're on edge, at one and the same time over-confident, arrogant and jumpy. Whenever I see a group of men like this, I feel sick and angry. It just spells danger; danger that I, my co-workers and women all over the world have to deal with. These men will each be given machine guns and packed into 3 or 4 transit vans which will drive behind the warheads.

To get back to the watch-and-wait routine: for 4 or 5, sometimes more days, you sit and wait, watched by the MoD police and their Alsatian dogs, and there is just the usual routine activity, or seemingly no activity at all. Then you leave, to carry on the rest of the day's work. This is when I realise how important it is to build your life on non-violence, always ready to resist. The convoy watch routine is not an interruption to the day's work – it is part of that day's work.

During this particular convoy watch, Esta and Aniko see two squat, dark blue lorries under police escort going into Burghfield. These lorries are probably carrying plutonium from Aldermaston.

Lisa is sentenced to 7 days in prison, in the middle of the state's preparations to put another batch of warheads on the road, for refusing to pay £204.00 to the state. Claire Pearson is also imprisoned for refusing to pay a £40.00 fine; she is locked up in Newbury police station until 8 o'clock at night.

Pleasanter interludes arrive over the week, for example when two East German women visit the camp. They are shown the silos area, which held the missiles trained on them and the people of their country. They are grateful to us for showing them this, and even more grateful that the silos are now empty.

Lisa is released on the 12th, just in time to hear the news that a Trident warhead convoy is in Burghfield. In the evening, she, Aniko, Annette and Claudia go to a meeting called by Greenpeace Ltd. in Tadley, one of the villages nearest to Aldermaston Atomic Weapons Establishment. As Aniko wrote in our diary, 'The whole meeting was based on whether Aldermaston's safe or not. I said that everyone agrees plutonium is the most dangerous substance known to humans, and this substance is being used to make Trident warheads at AWE Aldermaston. Trident is the most destructive weapon, designed to destroy whole continents. If the workers in Aldermaston trust the people who sat down and worked out how to make these weapons, they are signing their own death warrants.' Other people at the meeting speak about how the number of people dying from AWE Aldermaston-related diseases is a lot higher than is officially recognised.

This is still our perspective – not that Aldermaston should be made safe, but that it should be closed down.

Katrina and Lisa guide Annette and Claudia around Aldermaston and Burghfield, so that they too are aware of these awful places. This is becoming an important part of our work. We take women to Aldermaston and Burghfield to show these factories exist, and the thinking behind them exists, just like concentration camps existed. The two East German women leave the next day, and take the information and insights they've gained away with them.

The convoy leaves on the 17th, six days after it entered Burghfield to be loaded up with warheads. Aniko and Katrina go into Burghfield while the convoy is preparing to leave. Katrina is arrested for Criminal Damage, and both she and Aniko are taken to Reading police station. Aniko is released immediately, and Katrina is held from half past nine 'til 11.15. Whilst Katrina is being interviewed, her arresting officer is called away to take a phone call from Special Branch, who want information about the action.

Meanwhile, Lisa and Esta are outside Burghfield, witnessing the convoy as it leaves. Lisa recorded what happened next, in our Newsletter: 'The convoy, as we knew, stays overnight at RAF Wittering in Cambridgeshire. So that evening Aniko and I drove to Wittering to continue protesting against Trident. We arrived there at 8.00pm and found, because neither of us really knew the base, that we had to drive round it several times. To our confusion the base was huge and looked like it consisted of several separate parts. We finally decided on a place to head for, where we suspected the convoy vehicles to be.

'We made our way through wooded areas and little roads. Why is it, that if one doesn't know a place well, one always ends up at the dog-compound where all the dogs are barking madly? We hurriedly made our way, walked across fields and came to a small fence. Under the big yellow lights which we were heading for, there were two figures, obviously guarding the building behind the lights. We slipped under the fence only to find on the other side what I experienced as an almost 'intruder-resistantly' ploughed field. We stumbled across mounds of earth and vehicles started moving. So we went flat on our bellies, waiting. More movements, voices. Suddenly headlights were turned on and we found ourselves in the glaring light. Shouts. STAY WHERE YOU ARE, DON'T MOVE. We got up, and Aniko shouted, 'We are non-violent women, we are unarmed, we are going to walk towards you.'

'Two soldiers with automatic rifles appeared, and they were very nervous. We soon reached even ground and the weldmesh fence which encloses a compound with what looked like hangars or garages for big vehicles.

'The two soldiers who were guarding us asked our names and otherwise watched us closely as we walked up and down the weldmesh fence. There were soldiers inside the fence, and to me it looked a bit like what you can observe when you poke a stick into an ants' nest: determined little figures moving around, seemingly multiplying by the minute. They were many, they were armed and they were furious! I overheard an angry exchange between the soldiers who were inside the fence, some who wanted us off the premises by any means necessary, and the ones guarding us, who maintained that even though they did not like it, they had orders to wait until the MoD police arrived – which took a long time!

'Meanwhile we decided to have a look around. We climbed over the fence that we previously had slipped underneath, and walked further along the weldmesh fence. Finally the MoD police arrived and 'detained' us, to be ejected from the establishment. The young MoD who detained me shook noticeably while holding onto my sleeve.

'On our 3 hour journey back to Yellow Gate (we arrived safely back at 5am) we had a feeling of achievement: we now had an overall idea of the Wittering base and their security, a first step towards future resistance to the transportation of Trident nuclear warheads.'

Abigail arrives for her Means Enquiry the next day. She's held in Newbury police station until 8 o'clock at night, then released.

So February merges into March with the promise of Spring in the distance. Now women have followed the convoy a couple of times, and are sure of the route, and the fact that it drives through Reading. We feel we should let people in Reading know what we know. Aniko and Lisa go to Reading and distribute leaflets, describing the convoy and its route through the town. Ten days later, the people of Reading do indeed get a chance to see the convoy for themselves, as it leaves Burghfield on March 16th. It's a wet, drizzly day as Aniko and Katrina go into Burghfield twice, and are not arrested for Criminal Damage. Instead, the MoD police use violence to deal with Aniko and Katrina. Katrina is thrown over a barrier by two uncontrolled, hyped-up policemen. She makes a complaint about this, and is told by an MoD police Inspector, 'If you come in here, you should expect to be man-handled.'

The action resumes later that night, when Jan, Katrina and Aniko make the journey up to RAF Wittering. Aniko and Katrina enter the base where the convoy stays overnight, and once up to the superfence protecting the convoy, they are removed in a police van. The police demand to know Jan's I.D., but say they don't need Katrina nor Aniko's names, as they already know them. The green Cortina called Imbolc and the three women inside are followed by the police for the next hour of the journey back to the camp.

On March 30th, Katrina is in the Costing Office in London, claiming her costs from the libel case against the SUN. She described the ordeal in *DO YOUR OWN LIBEL CASE- How to Proceed with an Action for Libel – A Practical Guide with Encouragement*, the booklet she and Beth compiled: 'The Taxing Officer, who is judging how much should be awarded, sits and listens, looks at receipts, hears the represented Defendants and the unrepresented Plaintiff, me.

'There is a formula for doing this and it was clear that they, the Defendants and the Taxing Officer, had done it a thousand times before. The most important point was when the calculator came out, and my costs were slashed right down. We didn't get the costs we should have. What was worse was that the Wages for Housework Campaign, who had prepared an important part of the case relating to unpaid work, including the affidavit of my expert witness Selma James, were not awarded costs.

'At that stage, having been deprived of what is rightfully yours, you are left to salvage what you can from the ruins.

'It was classic mean-mindedness and I'm sure that the regulations are designed to protect the professional legal men and the men with power and money.

'It was explained to me that I couldn't hire anyone to do work for me. I could only be granted money for my McKenzie Friend's costs, at £8.50 an hour. Consider that the solicitors are awarded £70.00 an hour to prepare for hearings.

'The patriarchy is obsessed with not giving women money. The amount we manage with is so little, if we got more we could organise more effectively to overthrow it!'

After this, Katrina is invited to Presswise, set up by Clive Soley MP as a support and campaign group for people maligned by the press. The group has as one of its objectives a change in the libel laws, to allow Legal Aid for cases of defamation. Katrina goes to a meeting in the House of Commons in late March to encourage people to take out their own writs against newspapers who libel them.

April's full moon follows a sunny, windy day, a day Beth spends in court, supported by Katrina.

*Clerk of the court:* Would you agree that no arrangements have been made to pay [the Compensation and Costs ordered]?

*Beth:* Yes, I'd agree with that.

*Clerk:* Do you have anything to say about that?

*Beth:* Yes. This Compensation and these Costs arose from a non-violent action I took on Christmas Day a year and a half ago, together with Judith Walker and Margaretta D'Arcy. [Beth describes the mock village and the action.]

At the moment, people all over Britain and Ireland are disgusted by the IRA bombing in Warrington. This was a terrible, terrible thing. At Yellow Gate we condemn all violence, including IRA violence. The parents and families and friends of Jonathan Ball and Timothy Parry will never get over these childrens' deaths. The whole community in Warrington is mourning them. People in Britain and Ireland are calling for an end to the violence. I don't think the war in Ireland will end if we don't recognise that there is hurt and loss on both sides. There's mourning on both sides. Children and women and men have been killed by the British Army too. These are the names I painted:

Seamus Duffy, aged 15, killed August 1989
Sean Downes, aged 22, killed August 1984
Stephen McConomy, aged 11, killed April 1982
Peter McGuinness, aged 41, killed August 1981
Nora McCabe, aged 33, killed July 1981 (Nora was struck on the

head by a plastic bullet fired by an RUC officer.)

Carol Ann Kelly, aged 12, killed May 1981 (Carol was returning home from the local shop, carrying a carton of milk, when she was killed by 2 plastic bullets.)

Julie Livingstone, aged 14, killed May 1981

Henry Duffy, aged 45, killed May 1981

Peter Doherty, aged 40, killed July 1981 (he was killed by a plastic bullet as he stood at the window of his flat).

I've already served a day in custody at Devizes Magistrates Court for painting these names. I was never fined. I refuse to pay Compensation to the military for painting these names on the mock gravestones. My conscience doesn't allow me to pay Compensation to the military. They should never have removed the names from the mock gravestones – it was their decision to do so. They should have kept these names on the stones to remind the British Army of what they are doing in Northern Ireland. We made that mock graveyard a more truthful place.

*Clerk:* Do you realise what the consequences are of not paying this Compensation and Costs?

*Beth:* Yes. [The magistrates – 3 women – consult.]

Magistrate: Does you conscience not allow you to pay the Costs either?

*Beth:* No, it doesn't.

*Magistrate:* We're going to give you 7 days imprisonment, but we'll give you one day off for the day in custody at Devizes.

*Clerk:* You can't give a day off for that.

*Magistrate:* OK, that'll be 7 days then.

*Beth:* For a non-violent action against the war in Ireland? Well, that sentence rests on your conscience. My conscience is clear.

*Magistrate:* I'm happy for you that you're conscience is clear.

*Beth:* I'm happy too.

*Magistrate:* Just go with the policeman!

A Good Friday demonstration at Aldermaston has been planned by the peace network. The demonstration takes place in the pouring rain, but nonetheless, Lisa, Aniko, Katrina and Beth give out leaflets to the undeterred marchers. They meet a couple of people who were on the original Aldermaston marches, as were Peggy Walford with her twin baby boys, and Jean Hutchinson.

Another convoy of nuclear warheads leaves Burghfield on April 15th. It takes the back roads around Reading, after Lisa and Aniko's distribution of leaflets in Reading last month, about its route. Katrina, Abigail, Lisa, Aniko and I come back to the camp. We all prepare for our various roles in the forthcoming resistance. Abigail, Claire and I will hold the camp, while Katrina, Lisa and Aniko go up to Wittering. They arrange to meet Melanie at Stamford – the nearest train station to Wittering – and travel together from then onwards to set up a peace camp.

## PRESS RELEASE

'On Thursday April 15th 1993 at 8.00pm three women were threatened with a gun by a military guard, while non-violently protesting against the storage of Trident nuclear warheads at RAF Wittering in Cambridgeshire.

The women: Lisa Medici, Melanie Crawford and Katrina Howse, all from Yellow Gate, Greenham Common Women's Peace Camp, were threatened as they walked along the outer barbed wire defence surrounding the Trident warhead convoy.

Katrina Howse says: 'We had been singing loudly. I was horrified when an armed guard aimed his rifle at us and shouted twice, 'Stop! Don't move or I'll shoot!' It must have been clear to him that we were non-violent women. I shouted back to him to keep calm. It was obvious that we were women and we were not attempting to break through the inner defences to get to the convoy. He only put his gun down when I asked an MoD policeman to tell him to do so, and then only after the policeman told him several times.'

Lisa Medici explains: 'We were spotted approaching the outer security fence whilst walking across open fields. That was several minutes before we reached the outer security and it was not yet dark. I was deeply shocked when threatened by the soldier with a gun. All our attempts to defuse the situation seemed in vain, and he kept threatening us with the gun for several minutes until the MoD police arrived. The reaction of that soldier was in no way justified, given our non-violent approach.'

Arrangements are made to go to London on Monday, to meet with MPs and try to get a question asked in Parliament about the way non-violent protesters are treated. We have to set off early, and start by meeting Claire. We then go to picket the MoD building in Whitehall, with our banner that says WE, NON-VIOLENT WOMEN FROM GREENHAM COMMON WERE THREATENED WITH BEING SHOT, FOR RESISTING NUCLEAR WARHEADS. On seeing this, an older woman walking past gets very distraught. She shakes her head, saying, 'This government is terrible, terrible.' Katrina tells her the army is turning on its own people. The woman replies, 'It's going to get worse.' A nearby policeman says 'Don't ask me. I can't comment.'

When moved on from Whitehall, we go to Trafalgar Square, trailed by 3 policemen. We hold our banners at the lion's feet and distribute leaflets to keen-eyed tourists.

When a group of French schoolchildren watch us outside Downing Street, I can translate our message into French, 'Nous étions menacées d'être tiré, pour avoir resisté des têtes-nucleaires.' They linger awhile.

We meet Clive Soley, who tells us how to get a question asked, and into the House of Commons we go. At half-past 2, Ken Livingstone comes out, in the middle of a debate about the war in Bosnia. He agrees to ask a question. He will ask, 'Did this incident happen [as he describes it]? What were the instructions to the soldier?' The question is published in HANSARD on the 26th April, with the reply from Archie Hamilton: 'The women protesters were about 60 yd inside the station perimeter fence when they were challenged. I am satisfied that the action taken by the RAF and MoD police in removing them from the station was in accordance with MoD regulations.'

On May 4th, a Judicial Review rules no Compensation will be given to women who've served prison sentences as a result of being prosecuted under the illegal Greenham Common Byelaws.

A week later, Katrina defends herself against the charge that she caused Criminal Damage to a fence around AWE Burghfield in February. Margaretta, Aniko, Abigail and others support Katrina beforehand, when they display the TRIDENT ON TRIAL banner, and in the court. Aniko wrote in our Newsletter, 'Katrina explained to the court it was not enough to just stand and watch that morning of the 17th of February, when we knew that another convoy was preparing to leave.

'Both Katrina and myself entered this base on the 17th of February, our means of entry was through a hole in the fence which Katrina cut.

'Katrina knew she would be arrested and charged with Criminal Damage, but as she told the Court, she was impelled by her conscience. If she did not take action against Trident then she would be part responsible for the making of Trident. The convoy was delayed and therefore it was a successful action. Katrina said the action was taken in the spirit of hope, anger and belief that we can change the world and end the threat of nuclear war. It was a lesser thing to do, cutting the fence, than what was going on in that base. The action was an act of conscience; Katrina did not relish entering the Atomic Establishment but she had no choice.

'The new Criminal Justice Act is meant to prevent non-violent criminals from going to prison. The magistrates defined Katrina's crime as serious, therefore it was not in the category on non-violent crimes. Criminal Damage of £100.00 was so serious Katrina was given a 7 day custodial sentence. This was after a cat and mouse game – the magistrates were trying to drag out the case by delaying sentencing for a month. They wanted Katrina to agree to a pre-sentence report. This entails having an interview with a probation officer about one's record and then returning to court to be sentenced. This is akin to mental torture, being shackled for four weeks waiting to be sentenced. Katrina refused to cooperate with the pre-sentence report; this forced the magistrates to deal with her then and there. Katrina's strength was an inspiration for anyone who wants to work for change and a safer world. Her commitment to the struggle could not be dowsed, so the magistrates imprisoned her. The imprisonment, although always difficult, is no deterrent. A luta continua.'

A nuclear convoy enters Burghfield the next day. Sometimes people ask me, what can you do to resist the state when you're in prison? They've got you then, haven't they? I have always said no, you're resisting wherever you are. Women still check Burghfield when Katrina's in prison, we still organise to involve more women, and Katrina takes up the struggle inside prison. When she comes out, Margaretta meets her, and she's back into the routine of monitoring Burghfield with us all.

The convoy leaves at about 9.00am. It breaks down near Glasgow, one of the engines burnt out in the attempt to get to Faslane in a day, we discover later, from phoning Faslane.

Katrina and Aniko enter AWE Burghfield, after having driven to Wittering to see if the convoy had stopped there. They aren't charged, just released through the ugly, heavy gates at the front of the factory.

With another five carriers containing warheads up at Faslane, ready to be put on submarines as tall as Nelson's Column and as long as four football pitches, the start of the summer brings more women.

On June 4th, Lisa, Aniko and I go to meet Janet off a plane from Sweden. Since she won her appeal last year, she can apply to the Home Office for a month's visa to visit Britain. She started on this, almost as soon as she heard of the verdict, but it has taken until now for a visa to come through.

We are all very tense, waiting for her flight to arrive. We remember the last time Janet was at the airport, and we're also aware that her visa is subject to the discretion of Immigration Officials. It feels very much as if Janet is still entirely at their mercy, and we're all anxious to see her coming through customs. We keep leaping up, and dashing about to see if her flight's come in yet. Never mind! – as she eventually makes it through, to meet us. We are all a bit shaky, still, and can't quite relax, in case there's a tannoy message for Janet, hauling her back again. We have a coffee, and Janet tells us about the flight, and going through customs in the non-EEC queue, where everyone is subject to thorough scrutiny. We gradually calm down – enough to make it to the car, and back to the camp, where Abigail and Claire are only too pleased to welcome Janet.

I have a Means Enquiry on June 8th, for over £200.00 of fines. I am all prepared to be sent down for a couple of weeks. I tell the court I am not going to put money into the military. The strangest sentence follows – I am not to leave the court precinct until 4 o'clock! Aniko, who's supporting me in court, goes off to work, leaving me outside the WRVS tea shop reading a book. Janet pops in sometime after lunch, then I make my way back to the camp.

Things seem to be happening inside the ex-base, over the next few days. Aniko and I hear rumbling noises but can't see anything when we go in to have a look. The next day there's a military exercise, involving Chinook helicopters flying in and out. At the same time, there's an event for children put on by a police charity, and there are a lot of children in Building 92, the Commander's ex-offices. I would have thought it's too dangerous to do military exercises in the presence of children, but the RAF didn't seem too bothered.

Another convoy's in Burghfield on June 12th, when we go to check. There aren't many police around, which is quite unusual. Three days later the convoy leaves Burghfield, followed by Aniko and Katrina in the Cortina. The convoy, which we find out is carrying Tornado nuclear warheads, goes to a base in Norfolk near King's Lynn, called Marham, and this is where Katrina and Aniko are arrested under the Official Secrets Act.

There's another military exercise going on inside the ex-base today. Janet and Claire find armed soldiers outside one of the hangars. The doors to the hangar are closed, on Janet and Claire's appearance, but there's a tank in pieces outside the hangar. A 'Junior Citizens Scheme' is also in operation inside the Commander's ex-offices. It involves the Met. police, the fire brigade, ambulance workers and a lot of children. The children are being shown 'safety exercises.' They would be a lot safer a lot further away from nervous young men with guns.

Janet speaks about the military exercises when BBC breakfast TV come to do an interview about the future of the base. The BBC film crew tell Janet the base will be 'open to the public' on July 12th.

Katrina and Aniko are released at 11 o'clock the next morning. They're trying to catch up with the convoy, which has been seen near Honnington, as they find out by phoning Faslane peace camp.

It's pouring with rain; hard, heavy rain and there's a full-scale eviction of the camp. Five days ago, we bought a second caravan and installed it at Yellow Gate. Now the bailiffs serve notices on the caravans – if they're not moved by tomorrow, Newbury District Council will take them away. Janet goes in to see NDC, to get the order delayed until Monday, and she gets this in writing. Then we agree, on Janet's suggestion, to take the decision to evict the caravan to Judicial Review the next day.

Claire and I go up to the High Court and put in an application for Judicial Review. We spend a lot of time running up and down, from one office to another, but we get it done, just in time. I hand the bundle in to Mr Hendrey of NDC.

Katrina and Aniko return the next day, Saturday June 19th, after following the Tornado convoy. They're very tired. It is now near the summer solstice, and there's a feel of festivities in the air. However, as it turns out, we have other matters to deal with. The car breaks down on two consecutive days, after women go to check Burghfield.

Aniko and I talk to Mr Hendrey of NDC, who claims he never got the Judicial Review papers. He says the eviction will still go ahead, despite the Judicial Review. This seems to be really only a temporary measure to appease angry Newburyites, as later on in the day, two bailiffs arrive, without the police, so we don't evict the camp. Later in the week we're visited by Mr Tagg (legal officer) from NDC, who tells us the evictions will continue, and there'll be one the next day. He says he would like a meeting with us, and we agree to this.

At 5.00am, Katrina, Janet, Aniko and I leave for Burghfield. Janet and Katrina return at 9.00am to help with the eviction. Aniko and I wait outside Burghfield; also waiting are women from Nukewatch (successor to Cruisewatch) and BBC File on Four, who want to follow the convoy for a programme about the transportation of nuclear warheads.

The convoy leaves at ten to 10.00. As it drives slowly past us, we mark it with red paint. Aniko is arrested and taken inside the AWE. She is eventually released, after being charged with Criminal Damage, and together we go back to the camp. To get back, we walk through the ex-base, and inadvertently disrupt an armed MoD police exercise.

There has been no eviction, and we're all left asking the question, why were we told there would be one? It almost seems like we were told about the eviction so that we wouldn't leave the camp to mark the convoy and disrupt armed police exercises.

Janet, Katrina and I set up a peace camp at Wittering, after a brief rest. Katrina and I trespass on RAF Wittering. The MoD police are very hyped-up, and come tearing up to us in their van. We get driven out and dropped at the peace camp, at 2.00am. Four hours later, we get up and drive around the base. We wait for ages by the crash gate, as it is heavily guarded by armed RAF personnel and MoD police. At 11.30 everyone suddenly goes off duty; the convoy must have gone out through another gate to avoid us.

On July 1st Aniko and I are in Newbury Magistrates court, defending ourselves against charges of Criminal Damage to Aldermaston. No Costs or fines are imposed, but we're ordered to pay £400.00 Compensation. Janet leaves just before the end of the case to return to Sweden, and we are really sorry to see her go.

Judith and Randi arrive – Judith isn't here long, before she gets sent to prison for 7 days, for the FIBUA gravestones action. On the same day, July 6th, Katrina and Aniko speak to Mr Tagg to arrange a meeting with Newbury District Councillors. He tells us the next eviction will be on Thursday.

The July 12th Greenham Common Open to the Public Day is a bit of a non-event. The gate is opened up, but we seem to be the only ones attending. Ethel and Katrina walk down the Main Street with a banner saying IMAGINE A COMMON, and Aniko and I follow. We're trailed by the police, as usual.

Three days later, Margaretta has her appeal of the Criminal Damage charge arising from painting the mock gravestones in FIBUA heard in Swindon Crown Court. She makes the connection between the dehumanising effect of soldiers training at FIBUA and soldiers killing in Northern Ireland. The judge runs out of the court at this point. The court adjourns, for him to recover. When it reconvenes, the judge finds Margaretta Guilty. He asks for £100.00 Costs, on top of the existing £50.00 Costs and £150.00 Compensation.

The next day, Margaretta, Ethel, Erica, Claire, and Judith go into AWE Burghfield. They are found inside the base, and the police drive them out and drop them some distance away.

The convoy leaves at 10.30am on July 19th. It goes up the M25, onto the M10, through Stevenage, then onto the A1 and comes off at the A47 to Wittering. There are five enormous warhead carriers in the convoy, and just as they're driving into RAF Wittering, they are stopped. The Cortina has been driving in between the second and third carrier. Katrina and I get out of the car, walk calmly up to the vehicles, and to the best of our abilities cover them in red paint. Erica and Ethel also leave the car and join us outside the crash gates. We all sing, and shout MURDERERS! as the convoy finally enters. Katrina and I are not arrested at the time, but instead Aniko and Katrina are later picked up and taken to Corby police station. When I get to the police station, I say for the hundredth time that I painted the convoy. I was eventually arrested and interviewed. Both Katrina and I are charged and Aniko is not.

At the end of July, Ethel, Aniko, Judith and I go to Fairford Air Tattoo to tell people war is not a spectator sport. We are just about to start cutting the fence to get in, when 2 MIG Russian fighter planes crash. It is a terrible, frightening thing to see. The pilots had ejected and landed, not without injuries. One of the pilots was particularly badly injured. The debris lands very close to the quarter of a million people watching the tattoo and in the residential area around the base. We are all in a state of shock, as we realise what a narrow escape everyone had.

As women are beginning to gather for the memorial to Helen, on the 4th August, a woman called Shirley Burgess is killed near the same spot where Helen had been killed four years ago. She was cycling safely on the A339 with her friend Corrine, when a lorry tried to overtake her, and killed her. I try and do what I can to help her, and comfort Corrine, but Shirley is dead by the time the ambulance arrives.

We are all shaken, as we hold the memorial day for Helen. On Hiroshima Day, we hold a memorial for Hiro Sumpter, a Japanese woman who lived at the camp in the eighties. Hiro had died of cancer earlier in the year.

*Katrina* − Hiro worked very hard in her years at the Women's Peace Camp. She seemed happiest being busy, whether she was cooking a tasty meal in a huge pot over the fire, or cutting the fence to go in during our many actions inside the base.

1984, in particular, was the year she seemed so focused on taking non-violent direct action, going in again and again to disrupt the functioning of the base.

She had a confidence, even a joy, in taking non-violent direct action. This inspired confidence in other women.

She was undaunted and courageous as she enthusiastically tacked the USAF base. −

Over Hiroshima and Nagasaki days, 11 women cut through fence surrounding AWE Aldermaston. The first group of 8 on Hiroshima Day are arrested and taken to various police stations. Mary and Katrina were the first to go. They were taken to Newbury police station. Mary described what happened in our Newsletter: '. . . Not having been there for some years, I was shocked to find an order being made for my finger-prints and photograph to be taken. As I had given my name, claimed the bolt-croppers as my property, and stated that I had cut the fence, I could see no possible purpose in this. I therefore refused to cooperate. I was finger-printed and photographed while lying limp on the floor. My wrists were deliberately twisted the 'wrong' way, even after I explained this was causing me agony. I made a written complaint about this abuse at the first opportunity, and also about the decision to take finger-prints and photographs unnecessarily.

'On the 23rd May 1994 I received a response from the Police Complaints Authority denying that excessive force was used to take my prints and defending the decision to take them. However, they admitted that force should not have been used when taking my photograph, as this was 'in contravention of the Codes of Practice.' The Assistant Chief Constable conveyed 'his regret' about the 'discomfort' I experienced while being finger-printed, and his 'sincere apologies' for the photographing. 'The officers involved are to receive instructions...' and the custody sergeant is to 'discuss his handling of this incident and his failure to convey clear instructions with his Area Commander, from whom he will receive strong advice.'

Sarah was carried off to Reading police station, with the excuse that her solicitor was waiting for her there. She had not contacted a solicitor, and, funnily enough there was no one but the police waiting for her at Reading.

Claire, Frances, Jean, Aniko and I refused to be interviewed, furious that three women had disappeared in front of our eyes. We were quickly charged and released.

Sarah was released much later still, after a lengthy interview during which she was asked if she would leave the room while the tape-recorder was still running.

We had two days to recover until Nagasaki Day, when another 2 groups of women cut the fences again.

On August 13th, Aniko is due to defend herself in Reading, against Criminal Damage charges. The case is dropped, however, as it is not in the public interest to prosecute for Criminal Damage to a nuclear warhead convoy.

Throughout August, all the padlocks on the Main Gate have been coming off again, so that the Common really will be 'Open to the Public.' On September 3rd, Claire and Aniko are charged with Criminal Damage to the chain around the Main Gate.

There is also a nuclear convoy in Burghfield, non-violently resisted once again by two groups of women going into the base to disrupt the convoy preparations.

On the camp's 12th birthday on September 5th, Aniko and Claire are charged with Criminal Damage to fencing around AWE Burghfield. I am arrested and charged the next day; Aniko and I go in, and I take responsibility for cutting the fence. For the next three days, women go into Burghfield every day to stop the preparation of the convoy. The preparation most definitely does stop; I've heard tannoy announcements telling workers engaged in atomic weapons manufacture to go to their buildings, as there are intruders in the establishment.

The convoy leaves on September 9th, and is non-violently resisted.

There's yet another convoy in Burghfield on the 14th, and more incursions into that base then and on the 25th.

*Peggy's* statement: 'We were told the Cold War was over. The nuclear missiles had gone from Greenham Common and so you would like to believe all is well. Greenham Common is no longer an American nuclear base, but, where was the peace dividend? Where was the work for peaceful purposes taking place? So in May 1993 I came back to Yellow Gate because I knew the women hadn't gone away and I was very grateful they hadn't. Now, nearing my 75th birthday, having survived the blitz in Coventry 1941-1944, which I call the Hot War, through into the fifties through the Cold War, marching, protesting, Ban the Bomb, CND . . . in my own political structures I find personally there is not much time left to try and re-awaken the conscience of the British people to the awfulness of what is to come. Sometimes I ask myself, has Militarism overtaken Civilisation? The women of Greenham Common are still here and we are still working equally as hard now, as we did in the very early days against cruise missiles and there is no stopping now, we go on and on and on.'

At ten thirty in the morning of September 29th the convoy finally leaves Burghfield, and is non-violently resisted by Yellow Gate women. Lisa and Claire cover 2 warhead carriers with bright yellow paint and are charged with Criminal Damage. Aniko is charged with 'Going Concerned.' The police impound the Cortina and try to bribe Aniko into persuading Lisa and Claire to give their dates of birth, by saying if she didn't try, the car would not be available until the next day, and then only at a cost of £120.00. Lisa and Claire's shoes are kept for 'evidence'. An Inspector is eventually persuaded to give the women a lift to the car. He warns them to stay out of Bedfordshire!

The next day is set for the meeting between Newbury District Council and the camp about the evictions. At 9.30am the police and bailiffs turn up, to attempt to evict the camp. Lisa tells them about the Judidal Review and this afternoon's meeting. They aren't interested. The bailiffs say they've got orders, and don't know anything about any injunctions or meetings. Lisa is adamant that they contact NDC, which they do, and afterwards they say, 'We spoke to someone on the phone –

forget it.' They blame the mix-up on one department not knowing what the others are up to.

The following day, we are told by an MoD policeman who has come to ask whether we have seen a missing person that a rich property developer is very interested in the Common, but he was shocked to realise the Women's Peace Camp is still here. He would be prepared to pay vandals to wreck the camp and get the women out of his way, according to the MoD policeman.

The weekend of October 9th starts a whirlwind week for me. I arrive at the camp at half-past five on Saturday afternoon. I'm arrested half an hour later, and taken to Newbury Police station. Corby Magistrates Court had issued a warrant for me as I wrote a letter to enter a plea, instead of appearing in person. At about 3.00pm I'm packed off into a police car and driven to Corby police station, to appear in Wellingborough court on Monday. On Monday, I'm sent to Holloway because the magistrate didn't accept my reasoning that my experience of court had been that a letter is perfectly acceptable for a plea date. The magistrates also took an extreme objection to me not standing up in court. I'm remanded until Corby court sits on Thursday. Lisa, Aniko and Claire visit me on Tuesday, something which I really appreciate.

Thursday is also the day of the Judicial Review application regarding the evictions. The application is turned down. The judge said that after 10 years of being evicted, it is now too late for a decision to stop the evictions. Newbury District Council will be delighted, and once more have escaped coming under scrutiny from the legal system.

I am given Conditional bail from Corby court; I have to sign on at Newbury police station every day until the trial. I later get this changed to once a week. Katrina goes to Corby court the next day and is granted Unconditional bail until October 25th, when our case will be heard in Kettering Magistrates court.

The activity on Greenham Common is increasing. Several small businesses begin to move in to the buildings previously occupied by the military. We advertise as much as possible that the base is now open to the public, even going so far as to paint this in huge letters on one of the buildings by the Main Gate. We feel very strongly that now is the time for the people of Newbury and nearby to start taking fresh air and exercise on Greenham Common.

It is very important that the Common doesn't get colonised by the authorities, in any shape or form.

There's another police exercise, in October. This time it is a Hampshire Police Constabulary dog training exercise. Claire and Lisa very effectively disrupt this exercise, by walking right into it. The MoD police have to tell the Hants police that all they can do is escort the women off. The Hants police radio then gives out a message that the dogs are now following Lisa and Claire's scent and 'basically they've screwed it up for you.' We hope this will dissuade them from trying further exercises on the Common.

United Nations lorries and jeeps keep going in and out of the Common. We will have to work hard to get it really restored to the people.

In court on October 25th, Katrina and I are told to return to Corby on November 25th, and then we will be told when the trial will be. We leave the court wondering what on earth is in store for us, and as Katrina said in the diary, 'I can only warm to the next big scrap.'

Aniko is sent down for two weeks the following day, for refusing to pay £400.00 Compensation to the MoD for damage done to the fence at AWE Aldermaston in January. Aniko talks about how the state defines legal and illegal 'criminal damage' – these are political definitions which allow the extreme criminal damage of making nuclear warheads. She says whatever damage she did is absolutely minimal compared to what the MoD have done and are doing.

Katrina and Mary are in Newbury Magistrates court on November 10th, for their Hiroshima Day trial. Mary described the day in our Newsletter: 'A few members of Cor Corchion Caerdydd [Cardiff's Red Choir], including our baby Tomos were there in court to support as well as Aniko Jones, Isabel Strang and my daughter Zoe. The prosecution played the taped interviews of Katrina and myself in full. (The tapes were of the interviews conducted by the Newbury police as part of their investigation into the 'crime' of Criminal Damage we were charged with.) The prosecution wanted a summary of the tapes to be read out. However the summary was considerably different to the tape so we argued to have the tape heard. The value put on the damage that we caused was drastically reduced.

'Katrina cast doubt on the legality of the way the MoD took possession of AWE Aldermaston back in the 1950's. The MoD had been sufficiently panicked by previous legal proofs of their improper procedures to feel compelled to produce a 'loose minute' entitled Public Rights of Way – AWE Aldermaston and Burghfield. Katrina was able to show various probable rights of way on many maps, which might or might not have been officially 'stopped up.' These arguments won us leave to appeal. Aniko was called as a witness, and among other points she gave evidence that all of us involved in the action were working together. This made it possible for me to join my appeal with those of all the women.

'I used the illegality of Trident according to the Genocide Act as my defence. (The Genocide Act became law in Britain in 1969. It outlaws any weapon or act which could or was preparing to destroy any person or people because they belonged to a particular group, i.e. race, sex, creed or religion.) I claimed the danger to workers, local people and people on the route to and from AWE Llanishen in Cardiff and AWE Aldermaston as my legal excuse for cutting. Ray Davies, bass with Cor Cochion Caerdydd and County Councillor for Mid Glamorgan gave evidence on the radioactive nature of materials being transported by road between the two AWE's, and the danger this presented to the people of South Wales.

'We were fined a total of £207.00 each.'

Aniko and Claire are in Reading Magistrates court on November 15th, for their trial of Criminal Damage to the AWE Burghfield fence on the camp's birthday. The Crown Prosecution Service send statements with information about the code-word 'cutters' – given out so that personnel will take up 'defensive positions' when non-violent women enter the base. Both are found Guilty and will be sentenced on December 7th. On the same day, Katrina and I find out our case for painting the convoy in July has been dropped, as it is 'not in the public interest.'

On November 22nd, I am in the same court for Criminal Damage to the AWE fence on September 6th. I am found Guilty, and fined.

*Erica Mary Wilson* described the resistance to the next convoy, and her subsequent struggle for equal civil rights in custody and in court, in our Newsletter: 'Cutting the fence at AWE Burghfield on November 24th was a long overdue commitment to working against man's inhumanity to man. An additional trigger was our vehicle being surrounded by six policemen, as we waited for the convoy to leave AWE Burghfield, preventing us from tracking it. After a fruitless journey to RAF Wittering, a decision was taken by Katrina and myself to take direct action. We decided to cut down some sections of fence on return to Burghfield.

'We were subsequently arrested and charged with Criminal Damage. An issue had to be made throughout the procedures that if information was required they would have to accommodate to my partial deafness. This meant the police would have to face me, and when speaking to me, not interrupt or hold any cross-conversation, and they would have to cut out background noise. There was no understanding of deafness in the subsequent taped interview, so this made for a not very impressive tape, which was later played in court. Thankfully, court dates are written on the charge sheet so no misunderstandings over that.

'I was aware from previous court appearances my deafness would be an issue in tracking the proceeding. At the plea hearing I informed the court official of the position but we were still allocated a large court, with the witness box sited behind a large screen – a barrier to sound and cues from lip-reading. It was a relief that a solicitor was acting for us as I could hear little.

'Prior to the court case, I wrote a diplomatic letter to the court explaining the issues and requesting consideration from the magistrates and court officials. We were allocated a smaller courtroom and I was allowed to sit outside the witness box, nearer to the bench. However, this was not effective. There was no recognition of the need for facial vision and not moving while speaking. This resulted in a severely frustrating day. I coped as sign language users have to, by registering the non-verbal communication. In this instance, that between our solicitor and the Crown Prosecution person, mostly negative, was fascinating. Fortunately I was also able to catch up by reading the notes a colleague, Lisa, was taking, through the many adjournments.

'Subsequently I wrote a stronger letter to the court, stating I had been able to hear very little, indicating it was an issue of civil rights; I should be able to communicate in the proceedings. This would be especially critical during the cross-examination. Several lines of action were suggested, including the provision of an induction loop system, which can help those who can benefit from a hearing aid.

'On the second day of the hearing there was some direct acknowledgement of my deafness and needs by the magistrates and court officials. I was given dispensation to sit between the Crown Prosecution person and the witness box – a decided improvement. It also gave me the confidence to request a repeat of anything I couldn't hear. Although I was conscious of the court's needs it is demoralising to have to request repetition, owing to the non-provision of equipment.

'At the Means Enquiry I explained the issue of deafness. However, tension and anxiety levels were increased as I could hear very little of a colleague's Means test. After explanation to a sympathetic bench matters were dealt with effectively in explaining why I wouldn't be paying the £240.00 fine.

'Reception at Holloway was managed but with continual explanation of my deafness – draining! And a minor skirmish with one warder who was very put out because she had to come down a corridor to let me know she wished to speak with me. The rest of my stay was managed by women letting me know what information was being given and whether it was for me. There was no understanding from the establishment that for people with hearing loss communication through solid doors, down long corridors and around corners is impossible. It is demanding to continually state one is partially deaf and it is not a good feeling to depend on others for communication. It makes general conversation problematic. The cooperation from other women in cells meant I could participate in one-to-one relating. This freed me from continual confrontation with the system, when it wanted to communicate with me.

'A thought for reflection – what happens for a deaf person whose first language is British Sign Language, serving a longer sentence? I was given seven days. Legally a deaf person has a right to an interpreter in court. When facing the loss of freedom imposed by the court, I was not given, as is my right, equal treatment.

'There is a lot of education needed about deafness, as I discovered when I encountered a particularly ignorant male warder, and education also needs to be done in the rest of society as a whole. The one extensive conversation I did have about the issue was with a warder enquiring about the efficiency of hearing aids, as she was concerned for her own hearing loss.

'As a postscript, it has taken deaf activists over ten years and an appeal to the Court of Human Rights to get the issue of education, British Sign Language, and the need for access to information for deaf people recognised.

'The time I spent in prison certainly acted as NO deterrent, and I shall be taking on board deaf rights on further occasions. We would be proud to welcome any deaf activists interested in visiting the camp.'

At night it's -11C, and everyone feels the bitter cold. It is about this time that we hear that Blue Gate women are thinking of closing their camp very soon.

On 7th December, Claire and Aniko are sentenced at Reading Magistrates court for the September 5th action. They are given custodial sentences of 56 days each. Claire is taken to Holloway and Aniko is held overnight in Reading, for another trial the following day.

On 8th December, Aniko is hammered again. We are both in court for causing Criminal Damage to Burghfield in September. She is given a further 3 month sentence. On the way back from court, women discover a nuclear convoy in Burghfield.

December 12th sees an influx of women into the camp. A group of five women go to AWE Burghfield, where Margaret James cuts the fence to allow herself, Frances Vigay, Sarah Watson, Lisa Medici and Katrina to enter the establishment. Margaret, Frances and Sarah are arrested 'for their own safety' whereas the two camp women, Katrina and Lisa, are arrested for Criminal Damage. Margaret wrote in our newsletter: 'The blatant framing of the camp women would have been farcical but that it was a concerted, malicious attempt to take away women's freedom for an action they had not committed and obviously is part of the larger plan of trying to crush the camp.

'Once it became clear what was happening, I voluntarily made a statement taking responsibility for my action. Voluntarily should go without saying – women at the camp have always acted autonomously, while drawing strength and power from the knowledge that we do so collectively with other women.

'Over the next eight hours we consistently (it's easy to be consistent when you're telling the truth) and repeatedly stated that I cut the fence. We were all released with a view to prosecution.'

On the 13th, Katrina, Lisa and I leave to visit Aniko in Holloway. The car breaks down, on the North Circular Ring Road! Katrina and I continue on our way to the visit, while Lisa stays with the Cortina.

I have a Means Enquiry on the 14th, and am sentenced to 14 days. I am on the same wing as Aniko. I'm so glad to see her walking down the corridor. We spend about a week together, then I'm out again. She and Claire have their appeal heard in Reading Crown Court on the 16th. Claire's sentence is reduced to a £50 fine and she walks out of the court. Aniko's sentence is reduced to 3 months altogether, so she should be out on January 21st. She'll spend her birthday, Christmas and the New Year in prison. We give her all the support we can.

On the Winter Solstice, Erica and I ring her in East Sutton Park, an open prison in Kent.

Katrina goes up to London on the 29th, with documents for the High Court, to appeal their previous decision that we can't challenge the byelaws under which we have been evicted. We state during the case that we have squatter's rights for this land we have occupied for more than 12 years now.

Lisa and I go off to London, too, to celebrate the New Year with Claire; we ring Aniko, who seems happy to hear from us. Katrina and Peggy are celebrating Hogmanay on Greenham Common; the land that gives life to our work and dreams, the land that has still to be fought for.

# 1994
# ALL OUR TRIALS
## by Aniko Jones

J anuary 1994 was part of one of the wettest winters ever recorded. The two visible caravans on the A339 Basingstoke road were being battered by torrential rain. The sky was continually overcast, giving the impression of perpetual dusk. Day turned into night into day with very little demarcation and constant rain.

Apart from the rain making life more difficult there were other forces battering at the camp. There was the threat to the Common by speculators; the eviction order on the caravans; a full diary of court cases likely to be followed by imprisonment; and our very existence was under constant threat from the ever increasing number of Trident warheads being transported from AWE Burghfield in Reading to Faslane in Scotland.

Extract from the camp diary, 5th January, Katrina: 'Peggy and I walked on the Common, up and down the old runway. Even the surface of the Common by the runway is waterlogged. The rain is endless and is especially torrential all through the nights, beating down on the caravan roofs and on the tents. We give up on the fires for heating water because all the wood is water soaked. We plough through the mud. The camp is water logged. If it was not for the caravans we would all be continually soaked. All the more reason to fight in the High Court to keep them.'

Women are continually entering Greenham Common, reclaiming our right to walk on the land and to enjoy the early fruits of our victory. The visions of the Common being restored look more possible now than they have done over the past 50 years of occupation by the military.

Letters begin appearing in the NEWBURY WEEKLY NEWS from local people voicing their opposition to the Common being developed for industry.

On the 18th of January I am released from prison after serving 6 weeks of my 3 months sentence. I now have to serve the rest of my sentence in the community. This means if I commit an offence within the next 6 weeks I will not only be punished for that offence but I will have to serve the remainder of the original 3 months sentence.

This week, the local paper announces that the Ministry of Defence have made an application to remove Greenham Common and the rights attached to it from the Register of Common Land. If they are successful, development on the ex-base can go ahead. The article goes on – the application is complicated by the fact that in 1990 the MoD handed over £90,000 to the Commoners in an attempt to purchase the Commoners rights compulsorily. Some of the Commoners took the money, but several did not and still have full rights over the Common. Mike Thorne, of Newbury District Council, says they are relieved the application has been made, and hope the matter can be resolved speedily.

We make an appointment to see Philip Moate at the Berkshire County Council solicitors' department. We want to know the procedure for opposing the deregistering of the Common. The status of the Common and her rights had helped protect that land and had been a major element in the struggle to rid the Common of the military – now we need to fight off the developers to maintain the status of the Common.

On the 21st of January, two women from Blue Gate come down to the Sanctuary to announce Blue Gate will be closing. Later, our attention is drawn to articles in national and international newspapers claiming that the Women's Peace Camp on Greenham Common has closed down. These articles seem to have originated from women closely associated with Blue Gate. These articles did not make the distinction between the closure of Blue Gate and the closure of Greenham Common Women's Peace Camp as a whole. The media had a field day using this misinformation to yet again announce our demise. We had a lot of work trying to undo the damage.

On the 28th January, Lisa and Katrina go to check on the nuclear convoy inside Burghfield and find the convoy had left early in order to avoid resistance. Lisa and Katrina go on to Shire Hall in Reading to speak to Mr Moate. He informs the women that if the County Council are satisfied with the MoD's application to deregister the Common, they have to advertise their intention and the public then have 40 days to lodge their objections. An objection would mean the MoD will have to prove the grounds for deregistration are fulfilled, namely the Commoners rights are extinct. For instance, the MoD could argue that if for a sufficient period of time the land had been enclosed and the Commoners had not exercised their rights, then those rights will have lapsed.

We believe it would be difficult to show a voluntary acceptance of enclosing the land, with razor wire, armed guards patrolling and military Byelaws criminalising anyone who entered Greenham Common. We could also argue that despite these deterrents, women constantly entered Greenham Common and took the fence down –

preventing total enclosure.

Katrina and Lisa also speak with Mr Moate about Adverse Possession and how it might apply to the women living at Yellow Gate. If we could prove 12 years of constant occupation of the land we would gain the right to legally own it. This would help with our High Court challenge to the eviction order on the caravans.

While at Shire Hall, Lisa and Katrina research more of the history of AWE Aldermaston. It is a slow and frustrating process piecing together the story of what was once a glorious part of the country, now fully contaminated.

The month ends as it began, with continual rain and no let up with the work.

On 2nd February, Rosy is up before Reading magistrates for sentencing, which had been delayed for over a month because the probation service forgot to give her a date for her pre-sentence interview.

I have cooperated with the pre-sentence report procedure before, and while having an interview with a probation officer, she told me they did not like getting involved with 'political cases.'

Rosy was given the choice of a custodial sentence or 40 hours community service. Community service is seen as an act of recompense to society for the wrong done in committing a crime. We do not accept that our actions in resisting the state are wrong. We have nothing to recompense society for. The courts do not see our work at Yellow Gate as a service to the community. Rosy is given a custodial sentence of 3 weeks.

A few moments after Rosy has been taken to the cells, an MoD policeman approaches Katrina and informs her that the 5 women who went into AWE Burghfield on the 12th December 1993 and had been released with a view to prosecution will now receive summonses, legally forcing each of them to attend court to face charges of Criminal Damage.

As the month progresses, safety at AWE Aldermaston is being questioned publicly in radio and newspaper articles.

We begin to see more businesses being set up on Greenham Common. A Newbury District Council sub-committee has been set up to receive presentations from rival bidders for the land. English Nature argue for the restoration of the Common to heathland grazing. The Sporting Council would like to see a variety of sports facilities on the Common, including athletics tracks, cycling and motor sports, badminton, volleyball and basketball and even Nordic skiing. Sir Peter Michael and associates argue for mixed use, particularly emphasising employment. There were 18 responses from residents, many concerned about the noisy use of the Common, and asking for as much as possible to be restored to Common land.

Rosy is released from Holloway on the 10th of February. This is also the day of her appeal against the conviction and sentence she had just served. She has to go straight from prison to the Crown Court in Reading. Rosy's appeal was based on the fact she did not commit Criminal Damage to the Burghfield fence – I did. However, the appeal is not allowed, on the principle of 'Joint Enterprise.' We had both gone to AWE Burghfield with the intention of damaging the fence. It did not matter who had actually cut the fence. This is a new tactic by the MoD police. We had in the past tried to minimise the number of women charged with Criminal Damage when the intention was to gain entry into the bases.

The women charged with Criminal Damage for the actions on Hiroshima and Nagasaki Days 1993 appear in Newbury Magistrates Court over three days in the middle of February. (Mary and Katrina had been tried separately – see previous chapter.) Jean Hutchinson described the trials, on February 14th, 15th and 16th, in our Newsletter: 'A Stipendiary magistrate, Mr Davis, appointed by the Lord Chancellor, sat by himself to deal out what goes for justice in Newbury court. The case presented by all the women was articulate and substantive, containing real evidence of cause for alarm in the courts and throughout the land.

'The submissions were largely of five different kinds:1. The legal points: Section 5,2b allows the defence of 'lawful excuse' to the charge of Criminal Damage in certain circumstances within the Criminal Justice Act 1971. The common law defence was also submitted but dismissed, by omission at least, as the magistrate made no comment on it in his judgement.2. The legal status of AWE was put into question by references to a) the footpaths – their closure maps were produced, b) the Byelaws (which were used only once on women from Yellow Gate, befor a legal challenge in which the charges were dropped) and c) the original take-over of the land.3. The work of the AWE was also challenged under the Genocide Act 1969.4. Points regarding the dangerous condition of AWE Aldermaston were submitted. We did not cut the AWE's fence on the basis of 'it should be made safer' but on the basis it should be removed.5. Moral and religious arguments were offered which, of course, make the distinction between 'improving safety' and ending the whole operation for the sake of morality, legality and the lives of workers and the surrounding population. We know that the whole planet needs protecting from this monstrous blot on the landscape and from the weapons of mass destruction which it produces.

'Speaking in my defence I included most of the different kinds of submissions but concentrated mostly on the evidence of the 100 deaths of workers, plus the leaks from AWE Aldermaston.

'Reading some of the case histories of the deaths I felt it necessary to call for a moment of quiet memorial for the lives brought to an end by this nuclear activity of the state. One of the victims I referred to was Norman Davey, who worked at AWE for 30 years. He was a radiochemical analyst and was actually handling radioactive materials for 13 of those 30 years. Mr Davey was badly contaminated in a glove box accident in January 1965 which resulted in a particle of plutonium becoming lodged in his finger. His body monitoring in '81 and '82 had revealed a 'massive dose' of plutonium concentrated in the scientist's lymph nodes. The piece of plutonium in Mr Davey's finger was tiny, hundreds of times smaller than a pin head. However, the amount of plutonium in his body on his death was 1,000 times greater than would be expected in another human being. The jury at his inquest recorded an open verdict.

'The use of this case history and others was done in a sensitive way in order to bring the state of affairs – one hundred deaths in all – to the public eye and conscience.

'It has to be stated that the destruction of the prosecution's evidence was a cynical part of this case. It has happened before, but this time it included the destruction of a video plus a book which recorded details of the damage to the fence. We felt the Stipendiary magistrate should have dealt with this. Convictions of women were only achieved by their help. We know this is an old story but in this case their flawed justice was so blatant.

'On the evening of the 15th February the cases of Sarah Hipperson, Claire Pearson, Rosy Bremer, Frances Vigay, Aniko Jones and myself had been heard. Sarah Watson, Anna Goodson and Peggy Walford were preparing the last part of their defence when Margaret James, who was visiting the camp at the time, mentioned that she was doing a PhD on Particle Physics – this made her an expert witness on the dangers of nuclear material. This was good news after hearing the prosecution had dropped the charge of Criminal Damage on Aniko, Claire, Rosy and Frances who had cut the AWE fence on the 9th of August with Anna, Peggy and Sarah. The three women made strong submissions which were further strengthened by Margaret's evidence. She was able to describe the effect of plutonium on the human body. She made many other points effectively and the impact on the court and the magistrate was incalculable. (Margaret wishes to point out that she did not make any points that the other women had not already made, yet her evidence was given more credence because of the state's notion of a hierarchy of experts.)

'All the women heard over the 3 days were given 2 years' Conditional Discharges plus Costs of £1,000 (between us). No order for Compensation was made, despite the number of holes made in the outer fence and a hole in the inner intruder-resistant fence.

'All the women rejected the condition that they must stop this non-violent direct action for a 2-year period. The conditions that exist at AWE are such that we would be acting in an irresponsible way if we left unchallenged the work of producing warheads at AWEs and their apparent incompetence, revealed in this court case.

'We have appealed the conviction and sentence on the grounds that the cases need full and proper examination.'

Erica Wilson and Katrina are in Reading Magistrates for their Criminal Damage trial on the 28th February (see previous chapter). Katrina had done a lot of research on the existence of footpaths across the Atomic Weapons Establishment land at Burghfield; this case introduced the defence of legal excuse based on the existence of the footpaths for the first time. Katrina believes the footpaths still exist and that we can reclaim our right to use them. This means taking down any obstruction across the path, i.e. cutting the fence to gain entry.

Mr Kurtz, a solicitor, was engaged to provide the legal back-up and protection against the abuse of the law which constantly goes on in the court rooms.

The prosecutor tried to introduce a fax as evidence. The fax came from Aldershot, where the legal documentation concerning AWEs is kept, and tried to prove the footpaths had been blocked up legally. Mr Kurtz argued, under the laws of evidence, that the fax was not good enough. The prosecution were obliged to produce 'the best possible' evidence, a signed, certified copy of the document showing the blocking up of the footpaths. The prosecutor wanted to discontinue the proceedings – this meant they could restart the proceedings at a later date. Mr Kurtz argued to have the case dismissed. The prosecutor asked for a short break to consult with her boss, the head of the Crown Prosecution Service. She returned to argue for the case to continue, but asked for an adjournment, which she was granted. The date set was the 14th of March.

Early March brought the first breath of Spring. The sun shone for what seemed the first time in months. At last the heavy cloak of winter could be lifted from the tired shoulders of the women who had held the camp.

On the 14th of March, Katrina is fined £350 and Erica is fined £242 for cutting the fence at AWE Burghfield.

The weather turns very cold once more. The caravans are

shelter, but the walls are thin and the cold seeps through even our multilayered clothing. The thought of collecting water sends shivers through you. Collecting 3 or 4 water containers, taking them across the A339 road, filling them up at a stand-pipe and then pulling the heavy cold water back is exhausting. We wake up in the morning and have to break the frozen water before we can have a hot drink.

On the 16th March, Katrina walked down to the Sanctuary at 8.30am to tell me the car had been stolen. The bailiffs had woken Katrina earlier to say they had discovered our car in a ditch half a mile away. When we find the car, we discover a pair of binoculars has been stolen. The bailiffs pull the car out of the ditch. The engine starts first time!

The next day, Peggy and I go into London to see a solicitor about our appeals of the Aldermaston convictions and sentences we had received mid-February. Peggy wrote in the diary: 'We had a solid three hours, giving all the information for the appeal at Reading Crown Court. Michael [Schwarze] is to retrieve the tapes of the trial. It is unusual to have a magistrates court hearing taped....We called round to AWE Burghfield to check whether the convoy was in – we arrived back at the camp about 10.00pm to discover Trident had gone up to Scotland during the interval in which the car was stolen.'

Claire and I go into Burghfield on the 18th March. We did not trigger the alarm system and therefore had over an hour to explore the base. We passed a number of MoD police officers who did not see us because they did not expect to see us. Eventually we were arrested and released without charge. I left my bag in the base – Claire and I went back to retrieve it and in the process of entering we were spotted, arrested for Criminal Damage and charged.

On March 23rd and 24th, in response to the growing public demand for an inquiry into the safety of the Atomic Weapons Establishments at Aldermaston and Burghfield, Reading Borough Council held a community inquiry. Interested groups and individuals were invited to voice their concerns. John Cook, a Reading Borough Councillor, had visited the camp and invited us to submit our objections and fears about the AWEs. It was hoped this inquiry would put pressure on the government to hold a full-scale public inquiry into the safety of the AWEs. We at Yellow Gate felt it was important we had an input, to stress that the issue of safety is much wider than merely changing working practices and replacing old buildings. It covers our health, future and quality of life.

The inquiry was chaired by Helena Kennedy, whose remit was to discuss safety issues concerning people living by the AWEs.

Representatives from the AWEs attended to appease the public's concerns.

*Peggy Walford* – The Greenham Women were asked to give evidence on the second day of the inquiry. On the morning of the second day Katrina Howse, Claire Pearson, Rosy Bremer, Aniko Jones and I checked AWE Burghfield. We wanted to know if the nuclear convoy we had seen in Burghfield would be leaving that morning, and if it did we wanted to see if it was heading up north.

The convoy left at 10.00am and we followed it. While we were following the convoy, there was an attempt to push us off the road. We had signs on the car to attract public attention to what this military convoy is for; not to frighten, but to enlighten. The police were waiting for us when the convoy pulled off the road at Junction 10 of the A1. We did not pull off the road after it, as we were now certain it was going to RAF Wittering and we wanted to get back for the inquiry. On our way back we were pulled over by four police cars. The police wanted to search our car, but as they couldn't provide a reason why (as is required under the Police and Criminal Evidence Act), they couldn't carry out the search. They checked the driver's licence and we were told this was a normal spot check!

We arrived at Reading just in time and were the last to speak.

Katrina spoke of the connection between the poverty in Reading and the resources being poured into the AWEs. If the resources were spread fairly then the people of Reading would experience an improvement in their quality of life, especially the poor and unemployed.

Claire spoke of the routes the nuclear convoys take and of the dangers the unknowing public are exposed to. She also spoke of the inadequate facilities the emergency powers have to deal with a plutonium leak on the main routes the convoys take.

Aniko spoke of how the 'safe' radiation dosage a person can be exposed to is not based on scientific evidence but is a political decision. There is no such thing as a safe radiation dose, nor is there such a thing as a safe nuclear weapon.

I spoke of how Britain, after the 2nd World War (the Hot War) converted its war economy to a peace economy. We can do it again.

Over the two days of the inquiry, evidence was given of AWE Aldermaston using machines 30 years out of date. Last December there was a leak which was briefly mentioned in the local press. One scientist who was contaminated with plutonium died.

The politicians are not interested; we are told daily the Cold War is over. We ask, who is the enemy now? Why the need for these deadly weapons travelling up and down the country? There is no answer. There is no longer a Labour Party anti-nuclear policy; everyone seems to pretend the dangers have gone away, since cruise missiles left Greenham Common. This is not so – the Trident nuclear weapons are much more deadly than cruise missiles and there are many more Trident warheads. There is also the added danger of an accident when the warheads are transported on public roads. Where is the back-up if there is a major accident? How could the fire services and hospitals cope? These questions were asked at the inquiry but we didn't get any answers.

At the inquiry we met a woman who used to work at Harwell (a civil atomic research establishment) as a scientist. She later took us on a tour of Harwell, bringing a geiger counter with her. She showed us a weir in Sutton where toxic waste spills out, only to enter the Thames in the Henley area. She told us that in the area where she lives, the water is so contaminated that they use bottled water for everything.

I would urge the British people to write and protest to their MPs and make known their fears, ideas and solutions to these urgent problems which are all around, particularly near the AWEs. Stop this madness before it is too late. Make your desires known, play your part in exposing this madness. –

That night, Katrina, Claire and I drive up to RAF Wittering.

The 29th of March was the last day for the Ministry of Defence police on Greenham Common. They are to be replaced by private security guards. Katrina, Lisa and Claire walk into the police building during a photocall, displaying a banner which reads GOOD RIDDANCE. That night, we sawed the Main Gate off – one more symbol of the military's retreat.

April brought confrontation with the new security guards. On the 3rd, security guards try to intimidate Rosy and Lisa as they walk through the base to the Main Gate, accusing the women of Trespass and demanding to know their names. Rosy and Lisa refuse to give any information and continue on their way.

The following week, Claire and Anna went for a walk on the Common inside the ex-base. Claire wanted to show Anna the empty silos. Whilst walking in between the two outer fences around the silos, a man in a white estate car, later identified as an employee of Cottismore Construction, Headley, repeatedly drives at the two women, pinning them against the fence with the bumper of the car. He shouts, 'Have you ever heard of a psychopath?' as he continues to manoeuvre his car to pin each woman alternately against the fence. After several terrifying minutes during which the driver becomes more and more aggressive, he eventually reverses his car out of the area at high speed. Both women suffered injuries.

As Claire and Anna begin walking towards a hole in the fence, a second man in a blue estate car outside the silos threatens to send dogs into the corridor between the two fences.

A complaint is made to Newbury police, who claim it is not their jurisdiction to deal with Greenham Common, despite the fact the MoD police have now left. The women are sent to AWE Aldermaston, where the MoD police record the complaint, asking whether they had spray-painted the man's car. We later learn that after 'a full investigation,' they can proceed no further with the matter due to a 'lack of independent evidence.' Claire and Anna are seeking a private prosecution against the driver in an attempt to make him responsible for his behaviour. We are not all equal under the law and certainly not equally eligible for its protection.

The day following this attack, Claire, Lisa and I are in Biggleswade Magistrates Court, on trial for Criminal Damage to the Trident nuclear convoy.

We're surprised to discover that for national security reasons, the prosecution witnesses will be identified by number and not by name. We argue against this, pointing out that in the witness statements sent to us by the prosecution, names and addresses were given. Their omission in court gives the case a sinister atmosphere. In a barely audible whisper, the prosecutor asks the MoD representative in court if he could have the names of the witnesses made public, as their omission would be grounds for appeal. It was agreed we would have people with names give evidence.

Claire and Lisa admitted causing Criminal Damage by marking the Trident convoy with paint on the 29th September 1993.

I argue I was in the car and therefore not involved with the damage. The prosecutor introduces a House of Lords ruling from a terrorism case involving the IRA, in which the accused had given two bombers information about a particular pub and had driven the bombers to the site. The accused argued that as he did not know exactly what the bombers were going to do and neither had he seen a bomb he could not be guilty of being a bomber. The ruling stated the accused was a member of the IRA, knew their tactics and had a fair idea of what was being planned. By this ruling, I was found Guilty of Criminal Damage as I had driven the women to the convoy and as a member of Greenham Common Women's Peace Camp I would have had a fair of idea of their tactics.

The struggle to get the witnesses named, together with the use of this precedent, was disturbing. It was an effort to get the court to recognise our non-violence. We were dealing with a hostile, not a neutral bench.

The case went on for a second day. Lisa and Claire gave evidence and the police were challenged about their behaviour in September. We were all found Guilty. The court ordered pre-sentence reports on each of us. Lisa refused, but the magistrates would not sentence her there and then. We were ordered to reappear on 11th May.

Mid-April we are joined by Sue Adams for a week. Sue had travelled from Canada to spend time with us. The day after her arrival, the appeal of our unsuccessful application for a Judicial Review to examine Newbury District Council's eviction order on our caravans is heard in the High Court. Sarah, Katrina, Claire and I appear in front of three judges, again arguing the byelaws used to evict us are illegal, and are used selectively and inconsistently. The judges' decision was to endorse the former decision. The eviction notice is upheld. Our claim to rights of shelter and freedom from harrassment despite our political beliefs was not accepted. The next course of action open to us is to apply for Adverse Possession.

We're delighted when Sue buys the camp a fold-up ladder. The reason for this is the MoD have just completed building a wall at AWE Burghfield at the spot from which we monitor the convoy preparations. Now we either climb a tree or the new ladder in order to see over the wall.

On April 22nd, Claire and I enter a plea of Not Guilty to Criminal Damage to AWE Burghfield's fence from March. We're given bail conditions not to go on any MoD land or interfere with MoD property anywhere in the country.

Voting begins in South Africa's first non-racial elections on April 26th. We remember Irene Mkwayi, who never saw this day, and our thoughts are with Mrs Kotane.

On the 29th, Katrina, Sarah Watson, Margaret James, Frances Vigay and Lisa Medici enter their Not Guilty pleas to Criminal Damage charges from the December gathering action. The prosecution try to apply the same bail conditions Claire and I had received, but the women manage to argue the conditions are too vague, and walk out of the court with unconditional bail.

The 11th of May is the day Claire, Lisa and I have to return to Biggleswade Magistrates court for sentencing. Margaret comes to support, and witnesses Lisa and Claire being given a custodial sentence of 28 days, after refusing to do community service. It was what we expected and had planned for. I was sentenced to 3 months.

Holloway had changed its routine, so as to allow all women who want to do so to attend Education. This helps relieve the boredom and some of the oppression of the system. Education is a series of lessons ranging from pottery, Black studies, human studies, to languages, etc. The teachers seem dedicated to helping the prisoners – however, they are restricted by the prison system.

On May 15th, Sarah Hipperson, Peggy Walford and Katrina Howse went into the ex-base. They are challenged by the security guards and asked to leave. The guards then phone the MoD police in Burghfield and on their arrival, the women are told they are 'unwanted guests.'

Sarah Hipperson and Katrina travel to London to attend a Court of Appeal hearing on 17th May, challenging the Home Secretary's decision not to allow Compensation for prison served under the invalid Greenham Common Byelaws. Judge Bingham, Master of the Rolls, and two others turn down this test case appeal by Katrina. The judges explain one can only get Compensation if new or newly discovered facts come to light which prove the imprisoned person was innocent. The Byelaws have always been invalid, they argue, therefore this is not a new or newly discovered fact. Katrina told the NEWBURY WEEKLY NEWS, 'This decision confirms our experience of the way the courts continue to cover up for the government ministers. In denying Compensation for time served in prison the court is upholding the same arrogance that brought in the invalid Byelaws in the first place. But this is not the end, we will continue our struggle for Compensation.'

Trident is tested in the US Navy's Atlantic testing area, when a D5 missile is fired from the nuclear powered HMS Vanguard. Press reports speak of new plans to allow the missile to be used in a so-called limited way; armed with a single warhead (instead of up to 6 warheads on each missile), it could be used against 'smaller targets.' Some navy surface ship officers are reported as feeling this has made a nonsense of the billions already spent on the Trident system. So far, the Ministry of Defence have bought 44 of the 70 Trident missiles which will be our 'deterrent'.

We also learn that the eight transporters which carry the warheads from AWE Aldermaston to Coulport in Scotland were specially developed at a cost of £1 million each, but have a poor service record. The cost to the taxpayer has been estimated at £66,000 for spare parts alone.

In Holloway, I was suffering from either a slipped disc or a swollen hip joint squeezing on a nerve. I eventually asked the prison doctor for help. I was unable to sleep or stand up. I was given non-steroid pain killers, which had the effect of making me very drowsy and it seemed to take an enormous amount of will power just to get out of bed.

The women at the camp were organising for the August gathering and sending out leaflets.

On the 25th May, Lisa and Claire finish their sentence and I am transferred to Drake Hall in Staffordshire. All 3 of us decide to appeal our sentences, and I the conviction. At Drake Hall the pain killer dosage is increased – as is my tiredness and extreme lack of energy.

The end of the May brought some hot sunny days to the camp. Frances wrote in the diary: 'We got up and all gathered in the caravan to listen to a Radio 4 programme with Katrina talking about the camp's resistance over the years to the cruise missile convoys and now to Trident.'

I was listening to the same programme while cleaning the dining room tables in Drake Hall.

I was released from prison on 'licence' to attend Reading Magistrates court for our trial concerning Criminal Damage from March. I could go to court unescorted as long as I fulfilled certain requirements – mainly that I returned to prison after the case. I was driven to court in a taxi. We made a slight detour and stopped off at the camp. There I was able to give the surprised women a big hug before getting back in the taxi and meeting the women at the court. Katrina and Lisa were there to support Claire and I. We were found Guilty, despite there being no evidence of us committing the damage. We had a choice of a £125 fine or 7 days imprisonment. I refused to pay and had two days added on to my sentence. Claire asked for time to pay her fine, so delaying her time for imprisonment.

It was hard voluntarily walking back into Drake Hall, complying with a system I hated and wanted to dismantle. Having the support of my sisters enabled me to not let my resistance waver.

On the 14th June, Rosy Bremer and Erica Wilson were in court for non-payment of fines and sentenced to 7 days each.

The next day, Margaret James, Frances Vigay, Lisa Medici, Sarah Watson and Katrina are in Reading Magistrates court to fight their conviction for Criminal Damage. It is a two-day trial. Margaret James wrote in our September 1994 newsletter: '. . . in court, the police claimed that Katrina had bullied me into a confession. This statement was shown to be a lie; a police officer Skilling was quickly found who was quite prepared to say that in fact Lisa had cut the fence.

'The whole of the first day was taken up with Skilling's evidence. He gave an extremely detailed description of watching Lisa cut the fence. In questioning him, we reduced his evidence to the statement that in the time that it took him to run 19 feet, Lisa approached the fence, cut a 4-foot hole in it and got through. Now, we know that the police are slow and that Greenham women are extremely competent at cutting fences, but this was too much.

'The rest of the police started jumping ship and contradictory evidence was flying around the court room: who had arrested whom (one officer who claimed to have arrested me but hadn't, said that he thought he had because he was standing near me), what women had been arrested for and the nature of the security at the base.

'Eventually the case fell because it got to the point that if the police witness answered the next question, clear perjury would be committed. Full costs were awarded to all of us.

'It was a great achievement for us and it was satisfying that, on account of their trying to lie and frame other women they lost the conviction they could have secured (I said in court that I cut the fence and did so with lawful excuse i.e. to prevent genocide – the court didn't seem to care about that). Tremendous support was given in court by Sarah Hipperson, Anna and Jean.'

Letter published in June 23rd's NEWBURY WEEKLY NEWS:

I am writing to you from Yellow Gate Women's Peace Camp about the military exercises currently taking place inside the Common, behind locked gates. Last night (June 19th) several military vehicles and tanks went into the Common with lighting equipment and other military gear.

Today 2 women who were walking on the Common in order to determine the nature of the military presence found armed soldiers outside a hangar housing the tanks. More vehicles are going in this evening, so from all the evidence it looks like a fairly large scale exercise.

We know the Common has been used for army exercises after the cruise missiles left; most recently, in April, Ghurkas from Colchester spent several days inside the Common. Is the MoD going to restore the status of the Common as land available for everyone to enjoy or is it going to continue its stranglehold on this beautiful site?

Members of the public have every right to walk on the Common, and to appreciate all its beauty and abundance.

Whenever we exercise our freedom to enjoy the Common we are confronted by security guards who try to prevent us from entering or leaving. Today for example a security guard on a motorbike blocked off the nearest exit from the area around the hangars, where the military exercises were taking place. It is not up to these security guards to control who goes in and out, where when and how. Any fencing or building on the Common has been found to be illegal, so any attempt to protect the property, industry and military activity inside the Common has no legal validity as well as the obvious moral bankruptcy.

The Common is too precious a resource for us to allow it to be monopolised by the MoD and we cannot afford to slacken our vigilance and resistance to the privatisation of public land. Neither can we afford to believe the privatisation of the Common will write the military out of its history. They are here to stay unless we give them a clear message that there is no room on the Common any more for any military.

Readers who value their freedom, and the Common, must not let the military invade either. They would be most welcome to work with us against the colonisation of the Common.

Rosy Bremer

On June 21st, Katrina has a Means Enquiry at Newbury Magistrates Court. She refuses to pay £340 in fines and receives 14 days in prison. Lisa's diary entry: 'Katrina was excellent in court – even though the magistrates sat in the higher chairs in the elevated section, they had to look up to her.'

It is the Summer Solstice, and on the way to Holloway, the police car in which Katrina is travelling is stopped by a woman asking for help for her friend, who is delivering a baby! Katrina also leaves the police car, to join the happy crowd gathering – 'Thank the Lord, it's a girl!' someone exclaims. Someone else, on learning of Katrina's situation, pleaded (in vain) with the police, 'Oh, let her go!' Unfortunately, the journey had to continue. Both mother and daughter were fine, we later learned from a newspaper report.

On the last day of June, I am released from prison. On this day we learn that Newbury District Council have ear-marked £50,000 to help secure their future acquisition of Greenham Common. The Council will use the money to obtain advice from consultants on European funding, grants for the Common and legal guidance on buying the ex-base from the MoD.

In response to the report of the community inquiry into safety at the AWEs in March, Reading Borough Council established a campaign group. A new community forum is set up, of which we are to become members.

On the 7th July we have to send a letter to CND to respond to an article in the CND periodical, CAMPAIGN:

We are writing in response to an article titled 'Women and non violence, a Greenham approach' published in the Spring edition of CND TODAY.

We feel as women from Yellow Gate (the still existing and fully active Greenham Common Women's Peace Camp which has been open and active non-stop for 13 years) that this article was misleading. We draw your attention particularly to the following points:

The 'Greenham means . . .' list does not include a commitment to taking non-violent direct action against the military . . .

Several phrases in the article lead the reader to believe that Greenham has finished . . . The phrase, 'It is a sad time for those of us who are the last to leave' is extremely misleading since nowhere in the article is it made clear that the camp at Yellow Gate is still open . . .

*A luta continua* – Claire Pearson, Katrina Howse, Peggy Walford, Rosy Bremer.

The new Criminal Justice Bill begins to make its way through parliament. This new Bill is supposed to have the effect of stopping grassroots movements in this country and is therefore a testimony to the success of these movements. However, if this Bill is not challenged then it could have dire effects on people's liberties.

A lot has been written on the consequences of this Bill for hunt sabateurs and anti-road demonstrators. Very little is written about the effects on the 'peace movement'. This is an indictment of the 'peace movement', showing it up on the whole to be dormant and inactive. This means the activists who have kept up the effective resistance to Trident and militarism will bear the brunt of the Bill alone within the 'peace movement'.

There is a great deal of support for this new Bill because of the clever propaganda package presented to the public. Erosion of freedom is disguised as protection of property. The right to dissent against the abuses of power by the powerful is covered up as defending the rule of law.

Our ability to influence democratic institutions has been eroded by the military-industrial complex buying up, dismantling or disempowering those institutions which the electorate had an influence upon. The only way our voices can be heard is through demonstration and visible actions. This has become a powerful and effective means of ascertaining our rights to have a say in the running of our lives.

The camp has become a beacon drawing women from all over the world who wish to learn and participate in work for justice. This new Bill will criminalise us for being on this land (Clause 56) and not leaving. Clause 72 would criminalise us for returning within 3 months when 'asked' to leave. Magistrates could order the destruction of our goods.

We could be imprisoned under Clause 65 for holding our gatherings. Assemblies can be banned if the police 'believe' they may cause disruption of a community nearby. 20 people or more is considered an assembly. To incite or organise an assembly carries a 3 months prison sentence.

Clause 63 is designed to prevent 'aggravated trespass'. This could be used as a substitute for the Greenham Common Byelaws (1985) which fell foul of the legal and non-violent direct action challenges of the women at Greenham Common.

Under Clause 77 we would face prosecution for possessing information without authorisation which is not 'public knowledge' and could be of use to terrorists. The state does not have to prove the information could or would be used by a terrorist organisation, only that it is possible. In other words, any information the Government does not want you to know comes under this clause. Conviction carries a maximum sentence of 10 years.

Clause 26 hands power from the courts to the police to impose bail conditions. The police can even refuse bail.

We do not have to do anything to gain a conviction under these proposed laws. To commit an offence the police only have to prove intent. The removal of the right to silence means the police, through interrogation, could gain a lot of prosecutions from 'confessions.' Once in police custody it is difficult not to have your words misconstrued and confused through police tactics.Any evidence or facts needed to be taken into consideration for your defence have to be submitted while being arrested and during questioning. Any evidence produced later will not be accepted by the courts.

This Bill is challenging grassroots movements because we have been successful in strengthening the voice of the disenfranchised.

On the 24th July, women from the camp join an anti-Criminal Justice Bill march through London. The atmosphere was positive.

A National Audit Office report reveals the MoD have wasted more than £800 million building facilities for Trident in Scotland. The report reveals huge budget overruns, delays, mismanagement, lack of communication and design faults, including a failure to appreciate the cost of protecting the public from nuclear accidents.

To commemorate the 5th anniversary of the killing of Helen Thomas, women gather at Yellow Gate. Helen's family contributed to the memorial by sending flowers and a poem via friends who were travelling to Southampton on the 5th. The poem, in Welsh, was about Rosa Parks, a Black woman who had taken strong non-violent direct action* by saying 'NO' when told to move to the Black section of a bus in Alabama that was to take her home after a hard day's work. Helen's mother was to read the poem at the Eisteddfod at 1 o'clock, at the same time and on

* The first time I saw this refusal of injustice described as – and thereby included in the history of – non-violent direct action was in Wilmette Brown's book, Black Women and the Peace Movement (see Resources). -Editor.

283

the same day on which Helen had been killed five years ago. Mary Millington and Jean Hutchinson read the poem at Yellow Gate at the same time, in Welsh, followed by their translation into English.

The anger about the treatment of Helen in her death continues to surface – mostly I suppress it. This is not healthy, which is why it is important to have a memorial to Helen each year. This time allows us to remember and grieve. I feel in our struggle for justice we are carrying on Helen's work. At the age of 22 she had already given a lot to our struggle and the struggle for Welsh autonomy – we have to build on that.

One piece of work we had to deal with on the 5th was our response to learning that the United Nations' were planning to hold a women's conference in Beijing. We sat underneath the poplars and composed a letter to the Secretary General, Gertrude Mongella:

Yellow Gate

Dear Ms Mongella,

As women who are gathered here today to commemorate the life of Helen Thomas, who was active in protests against the Tiananmen Square massacre in June 1989, we wish to express our dissent from the decision to hold the Fourth World Conference on Women: Action for Equality, Development and Peace, in Beijing during September 4-15th 1995.

Shortly after her work outside the Chinese Embassy, London and at Greenham Common to support the non-violent encampment in Tiananmen Square, Helen was killed on the 5th August 1989 on the road outside the peace camp by a West Midlands Police horse-box vehicle.

Throughout the month of June 1989, we worked in solidarity with the non-violent encampment in Tiananmen Square, enjoining our non-violent encampment with theirs.

We continue to align our efforts with all those who are imprisoned in China for their defence of non-violence and democracy, and with the families and friends of those killed. Until they are allowed to express their views freely, without risk of being silenced by death or imprisonment, we believe that Beijing is an unfit venue for any discussion.

We are non-violent, non-aligned, anti-racist, anti-nuclear autonomous women.

[signed] Sarah Hipperson Frances Vigay

| | |
|---|---|
| Rosy Bremer | Claire Pearson |
| Zoe Harper | Jean Hutchinson |
| Klaske Rast | Katrina Howse |
| Beth Junor | Janet Tavner |

Peggy Walford        Aniko Jones
Clare Downs

On August 6th, following our Workshop at the camp, 6 women take non-violent direct action at AWE Burghfield. Katrina Howse, Jean Hutchinson, Rachel Bird, Sarah Hipperson and Frances Vigay take down 9 sections of fence around the Atomic Weapons Establishment. All are all charged with Criminal Damage and bailed to appear at Reading Magistrates Court on September 12th.

On Nagasaki Day, 7 women: Claire Pearson, Rosy Bremer, Peggy Walford, Katrina Howse, Klaske Rast, Sarah Hipperson and Jean Hutchinson chain themselves to a fence inside AWE Aldermaston. After having been cut from the fence and escorted off the premises by MoD police, the women continue to hold a vigil outside the fence for some time.

Letter from Mrs Thomas:
Dear All,

Thank you all for your kind words of support on August 5th. It was good to hear that so many of you had got together at Yellow Gate to remember Helen. My heart was there with you.

August 5th was a very memorable day for me too. For the first time since we started competing as a recitation party at the Eisteddfod, we went through preliminary tests and reached the stage with two other parties. That in itself was quite an achievement; it was a bigger shock still to get 1st prize! We were reciting on stage just after 1pm and I felt Helen was there with me.

Just an hour later, the name of the chaired bard was announced. He was Emyr Lewis [the solicitor who had worked with Mrs Thomas to reopen the inquest into Helen's death]. For all this to happen on August 5th was very moving.

Anne and Norma, who very kindly called on their way to Southampton, were thrilled to learn of our success. They told their mother on the phone of the welcome they received from you all.

Anne was our tutor, and as I am sure you will all agree, the poetry she had chosen for us to recite was very moving.

I hope I will be able to visit you very soon...

All my love and very best wishes,

Janet & family

On August 13th, Janet, Rosy and Peggy go to London to join the Troops Out march, to show our solidarity with the people of Northern

Ireland and to reaffirm our stand against the British army's occupation of Northern Ireland.

In September, we complete our preparations for our celebration of 13 years of resistance. The newsletter was made ready, the banners put up. Katrina wrote in our newsletter: 'It is a sign of the strength of the camp, and that means all of us who keep it going, that the camp is still active and developing after 13 years. We have all made a commitment here, and invested so much of our lives against great odds.

'The land has to go back to Common land and be taken out of the hands of the Ministry of Defence. The MoD have so far had their application to de-register the Common sent back to them by Berkshire County Council. It's only a matter of time before it's accepted, and the MoD try to sell the land to property developers. This we will resist by opposing them in the courts and on the Common.

'This work travels alongside all the work against Trident. Our main focused non-violent direct action is against Trident nuclear warhead production and transportation. There will be continuous refurbishment of Trident at Burghfield and Aldermaston even after completed production.

'13 years on it's clear any solid opposition to nuclear weapons has to be part of a collective commitment. It's been a long haul, it's going to carry on being a long haul. This year has shown me, yet again, how the military are determined to break our resistance to Trident with all the state power they can muster. Just look at all the prison that has been inflicted on women this year, particularly on Aniko Jones. Also, 5 of us had a 'Going Concerned' Criminal Damage charge dumped on us for going into AWE Burghfield last December. A PC invented the story that Lisa had cut the fence, when she hadn't, and he asserted this in the Magistrates Court. The case collapsed after 1½ days of trial this June. The prosecution had to seek permission to drop the charges from a 'top' MoD official at Whitehall. The man's name is reputed to be Cyril Foster. This confirmed my suspicion that the charges against us are being orchestrated at a top MoD level, where the military dictatorship is very secretive and protective of itself. There was selective intimidation of Lisa and I that December night at Burghfield. We were women they knew as camp women, and they try to individually break camp women. In the end the 5 of us were so strong together that the top level man put a Going Concerned charge on us all. This fell through and exposed him. It took us 6 months of fighting this charge before he was exposed by the failure of the prosecution.

'Beyond one name is a whole military dictatorship: there isn't even a pretence, or thin hope, that we can vote nuclear weapons and the military out of power. We need more women to join us so we can stand firm and face this dictatorship with more support. We stopped cruise missiles, we can do the same to Trident nuclear weapons. This is what the military most fear.

'The Audit Office have revealed that the MoD spent £1.9 billion on the buildings for Trident. This was an overspending of £800 million. As usual there is no criticism or questioning, it is accepted that the MoD can have all that money for a totally destructive weapons system. Meanwhile Rwandan refugees are dying in their thousands with little help from western military states – they did nothing to stop the genocide in Rwanda. We cannot endure this system ruled by a power mad military.

'A small group of committed women can do so much to oppose these dominant values. The Cyril Fosters don't want us to know how effective we are, and that we are getting stronger. Join us.'

On the 13th September, Claire is given a 7 day prison sentence for refusing to pay a £40 fine.

On the 15th, Katrina finds a pro-fascist leaflet has been slipped into her caravan.

The Trident nuclear convoy leaves Burghfield on the 19th September. While following it, we are stopped by Biggleswade police on 'suspicion of a possible breach of the peace' and held for over 3 hours in a police cell until the convoy has reached RAF Wittering. We return to the camp to discover a letter sent to us from Exeter district, warning/threatening us: 'There will be an attempt to disrupt the peace camp's peace activities. Violence may be used. Men will be involved as well as women. – A Pacifist.'

Very early in the morning of the 20th, we begin following the convoy once more. Katrina and Rosy blockade it, are arrested and then de-arrested once the convoy is on its way again. We continue following it, continually being stopped by the police in every county we enter, sometimes even twice in one county. We follow the convoy up to Scotch Corner [North Yorkshire], informing people on the route that this unmarked military convoy carries nuclear warheads. At Scotch Corner we have to leave – we have little money and we're low on petrol. It was hard to watch the convoy continue its journey up to Scotland, with more warheads to be put on the Trident submarines.

As the winter draws in, I have to serve another sentence – 7 days from the 27th September. We continue our resistance to the Criminal Justice Bill. We are privileged to be joined by three women from Holland, who tell us about a 'Walk for Mother Earth' coming to England in 1995. We continue our regular incursions into AWEs Aldermaston and Burghfield. Katrina requests independent legal observers from the European Court of Human Rights to monitor the next trial at Reading Magistrates Court, in light of our past experiences in this court.

The concerns for safety in AWE Aldermaston come to a head when a Health and Safety Executive (HSE) inspection finds inadequate precautions are being taken to prevent a runaway nuclear chain reaction; a Prohibition Notice is immediately issued to halt operations in one area of the plant. 65 deficiencies in all were found. 19 recommendations require immediate attention. One of the HSE's primary recommendations is that the Secretary of State for Defence should waive AWE's immunity from licensing under the Nuclear Installations Act.

At the end of October, we learn that the MoD plan to return 900 acres – all of Crookham Common and the majority of Greenham Common – to public ownership via the Council. There are two important areas not included in the deal: the former nuclear silos area, still subject to inspection by Russian delegates under the INF Treaty, and the partly built up area of around 144 acres which encompasses most of the buildings on the ex-base, which the MoD want to develop commercially.

The trial for the Hiroshima Day action at AWE Burghfield runs for two days at the beginning of November, then is adjourned until the 10th for judgement. In the interim, a representative from the Ministry of Defence visits the camp to inform us their application to de-register Greenham Common has been accepted by Berkshire County Council. He presents the de-registration as a *fait accompli*, as the Commoners have sold their rights. He is informed we will oppose the application. After making enquiries at Berkshire County Council, we find out that in fact the application to deregister had not been accepted.

On the 11th, Sarah Hipperson, Jean Hutchinson, Katrina Howse, Frances Vigay, Rachel Bird and Peggy Walford are each found Guilty of Criminal Damage to the Burghfield fence. Katrina is fined £400, Sarah and Jean £300, Frances, Peggy and Rachel £250.

The year ended as it had begun, with torrential rain beating down on the caravans. We are still here, still true to our principles, still living our politics. Neither the rain nor the state has dampened our fires.

# 1995
## *(January 1st – Nagasaki Day, August 9th)*
# COMMON SENSE
## by Rosy Bremer

1995 begins with a beautiful, sunny sub-zero morning. There's snow on the ground, and an exceptionally cold wind whipping over the Common. Janet's at the camp and it's a great pleasure to have her here, enjoying the magic of the new year. Aniko is too ill to join in the celebrations or appreciate the quiet snow falling all around.

On New Year's Day I go for a walk in the ex-base. We don't get long to match the calm, unhurried weather, as there are helicopters flying around the Common and military vehicles entering. Janet checks Burghfield, as often the military synchronises its air and road manoeuvres. A final check on the 6th of January shows the convoy is in, waiting to be loaded.

We are also busy trying to find out exactly what Newbury District Council are planning for the Common. We meet with Mike Thorne, assistant director of development services at Newbury DC, to find out about a conference called *Planning and the Peace Dividend – Unlocking the Defence Estate.* Mike Thorne tells us he can't give us an invitation to the conference, but can give us the conference organiser's address. We contact the organiser who tells us we cannot attend unless we can pay £155 to register. From then on, we decide to organise a picket of the event. Our reasoning is explained in our leaflet, distributed to those attending, *What's the point of a picket?*

COLLUSION – Newbury District Council has a history of colluding with the MoD's requisition of Greenham Common for use as a military base; most notably a nuclear military base. No doubt other authorities have also given permission, tacitly or otherwise for the military to move in on public land.

In the '30's Greenham Common was declared a Site of Special Scientific Interest, to be protected from development . . . The Common hit the headlines in the early eighties, because of the inspired protest against cruise missiles. The women who made Greenham a key issue and resisted the criminal abuse of the Common faced prison sentences, eviction after eviction and harassment, for their efforts.

The local council fully sanctioned the evictions, to remove the voice of opposition to the theft of Common land. One of the evictions was even entitled *The Final Solution.* Now that cruise has gone, it's time for our work to be acknowledged.

EXCLUSION – Our work has made this conference possible. We

challenged the MoD on Greenham Common, we stopped cruise missile deployments on Salisbury Plain, we took the MoD to court, and we won. Where is the recognition of the vital role women have played, in restoring the Common? We cannot speak about our invaluable experiences because we haven't got £155. Newbury District Council and other consultants/authorities/planners, some of whom have worked flat out to stop women opposing the military takeover of Greenham Common are suddenly the experts. We must have a fair hearing in any discussion of the peace dividend; without our resistance there would be no mention of a peace dividend.

FRAUD – There is no peace dividend. There will be no peace dividend until the British state has stopped producing Trident nuclear warheads. At the expense of health, education and shelter, our government is spending over £30 billion on another genocidal weapon system. This must be challenged and highlighted whenever there is talk of unlocking defence estates. Women who have worked for years and years to get what the state has taken from the MoD are not included or recognised, when we could give specialist evidence on the peace dividend that is due to us. That is what we have to say; there is no peace without justice, and justice means a fair hearing. Even for the poor. We continue to work to expose and resist the military; we will continue to reclaim the Common.

Unusually, the Trident convoy leaves Burghfield on a Sunday, the 8th of January. Frances Vigay and Aniko drive up to Wittering and trespass once the convoy's in the vehicle compound. They arrive back at the camp in the early morning, very tired but satisfied they've done all they could to resist.

Katrina has two court appearances, one a Legal Aid appeal, the other a Means Enquiry which she manages to have post-poned *sine die* (without date) pending the outcome of the appeal of the convictions arising from the Hiroshima Day 1993 action.

We also have a meeting with Newbury District Council in January about plans to create a museum on Greenham Common. Sarah, Jean, Katrina and Aniko attend on behalf of the camp. Other groups in attendance include representatives from Bradford University Peace Studies Department, the Allied Forces Group (a local military vehicles trust), Commons Again, Greenham Retailers Association for Trade (GRAFT) and Reading Mediation Centre.

We all feel it is an historic meeting, in that we had been invited by Newbury District Council to give our expertise and have our work recorded. At the same time, we are aware that our story is not yet over and we have concerns regarding whether our history will be accurately

*. . . The following day, the Walk for Mother Earth arrives at the camp.*
*It's such a dismal, drizzly day . . .*

represented and recorded. It is most definitely not in the state's interest to give us a platform. The months ahead reveal just how complex the power politics regarding the proposed museum are.

Before the month is out, Newbury District Council unanimously votes to grant a further £50,000 to the Greenham Common sub-committee to spend on consultants' fees and publicity.

At the beginning of February, solicitor Mike Schwarz visits to discuss the forthcoming Aldermaston appeal. He tells us he's never come up against so many brick walls, in trying to get evidence out of the MoD.

On the same day, Sarah, Katrina and Aniko go to Shire Hall in Reading to meet with Mr Moate again. Mr Moate explains the land-swap proposed by the MoD in light of their failed applications to deregister the Common. The proposed land-swap scheme would permit industrial development on the built-up area, and put Commoners rights on an area of land outside its surrounding fence.

In Reading Crown Court, we appear before Judge Lait once more, this time for directions concerning the Aldermaston appeal. We are told to prepare our skeleton arguments for the end of March. The hearing is set for July 3rd and is timetabled to last until the 7th. Aniko and Peggy are represented by a barrister, Rajiv Menon, who shows a lot of enthusiasm for the case.

We begin preparing for the arrival of the Walk for Mother Earth. Aniko prepares the ground with the Council, and manages to obtain permission for the Walk's mobile exhibition to park in the Council's car park. The Council will pay for this, and will also arrange for a talk to be held in the Town Hall. (The Council later says the car park is too small, and arranges for the exhibition to be shown at a farm 10 miles outside Newbury.)

We send out invitations to local environmental/peace groups to meet the walkers at the camp.

We first meet the walkers on the 19th February, at their last overnight stop before they will reach Greenham Common. When we arrive, the walkers are huddled in a circle, discussing how best to support those of their group who have been denied entry to the country. Those from Sri Lanka were refused visas to enter Britain; a Blackfoot Native American man was removed from the country after holding a placard in Portsmouth ferry terminal protesting the decision to refuse entry to the Sri Lankan walkers.

The following day, the Walk for Mother Earth arrives at the camp. It's such a dismal, drizzly day that we get up early to prepare a hearty broth to warm the walkers when they arrive. Both the camp banners and Katrina's latest art-work banners are hung from the trees.

Just after midday, we see a colourful, vibrant group walking along the A339 road. Someone is playing a squeeze-box and a couple are beating on tambours. We hold hands in a circle at the side of the road and sing, to welcome them. The broth is dished out, and then we give an in-depth talk about our history.

Together we then walk into the ex-base through the Main Gates, up the High Street and along the former runway to the empty silos. We pause before entering, as Sarah describes some of the actions women have taken to remove fencing from the Common. She says if we had been faced with a concentration camp, we would have wanted to do whatever we could to help people to survive. An atmosphere of evil still pervades the area, although the walkers have brought in a joyous, celebratory energy.

With the rain still falling, we wind our way back to the camp. We are privileged to have most of the women in the walk stay overnight with us. A mixed group goes into the Friends' Meeting House in Newbury for the night.

We get up at 5.00am the next morning to be in good time to get into Aldermaston before the workers begin arriving. We also plan to blockade the factory as they arrive. We arrive at the Atomic Weapons Establishment before seven. A group of women walk under the barriers at the Construction gate. This corridor leads to the A90 building, where plutonium is machined into the form in which it will be put into warheads.

We get about a quarter of a mile into the Construction corridor before the police arrive with dogs. Some of the police are wearing military clothing over their uniforms. They say they're doing this 'because its cheap.' We stay for about three quarters of an hour, before we're put into MoD police minibuses and driven out of the base. We remain at the Construction gate, turning back the traffic trying to enter. The MoD put a CLOSED sign on the gates.

The kitchen bus accompanying the walkers brings us hot tea and coffee and later soup and bread for lunch. We take it in turns to blockade the other gates. After lunch, we all go round to the Main Gates, where the mixed group have been blockading. We walk in through the two huge gates past the armed guards, only to be stopped just before we reach the Main Street.

At this point the MoD police close the gates, enabling four of us to chain ourselves to the gates, while other women form a blockade in front of us. Two of us have our hands cut when the chains are removed by someone in military uniform. Another woman is knocked to the ground by a car during the mixed blockade. Complaints are registered, but we are informed 'there are no first-aid facilities in the Establishment.'

It is inspiring to show such international opposition to Aldermaston. We must say goodbye on the 22nd, and get back to holding the camp on our own again.

On the 24th February we hear that the convoy is in Burghfield with five warhead carriers.

On the 27th, Katrina, Peggy and I go into the former USAF Headquarters building with some of the core group of the Museum Committee. We discuss whether the building is suitable for conversion to a museum. We go into the 'decontamination suite' with its metal showers, reminiscent of records we have seen of the concentration camps. We are disturbed by the visit, not least because whilst this building is about to be made into a museum, Aldermaston and Burghfield are still producing nuclear weapons.

The convoy leaves for Faslane on March 2nd. We leave for RAF Wittering at half past four the following morning, to arrive just as it's getting light. It's a crisp, frosty morning, the ground is absolutely frozen as we make our way through the fields to the vehicle compound. We meet the convoy exiting at half past ten and follow it. The military know they can never be confident of carrying out their manoeuvres unopposed. They plant police outriders on the A1 who try and slow us down. It's not so impossible to shake the military's confidence.

Katrina has an exhibition of her banners in Reading. She, Sarah and Aniko go to the opening night on the 5th of March. By all accounts it was exhilarating to be surrounded by the art-work born of Katrina's struggle against the military.

We all get a shock the next day, when Katrina tells us the MoD have put up a new fence, inside the Common. This is to separate the 144 acres of land marked for development from the rest of the Common. We know from past legal experience that it is illegal to erect any fence on Common land. Sarah and Katrina go to see Stuart Tagg at Newbury District Council, who says he knows about the fencing and that the MoD are entitled to put such a fence on the Common. We suspect they won't be asked for planning permission. Katrina and Sarah resolve to take the battle into court.

Aniko goes to Berlin on March 25th for an international conference on direct action. She had been invited after one of the organisers heard her speaking about non violence at a meeting to organise actions against the Criminal Justice Act. She returns on the April 3rd to report a very good response to her presentation about Greenham.

Preparations begin for our Beltane Walk, amidst numerous meetings and regular checks for the nuclear convoy. This walk is to be a sacred walk from Whitehorse Hill, Uffington, along the Ridgeway Path to Avebury Stone Circle, then by transport to the Atomic Weapons Establishments at Aldermaston and Burghfield. The leaflet for the walk affirmed 'it's time to go from AWE for creation, our lives and the natural world, to AWE's, to stop Trident.' Our preparation includes the composition of new songs, another creative expression of our politics and vision. These are all compiled into a songbook which is photocopied the day before the walk begins.

Teresa Smith, who lived at the camp in the early '80's with her 7-year old daughter Elisabeth, had written to ask Katrina to carry her poem *Sheila na Gig* with her on the walk. In an interview with Janet Tavner at Yorkshire Sculpture Park in 1990, Teresa spoke of her time at the camp*:

*Teresa Smith* – I was living in a semi-detached house on a middle class estate at the edge of a town which saw itself as middle class. I'm not middle class and my daughter was going to a school which upheld middle class values. It's the only school I've ever met where they have a regular parents prayer meeting to pray for the school. This is in a state school.

Because I opted my daughter out of religious education I was

* This tape recording was transcribed by Frances Vigay.

therefore considered to be depriving her and I was considered unusual and queer, you know, queer in the sense of weird, peculiar. I opted Elisabeth out of religious education not because I objected to her being taught about religion, but because they were not teaching her adequately.

I was supposed to be receiving maintenance from my husband who was living abroad, from whom I was separated. He chose not to send it so I was living on Supplementary Benefit, which was a low level, inadequate to allow me to heat the house. We'd heat the house for an hour before Elisabeth came home so that it was a warm house for her to come into; we'd spend the evening at a friend's house and share her heating, then go home, have that hour or so while the house remained warm before she went to bed, so she'd go to bed in the warmth. We couldn't afford to heat it at other times.

We were vegetarian in those days, simply because we could not afford meat, and we often couldn't even afford good vegetables.

So there was that attraction of the camp, that it would be cheaper living at the camp than trying to live on your own. It would be less isolating for me particularly to live in an area of like-minded women, where I didn't have to think, either I can get a childminder or I can stay at home with my daughter. That was a real attraction, the fact that these things which were denied me by the poverty of the social security system and the poverty of town living, especially these London dormitory towns that see themselves as so middle class, would not be denied us at Greenham. That sort of cultural poverty and plain financial poverty was solved for me by going to Greenham.

Also, I had been politically involved before I was married and it was a way to be politically involved that didn't clash with my responsibilities to Elisabeth. It was a real release when I realised that it wasn't either I looked after Elisabeth or I went to Greenham, but I could actually take Elisabeth to Greenham with me and I could make my voice heard. The influence I had at Greenham had to be a behind-the-scenes thing, but I could do that and it didn't clash with being a mother and bringing up a daughter.

I visited a couple of times during '82, I was at the big December action in '82, then I came back again at the very end of December '82. We came down to live late January '83 and we lived at the camp continuously until the following August.

At first, I was really worried about keeping Elisabeth warm, and about how on earth to keep her dry in all this weather. Of course in time I relaxed, she got more sensible as she began to learn about things, and I relaxed more as I began to learn about the launderette in Newbury, and such like.

The school was always very helpful. I didn't put Elisabeth into school immediately. I said we'll come and we'll stay a couple of weeks and if it works out then we'll stay on, and I'll put you in the local school. In fact she started school the following Monday.

During the course of that week, Io, Mairi, Mary, Hiro and one or two others started to build a camp at Green Gate. Elisabeth went over and helped them with the building and took me up there. It was established at that time only for women who had already been some time at the camp, much the way the Sanctuary is used now. I asked about being able to live there. They said yes, that was fine, because they knew my commitment. That was good. Elisabeth could come back and live what for her would be a normal life out of the public eye, with a steady group of women, so that she was able to make relationships and that was important for her.

The lie of the land at Green Gate was wonderful because she could go across the Sanctuary, over the stream and up the other side. She roamed wonderfully, and would make all sorts of games. She just assumed that every woman was her potential equal and potential friend, and so they would go off. When I wanted her I could just stand at the side of the camp and call across this great bowl it was, with the Sanctuary at the bottom of the bowl; my voice would carry and she would come from such a long way away. I'd sit down and wait and five minutes later Elisabeth would appear: 'Yes Mum, what do you want?' and that was good.

When we went back to living in a house I noticed that whereas before, when she'd been colouring in a book, she sat at the edge of the room; then, she occupied the whole of the room. She learnt to occupy the whole space and not just scrunch herself up in a corner of it, the way girls use a school playground. Girls sit around the edge of the playground while the boys use the middle of it.

Even now [15 years], she isn't intimidated by adults. She still treats adults as her equals and there's no way they can talk down to her.

From the minute I knew Elisabeth's father was anti our being at the peace camp, I realised that any action I took that got into any sort of records would not be good for me or for Elisabeth. I didn't take part in arrestable actions. I did go into the base once – we planted sunflower seeds and lily of the valley.

On April 1st, which fell on a Saturday, the women had a typical action that showed up the stupidity of the male machine and the creativity of women's protest: they had a teddy bear's picnic inside the base, dressed up as teddy bears. Rupert Bear went, and Paddington Bear went, and there was a cat and there was a pantomime cow in two parts called Daisy, and various others. I took all the women's leftovers from the fur fabric they'd made their outfits from and put them all together into an outfit for Elisabeth. She was a legal observer, so that she was dressed up and was a part of it but not in a way that she could get into any trouble with the law or anything. We stayed outside and we saw what happened and really entered into it.

I happened one day to walk over from Green Gate to Yellow Gate – the shortest route is to go halfway along the fence and the other half along the road. I noticed these two rather small planes parked exceedingly close to the fence, so when I got to Yellow Gate I went to Sarah [Hipperson] who was a good person to go to, and said, 'Do you know I think they're ever so careless the way they've left a couple of their planes very close to the fence with only one soldier sitting in front of them.' The next day I had to go back to Kent to look after my house. Coming back in the evening, I got a newspaper at Paddington station. I don't think the headline was quite like the badge that said 'bye bye blackbird' but I saw that various women had gone in and painted these spy planes. That was the sort of thing I would do. I would see what could be done.

I believe the spiritual work we did at the camp was essential. I think it grew out of the women living with the elements. We lived under the stars, we knew when it was full moon because the nights were lighter and we knew when it was new moon because they were darker. We knew the time of year, we knew what the weather was doing, we felt it. You can't be that close to the Earth herself without recognising your connection. That is what spirituality is about, recognising that there is a oneness in everything. This was where our strength came from, in recognising this oneness, and this is where the principle weakness of the base comes from.

The whole patriarchal mindset which is the military mindset is that 'we say something has to be so and it will be so, and if necessary, we will back it up with our force' and so then 'our force' means our fists, our guns, and whatever they can create, but it's always an extension of themselves. Now, they couldn't understand that they'd tell the women, 'You must get off the Common,' and they would back it up with their force, which in this case meant the men with their muncher machines [rubbish lorries used in the evictions] and they'd think they'd done it because they'd used all their force and they'd moved us off the land. We'd come back, and they couldn't understand that.

We were not using our strength and making weapons which became an extension of ourselves. What we were doing was becoming an extension of the power of the Earth herself and I think that, at its best, is what we were after doing. I don't know whether any of us could have put it into those words then . . .

In the July when we had some blockades...we decorated the police vans with bracken and they kept taking it off, telling us that if we put it on again it was assault and they would arrest us. We were just not taking it seriously and we were being ever so light-hearted about it – 'don't you like art?' and 'beautify your vehicles!' and 'how is that incompatible with being a policeman?' and such like. The women started dancing and made a circle. That was the most powerful circle ever. Before that circle ended I'm sure I wasn't the only person who could actually see the reality that would be where the base had been, a place of green trees, green bracken and picnic seats . . . I'm convinced that that is what it will be in time. It was at that moment I knew that whatever else happens on the way, we've won. You know, it's going to go, and it'll go back to something green. –

Katrina wrote to Teresa to tell her about the Beltane walk. Teresa could not go on the walk because she was fighting cancer.

'Dear Teresa,

'Thank you for your letter which I received just before the Beltane walk. I hope the hospital appointment gave something helpful . . .

'The walk was tremendous, I hope our postcards conveyed something of the feeling.

'We were altogether 13 women . . . I feel that was magical, and synchronistic . . . We all gathered together on White Horse Hill, which again I realise is marvellous. I also realised again that the White Horse is not a White Horse but a Dragon. The fire coming out of her mouth was so obvious from standing on her eye.

'We walked to Wayland Smithy. What a wonderful construction it is, very private, and sacred. Sarah was particularly moved by Wayland Smithy. Most of us seemed to be awed by it – Her.

'Then we moved on to our 1st night camping, Fox Hill just below Lydington Castle. A wild and cold night, with Sarah in the little caravan, the rest camping. Well, this account isn't realistic without you knowing that the police tracked us, plainclothes and in a panda car, right from White Horse Hill. They kept wanting to know what we were doing. At one stage they thought we were going to walk to Stonehenge and reclaim Salisbury Plain.

'At Barbury Castle the RAF police thought we were going to reclaim RAF Wroughton.

'At Silbury Hill we were observed by very thuggish plainclothes police, and then two, a woman and a man with metal sticks (!) raced up the Hill like they were paratroopers. We were camped at the bottom – Beth, Mary and Aniko raced after them and interviewed them at the top. They hadn't had time to get to the tents at the top, but what would they have done up there alone, looked for boltcutters? Planted something? They didn't get the chance, the verdict was they were definitely police...

'Back to the first night – Mary arrived in the morning, as well as Fiona and Aniko and we walked up past Lydington Castle, along the downland hills and down into Ogbourne St George . . . Up to Barbury Castle – this is such a beautiful stretch of the Ridgeway because you climb up higher and higher, up the chalk downs. It is both spectacular but also warm country. I think we all felt inspired by it. Francine was delighted with the word *undulating* . . .

'That night there was a cold and freezing wind; we looked out from the heathland over the plain below us, with Barbury Castle's strong, historic presence above us.

'By the next morning, which was bright and clear, I really felt I was on a pilgrimage . . . at Avebury we moved from stone to stone, focusing on the ritual specifically to stop Trident. Sarah read out your letter of many years ago which explains the true meaning of 'meekness' . . . Beth read a poem by Alice Walker. I read your poem at the last stones, in the area of the great barn. *Sheila na Gig* had a very poweful resonance, right from the title. I think the physicality of the poem, Earth and women, our bodies, makes it a very moving, deep work. The basic, powerful language, earthy and strong – a beautiful poem, Teresa, and wonderful to read! Love of life, a respect and wonder and awe in every line!

'Then we slept on top of Silbury Hill, and in the morning went back to Greenham. Actions happened – Sarah, Rosy, Mary, Fiona and Dorette cut the fence at Aldermaston. 3 sections down, 2 others cut, right by the main road. 5 of us went in, and while waiting for women to be charged, Frances and Henny doublehandedly blockaded Aldermaston's Main Gates. Under the full moon we blockaded, sang and danced the Sowetan Earth Dance. The first woman, Fiona, was charged at 9.50pm, two minutes after the height of the full moon . . .'

We try and wind down over the next couple of days, and adapt once again to the camp routine.

Our court case to stop the land-swap and get the fence inside the ex-base taken down begins, with a pre-trial hearing in the County Court. The MoD and Newbury District Council try to get the case thrown out, but do not succeed. A date is set for another hearing: July 31st.

Katrina learns that Teresa Smith died on the 16th of June, and writes in the diary: 'Her condition got much worse and with friends and family around her, she died. She has left a very brave, gutsy daughter . . . Always, Teresa remained undefeated. Dying with cancer, her spirit seemed to be as strong as when she knew she was in her last stage. I feel very grateful that I knew Teresa and that I was part of her journey in her spiritual 'gang'. Her son, Michael, and daughter, Elisabeth need all the support they can get and would like. Blessed be to them. Teresa understood so much about matriarchal wisdom, lived by it, and communicated it. For me she is an example of how to live rightly and freely.'

Our Aldermaston appeal begins in early July and lasts 7 days, during which time a convoy of Trident warheads leaves Burghfield. Our suspicions had proved exactly right, and our preparation had paid off – we could resist the convoy and still appear in court. We manage to get across the evidence we want to be heard, so that our integrity as a group and as individuals shines out, as does the fact that we take reasonable action, in such an insane world. The judge does not give a verdict, saying it is 'not an uncomplicated matter,' but later promises to do so in September.

In the County Court on the 31st July, the MoD appear with no defence prepared. The judge explains they are perfectly entitled to reserve their position. Katrina argues well on several points. However, Judge Davidson strikes out the proceedings against Newbury District Council and gives the MoD 21 days in which to prepare their defence. We are to return on September 25th.

The sixth anniversary of Helen Thomas's death falls on a Saturday once more, the weekday on which Helen was killed.

*Janet Thomas* – It is now six years since Helen's death. That terrible moment on the afternoon of August 5th 1989 will remain with us and indeed with many others, for a long, long time.

So many people's lives have been affected by Helen's death. She was a bubbly, lovely, wonderful young woman who had so much to offer.

She had decided that she wanted to work for peace and justice in the world. How sad it is that she paid the ultimate price for what she so strongly believed in. It hurts so much to think that one of her priorities in life was denied her in death. All we wanted from the inquest into her death was the truth. Was that too much to ask? It obviously was!

The *hiraeth* for Helen will be with us for ever. The frustration and anger left by the injustice of the inquest stands in our way and obstructs us from our memories and peace of mind. –

August 6th 1995 is the 50th anniversary of the dropping of the first atomic bomb in wartime, on the population of Hiroshima. We wake to hear on the radio news that the mayor of Hiroshima has apologised for Japan's role in the Second World War. He is calling for total nuclear disarmament. The British state reacts by saying this is not an apology from the Japanese government; doubt is also cast on the sincerity of the message. We discuss these developments at length, before 5 women leave the camp to remove 9 sections of fence from AWE Aldermaston. All are arrested and charged.

On Nagasaki day, a group of ten of us blockade the Construction gate and the Main Gates of Aldermaston.

# EPILOGUE

We now begin to prepare our next newsletter, in an attempt to record our work and distribute an accurate account of who we are and what we are doing. All our words cannot be captured – our replies to charges, our painted messages, our discussions, thoughts, challenges in courts, our banners, leaflets, letters, songs, stories and poetry. Once again, Katrina will produce just the right illustration for the cover, which will compensate in large part. Our language, so much a part of all our non-violent actions, seems painfully inadequate at times.

During the August gathering which ended Rosy's final chapter, we've been joined by Mary Millington, who wrote of Helen Thomas in our 1989 newsletter: '. . . I felt a great liking for a woman who could make clear, in a first conversation with someone, who she was and what she stood for, without either placating in any way, or causing offence.

'She started me thinking: why are we in England not taught the language of the country next door? The answers go back into English colonialist history, and still continue today.

'I want to learn Welsh, both in memory of Helen, and for my own benefit.' This desire is being fulfilled:

*Mary* – I started learning on my own with a book and a tape which Helen's friend Joe gave me, then was directed towards a residential weekend for Learners at Llangrannog in West Wales by Gill Stephens of Cymdeithas yr Iaith Gymraeg (the Welsh Language Society), when she visited Yellow Gate after Helen's death. Since then I have attended the weekends at Llangrannog almost every spring and autumn, and have progressed from blithering idiot in the beginners' class to the bottom of the 'bron yn rhugl' (almost fluent) class. I moved to Wales in 1992, and have been greedily chomping my way through the various courses available ever since. I obtained my TGAU Cymraeg Ail Iaith (GCSE) last year, and will be starting an 'A' Level course this September.

People ask me why – why does an English woman like me want to learn Welsh? And I ask myself the same question. Becoming fluent and literate in Welsh will not bring Helen back. One more English learner getting the language a bit wrong will not further its cause at all.

One answer is: I am learning Welsh to please myself, because it sounds so lovely and is transforming the shapes of my thoughts and extending my experience.

But the chief and original reason is the influence of Helen Thomas and all she stood for; how we at Greenham answered her need to make a stand for peace in the world and for women, and how she influenced us with her sense of identity bound up with her language and her strong love for her country.

'O bydded i'r heniaith barhau.'
(Anthem Cymru)

Long may the ancient language continue.
(Anthem of Wales)

✳✳✳

What more can one ask from words and images, than that they transform the shapes of one's thoughts, and extend experience?
*A luta continua.*

-NOT THE END-

.

# NOTES

*Who we are –*

We are young and old, in our twenties, thirties, forties, sixties and one seventy year old woman.

We are working class women and middle class women.

We are lesbian, heterosexual and celibate women, acknowledging that the first two categories can also be celibate.

We are women of different abilities.

At times in our history we have been Black women and white women.The only descriptive category which includes us all is the one which recognises we are all autonomous women. Within this autonomy, we agree upon and are influenced by a set of clearly defined principles: we are non-violent, non-aligned and anti-racist.

*What you can do –*

Any proceeds from the sale of this book will go direct to the camp.

All women who share our principles are welcome to visit or stay at the camp for any period of time. Children are welcome with their carers.

Men who are able or willing to work with autonomous women are welcome to visit the camp during daylight hours, or to write to the camp enquiring how you may support our work.

Financial support is much needed and appreciated. We do not have offices/Foundations/national or international representatives collecting funds on our behalf. All donations should be sent directly to us, at our postal address below. Cheques should be made payable to 'Greenham Common Women's Peace Camp'.

We produce regular Newsletters, usually twice a year. If you wish to be put on our Newsletter mailing list, please write to let us know, enclosing £1.50 per issue to cover our copying and postage costs.

Our postal address –
Yellow Gate,
Greenham Common Women's Peace Camp,
nr. NEWBURY
Berkshire
England
RG19 6HN

Tel. 0374 136728, between 8.00-9.30pm each evening. Please note this is a mobile phone, and calls are charged at a higher rate.

## 1984

1. HANSARD, House of Commons, 14 February 1984, Vol. 54, c117-8.
2. HANSARD, House of Commons, 13 March 1984, Vol. , c272-3.
3. HANSARD, House of Commons, 3 April 1984, c445w.
4. Radio Four 'World at One', April 4 1984; see also Letters to the GUARDIAN, Saturday April 7th 1984.
5. HANSARD, House of Commons, 5 April 1984, Vol. 57, c1241-4.
6. HANSARD, House of Commons, 24 July 1984, Vol. 64, c593w.
7. Information from The Annual Register, 1984.

## 1985

1. Hearing before Electoral Registration Officer, Mr W J Turner, 7th January 1985 in The Council Offices, Market Street, Newbury.
2. Appeal, Newbury County Court, between: George Anthony Meyer (Second Respondent) and The Electoral Registration Officer for the District of Newbury (First Respondent) and Hipperson, Johnson, Griffiths, Griffiths, Green, Dennett and Howse (Appellants).
3. Bundle No. 2 Papers from Memery, Crystal & Co., Solicitors 31 Southampton Row, London WC1B 5HT
4. HANSARD, House of Commons, 6th February 1985, Vol. 72, c945-956.
5. House of Commons 2nd Report from the Defence Committee, Session 1984-85, "Security at Royal Ordnance Factories and Nuclear Bases", printed 13 February 1985 by HMSO (HC 217).
6. Keesings Contemporary Archives, Vol. XXXI, p. 33507.
7. ibid, p. 33507.
8. ibid, p. 33507.
9. As reported in the TIMES Law Report (p. 24), May 2nd 1985.

## 1986

1. Information about the bombing of Libya and the events preceding it from: Keesing's Contemporary Archives, Vol. XXXII, June 1986, pp. 34456 – 34457.
2. From a report compiled by the Wages for Housework Campaign, 71 Tonbridge Street, King's Cross, London WC1H 9DZ.
3. See 'Letters' to SANITY, July 1986.
4. HANSARD, House of Commons, Vol. 89, 13 January 1986, c793.
5. HANSARD, House of Commons, Vol. 89, 13 January 1986, c842.

## 1988

1. From 'A New Kind of Sus,' statement of 26 February 1988 produced by King's Cross Women's Centre.

2. From April 1988 Yellow Gate newsletter, p.21.

3. This discussion is recorded in full in the April 1988 Yellow Gate newsletter, pages 41-49, incl.

4. From April 1988 Yellow Gate newsletter, pp 33-40, incl.

5. The GUARDIAN, Wednesday April 20th 1988, page 2.

6. HANSARD, House of Commons, 29 April 1988 c310-11w.

7. From September 1988 Yellow Gate newsletter, pp 57-58.

8. ibid, pp58-59.

9. See previous chapter, re. disruption of postal delivery by camps on the north side of the base. In the Spring of 1988, Mrs Mkwayi was able to travel to Europe to accept an honour on behalf of Mr Mandela. She was also able to spend some time in London, and sent a first class letter from London to Sarah Hipperson on the 7th March, with this happy news. The letter lay in a van at Woad Gate until 24th March, 10 days after Mrs Mkwayi had returned to South Africa.

### YOU CAN'T KILL THE SPIRIT

1. Affidavit of Douglas Conway presented in the application by Mrs Janet Thomas for Judicial Review of the Inquest held on 12th September 1989 into the death of Helen Thomas; High Court of Justice, Queen's Bench Division, April 23rd, 1991.

The affidavit is reproduced in full in our September 1991 Newsletter.

2. Affidavit of Katrina Howse presented in the application by Mrs Janet Thomas for Judicial Review of the Inquest held on 12th September 1989 into the death of Helen Thomas; High Court of Justice, QBD, April 23rd, 1991.

3. ibid.

4. House of Commons, Second Report from the DEFENCE COMMITTEE Session 1983-84: The Physical Security of Military Installations in the United Kingdom. Vol. II

(London: Her Majesty's Stationery Office)

5. The workshop at the December gathering was tape-recorded and transcribed. Much of the transcription appeared in our APRIL 1990 Newsletter.

6. HANSARD, House of Commons, 23 July 1990, c70w.

7. From the affidavit of Aniko Jones submitted in the libel action against the SUN.

# RESOURCES

*Black Women and the Peace Movement*, Wilmette Brown (Bristol: Falling Wall Press, 1984).

*Tell Them Everything*, Margaretta D'Arcy (London: Pluto Press, 1981).

*Awkward Corners*, John Arden & Margaretta D'Arcy (London, Methuen, 1988). See essay, 'Power to the Sisters!'

*Greenham Common: Women at the Wire*, Barbara Harford & Sarah Hopkins, eds (London: Women's Press, 1984). This is the book concerned with the early history of the Women's Peace Camp which we recommend.

*Pacific Women Speak – Why Haven't You Known?* (Oxford: Green Line, 1987)

*Camp Newsletters:*

> *Six Years* – September 5th, 1987
> *Take Action on Racism* – December 1987
> *In Struggle* – April 1988
> *Seven Years* – September 5th, 1988
> *Holding Our Ground* – April 1989

*We Are Mourning the Death of Helen Thomas* – September 5th, 1989

*Resist the Military* – December 1989 – this handbook on non-violence was translated into French, German, Swedish and Welsh.

> *Moving On* – April 1990
> *No More Wars* – December 1990
> *Ten Years* – September 5th, 1991
> *Justice and Equality Worldwide* – August 1992
> *I Am A Witness To Your War Crimes* – June 1993
> *By Our Actions We Are Free* – September 5th, 1994

These back copies of our Newsletters are available for reference only at the camp. See above for details of how to subscribe.

*Oral History:* The Imperial War Museum in London holds tape-recordings of several Yellow Gate women's accounts of events at the camp.

See also: *The Richard Dimbleby Lecture 1992 – The Judiciary in the Nineties* (London: BBC Education, 1992).

Tony Benn, *The End of an Era, Diaries 1980-90*, ed. Ruth Winstone (London: Hutchinson, 1992).

For a backlist of books available from Working Press, send sae to: Working Press, 54 Sharsted Street, LONDON SE17 3TN.

*The silos which once housed 101 cruise missiles, protected night and day by armed guards, now lie empty, rusty and disintegrating.*
*Nature is reclaiming and cleansing the area.*